Adobe
ACROBAT 7
IN THE Office

DONNA L. BAKER

Adobe Press

Adobe Acrobat 7 in the Office
Donna Baker

This Adobe Press book is published by Peachpit Press.
For information on Adobe Press books, contact:
Peachpit Press
1249 Eighth Street
Berkeley, CA 94710
510/524-2178, 510/524-2221 (fax)
www.adobepress.com

To report errors, please send a note to errata@peachpit.com. Peachpit Press is a division of Pearson Education. For the latest on Adobe Press books, go to www.adobepress.com.

Editor: Karyn Johnson
Production Editors: Alan Reade, Myrna Vladic, Pat Christenson
Compositors: Jerry Ballew, Tina O'Shea, Owen Wolfson
Indexer: Karin Arrigoni
Copy Editor: Rick Camp
Proofreader: Barbara McGowan
Interior Design: Karen Kemp
Cover Design: Charlene Charles Will

ISBN 0-321-32182-0

9 8 7 6 5 4 3 2 1

Printed and bound in the United States of America

For Terry

Acknowledgments

I want to thank my usual cast of characters for helping me bring this book to life. Thanks to Terry for being the super guy he is (and for the spiffy new coffee pot). Thanks so much to my girl Erin for getting a job and finally moving out of the house so I have time to work! Thanks to my dogs for keeping me company, to Deena for keeping me amused, and to Tom Waits for filling my soul.

What can I say about the Peachpit folks? I have truly enjoyed the experience of writing this book, which grew from a simple concept to this very fine finished product. Special thanks to Karyn Johnson for her masterful editing, to Becky Morgan for her ongoing support and clarity of vision, to John Deubert for his salient tech editing, and to Alan Reade for translating my "What if we do this?" questions into reality. Finally, thanks to Adobe for the latest incarnation of one of my favorite programs. It's come such a long way in such a short time.

Contents

Chapter 3   Building a Slideshow Presentation with Picture Tasks   51

Chapter 4   Creating an Interactive Map   65

Chapter 5   Creating Online Content in Acrobat   91

Chapter 6   Managing a Print Job   113

Chapter 11   Working with Technical Drawings   279

Chapters Available on the Web site:

Bonus Chapter 1—Building a "Wow!" Résumé
Bonus Chapter 2—Creating a Layered Brochure
Bonus Chapter 3—Constructing a Form Using Adobe Designer
Bonus Chapter 4—Creating an Interactive Catalog

Introduction

What do college students, software product managers, and deli owners have in common? Aside from the obvious answer that they are presumably human? My answer is that they can all, in one way or another, make their lives simpler and more productive using Acrobat 7 Professional.

Everybody who uses a computer has seen and worked with PDF (Portable Document Format) documents. We all know they are used for viewing documents that look and print like the original, complete with formatted text, images, and layout structure. But that, my friends, is the mere tip of the iceberg. Consider these questions:

- Are you tired of running around the office, report draft in hand, making sure everyone has reviewed it and given you feedback?

- What if you are a government employee and looking for a way to send plans and proposals to a select group of decision makers, while ensuring that the content is secure from unauthorized viewing? Do you hand deliver or send couriers?

- How can you write a manual that incorporates your material and provides links to your accessory information, such as data tables, interviews, information from Web sites, and other sources?

- What if your business wants to create an order form for your customers that can be filled out and e-mailed back to you, shortening the ordering and fulfillment process, thereby increasing your customer's satisfaction and, ultimately, your bottom line?

- And what about pictures? Sporting your new digital camera, you take numerous pictures of your products or services in action—how can you easily share them with colleagues and customers?

The answers to all these questions can be found in Acrobat. You just need to know how to find them.

Is This Book For You?

This book is for anyone who works in an environment where document control and management is an issue. That includes a lot of people! This book is written from a number of perspectives and directed at business persons of all types. However, this book is *not* written for the computer novice. I have assumed that you are familiar with your computer and have some experience with the software that coordinates so handily with Acrobat 7.

Some of the projects in the book contain a few details about working in software applications that are outside the suite of Microsoft Office products and Adobe Acrobat. For example, in a few places where I found it might be helpful to share some tips for working with files in Adobe Photoshop or InDesign, I've given some instructions. However, you don't need to have those applications to follow along: In addition to the files generated by these programs, I have also included the PDF versions. These projects are useful for anyone with basic office software packages, including those who want to use them for their personal projects. The book assumes you are using Acrobat 7 Professional to build the projects, but anyone with the Adobe Reader will be able to view and use the projects once they are created.

Goals of This Book

There are over one-half billion copies of Acrobat Reader and Adobe Reader spread across the planet. That's a lot of people who have the capability to see your work. With the introduction of Acrobat 7 Professional and its expanded functionality, now more than ever you can distribute your content easily and safely and allow your users to interact with your documents.

Simply because it is so functional in such a broad range of areas, Acrobat can be very intimidating. And when you have a deadline that's fast approaching, it's even more daunting a task to figure out how Acrobat can best serve your needs.

That's where this book comes in. *Adobe Acrobat 7 in the Office* is a guide to using Acrobat in your office, just as its title says. In these pages, you will find a collection of case studies and scenarios that might match your own. While you may find your exact scenario portrayed in this book, it's more likely you will read about some process or task that is on your to-do list and learn how to use Acrobat's power to make your workday more productive. As I mentioned, Acrobat can be used in so many ways that it can overwhelm the new or casual user, or even those who use it for some situations but haven't had the opportunity for a full exploration of the program. By identifying particular problems and then showing you how they can be solved using Acrobat, this book allows you to take these lessons and concepts and apply them to your own circumstances.

You won't find a lot of step-by-step instructions for completing common tasks in this book, such as how to save a document. There are a number of very good books you can read that can help you do that. Nor are there instructions for working with any of the source programs that can be integrated with Acrobat, aside from the how and why of preparing documents for use in Acrobat. For example, you'll see how to use Microsoft Word styles to generate a PDF bookmark set, but you won't learn how to use Word styles in this book.

How to Use This Book

This book isn't meant to be a manual, nor is it meant to be read from cover to cover—although you're more than welcome to read it all! Instead, it looks at a range of scenarios that you may face in your workplace and shows you how Acrobat can be used to help you solve many common workflow and document management problems.

Chapter 1, "Getting Your Bearings," describes how the program works from a functional standpoint. In this chapter, you will see how the Acrobat program is structured and how to manipulate its features. The chapter is also designed to give you terms of reference—Acrobat has many panes, panels, dialogs, and tools that can be used in combination or chosen based on how you like to work. The rest of the chapters refer to these objects, but they don't provide specific details on how to access them. If you are interested in working with one of Acrobat's navigation features, such as bookmarks or pages, you have to know where to find the Navigation pane. Chapter 1 tells you where to find it.

Some processes and techniques are used in more than one chapter, simply because they are so useful. The particulars of using a process vary according to the needs of a project, and that is the approach I've taken in this book. For example, working with binders is a great way of combining content produced from a wide range of programs into a single PDF document, and that process is incorporated into several case studies. How the content is used after it is put into a binder varies according to the problem at hand.

Make the Program Work for You

We are all becoming accustomed to working on projects as teams; sharing and collaboration is a workday reality. We are also accustomed to using multiple pieces of software to get our work done. You will be amazed at what you can do with a single program. Before digging into a whole range of ways in which you can use Acrobat to make your workday smoother and your work more efficient, I want to touch on some other ways you can make the program work *for* you.

One of Acrobat's strengths is the ability to perform so many of the same functions in different ways. As you learn to work in the program, consider what you are doing and think about how you work in other programs. For example, are you always on the lookout for shortcut menus wherever you go? If so, you can use them in Acrobat. Are you very visual, and do you rely heavily on toolbars to locate tools and functions? Or are you the methodical type, organizing your world into folders and subfolders? Acrobat's got you covered. Maybe you like to bypass the program interface altogether and have mastered the graphic designers' world of mouse-click right hand/keystrokes left hand. Acrobat's got that covered too.

Conventions Used in This Book

Well, the folks at Adobe are looking out for you and have a whole bunch of ways to let you work according to your needs. In this book, I generally only reference tools on toolbars and shortcut menus to make it easier to follow along; in cases where a command is only available from a menu, that is included as well. Although the screenshots show the Windows version of Acrobat, the commands throughout the book are given for both Windows and Macintosh.

Here's an example of how instructions are presented in the book. Suppose you are reading about cropping a page. You can access the same command in these ways:

- Right-click (Windows) / Control-click (Macintosh) the page in the Pages pane to display the shortcut menu, and choose Crop Pages (**Figure 0.1**).

- Click the Options button on the Pages pane to display the menu, and choose Crop Pages.

- Choose Document > Crop Pages from the main program menu.

- Click the Crop tool on the Advanced Editing toolbar.

- Press the "C" key on the keyboard to activate the Crop tool, if the single key accelerator preference is set in the General section of the Preferences dialog.

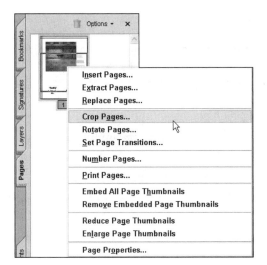

Figure 0.1 *Shortcut menus are used to find many program functions.*

Although all these methods work equally well, describing them all for each operation throughout the book is repetitious and, I imagine, rather boring to read.

Online Content

The chapters in this book are based on projects that include one or many documents in a variety of formats. The source material for these projects is available free on the *Acrobat 7 in the Office* Web page: www.donnabaker.ca/downloads. Click the ☀ to open the book's PDF Web interface.

Each chapter's projects come in two or more forms—as the raw documents, and as the completed PDF document. In most cases, there is at least one interim PDF document as well. There are also many accessory files, such as source images, text files where a project calls for using a block of text, and text files for any bits of JavaScript used in the projects. The files available for download are indicated in the text with an icon in the margin ☀.

For example, in the Chapter03 folder, you will find four JPEG images, a WAV music file, and three PDF files, each named both according to its function and the chapter's scenario. That is, in Chapter 3, Susan first creates a PDF document named susan_raw.pdf; the file named susan_slideshow.pdf is a slideshow file; and the final version after reducing the file size is named susan.pdf.

All chapters include project files, which are listed prior to where they may be helpful if used. It isn't necessary to download and work with the files for the projects to be useful though. They are only there to help you visualize the project details and assist you with creating the sample. Additionally, several bonus projects are included on the Web site, which take some of the case studies found within the book even further.

Not only are all these files available for the chapters in the book, but also you'll find four extra bonus chapters online. These bonus chapters are full-length projects that show more of Acrobat's features.

Now, let's look at all those great features in Acrobat you've heard about.

1

Getting Your Bearings

Acrobat 7 Professional is a feature-rich program, but this wealth of riches can be confusing to those unfamiliar with all it can do. And it can do a lot! Acrobat can be used for many things, ranging from preparing cohesive documents using content from multiple sources, to sharing and reviewing documents in a workgroup, to securing and mailing documents and attachments, to creating and distributing intelligent forms, to preparing collections and organizing groups of documents, to.... If you are getting the impression that Acrobat 7 covers a wide spectrum of functions, you're right.

In this chapter, we'll take a quick tour of the program and look at some of its features and tools. If you're interested in customizing the interface to make your work in Acrobat more efficient, there are tips that appear later throughout the book that you can follow.

Introducing Acrobat 7 Professional

Adobe has produced a stellar product in Acrobat 7. For the first time, you can enable content created in Acrobat 7 Professional to be commented and marked up in Adobe Reader, effectively opening up one of Acrobat's strongest features to millions more users.

Here are some of the highlights of Acrobat 7 Professional:

- Create PDF documents from more Microsoft Office programs, such as Access and Publisher (Windows).

- Create PDF documents from engineering programs, including AutoCAD and Microsoft Visio (Windows). Acrobat also includes Measuring and Drawing Markups tools.

- Embed object-level data in Visio drawings that are converted to PDF (Windows).

- Set up and maintain collections of documents within Acrobat using the Organizer.

- Attach external documents to your PDF document, which can be extracted and saved from the document as separate files.

- Create and control security policies through the new Managing Security Policies window, including the use of policy servers.

- Create interactive forms with Adobe Designer, included with Acrobat 7 Professional (Windows).

- Enable Commenting tools for Adobe Reader 7 users, and manage your reviews using the Tracker window.

- Make documents accessible for use on screen readers and other assistive devices through the Accessibility Setup Assistant wizard and other new tools.

- Use the Print Production tools to create a PDF workflow for high-resolution output according to PDF/X publishing standards.

- Build document collections that comply with proposed PDF/A archival standards.

Acrobat Versions

Acrobat comes in several versions, each useful for working with documents in different ways. This book concentrates on Acrobat 7 Professional. Because there are differences among the features available in the various versions of the program, some of the most important features and which versions of the program they apply to are listed in Table 1.1. The table includes Acrobat Elements, which is a specialized version of the program for enterprise environments; Adobe Reader 7; and both Acrobat 7 Standard and Professional versions.

Table 1.1 Acrobat Versions and Their Features

	ADOBE READER 7	ACROBAT ELEMENTS	ACROBAT 7 STANDARD	ACROBAT 7 PROFESSIONAL
View, search, and print PDF files	X	X	X	X
Enable Adobe Reader 7 users to work with Commenting tools				X
Create PDF documents from all applications that print		X	X	X
Combine source documents into a PDF document			X	X
Use content from Microsoft Office programs, including Word, Excel, PowerPoint, Outlook, Internet Explorer, Access, and Publisher (Windows)			X	X
Manage document reviews			X	X
Use security such as passwords and certificates		X	X	X
Use content from AutoCAD, Microsoft Visio, and Microsoft Project (Windows)				X
Convert layers and object data in technical drawings (Windows)				X
Preflight high-end print jobs				X
Build intelligent forms using Adobe Designer (Windows)				X

The Interface

Like most programs, Acrobat Professional has an interface composed of menus, toolbars, and a variety of work areas or panes (**Figure 1.1**). Many features and functions can be accessed through the interface in a number of different ways, or the shortcut keys can often be used instead. Whichever method you choose really depends on what you feel comfortable with and how you like to work.

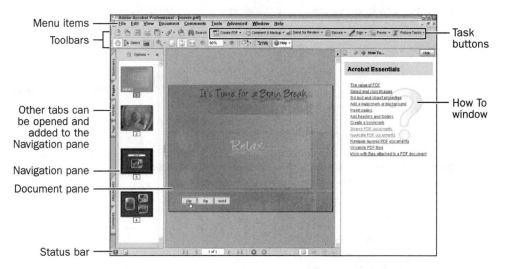

Figure 1.1 *Acrobat 7 Professional's interface is made up of several components within its program window.*

It's important to take some time to learn about the features and understand how the program works for two main reasons:

- Knowing the features available lets you incorporate more of them into your projects.

- You will work faster and smarter when you learn to use the program and customize it to meet your needs.

The Program Window

When you open Acrobat 7, the default program window shows several components. You can configure the layout by displaying or collapsing panel groupings. You may find that it's easier to focus on your document at hand if you hide some of the panes or toolbars from view.

But for now, take a few minutes and tour the program. Open the Navigation pane tabs, click the Task buttons, check out the toolbars' contents. You're bound to find something interesting! When you come across a feature of interest, make sure to experiment with it.

Acrobat's program window is made up of multiple sections, all intended to make life less complicated. You see menus and toolbars across the top, which contain tool icons and pull-down selections. The remainder of the program window is made up of different panes, with the Status bar at the bottom of the window. The Main menu displays across the top of the program and contains many common menu item headings such as File and Edit, along with Acrobat-specific headings, like Document and Comments (**Figure 1.2**). Many of the menu items are also available from Acrobat's toolbars. The name of the open, active document is shown at the top of the program window.

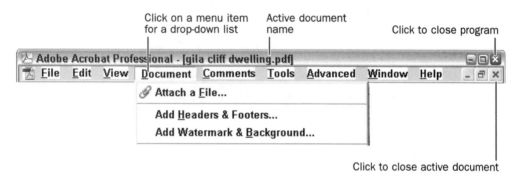

Figure 1.2 *Select program functions from the Main menu.*

Window Panes

Most of the program window is divided into three panes (**Figure 1.3**). You can resize the panes by dragging their vertical separator bars left or right. These are described here in the order they appear in Acrobat's default view:

- **Navigation pane.** The tabs along the left side of the program window are called the Navigation pane. Use the different tab views to manage and control your document's content.

- **Document pane.** Your document displays in the Document pane; use the horizontal and vertical scrollbars to move the view of the document in the pane.

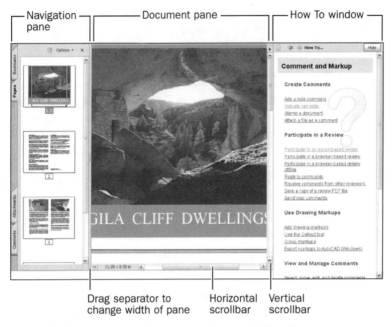

Navigation pane — Document pane — How To window

Drag separator to change width of pane — Horizontal scrollbar — Vertical scrollbar

Figure 1.3 *The program window contains three resizable panes.*

- **How To window.** Display or hide the How To window at the right of the Document pane. This window contains links to common tasks as well as the program's complete Help files. The How To window's area is also used to display Search information and the results of Accessibility testing.

The Status Bar

The Status bar runs across the bottom of the program window. Here's where you can change your layout, determine page size, and navigate quickly. There are several components located here:

- **Navigation tools.** Use the controls on the Status bar below the Document pane to move between pages in the document; you can also track your view history using the arrow buttons. The number of the visible page and the total page count are also shown here (**Figure 1.4**).

- **View buttons.** The two green View buttons are located to the right of the Navigation tools. Use the buttons to move through the pages in your document, jumping from view to view. Click the Previous View (the left arrow button) to go to the last document page and magnification you looked at in the Document pane; click the Next View (the right arrow button) to

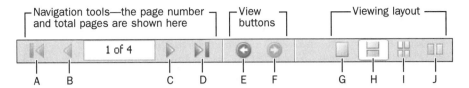

Navigation tools—the page number and total pages are shown here

View buttons

Viewing layout

A B C D E F G H I J

A. Go to first page **B.** Go to previous page **C.** Go to next page **D.** Go to last page **E.** Previous view **F.** Next view **G.** Single-Page view **H.** Continuous view **I.** Continuous-Facing view **J.** Facing view

Figure 1.4 *Move through a document using the Navigation tools or the View buttons—change the viewing layout depending on the structure of your document.*

move to the next document page and magnification. These buttons are disabled in the program until you have moved from the initial page you see in the document to another page or magnification.

- **Viewing layout controls.** At the right of the Status bar you can change the viewing layout, such as single or continuous pages, or pages laid out side by side as in a book, each indicated by a different icon. In Figure 1.4, the layout view is Continuous (the Continuous view icon is highlighted).

- **Special status.** Special features of the document, such as layers or security, are indicated by icons at the left of the Status bar. You can also select an icon to show a full-screen view of the document; or if you prefer to remove only the toolbars from the view, you can do this here as well.

- **Page size.** Move your pointer over the left lower edge of the Document pane to see the page size in a pop-up tooltip (**Figure 1.5**). The tooltip shows the dimensions when the full page width is shown in the Document pane. If the view is magnified and the scrollbars are visible, the page dimensions are displayed on the horizontal scrollbar (**Figure 1.6**).

11.00 x 8.50 in

Figure 1.5 *Special features of the document are shown on the program window, along with tools for controlling how your document is displayed.*

8.50 x 11.00 in   1 of 2

Figure 1.6 *The page dimensions are shown on the horizontal scrollbar when it is active.*

Toolbars and Task Buttons

Acrobat contains a large number of toolbars. These are made up of icons, some of which show pull-down arrows that contain submenus. Most of the tools are also available from the Main menu (**Figure 1.7**).

Figure 1.7 Click the pull-down arrow to reveal subtoolbars, available next to many of the icons within toolbars.

Acrobat contains a collection of toolbars as well as subtoolbars available from the View > Toolbars menu. You can spend a lot of time opening and closing toolbars using the menu. Save a couple of mouse clicks by working in the toolbar well, which is the area at the top of the program window that displays the toolbars. Right-click (Windows) / Control-click (Macintosh) in a blank space on the toolbar area to display the same options as those available from the Toolbars submenu (**Figure 1.8**).

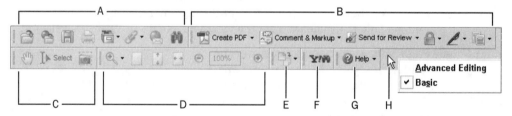

A. File toolbar **B.** Task buttons **C.** Basic toolbar **D.** Zoom toolbar **E.** Rotate View toolbar **F.** Search the Internet toolbar **G.** Help toolbar **H.** Right-click/Control-click an empty space on the toolbar (the toolbar well) to open the list of toolbars

Figure 1.8 All the toolbars and display options are available from the toolbar well.

To refer to a tool or toolbar name quickly, move your pointer over the vertical hatched lines at the left of a toolbar to display its name in a tooltip or pause your pointer over a tool to show its name there (**Figure 1.9**). While you are learning to work with Acrobat, you can show the labels next to the tool icons, but you may want to hide them when you become more proficient in order to maximize working space. To do this, choose View > Toolbars > Show Button Labels, and then select the Default, All, or No button label options.

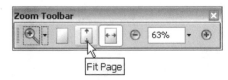

Figure 1.9 *If you are unsure about a tool's or toolbar's name, you can display it in a tooltip by rolling the pointer over the icon.*

Tools for Your Type

You can handle Acrobat's toolbars the same way in which you handle your physical desk. Which group do you belong to?

- **Neatniks.** Lock the toolbars if you are the type of person who needs everything placed just so in order to function. You can customize the tool layout, and once the program is arranged to your satisfaction, choose View > Toolbars > Lock Toolbars (or select the command from the toolbar well's shortcut menu). The separator bars between the individual toolbars disappear. You can't lock floating toolbars—those you have pulled off the toolbar area—nor can you add them to a locked toolbar.

- **Some Tidiness Necessary.** Some people like things surrounding them during the workday and then like everything back in its place before they go home. Choose View > Toolbars > Default to reset the toolbar arrangement to the program default.

- **The Rest of Us.** I'm sure I'm not alone as a person who usually leaves things as they are when I quit work for the day. Often, seeing what I was working with the day before triggers my to-do list. The same can be said of toolbars. When you close and reopen Acrobat, the arrangement of toolbars and Task buttons remains as you last set them.

Task Buttons

Each Task button contains a set of commands for performing a particular function, such as creating a PDF or commenting on a document (**Figure 1.10**). They are different from toolbars in that they contain related commands instead of related tools. Each Task button also includes a command to open its corresponding How To window, which contains information on using the commands. Open a Task button by choosing View > Task Buttons and selecting the appropriate Task button. Display the Task button's bar by choosing View > Task Buttons > Show All Task Buttons.

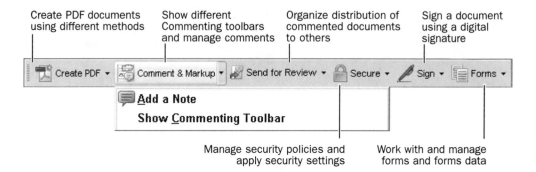

Figure 1.10 *Each Task button contains a group of related commands for performing a specific type of task.*

Click the Task button's pull-down arrow to display its menu. Acrobat contains a set of six Task buttons:

- **Create PDF.** This Task button contains commands for generating PDF documents using different methods, such as documents or scans.

- **Comment & Markup.** Here you'll find commands for things like showing the different Commenting toolbars and managing comments.

- **Send for Review.** The Send for Review task button's menu contains commands for managing a review cycle, such as starting a new review or opening the Tracker, a window used for managing reviews.

- **Secure.** On this Task button's menu, you'll find different commands for using and managing security policies.

- **Sign.** Use the commands on the Sign task button's menu to add secure signatures to a document.

- **Forms.** The Forms task button's menu contains commands for creating and editing forms as well as other forms-related tasks.

Opening and Saving Documents

Unlike most programs you may have experience with, you won't find a "New" command in the File menu. You don't create blank documents in Acrobat and then add content as you would with many programs. Instead, you open existing PDF documents, or create new ones in several ways.

The only type of document that opens instantly in Acrobat is a PDF, but Acrobat can *convert* many types of documents automatically when you open them by choosing File > Open. For example, if you open a Microsoft Word document in Acrobat 7, it goes through an automatic conversion process before the file is displayed as a PDF. You can also use the Create PDF Task button's commands for creating a PDF in a variety of ways **(Figure 1.11)**. The options include creating a PDF from a file, from multiple files, from a scanner, or from a Web page. You can also create a PDF from a snapshot (From Clipboard Image in the drop-down menu), which is a selected area of the document pane that is copied to the system clipboard.

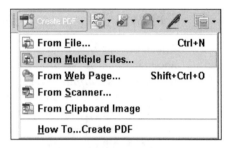

Figure 1.11 *The Create PDF Task button offers a number of ways to create a PDF in Acrobat.*

You can save a PDF document in the usual way—that is, by using the Save command on the File menu. However, you can also generate a wide range of other file formats in Acrobat. Choose File > Save As to open the Save As dialog. Click the "Save as type" pull-down arrow and choose an option from the list **(Figure 1.12)**. Once you make a selection, you can click the Settings button to configure most types of files.

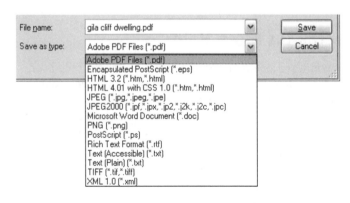

Figure 1.12 *Acrobat lets you save a document in a wide range of file formats.*

"How To" Stop Along the Way

Check out the offerings in the How To window when you are first learning about Acrobat or learning how to use a new feature (**Figure 1.13**). The How To window lists common tasks and contains information groupings on special topics such as print production or working with forms. Select a topic to display a list of common tasks or functions associated with that topic.

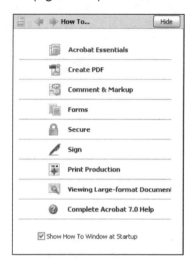

The How To window displays by default when you open Acrobat. When you are familiar with the program, you can deselect the Show How To Window at Startup check box on the How To window to hide it. If you want to revisit the How To contents, select Help > How To > and choose a topic title. Or you can click Help in the default toolbar setup and select a topic from the pull-down menu in order to open it in the How To window's area of the program window. If you want to restore the default How To window's appearance, click the How To Home Page icon ▓ in the How To window.

Figure 1.13 *Click one of the main topic areas on the How To window to open a list of topics.*

Mining the Depths for More Help

If you didn't find what you were looking for in the How To window, help is on the way! Use Acrobat's main Help feature to find in-depth information that goes beyond the step-by-step instructions on basic program functions. Choose Help > Complete Acrobat 7.0 Help or press the F1 key to open the Help files in a separate window.

You can access information in three ways with Acrobat's Help feature—by Contents, Index, or Search. Use the option that suits how you work and your Acrobat knowledge level. If you are a very systematic person, the Contents tab will guide you from general to specific topics. Use the Search tab if you are familiar with the program and want to find a specific topic. If you aren't sure what you are looking for, type a term in the Index tab and watch the headings that display—you may find a heading that triggers a mental connection to the precise topic you need. Here is how to use each one:

- **Contents.** The Help files open to the Contents listing by default. Topics are arranged in a hierarchy; a (+) next to a topic means there are subtopics. Click the (+) to display the nested contents—the sign will toggle to (–), meaning the topic is expanded (**Figure 1.14**).

- **Search.** Type the search term in the "Find topics containing" field, and then click Search. Topics containing your search term are listed in the pane at the left of the Help window. Click a topic to display the content in the main pane; each instance of the search term is highlighted. If the highlighting is distracting, click the main pane of the Help window to deselect the highlights.

- **Index.** Type the first few letters of the term in the field at the top of the Index pane. Matching listings are displayed in the body of the window (**Figure 1.15**). Use the navigation options at the top left of the window to make your way through the file—the arrows take you back and forth through the pages you've visited. Click the Printer icon to print the topic displayed in the Help window; click the plus (+) or minus (–) icon to zoom in or zoom out of the Help window for easier reading.

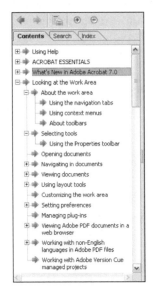

Figure 1.14 *The Contents tab is an easy way to find information if you are familiar with Acrobat.*

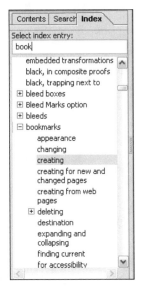

Figure 1.15 *Use the Index to display a list of topics alphabetically.*

If you are working on a delicate operation and need to refer to a search page repeatedly, don't close the window. Instead, minimize it—when you reopen it, the last content displayed is visible. Since the Help files are a separate window from the program, you can arrange both Acrobat and the Help files on your desktop for ease of use.

Making Your Exit

We have come to the end of the tour, as well as the end of this chapter. Close Acrobat as you would any program. When you reopen the program, the toolbars are arranged as you last left them. The Navigation pane, on the other hand, may or may not be displayed in the same way. Acrobat allows you to specify how you want its navigation features to display when a file is opened. For example, along with the document, you can show the Bookmarks, Pages, or the Attachments pane. Settings are not constant; that is, you decide how the navigation features are displayed on a file-by-file basis.

Now that you've seen how some of the tools and features work in Acrobat 7 Professional, you're ready to dive in and have some fun. The projects in this book show you how to use this extraordinary program to make your work and life a whole lot easier!

2

Building a Sales Proposal from Multiple Files

We often find ourselves overwhelmed by the number of programs and file formats we're inundated with on a daily basis. Suppose you wanted to view a Microsoft Word document, Excel spreadsheet, and PowerPoint presentation as one document. You could cut and paste content from one program to another, but wouldn't it be nice to have the luxury of using each document's structure? Or what if you needed to e-mail a single presentation, and it had to include Web pages from your company Web site, a table from your coworker's PowerPoint presentation, and sample book pages that had been saved in InDesign?

One of Acrobat's biggest contributions to creating order in the office is its ability to create a single document from a variety of sources. In this project, you'll see how to merge a PowerPoint presentation, a Word document, an Excel spreadsheet, content from a Web page, and other sources into a single PDF document. Combining the material into one cohesive PDF document saves a lot of time when you don't have to repurpose the material manually.

You'll also use the Snapshot tool in this chapter, as well as change the size and content on some of the pages. To finish the job, you'll use bookmarks as navigation aids to give your readers direction as they make their way through your document, and you'll add page transition effects as a finishing touch. As a bonus, you'll also see how to create a PDF in InDesign.

Doggone It!

Joe and Jim Percy are twin brothers. In addition to their genetic makeup, they also share a love of dogs and a passion for business. After graduating from college several years ago, they decided to start a business together. They cast around for ideas and came up with the concept of selling a spray cleaner specifically designed to remove pet stains from virtually any surface. Although there were other products on the market, they felt their drive, coupled with their knowledge of pet owners and their needs, would be instrumental in the development of their business, Doggone It!

They were right. After five years of crisscrossing the country displaying and selling Doggone It! at dog shows, they are now seeing the fruits of their labor. Having seen Joe and Jim at their most recent dog show, the representative of a major pet supply chain store just called the brothers with an offer to discuss distributing their product, telling them the company's buyer would be flying in the next day to talk to them.

In preparation for the upcoming meeting, the brothers need to prepare a sales proposal to present to the company's representative. Joe and Jim may be big on ambition, but they are suddenly short on time!

They want to include information from several sources, including part of a PowerPoint presentation they run at dog shows, some financial information on a spreadsheet, customer testimonials and other information from their Web site, and a print ad they have started using in various publications.

They need the presentation to look polished and work well, but they don't have either the time or the inclination to reproduce all the material in a single format. They also need the presentation to be useful both onscreen and in print.

Steps Involved in This Project

The logical solution for the Percy brothers is to work in Acrobat. With Acrobat, they can produce a presentation document that will meet their requirements in the short amount of time they have (**Figure 2.1**).

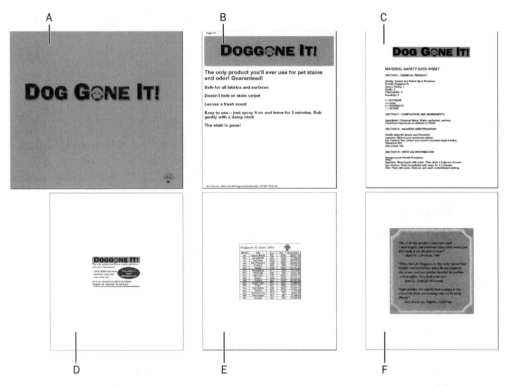

Did you know you could **A.** convert PowerPoint slides directly to PDF **B.** Use all or a portion of a Web page in a PDF **C.** Convert Word documents into PDFs from Word or Acrobat **D.** Easily convert an InDesign advertisement to PDF **E.** Include an Excel spreadsheet or part of a spreadsheet in the final PDF **F.** Convert just an image from a Web page to PDF.

Figure 2.1 *The Doggone It! presentation document includes material from a wide range of programs.*

To create their presentation, Joe and Jim need to do the following:

- Extract the slides they want to use from their PowerPoint presentation and convert them to PDF.

- Convert pages from their Web site, including customer testimonials extracted from a page on their Web site.

- Use InDesign's PDF conversion settings to create a PDF version of their advertisement to include in the presentation.

- Create a binder PDF that includes the converted documents as well as several other documents that they decide they need to round out the presentation. The other documents include a Word document, an image, and an Excel spreadsheet.

- Extract a portion of the spreadsheet using the Snapshot tool and create a separate PDF document, which is then used to replace the full spreadsheet page in the main document.

- Adjust the sizes and content on some of the pages.

- Reorder the presentation and configure bookmarks for the document.

- Add transitions to the document's pages for added interest.

To start constructing their document, Joe and Jim decide they'll choose the best slides from their dog show PowerPoint presentation and convert them to PDF.

Creating a PDF from a PowerPoint Presentation

Joe and Jim use a PowerPoint presentation running in a loop as part of their dog show booth display. They could work from within Acrobat to convert the presentation (see the sidebar "Taking the Long Way" for further information). However, since they only want to incorporate three of the presentation's slides in the sales presentation, it's easier to work from PowerPoint and use its PDFMaker for the conversion.

When you install Acrobat 7, the program also installs menus and toolbars in Microsoft Office programs. These plugins, called PDFMakers, have some settings particular to the type of program they are installed into as well as collections of common settings shared by the Adobe PDF printer, Acrobat Distiller, and Acrobat.

Preparing the Presentation for Conversion

The segment of the presentation the brothers use for dog shows contains a set of five slides. They want to use only the first three slides as a PDF document. You can't select pages/slides to convert as you might for a printer, but you can hide the other slides in PowerPoint before converting the file.

 Download the original PowerPoint presentation named **doggoneit.ppt** if you want to experiment with selecting and converting PowerPoint slides. Download **doggoneit_ppt.pdf** to see the converted presentation.

Follow these steps to hide slides in the presentation:

1. In either the Normal view or the Slide Sorter view, select the slides you wish to hide. Slides 4 and 5 in the sample project need to be hidden.

2. Choose Slide Show > Hide Slide, or right-click/Control-click on the selected slides and choose Hide Slide.

3. You see the slides' numbers display a strikethrough, indicating they are hidden (**Figure 2.2**).

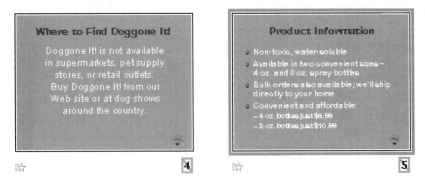

Figure 2.2 *Select the slides to hide in PowerPoint.*

The other feature that Jim and Joe decide to change is the page size. The PowerPoint PDFMaker uses the page layout assigned to the presentation in PowerPoint. They are going to use the slides as part of a document that uses regular letter-sized pages, so they want to define the width of the page to correspond with the rest of their PDF document's content. Although they can crop the presentation's pages in Acrobat, they decide instead to change the page size before conversion.

Follow these steps to change the page size of the PowerPoint presentation:

1. Choose File > Page Setup to open the Page Setup dialog.

2. Click the Slides sized for pull-down arrow and choose Custom.

3. Set both the Width and Height fields to 8.5 inches; leave the Slide orientation at its default Landscape setting.

4. Click OK to close the dialog.

WHY NOT JUST CHOOSE A PORTRAIT ORIENTATION?

If you choose the Portrait orientation, you'll have the correct width and height of a regular letter-sized page, but the content will be distorted. Using this method, the images are not scaled proportionally, so the logo is stretched vertically (**Figure 2.3**). By cutting the width of the page and leaving the height, PowerPoint maintains the Landscape orientation and doesn't distort the content. You'll find that the content of text boxes is shifted as the page width is decreased. If you resize a presentation using this method, check your text boxes' contents before converting.

Figure 2.3 *Resetting the page size and orientation distorts the page's content.*

Converting the Presentation

Next, set the PDFMaker's conversion settings by choosing Adobe PDF > Change Conversion Settings. This opens the Acrobat PDFMaker dialog, which in PowerPoint displays two tabs for choosing general settings and security.

The default Conversion Settings option is Standard, which is what is used in this project. You can select or deselect a variety of options for both the PDFMaker and the Application Settings. The default options are shown for the PDFMaker settings at the top of the dialog (**Figure 2.4**).

In the Application Settings, only these options are required:

- Add bookmarks to Adobe PDF

- Enable accessibility and reflow with Tagged PDF

- PDF layout based on PowerPoint printer settings

You'll see there are also options for converting animation and slide transitions. The Percys don't need animations, so these options can be deselected. You'll also note there is a setting called Convert hidden slides to PDF pages. Having this option deselected means the slides hidden earlier won't be converted.

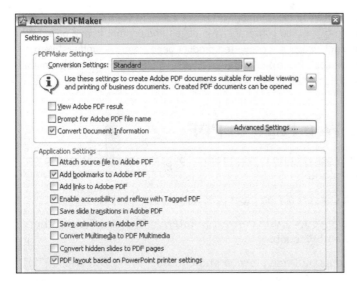

Figure 2.4 Choose Application Settings in the PDFMaker.

This is a quick trick that saves time later because you won't have to delete any pages you don't want to use from the PDF document.

NOTE For the PDFMaker in the Mac version of PowerPoint, the animation conversion options are not available.

After you click OK to close the Acrobat PDFMaker dialog, it's time to convert the file. Click Convert to Adobe PDF 🖼 on the PDFMaker toolbar, or choose Adobe PDF > Convert to Adobe PDF. The presentation's slides are processed and converted to PDF.

Next, it's time to convert the content from the Doggone It! Web site.

> **TAKING THE LONG WAY**
>
> From these steps, you see how to work with both PowerPoint and PDFMaker settings to convert just what is needed. If you don't change settings, you can work in Acrobat to achieve the same outcome, but you'll have to crop the pages to width and delete the extra slides from the converted presentation.

Creating PDF Documents from Web Pages

Doggone It! has a Web site that Joe and Jim use to sell their product. They are going to use the PDFMaker that Acrobat installs in Internet Explorer to convert the homepage of their site, one of their product pages, and a portion of another page to PDF so they can include these with the sales package.

Click the **Doggone It!** link next to the Chapter02 download files to open the Doggone It! Web site if you would like to practice converting Web pages and content from a page to PDF. Download **8 ounce.pdf**, which is a converted product page from the brothers' Web site you can use in the project. Download **Doggone It!.pdf**, which is a converted segment of the Percy's homepage converted to PDF to use in the project.

Converting a Web Page to PDF

Joe and Jim decide to convert one of the product pages from their Web site to include in the presentation.

Follow these steps to convert a Web page to PDF:

1. Open the Web page you want to convert in Internet Explorer. The brothers open the Doggone It! Web site.

2. Click the PDFMaker's pull-down arrow and choose Convert Web Page to PDF (**Figure 2.5**).

3. In the dialog that opens, name the file and select a storage folder. By default, Acrobat uses the Web page's name as the filename. The Web page being converted is named "8 oz bottle," and that name is also used for the PDF document. The project's file is named 8 oz bottle_web.pdf.

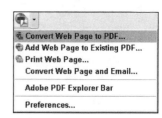

4. Click Save to close the dialog and create the PDF.

Figure 2.5 *Choose options from the Internet Explorer PDFMaker.*

> **TIP** By default, the PDF document opens in Acrobat. If you don't want to review the document and then close it, deselect the "Open in Acrobat when complete" check box at the bottom of the dialog.

Converting Selected Content From a Web Page to PDF

Next, the brothers want to select a portion of a page to convert to PDF. They can select text, images, or both.

Follow these steps to convert a selection from a Web page:

1. Open the Web page to be converted in Internet Explorer.

2. Click and drag to select the text and images to be converted (**Figure 2.6**).

Figure 2.6 You can convert selected content on a Web page to PDF.

3. Right-click/Control-click anywhere on the Web page (it isn't necessary for the pointer to be over the selected content) to open the shortcut menu, and choose Convert selection to Adobe PDF.

4. In the Convert Web Page to Adobe PDF dialog, you see the page name used again as the default PDF document name; you also see the "Only convert selection" check box is active at the bottom of the dialog (**Figure 2.7**). Click Save to convert the document and save it as PDF. The project's file is named 8 oz bottle_web.pdf.

Figure 2.7 Make sure the "Only convert selection" option is checked to convert only the content you select on the page.

NOTE Converting selected content from a Web page is a handy way to save content without saving navigation frames or advertising.

CONVERTING AN ADVERTISEMENT IN INDESIGN TO PDF

In recent months, Jim and Joe have started placing ads about their product in some dog enthusiast magazines. Their ad is designed in InDesign CS, and they'd like to include a PDF version in their presentation. InDesign documents can't be produced in Acrobat by using the Create PDF from File method; they must be converted in the native program.

 Download **doggone_ad.ind** if you work with InDesign CS and would like to experiment with converting to PDF.

To convert a document to PDF in InDesign CS, follow these steps:

1. Open the document in InDesign.

2. Choose File > PDF Export Presets > [Print]. InDesign offers a number of presets.

3. The Export dialog opens, and the file's name and original folder location are shown by default. Choose an alternate name or storage location if desired, and click Save.

4. The Export dialog closes and the Export PDF dialog opens. In this dialog, you can adjust various settings for the document, such as Acrobat version compatibility (shown on the General settings tab); downsampling options for images on the Compression settings tab; Printer's marks and bleed settings on the Marks and Bleeds settings tab; and Advanced options such as color space and fonts in the Advanced tab. You can read a summary of the settings in the Summary tab.

5. Leave the default settings as they are on the Export PDF dialog, and click Export. The dialog closes and the PDF document is generated.

PDF CONVERSIONS IN QUARK

In Quark, choose File > Save Page as EPS to save the file in the EPS (Encapsulated PostScript) format. Open Acrobat Distiller and choose File > Open in Distiller, or drag the file to the Distiller window to create the PDF file. Learn more about working with Acrobat Distiller in Chapter 6.

Combining Documents in Acrobat

Many of the documents for the presentation package are now converted to PDF. Jim and Joe also want to use an Excel spreadsheet, a Word document, and a JPEG image, which they'll convert in Acrobat.

You can easily convert many types of source documents, such as Word documents or Excel spreadsheets, from within Acrobat. The last conversion settings you choose in a program's PDFMaker are the settings used for converting the document to PDF in Acrobat. In the Percys' case, while they could convert each document from within its respective application, they are working in Acrobat as they are also combining other content, and it's quicker than opening both Word and Excel to convert files and then closing the programs again.

Download these additional files if you want to create the binder document as described in the project: **doggone_ad.pdf**, which is the converted InDesign CS advertisement; **sales.xls**, the Excel spreadsheet used in the project, **customers.jpg**, which is a copy of the image used on the Doggone It! Web site, and **doggone_specs.doc**, a Word document that lists product specifications. The basic combined PDF document is also available, named **Binder1.pdf**.

To create a single PDF document from a number of documents, follow these steps in Acrobat:

1. Click the Create PDF task button's pull-down arrow. You see there are several options, including From File, From Multiple Files, From Web Page, and From Scanner. The final option, From Clipboard Image, is inactive unless there is existing content on the clipboard, as you'll see later in the chapter. Choose From Multiple Files; the Create PDF from Multiple Documents dialog opens.

2. Click Browse to display the Open dialog, and select the files to use for the project. The files selected are shown in **Figure 2.8**. The list includes the PDF documents created so far in the project, as well as one Word document, one Excel document, and a JPEG image.

3. Click Add to dismiss the Open dialog.

Name	Size	Type ▲
📁 source		File Folder
📁 website		File Folder
8 oz bottle_web.pdf	17 KB	Adobe Acrobat 7.0 Document
Doggone It!_web.pdf	18 KB	Adobe Acrobat 7.0 Document
doggone_ad.pdf	87 KB	Adobe Acrobat 7.0 Document
doggoneit_ppt.pdf	59 KB	Adobe Acrobat 7.0 Document
customers.jpg	69 KB	JPG File
sales.xls	23 KB	Microsoft Excel Worksheet
doggoneit.ppt	71 KB	Microsoft PowerPoint Prese...
doggone_specs.doc	51 KB	Microsoft Word Document

Figure 2.8 *Select the files you want to combine into a single PDF document.*

The selected files are added to the Files to Combine column on the Create PDF from Multiple Documents dialog (**Figure 2.9**).

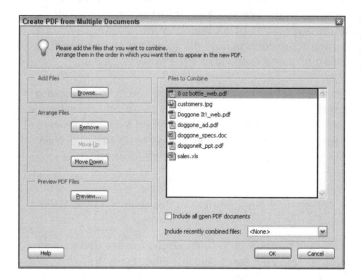

Figure 2.9 The selected files are added to the window in the Create PDF from Multiple Documents dialog.

4. To modify the order of the content, click a file and then click Remove (to delete it from the list) or the Up or Down button to adjust the selected document's order. In the sample project, Joe and Jim decide to leave the files in their original order—sorted by file type—and will adjust them later in the Pages pane.

5. Click OK to close the dialog and start the document processing. The files that are already PDF documents don't need processing. The Acrobat window becomes blank, and you see a number of progress bars as the PDFMakers for Word and Excel process their respective files; Acrobat processes the JPEG image.

6. The Save As dialog opens when the documents have been converted. Acrobat names the combined document Binder1.pdf, which is the name used for the sample project, and stores it in the source files' folder by default.

7. If you prefer, rename the file and choose a different storage location, and then click Save to dismiss the dialog and open the document in Acrobat.

One of the documents added to the Binder1.pdf is an Excel spreadsheet. Jim and Joe want to use only a portion of the spreadsheet in the presentation. That's next.

Modifying a Spreadsheet PDF

One page of the presentation document is an Excel spreadsheet that shows the business' sales figures for the first quarter of 2004 (**Figure 2.10**). Jim and Joe realize it doesn't make good business sense to show their profit for the quarter, although it is shown on the spreadsheet.

Doggone It! Sales 2004									
Month	City	4oz	8oz	Total Sales	Cost 4oz	Cost 8 oz	Profit 4 oz	Profit 8 oz	Total Profit
Jan	Laguna Beach	722	1500	21,531.78	880.84	3,660.00	4,165.94	12,825.00	16,990.94
Jan	Long Beach	450	1452	19,102.98	549.00	3,542.88	2,596.50	12,414.60	15,011.10
Jan	San Diego	1200	1600	25,972.00	1,464.00	3,904.00	6,924.00	13,680.00	20,604.00
Jan	San Francisco	1400	1845	30,062.55	1,708.00	4,501.80	8,078.00	15,774.75	23,852.75
Jan	Portland	889	992	17,116.19	1,084.58	2,420.48	5,129.53	8,481.60	13,611.13
Jan	Seattle	1020	1550	24,164.30	1,244.40	3,782.00	5,885.40	13,252.50	19,137.90
Feb	Philadelphia	677	599	11,315.24	825.94	1,461.56	3,906.29	5,121.45	9,027.74
Feb	Pittsburg	458	748	11,421.94	558.76	1,825.12	2,642.66	6,395.40	9,038.06
Feb	Allentown	799	1024	16,838.77	974.78	2,498.56	4,610.23	8,755.20	13,365.43
Feb	Boston	1025	1555	24,254.20	1,250.50	3,794.20	5,914.25	13,295.25	19,209.50
Feb	Portland	644	1600	22,085.56	785.68	3,904.00	3,715.88	13,680.00	17,395.88
Mar	Grand Forks	555	1420	19,485.25	677.10	3,464.80	3,202.35	12,141.00	15,343.35
Mar	Pierre	622	1852	24,701.26	758.84	4,518.88	3,588.94	15,834.60	19,423.54
Mar	Des Moines	499	1225	16,950.76	608.78	2,989.00	2,879.23	10,473.75	13,352.98
Mar	Wichita	844	1020	17,109.36	1,029.68	2,488.80	4,869.88	8,721.00	13,590.88
Mar	Oklahoma City	1200	752	16,652.48	1,464.00	1,834.88	6,924.00	6,429.60	13,353.60
Mar	Albequerque	944	887	16,346.69	1,151.68	2,164.28	5,446.88	7,583.85	13,030.73
Mar	Amarillo	863	655	13,230.82	1,052.86	1,598.20	4,979.51	5,600.25	10,579.76

1st Qtr Profit $275,919.27

Figure 2.10 *The spreadsheet contains information that Jim and Joe don't want to include in the presentation.*

They decide to use Acrobat's Snapshot tool to capture the part of the spreadsheet they would like to include in the finished presentation, create a separate PDF document from the snapshot, and then incorporate that into the Binder1. pdf document.

Capturing Content from a Page

Acrobat offers the Snapshot tool, which is a handy way to capture some of the content from a page and use it to create a separate PDF document.

To capture a portion of the spreadsheet, follow these steps in Acrobat:

1. The Zoom toolbar is one of Acrobat's default toolbars, but choose View > Toolbars > Zoom if it isn't displayed in the program. Set the view to 100% on the Zoom toolbar (**Figure 2.11**). You can either click the (+) or (–) button until the view reads 100% or click the value pull-down arrow and choose 100% from the list.

Whatever size is shown in the Document pane when you capture the snapshot is used in the subsequent PDF document. If you convert at 100%, there is little or no distortion of the appearance.

Figure 2.11 *Set the view using tools on the Zoom toolbar.*

2. Click the Snapshot tool ▣ on the Basic toolbar.

3. Drag a marquee on the page around the content you want to capture (**Figure 2.12**).

4. Acrobat tells you the content has been copied to the clipboard; click OK to dismiss the message dialog.

Next, you'll create a PDF document from the content on the clipboard.

Using Clipboard Content

Acrobat stores content captured with the Snapshot tool on the system clipboard. If you'd like to see it, choose Window > Clipboard Viewer to open the ClipBook Viewer. You see the captured portion of the spreadsheet is shown (**Figure 2.13**). Close the Viewer window.

Download **clip.pdf** if you prefer to work with the segment of the spreadsheet as described in the previous section.

Next, follow these steps to create a separate PDF document from the captured content:

1. Click the Create PDF task button's pull-down arrow and choose From Clipboard Image.

Doggone It! Sales 2004					
Month	City	4oz	8oz	Total Sales	Cost 4oz
Jan	Laguna Beach	722	1500	21,531.78	880.84
Jan	Long Beach	450	1452	19,102.98	549.00
Jan	San Diego	1200	1600	25,972.00	1,464.00
Jan	San Francisco	1400	1845	30,062.55	1,708.00
Jan	Portland	889	992	17,116.19	1,084.58
Jan	Seattle	1020	1550	24,164.30	1,244.40
Feb	Philadelphia	677	599	11,315.24	825.94
Feb	Pittsburgh	458	748	11,421.94	558.76
Feb	Allentown	799	1024	16,838.77	974.78
Feb	Boston	1025	1555	24,254.20	1,250.50
Feb	Portland	644	1600	22,085.56	785.68
Mar	Grand Forks	555	1420	19,485.25	677.10
Mar	Pierre	622	1852	24,701.26	758.84
Mar	Des Moines	499	1225	16,950.76	608.78
Mar	Wichita	844	1020	17,109.36	1,029.68
Mar	Oklahoma City	1200	752	16,652.48	1,464.00
Mar	Albequerque	944	887	16,346.69	1,151.68
Mar	Amarillo	863	655	13,230.82	1,052.86

Figure 2.12 *Drag a marquee with the Snapshot tool around the content on the page.*

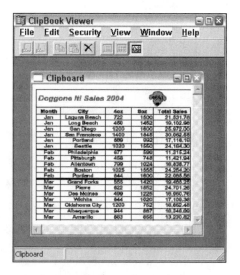

Figure 2.13 *You can see content captured with the Snapshot tool on the ClipBook Viewer.*

You see now that the option is active on the toolbar—earlier in the project, when you built the binder document, this option was disabled because there was no content on the clipboard.

2. Acrobat automatically converts the clipboard image to a new PDF document.

3. Choose File > Save to save the document (the project's file is named clip. pdf) and close it.

Now you have two documents open in Acrobat—Binder1.pdf and the new clip. pdf document.

Revising the Binder Document

The final stage of the process is to replace the existing spreadsheet page in the sales presentation document with the newly created spreadsheet segment.

You can download the modified binder document named **Binder2.pdf** to see how the extracted portion of the spreadsheet is integrated into the binder document.

Follow these steps in Acrobat to replace the file in the binder document with the new one:

1. Select the Pages tab at the left of the program window to display the Pages pane.

2. Click the existing spreadsheet page to select it (**Figure 2.14**). You see the page's thumbnail and its page number are highlighted with a gray outline, indicating it is the selected page.

3. Right-click/Control-click the thumbnail to open the shortcut menu and choose Replace Pages (Figure 2.14).

You can also select the command from the Pages pane's Options menu, or by choosing Document > Replace Pages. As you are already working in the Pages pane, it's simpler to select the command from the pane's Options menu.

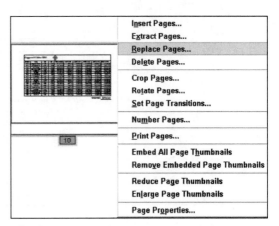

Figure 2.14 Select the page to be replaced in the Pages pane.

4. In the Select File With New Pages dialog, choose the spreadsheet segment PDF named clip.pdf, and then click Select to dismiss the dialog.

5. Next, the Replace Pages dialog opens. You see that the Original section of the dialog lists the Replace Pages as 10 to 10 of 10 in the Binder1.pdf document, meaning only page 10 will be replaced.

The page number is inserted in the dialog automatically because it was the page selected in the Pages pane before the Replace Pages process started. You also see that the Replacement section of the dialog lists Pages 1 to 1 of 1 in the clip.pdf document because the replacement document has only one page.

6. Click OK to dismiss the dialog; a confirmation dialog opens asking if you are sure you want to replace the page. Click Yes; the dialog closes and the page is replaced, as you can see both on the Document pane and in the Pages pane's thumbnails (**Figure 2.15**).

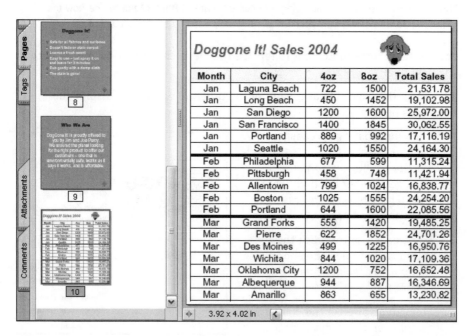

Figure 2.15 *The spreadsheet page is replaced with the new PDF document showing just the captured content.*

7. Save the document with the new content.

The sample project is saved as Binder2.pdf to differentiate the versions of the document.

Now that the content is assembled, it's time to reformat the sizes of some of the pages.

Changing Page Sizes

There are pages in the project that should be modified to be more consistent with the appearance of the rest of the project. These are

- The converted JPEG image

- The page created from the snapshot

In this section of the project, the brothers are working with Advanced Editing tools. To make the process quicker, choose Tools > Advanced Editing > Show Advanced Editing Toolbar (**Figure 2.16**). Drag the toolbar to dock it with the other toolbars at the top of the program window. Joe and Jim modify the image and spreadsheet segment pages using the Crop tool and the Crop Pages dialog.

Figure 2.16 *Open the Advanced Editing toolbar to save time as you work on page details.*

Follow these steps to resize the page of the converted JPEG image:

1. Click the JPEG image's thumbnail in the Pages pane to select it (**Figure 2.17**). You see the thumbnail and its page number are framed with a gray border, indicating the page is selected.

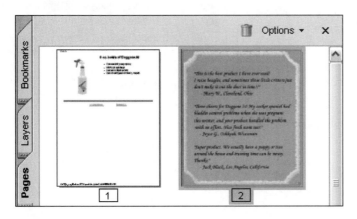

Figure 2.17 *Select the thumbnail of the JPEG image's page.*

2. Double-click the Crop tool 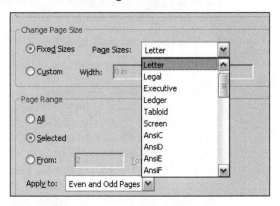 on the Advanced Editing toolbar to open the Crop Pages dialog.

   Alternatively, you can choose Crop Pages from the Pages pane's Options menu.

3. At the upper right of the Crop Pages dialog, the preview of the page shows its current size, which is roughly 5.5x6 inches.

   Leave the default settings in the Crop Margins and Margin Controls sections of the dialog. Crop Margins and Margins Controls both use values of 0 in for all sides; you don't want the image's dimensions to change.

4. Click the Page Sizes pull-down arrow and choose Letter from the list (**Figure 2.18**). You see the page size is now changed in the preview area of the dialog.

5. Check that the Selected option is chosen in the Page Range section of the dialog—it is selected automatically if you selected the page's thumbnail in the Pages pane.

Figure 2.18 *Choose a page size option from the pull-down list.*

6. Click OK to close the dialog and resize the page. In the Document pane, you can see the page is now resized and the image is centered on the page (**Figure 2.19**).

7. Repeat the same steps using the spreadsheet segment, and save the document after you have successfully changed the page sizes for both the JPEG image and the spreadsheet segment.

TO RESIZE OR NOT

There is no hard-and-fast rule regarding uniform page sizes. However, using a uniform page width is easier for the viewer because the individual pages seem more proportional.

The next adjustment to be made is to the advertisement page.

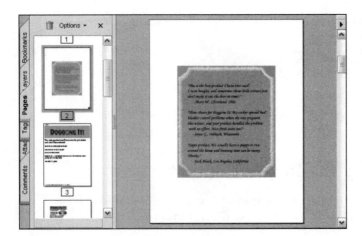

Figure 2.19 *The image's page is resized to a letter-sized page.*

Tweaking Content on a Page

The advertisement was converted from an InDesign CS document and was automatically placed at the upper left of the page. Joe and Jim would like it placed at the center of the page. They will use another Advanced Editing tool along with a simple trick to place the content correctly at the center of the page.

Setting a Selection Preference

Before working with the page, you'll need to set one of the program preferences by following these steps:

1. Choose Edit > Preferences (Acrobat > Preferences) to open the Preferences dialog.

2. Click the General category in the column at the left of the dialog to show the General preferences.

3. Click the Select Tool Options pull-down arrow and choose Images before text (**Figure 2.20**).

4. Click OK to close the dialog.

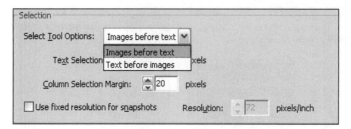

Figure 2.20 Set the Selection preference to touch up the content of the page correctly.

Repositioning the Page's Content

To modify the position of the advertisement's content on the page, Joe and Jim go once more to the Advanced Editing toolbar.

Follow these steps to move the content to the page's center:

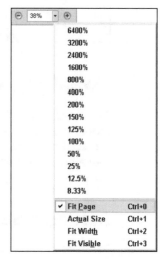

Figure 2.21 Select the view from the Zoom toolbar to display the full page in the Document pane.

1. Click the page's thumbnail to select it in the Pages pane.

2. On the Zoom toolbar, click the View pull-down arrow to open the options pull-down shown in **Figure 2.21**. Select Fit Page. The full page shows in the Document pane.

3. If you then look at the page's thumbnail in the Pages pane, you see a red bounding box overlaying the entire page; you can also resize the view to the full page by dragging a corner of the red bounding box (**Figure 2.22**). The larger you drag the size of the box, the more of the page is shown in the Document pane. It's faster to choose the view from the Zoom toolbar.

4. Click the TouchUp Object tool 🔲 on the Advanced Editing toolbar.

5. Drag a marquee around the page's content on the Document pane (**Figure 2.23**).

6. Release the mouse. You see each object within the page is identified by a gray bounding box (**Figure 2.24**).

7. Press Ctrl-X/Command-X to delete the selected objects.

8. Press Ctrl-V/Command-V to paste the content back on the page. Acrobat automatically places it at the center of the page.

Nice trick! The document's content is complete. All that remains is sorting the pages and checking the bookmarks.

Figure 2.23 *Drag a marquee around the content with the TouchUp Object tool.*

Figure 2.24 *All the objects within the marquee are selected.*

Figure 2.22 *You can also resize the view using the bounding box overlaying the page's thumbnail in the Pages pane.*

OH NO! WHAT HAPPENED?

If you select content, then delete and paste it back into the page, you may encounter one or two unexpected events. Here's what can happen:

- The advertisement contains a group of objects—a black ellipse with text overlying it. If the Select Tool Options preference isn't set to select images before text, then logically the text is selected before the images. When the objects are pasted back to the page, the text is placed before the image. In that case, the text is beneath the black ellipse unless you modify the preference.

- When you paste content back into a page, it is placed at the center of whatever has been identified as the page's size. When the entire page is visible in the Document pane (when the red bounding box in the Pages pane covers the entire page), the content is pasted to the center of the page, as you would expect. If, on the other hand, only a portion of the page is showing in the Document pane (and the bounding box in the thumbnail view in the Pages pane covers only a portion of the page), Acrobat pastes the content back into the center of the selected area.

Sorting Pages

The binder PDF was created using the documents as selected from the storage folder. They now need to be reorganized into their final order. You can quickly adjust the page sequence in the Pages pane for this type of project because the content is very visual and it's easy to distinguish the content on the thumbnails.

Before modifying the sequence in the Pages pane, drag the right border of the pane to the right to increase the size of the pane until you can see all of the thumbnails. If you are having difficulty seeing the content of the thumbnails, click the Options button at the top of the Pages pane and choose Enlarge Page Thumbnails. You can choose the command repeatedly until you can see the thumbnails clearly.

The "before" layout of the presentation document follows this layout:

- The product page from the Web site

- The converted JPEG image

- The homepage from the Web site

- The InDesign advertisement page

- The two-page Word document containing the product specifications

- The three-page PowerPoint presentation

- The segment of the spreadsheet

To move a page in the document, click and drag the thumbnail in the Pages pane. You can also Ctrl-click/Command-click to select several thumbnails at once. As you drag a thumbnail, a vertical bar is displayed that indicates the new location for the pages once you release the mouse (**Figure 2.25**). In the figure, which shows the "before" layout, pages 7, 8, and 9 are selected; the vertical indicator shows that when the pointer is released, the three pages will be moved to the start of the document. This is their intended location.

Move other thumbnails as desired (**Figure 2.26**). In Joe and Jim's project, the final page order is

- The three-page PowerPoint presentation

- The homepage from the Web site

- The product page from the Web site

- The two-page Word document containing the product specifications

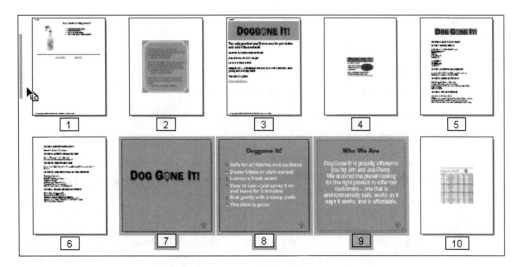

Figure 2.25 *Select one or more thumbnails and drag them to a different location in the layout; you see a vertical indicator at your pointer's location.*

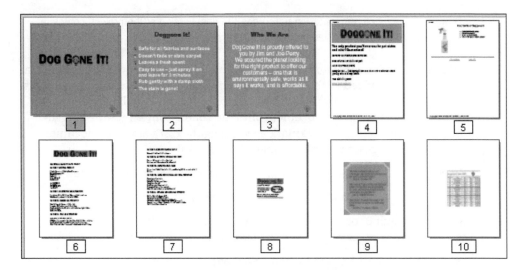

Figure 2.26 *The "after" layout of the document shows the final locations of the pages in the Pages pane.*

- The InDesign advertisement page

- The converted JPEG image

- The segment of the spreadsheet

Save the document to preserve the reordered pages.

The final phase of the project is to organize the document's bookmarks and to set its opening view.

Modifying the Document's Bookmarks

Bookmarks are navigational links listed in the Bookmarks pane that display page content in the Document pane when clicked. To view the document's bookmarks, click the Bookmarks tab in the Navigation pane to open it. If there are long bookmarks, as in this project, click the Options button at the top of the Bookmarks tab and choose Wrap Long Bookmarks from the pull-down menu; bookmarks whose character length exceeds the width of the pane are automatically wrapped to the next line so you can read the names clearly.

 Download **doggoneit_presentation.pdf** to see the final version of the project, complete with page sizing, sorting, bookmarks, and page transitions.

When the binder document was created from a number of other documents, a bookmark was added to the binder for each document. In addition, bookmarks were added for the converted Web pages, quite a number of bookmarks were converted with the Word document, and the source content for the spreadsheet was given its own bookmark as well (**Figure 2.27**). Since the document has only ten pages, that's far too many bookmarks!

You see several different icons in the Bookmarks pane. These indicate

- A separate page added to a Binder or the binder itself

- The default Bookmark icon, displayed when a new bookmark is added in Acrobat or pages are converted using Word headings or styles

- Web bookmarks created when a Web page is converted to PDF

Bookmarks are organized in a *hierarchy*. That is, there are parent bookmarks, which can have child bookmarks, which in turn can have child bookmarks of their own, and so on (shown in Figure 2.27). You can use an unlimited number of bookmark levels—three is the optimal number to use and still be able to display properly in the Bookmarks pane. Remember that if you delete a parent bookmark, any dependent child-level bookmarks are also deleted.

BOOKMARKS GOT YOU DOWN?

There are only ten pages in this document. Instead of modifying all the existing bookmarks, it may be simpler to delete them all and then add and configure a new set of bookmarks altogether. In the project, we'll take the long way round.

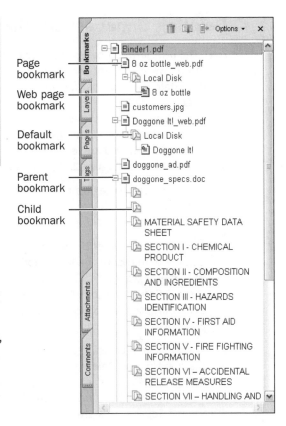

Figure 2.27 The document's numerous bookmarks are derived from different sources.

Open and close the hierarchy to show and hide dependent levels of bookmarks as you work with them. A bookmark that shows a (+) to the left of its icon means it contains content; a bookmark that shows a (–) to the left of its icon means that it is fully expanded, showing all its content.

You can approach "bookmark surgery" any way you like, but it's easiest to follow these steps:

1. Delete any bookmarks you don't want to use first.

2. Test the view of the bookmarks by clicking them and seeing the page layout in the Document pane.

3. Change the order of the bookmarks to match the document's page order.

4. Add new bookmarks if necessary.

5. Rename the remaining bookmarks.

6. Retest and reorder as necessary.

Joe and Jim have to follow all the steps to get their bookmarks in order.

Deleting Unnecessary Bookmarks

First, the brothers remove bookmarks that aren't necessary for the document. To delete a bookmark, click it to select it in the Bookmarks pane and press Delete. You can select more than one bookmark at a time by holding the Ctrl/Command key and clicking the bookmarks (**Figure 2.28**).

In the Bookmarks pane, Jim and Joe follow these steps to delete bookmarks:

1. Click to select the entire set of child bookmarks of the Word document, doggone_specs.doc, and press Delete to remove them (the bookmarks are shown selected in Figure 2.28).

2. Click to select the sales.xls bookmark and press Delete to remove it (**Figure 2.29**). You see that the bookmark and its child bookmark named Source Data are both removed.

3. Click the two bookmarks named Local Disk as well as the bookmark named Source Data (**Figure 2.30**). Delete the bookmarks; you see the child bookmarks of the two Local Disk bookmarks are also removed.

There are ten bookmarks left in the list at this point (**Figure 2.31**). The bookmark named Binder1.pdf at the top of the list isn't required, but you can't delete it now without removing the rest of the bookmarks because

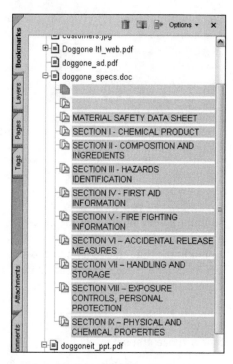

Figure 2.28 *Select more than one bookmark at a time for deletion; the Word bookmarks are selected in the image.*

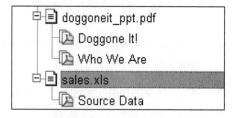

Figure 2.29 *Delete the bookmark for the original spreadsheet document.*

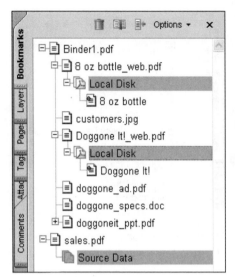

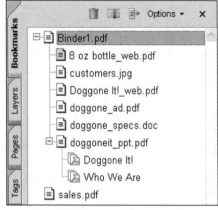

Figure 2.31 *The remaining list of bookmarks is much shorter than the original list!*

Figure 2.30 *Remove other extra bookmarks from the Bookmarks pane.*

they are dependent bookmarks. You'll have to reorder the bookmarks first. But before you do that, you'll first want to rename the bookmarks so that they are easily understood.

Renaming the Bookmarks

Now that the list has been weeded out, test the remaining bookmarks to see what page each bookmark is linked to. Click the bookmark in the Bookmarks pane; the corresponding view is shown in the Document pane.

You have to change the names of many of the bookmarks to make them more understandable. When you create a binder PDF document, each document is assigned a bookmark using the file's name, which isn't always the optimal name for understanding the content.

To change the name, click the existing name in the Bookmarks pane to make the text active, then type a new name (**Figure 2.32**).

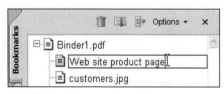

Figure 2.32 *Click a bookmark's name to make the text active.*

Click each bookmark in turn to see the content it displays, and then change the names to reflect the page's content (**Figure 2.33**). Leave the Binder1.pdf bookmark for now; it's changed in the next step.

Reordering the Bookmark List

The next step is to make the bookmarks of equal rank. If you look at the list of bookmarks, only the Binder1.pdf and Doggone It! bookmarks are first-level bookmarks (shown in Figure 2.33), meaning they are not a dependent of any other bookmark. The other bookmarks in the list are dependent bookmarks of either of the two parent bookmarks.

To change the ranking of a bookmark, click the bookmark to select it, holding down the mouse button. You see a horizontal bar and a pointer arrow (**Figure 2.34**). Drag it to the left and release the mouse; the bookmark's level is changed in the hierarchy.

Continue moving all the bookmarks until the entire set is of equal rank (**Figure 2.35**). The order of the bookmarks varies according to the sequence in which you select and move them.

When you click the original Binder1.pdf bookmark, the product page from Joe and Jim's Web site is shown in the Document pane because that was the first document added to the binder document earlier in the project. With the Binder1.pdf bookmark selected in the Bookmarks pane, press Delete to

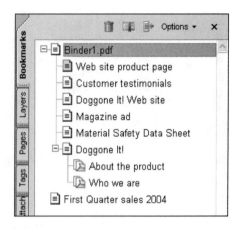

Figure 2.33 *Rename the bookmarks according to the pages' contents.*

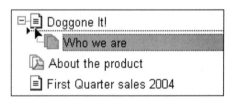

Figure 2.34 *Drag a bookmark left to raise its level in the bookmark hierarchy.*

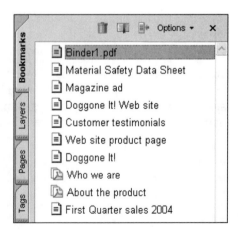

Figure 2.35 *The set of bookmarks are now at the same level.*

remove the bookmark because it no longer has any dependent bookmarks and isn't required in the project.

NOTE There are ten pages in the document and nine bookmarks—the Material Safety Data Sheet covers two pages.

Next, change the order of the bookmarks to match the page order in the document. At this point, the bookmarks link to the correct pages, but their order in the Bookmarks pane doesn't match the page order. The final arrangement of bookmarks is shown in **Figure 2.36**.

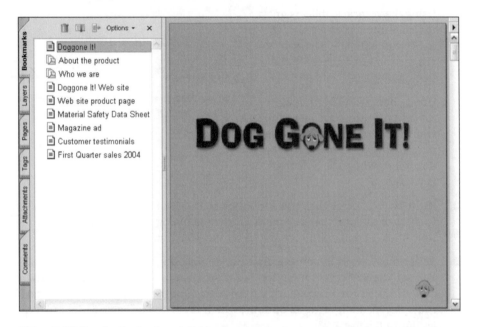

Figure 2.36 *Reorder the bookmark list by dragging the bookmarks to their correct locations; clicking a bookmark shows the corresponding page in the Document pane.*

Resetting the Bookmark Views

For many of the bookmarks, the default view is correct. That is, clicking the bookmark shows the full width of the page in the Document pane. The bookmark's link is called an *action*, meaning some event occurs in the program in response to your viewer's interaction with the bookmark—in this case, clicking the bookmark produces the action that displays the content in the Document pane.

If you click through the list of book-marks, you'll notice that the adver-tisement page isn't displaying its content correctly (**Figure 2.37**). Instead of appearing at the center of the Document pane, the advertisement is shown lower on the pane.

Follow these steps to reset the book-mark view for the advertisement page:

1. Using the vertical scrollbars, move the page into its correct view in the Document pane. You want to see the content centered in the Document pane.

   Don't change the Zoom mag-nification setting, because you want the page to have the same magnification as the rest of the document when the bookmark is clicked.

Figure 2.37 *The modified page doesn't display its view correctly in the Document pane.*

2. Right-click/Control-click the bookmark in the Bookmarks pane, and choose Properties to open the Bookmark Properties dialog, or choose Properties from the Options pull-down menu on the Bookmarks pane.

3. Select the Actions tab on the dialog to display the bookmark's link action. You see the Select Action option is set at "Go to a page view," which is the default action for a bookmark. At the bottom of the dialog, the link action is displayed, along with its options, which are listed as Page: 8, Zoom level: Fit Width (**Figure 2.38**).

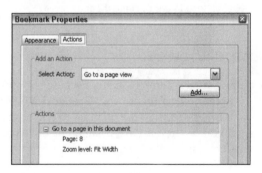

Figure 2.38 *Choose settings for the bookmark's link in the Bookmark Properties dialog.*

4. Click the "Go to a page in this document" action to select it, and then click Delete. The action is removed from the document; you need to replace it to reset how the page is seen when the bookmark is clicked.

5. Click Add. The Create Go to View dialog opens (**Figure 2.39**). You can set the view for the page, as described in Step 1. (You can also set the page prior to opening the dialog.)

6. Click Set Link. The dialog closes, returning you to the Bookmark Properties dialog. The "Go to a page view" action is replaced on the dialog, using the same characteristics as those shown in Figure 2.38. That is, Page: 8, Zoom level: Fit Width.

7. Click Close to dismiss the dialog.

8. In the Bookmarks pane, click another bookmark and then click the advertisement page's bookmark again to see the content centered in the Document pane.

Figure 2.39 *Follow the directions in the dialog to set the view for the bookmark to link to if you didn't set the view before opening the Bookmark Properties dialog.*

NOTE From the Actions tab, you can select an action and then click Edit to reset its values. For the bookmark, resetting the values doesn't change the actual appearance of the page's view; you must replace the action.

The final process in using bookmarks in a document is to set the view the user sees when the document opens.

Setting the View

There are several ways you can specify how a document displays when it opens. By default, only the first page of the document is displayed in the Document pane, and none of the Navigation panes are open. You might instead choose to also display the Bookmarks, Pages, Attachments, or Layers panes.

Using an appropriate view option shows your viewers the important navigation content in your file immediately on opening it—they don't have to open any panes themselves, and they'll recognize quickly that you have gone to the trouble of adding a navigation system.

Follow these steps to set the view:

1. Set the width of the Bookmarks pane and the Document pane as desired.

2. Choose File > Document Properties to open the dialog. Click the Initial View tab (**Figure 2.40**).

3. Click the Show pull-down arrow and choose Bookmarks Panel and Page.

4. Click OK to close the dialog.

5. Save the document, and then close and reopen it. You see the Bookmarks pane displayed, and the full width of the page is shown in the Document pane, as shown in Figure 2.36.

Figure 2.40 *Choose an option to display when the document opens.*

At this point, the presentation is essentially done. With just a few minutes before it's time to leave for their presentation, the brothers decide to add one last finishing touch. They want to add transitions to the pages to add a bit of visual interest to the presentation, and they decide to present the document in full-screen mode as well.

Using Page Transitions

Joe and Jim decide that they'd like to present the information to the client in a full-screen view and later send him the PDF so that he can navigate through their information using the bookmarks.

You can add transitions in Acrobat and configure them according to how your document is designed. For example, you can specify that the pages turn automatically or in response to a mouse click. In this project, the pages will turn in response to a mouse click because some pages, such as the technical specifications and the spreadsheet, have more content than can be seen or described in a few seconds.

NOTE To see an example of a slideshow that runs automatically, check out the project in Chapter 3.

Adding Transitions

Adding transitions gives the brothers the option of showing the presentation using the Full Screen view, as well as a more interesting way to change pages.

Follow these steps to add the transitions:

1. Choose Document > Set Page Transitions to open the Page Transition dialog.

2. Click the Effect pull-down arrow in the Page Transition area and choose an option from the list. The project uses the Wipe Down effect (**Figure 2.41**).

    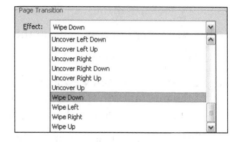

    If you prefer, you can choose from numerous other effects, including box in/box out options, other wipes, fades, blinds, cover/uncover effects, and so on.

    Figure 2.41 *Select the transition you'll use in the presentation from the pull-down list.*

3. Select the page range to apply the effects to. The default applies the transition to all pages; use the default in this project (**Figure 2.42**).

4. Click OK to close the dialog and add the transitions to the page.

You can't see the transitions in the program window. Use the Full Screen view to test the project's effects.

Figure 2.42 *Specify the speed of the transition and whether you want the pages to turn automatically in the dialog.*

Viewing the Slideshow

The last step in the project is to test how the slideshow runs. Acrobat 7 includes an option that lets you show just the content of a document against a solid background. Removing the program's interface allows you (and your viewers) to concentrate on the content rather than being distracted by the surrounding toolbars, menus, and other program items.

Follow these steps to view and run the slideshow:

1. Display the first page of the document in the Document pane.

2. Click the Full Screen view icon ![icon] on the Status bar at the bottom left of the program window. The program interface is now removed from the screen, and the page is shown against a black background (**Figure 2.43**).

3. Click the left mouse button to advance through the slides/pages.

4. Press the Esc key to return to the regular program interface.

Figure 2.43 The document's pages are shown at full-screen size against a black background.

SETTING A DOCUMENT TO USE FULL SCREEN VIEW AUTOMATICALLY

Just as the brothers set the document to automatically display the Bookmarks pane and the document when it opens, they can also specify that the file opens as a slideshow in the Full Screen view automatically.

Follow these steps to create an automatic slideshow:

1. Choose and customize a slide transition (described in the "Using Page Transitions" section).

2. Choose File > Document Properties to open the dialog, and then click Initial View.

3. In the Document Options area of the Initial View dialog, click the Show pull-down arrow and choose Page Only. If you leave the settings used in the project, you'll also see the Bookmarks pane when the slideshow is viewed.

4. Click the Open in Full Screen mode check box in the Window Options section of the dialog.

5. Click OK to close the dialog.

There are several options on the dialog for hiding content, but unless your viewers know keyboard shortcuts or you add additional content such as navigation buttons, they won't be able to see the entire program interface when the slideshow is finished and they return to the regular Acrobat interface.

If you have hidden the toolbars, from the program window the user can click the Show Toolbars button ⊞ on the Status bar at the lower left of the program window to toggle the toolbars on.

To test the slideshow, save and close the document and then reopen it. Any transition set in the program is used when the slideshow displays. The pages are seen against a black background by default. Press Esc to exit the slideshow and return to the basic program interface.

Changing the Presentation's Background Color

Joe and Jim are fine with the default black background color for the presentation, but they could change it if they wanted to add some color.

Follow these steps to change the background color of the slide presentation:

1. Choose Edit > Preferences (Acrobat > Preferences) and select the Full Screen listing to display the options.

2. In the Full Screen Appearance section of the dialog, click the Background Color color swatch to open a color palette, and then choose a custom color.

3. Click OK to dismiss the dialog and set the background color.

The job is done! And for a happy ending to the chapter, Joe and Jim make their presentation, are offered an enormous contract, and go on to be major players in the pet care industry.

What Else Can They Do?

There are some additional features Jim and Joe could add to their presentation document if they had more than a few hours to prepare for their meeting. They could customize the bookmarks' text using color or bold/italic text, as described in Bonus Chapter 1, "Building a Wow! Résumé," available on the book's Web site.

They might like to add text labels to some of the pages using the TouchUp Text tool, which is described in Chapter 9. In addition, they could add a header or footer to the pages to add a unifying element to the project, and add page numbers as well to tie the presentation together. Learn about footers in Chapter 14 and page numbers in Bonus Chapter 1 on the book's Web site.

All in all, in the short amount of time available, they prepared a valuable and usable document.

3

Building a Slideshow Presentation with Picture Tasks

Suppose you need to present a series of photographs to a committee that will decide which one belongs in a company brochure. Or imagine that you are preparing a collection of shots, one of which will appear in a newspaper ad. How can you present the selection of possibilities to a client in a way that is both professional and interesting?

Acrobat 7 includes a plug-in called Picture Tasks that allows you to easily manage a group of images and prepare different types of output, including a slideshow and various print options. In this chapter's project, you'll learn how to use the plug-in to create a slideshow and customize it, as well as to send the final product automatically by e-mail from within Acrobat. Your viewers will be able to see the slideshow using Acrobat or Adobe Reader—a slideshow is viewable in Acrobat version 5 or newer and Acrobat Reader version 5, as well as in Adobe Reader, which replaced Acrobat Reader in version 6 of the program. Bonus material on the book's Web site shows you how to print pictures with various layouts.

Picture This

Let's look at Susan Jenkins's predicament. Susan is a busy assistant at Picture This, a small suburban advertising and marketing agency that specializes in customizing calendars, placemats, and other marketing items for local businesses.

Susan has mastered the art of transferring images from her camera to her computer. Working with a simple image manipulation program she received with her camera, she can organize, correct, and store hundreds of images at a time. Susan is responsible for showing her images to the company's client, and therein lies her problem. She has been in the habit of attaching images to e-mails to send to her clients, but she doesn't like searching for, attaching, and keeping track of the images. She doesn't find this method particularly convenient—either for herself or her e-mail recipients, who are forced to open, save, and organize these images themselves. More importantly, Susan would like to present these images to her clients in a more professional and interesting format.

What Susan needs is a quick way of assembling a collection of images in a format useful for online distribution via e-mail. She might decide to jazz up the way the images are presented, perhaps even adding date captions and music before sending the file to her client, Carter Motors (**Figure 3.1**).

Acrobat 7, of course, can help Susan solve her problem. In fact, there are two ways you can use Acrobat to produce a slideshow, depending on the format of the images you intend to use. One method is to create a slideshow manually, which you can do if you don't have JPEG files to work with (see the sidebar, "Working with Other Image Formats"). This method involves adding your own transitions, using various tools to add captions (and music if you like), and setting the document to correctly display the slideshow. See Chapter 2 for more details on displaying a presentation.

The simplest method, which is covered in this chapter, is to use Picture Tasks, a plug-in that is activated when you use JPEG images in Acrobat.

Steps Involved in This Project

Susan can work entirely from within Acrobat's Picture Tasks plug-in to create the presentation as well as different print versions of her images. She can also e-mail the presentation right from Acrobat.

First, she plans to import the images into Acrobat in a binder, or combined PDF document. After using the Picture Tasks' features, she'll have a slideshow complete with a title, slide transitions, and music.

You can select a title and add it to the slideshow automatically with Picture Tasks.

Playback buttons let your users easily control the presentation.

Carter Motors Winter Ad

Images can be easily converted to PDF.

You can add and choose a background for the assembled slideshow.

Figure 3.1 *The project's slideshow contains a number of winter images.*

To create her slideshow, Susan needs to

- Import the group of images into Acrobat, where they are converted to PDF

- Open the Picture Tasks' Export to Slideshow dialog and configure the slideshow's contents, adding a title, transitions, and music

- E-mail the slideshow PDF to her client

You can work with a range of image formats in Acrobat. Susan is working with JPEG images, so we'll focus our discussion on that format.

WORKING WITH OTHER IMAGE FORMATS

If the images are not in JPEG format, or if Susan wants to use more transition options, include additional text, or control the compression of the images in the slideshow manually, she can create the slideshow in Acrobat without the benefit of the Picture Tasks plug-in. This is what she needs to do:

- Add transitions to create a slideshow in Acrobat. For more on transitions, see Chapter 2.

- Add captions using the TouchUp Text tool. For more on the TouchUp Text tool, see Chapter 9 and Bonus Chapter 4.

- Add music using the Attach Sound tool. Read how to use the Attach Sound tool in Acrobat's Help files.

- Set the document to open in Full Screen view (see Chapter 2).

- Downsize the images in the finished presentation, producing a smaller file. This technique is discussed in Chapter 4.

- E-mail the presentation to her client. This is covered later in this chapter.

WORKING WITH JPEG IMAGES

JPEG (Joint Photographic Experts Group) is a file format often used with grayscale or color images, including photographs. It is a type of compression, which means the file size is reduced by combining the pixel content in different ways.

JPEG compression is called *lossy* compression because it removes image information from the file to make the file smaller in size. The compression process increases the size of pixels and applies a mathematical formula to approximate the color in each larger pixel. As a result, the quality of the image can be reduced. It's important to strike a balance between the file size and the quality of the image.

Acrobat uses five levels of JPEG compression. Image quality and file size are inversely proportional. That is, the higher the quality of the image, the larger the file size; the lower the quality, the smaller the size.

Both high and maximum compression levels produce very clear, crisp images. On the other hand, Minimum and Low levels can be distorted and display a boxy appearance. Sometimes the distortion is so great it's difficult to determine what is in the image (**Figure 3.2**).

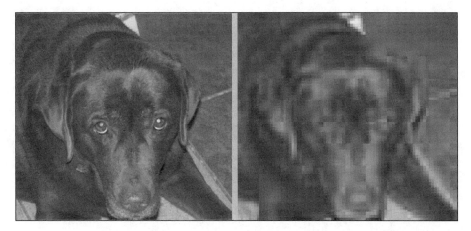

High resolution (large file size)   Minimum resolution (small file size)

Figure 3.2 *Although you may get a small file size, an image can become unrecognizable if compressed too much.*

Assembling the Files

Susan can construct her entire presentation, including captions and music, from within Acrobat. In so doing, she'll work with a very helpful Task button to create her PDF, named—appropriately—the Create PDF task button.

NOTE Task buttons are different than toolbars. Acrobat has a large collection of toolbars, each containing icons for a range of similar commands. Task buttons are collections of commands you would commonly use to perform different types of tasks, such as creating a PDF document, commenting and marking up a document, or building forms.

Download the four JPEG images named **carter1.jpg** through **carter4.jpg** if you want to practice loading and arranging files for the slideshow. Download **susan_raw.pdf** to see how the files were combined.

Follow these steps to create the PDF document:

1. Click the Create PDF task button to open its pull-down menu, and choose From Multiple Files (**Figure 3.3**). If the Task button isn't displayed, choose View > Task Buttons > Create PDF. The Create PDF from Multiple Documents dialog opens.

Figure 3.3 *Select a method for creating a PDF file from this menu.*

2. Click the Browse/Choose button to open a file browser dialog, and locate the files you want to use for the slideshow.

3. Select the files, and click Open to dismiss the file browser dialog and load the files into the Create PDF from Multiple Files dialog (**Figure 3.4**).

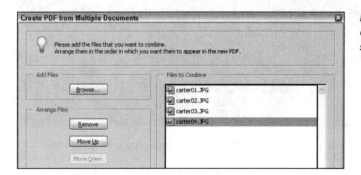

Figure 3.4 *Assemble and order the images for the slideshow in the dialog.*

4. Rearrange the order in the dialog by clicking a file in the list and then clicking the Move Up or Move Down buttons, or drag the file up or down in the list. Click Remove if you want to delete a file from the list.

5. Click OK to close the dialog; a Save As dialog opens, along with an Adobe Acrobat information dialog. Click OK to dismiss the Adobe Acrobat dialog (we'll come back to it shortly).

6. In the Save As dialog, name the project and select a storage folder. By default, Acrobat names the file Binder1.pdf. Susan names her file susan_raw.pdf (**Figure 3.5**).

7. Click Save to dismiss the dialog and open your document in Acrobat.

Picture Tasks

As part of the document creation process (Step 5 above), you see a dialog named Adobe Acrobat that describes Picture Tasks (**Figure 3.6**). Picture Tasks is a separate plug-in that is not always present in Acrobat. The plug-in is launched when your document is created in Photoshop Album or Photoshop Elements (version 2 or newer), or in Acrobat using JPEG images, as in this project.

Figure 3.5 *Name and save the slideshow file, named Binder1.pdf by default.*

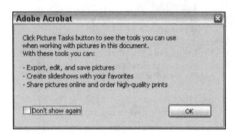

Figure 3.6 *Picture Tasks may be enabled depending on the image format.*

When the Picture Tasks plug-in is activated, several changes are made to the program:

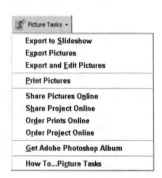

- The Picture Tasks button appears on the Task bar. It includes a pull-down menu that lists Picture Task options (**Figure 3.7**).

- Picture Tasks is now included in the View > Task Buttons menu (**Figure 3.8**).

- A How To window displays at the right of the program window containing several links to information about what you can do with Picture Tasks.

Figure 3.7 *You can choose from a number of functions on the Picture Tasks menu.*

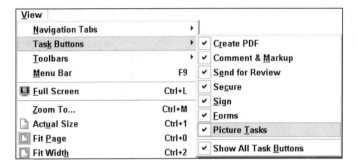

Figure 3.8 Picture Tasks is included in the Task Buttons pull-down menu.

Picture Tasks How To Window

You can work directly from the Picture Tasks How To window to do a number of tasks (**Figure 3.9**). For example, you can

- Create a slideshow automatically through a single dialog

- Export the pictures from the document and either save them or edit them in an image-editing program

- Print the pictures using a number of different page layouts

- Choose from several online functions for sharing or ordering online

In this discussion, we'll focus on creating the slideshow, and then we'll take a look at how the pictures in the slideshow can be printed.

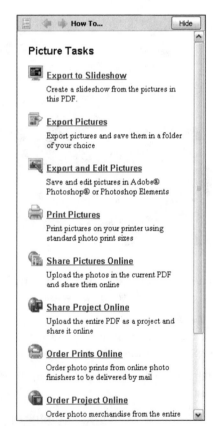

Figure 3.9 The Picture Tasks How To window contains a list of links to different options and processes.

Creating a Slideshow Using Picture Tasks

To begin working with the Picture Tasks How To window, click a function in the list. The appropriate dialog opens. Click the Hide button to close the How To window if you find it takes too much room on the program window. You can reopen the How To window by clicking the Picture Tasks task button and choosing How To Picture Tasks from the pull-down menu.

Download the **susan_slideshow.pdf** file to view the finished slideshow after it was created with Picture Tasks. If you want to build the slideshow yourself and then add an audio file, download the **snow.wav** file to insert into the slideshow.

Picture Tasks contains an option that lets Susan build a slideshow through a single dialog, making her job easier and the task quicker.

Follow these steps to create a slideshow directly from the Picture Tasks How To window:

1. Click the Export to Slideshow link on the Picture Tasks How To window, or click the Picture Tasks button and choose Export to Slideshow from the pull-down menu. The Export to Slideshow dialog opens (**Figure 3.10**).

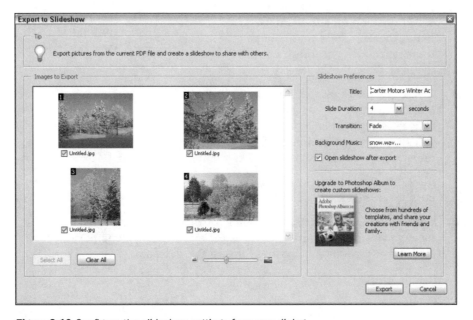

Figure 3.10 Configure the slideshow settings from one dialog.

2. Click the check boxes beneath each thumbnail of the document's images or click the Select All check box to select the set of pages automatically. (Click Clear All to remove all the check boxes if you want to start the selection process over.)

3. Click the Title field and type a name for the slideshow, which will be shown on the first page of the slideshow when it plays.

4. Click the Slide Duration pull-down arrow and choose a time for displaying each slide. You can choose from several options, ranging from 1 to 30 seconds.

   For a slideshow used to present images, as in this example project, 4 or 5 seconds is a sufficient length of time for viewers to see each image.

5. Click the Transition pull-down arrow and choose from one of several transitions, which are animations used to change the view from one image to another (**Figure 3.11**). For example, the Fade transition fades one image out as the next fades in; the Wipe transition slides one image out as the next slides into place.

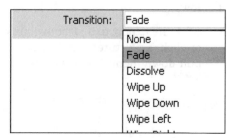

Figure 3.11 *Choose from several transition options.*

6. If you like, click the Background Music pull-down arrow and choose Select to open a browse dialog. Locate a music file and select it; you see its name listed in the field. Susan uses the snow.wav file for her project. The default option for Background Music is None.

7. Click the "Open slideshow after export" check box to view the slideshow once it is created.

8. Click Export to dismiss the dialog, and open a Save As dialog. Rename the file if you wish (it automatically uses the existing PDF filename) and select the storage location. Click Save to create the slideshow.

NOTE You can only use sound in WAV, AIFF, or MP3 formats. Acrobat embeds the sound in the PDF document in a format that plays in both Windows and Mac. Music files add considerably to the file's size.

Figure 3.12 *Slideshows created with the Picture Tasks plug-in automatically include a control panel.*

If you chose the option "Open slideshow after export" on the Export to Slideshow dialog, when you save the file, the slideshow runs. The slideshow displays a semitransparent control panel at the upper-right corner of the window (**Figure 3.12**). Click the controls to control the slideshow's playback, or let it run as programmed.

When the slideshow finishes, it closes and returns to Acrobat. An Adobe Picture Tasks dialog displays (**Figure 3.13**). Click Play to replay the slideshow, or close the dialog.

Figure 3.13 *A dialog displays in Acrobat when the slideshow ends.*

A SHORT COMMERCIAL MESSAGE

The Export to Slideshow dialog also includes a Learn More button. Click the button to open an Online Services Wizard describing Photoshop Album, which is another Adobe product. Use Photoshop Album to organize and catalog images, make corrections, and distribute finished projects. Photoshop Album projects include the slideshow and picture layouts used in this project. You can choose options from the Online Services Wizard to either buy the product or download a trial version. The Picture Tasks plug-in is based on some of the functionality found in Photoshop Album.

Reducing the File Size for E-mail

One of Susan's goals is to prevent sending massive e-mails, so it's important to consider the file's size.

 If you want to try compressing the slideshow yourself, use the file **susan_slideshow.pdf**. Download the **susan.pdf** file to view the final slideshow after reducing its file size.

To quickly check a document's size, choose File > Document Properties. In the Document Properties dialog, select the Description tab (**Figure 3.14**). In the Advanced section of the tab, you see details about the document, including its size. Susan's presentation is about 3.2 MB. For recipients with dial-up Internet connections, a file that size could require quite a long download time!

NOTE In the Document Properties dialog you can add information about the document such as a name, author, and so on, as shown in Figure 3.14.

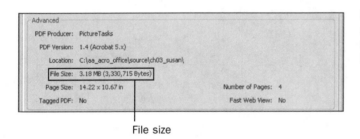

File size

Figure 3.14 Check the size of the finished document in the Advanced section of the Document Properties dialog.

There are two ways you can reduce the file size of a document. One way is through a simple command, the other is through an advanced feature called the PDF Optimizer, which is described in Bonus Chapter 4 on the book's Web site. Here, we'll limit the discussion to the simple method.

Follow these steps to reduce the file size:

1. Choose File > Reduce File Size to open the Reduce File Size dialog. The default setting for this command is compatibility with Acrobat 5.

2. Click the "Make compatible with" pull-down arrow to choose another Acrobat version (**Figure 3.15**).

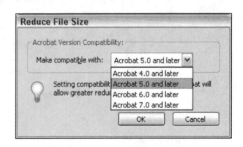

Figure 3.15 Choose a version compatibility option in the Reduce File Size dialog.

NOTE The higher the version number you choose, the more the file size may be reduced, depending on the document's content. However, if your client is using an older version of Acrobat or Adobe Reader than the option you select, they may not be able to see the content or some of the features of the document.

3. Click OK to close the dialog. A Save As dialog opens, using the default name of the presentation.

4. Type a name for the copy and click Save to process and save the file. The copy opens in Acrobat.

NOTE Acrobat recommends you first save a copy of the document when you use the Reduce File Size command; in some cases, the resulting document is compressed too much, resulting in distorted content, especially images.

Based on the content of the document as well as the compatibility version you choose, you may see a dialog similar to the one shown in **Figure 3.16**. In this presentation, for example, there are two issues:

- The presentation uses JavaScript to activate the controller and the slide transitions, which may be a problem for viewers using old versions of Acrobat or Acrobat Reader.

- The slideshow was created using the Picture Tasks process. As part of the process of reducing file size, images are modified automatically; when Picture Tasks is used to create the slideshow, image optimization is omitted.

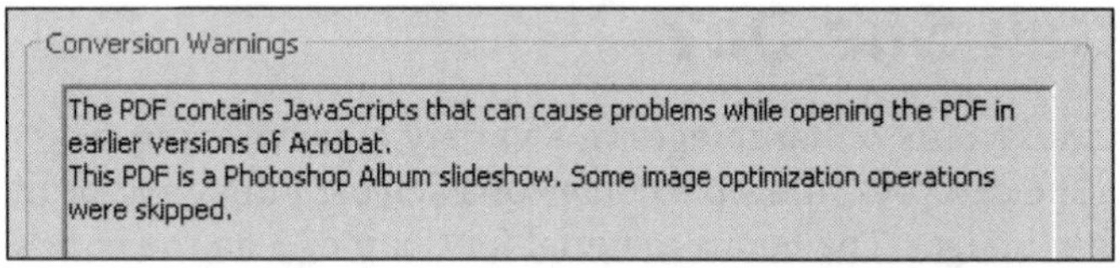

Conversion Warnings

The PDF contains JavaScripts that can cause problems while opening the PDF in earlier versions of Acrobat.
This PDF is a Photoshop Album slideshow. Some image optimization operations were skipped.

Figure 3.16 *After the file is processed you may see a Conversion Warnings dialog listing problems or notes about the conversion process.*

The original presentation started at a size of more than 3 MB; after reducing the file size using any of the Acrobat 5, Acrobat 6, or Acrobat 7 compatibility settings, it is reduced slightly and decreases download time a bit.

Sending the Presentation

The last step in the process is sending the PDF presentation. Again, Susan can work entirely in Acrobat—she doesn't have to open her e-mail program and search through her computer to find the presentation file.

Follow these steps to send the presentation:

1. Choose File > Email. An e-mail dialog opens, with the presentation attached (**Figure 3.17**).

2. Type the recipient's name in the To field or click To and choose the recipient's name from the address list.

3. Click Send to close the dialog and send the presentation on its way. It's that quick!

NOTE Depending on your operating system and configuration, you may see a dialog stating that the e-mail has been sent to your e-mail client.

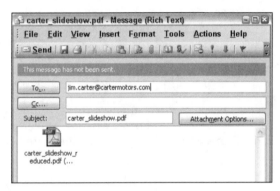

Figure 3.17 *Use Acrobat's commands to automatically attach the presentation to an e-mail message.*

What Else Can She Do?

Susan can produce print layouts of her images in a variety of ways using the Picture Tasks plug-in. She can print multiple copies of a selected image or print a contact sheet of all her images. The bonus material for Chapter 3 on the book's Web site shows you how to work with other Picture Tasks. If Susan is really serious about sending presentations in a very compact format, she can use lower-resolution JPEG images when she is constructing the presentation. If the source images are at a lower resolution, each source image contributes less to the overall file size.

She can also build the presentation manually. Rather than using the Picture Tasks feature, she can work with a number of commands, actions, and other features to create much the same presentation as that produced automatically using Picture Tasks. When building a presentation from scratch, you have more control over the individual components. For example, you can *optimize* images, which is a method of compressing them to a level best compatible with the way they are used in a manual presentation, an action that can't be done using the Picture Tasks method. Read about creating a slideshow manually in Chapter 2.

4

Creating an Interactive Map

A full-featured PDF document—that is, one containing a navigation structure—more closely resembles a Web page than a simple document. Within a PDF document, you can add buttons, links, and bookmarks, providing a path for your users to make their way through your document.

Unlike a Web page, which sometimes can contain broken links or images that don't load, a PDF document maintains its appearance and integrity at all times, making Acrobat 7 a great option for creating a wide variety of structured documents.

In the project in this chapter, you'll see how to create an interactive "map." The interactive part comes from the various buttons used to display pop-up images and text. You'll learn how to draw the buttons and add actions to them. The images for this project are created in Photoshop, and you'll see how to convert them to PDF in Acrobat. Bonus content on the book's Web site (www.donnabaker.ca/downloads) for this chapter shows you how to convert an image to PDF in Photoshop And you don't have to worry about protecting the content of the map; you'll learn about adding security to the finished document as well.

Fleur-de-Lis Travel

This is the story of an up-and-coming boutique travel agency in New Orleans, owned and operated by one Amanda Marshall and her former college room- mate. The company, Fleur-de-Lis Travel, specializes in providing an immersive experience for its guests, including customized tours, airport limo service, and boutique hotels.

Amanda has discovered that many of her prospective clients learn of her services through its Web site. She's spiced up the Web site presentation and is using an interactive HTML page both to illustrate a few of the area's most famous attractions and to provide custom tour ideas. The Web page contains pop-up images and rollovers, but that isn't working as well as Amanda would like. She wants the entire presentation to be available immediately, without waiting for downloads; she's also concerned that some of the site's most important design features might be hidden by pop-up blockers.

One of Amanda's concerns is the integrity of the presentation. For Fleur-de-Lis Travel, presentation is everything, and Amanda needs to be sure that the effort she makes in building an interactive map will result in a flawless document that can be used online.

Amanda looked at the option of creating a Flash presentation, but decided against it for a couple of reasons. She wasn't sure if her clients would be inter- ested in waiting for a Flash presentation to load, and although she's worked with Flash in the past, it's not her forte. Acrobat, on the other hand, is a pro- gram she is quite comfortable with.

Amanda has an interesting job ahead of her! She plans to create an interactive PDF file that contains the image of a New Orleans map, which serves as the background for the project, as well as a set of six visible buttons. When the prospective clients visit the Web page, they can simply click a button to see both a photographic image and a block of text describing a city landmark (Figure 4.1).

Steps Involved in This Project

In addition to building the set of buttons and pop-ups, Amanda decides at the end of the project to add a background for the text pop-ups, which is done in Photoshop directly from Acrobat. If you don't work with Photoshop, you can work with a different image editing program. Finally, she adds security to pro- tect the content of the document.

In Acrobat, you can make images pop up when a user moves the mouse over an interactive button.

You can also create special buttons for text to pop up.

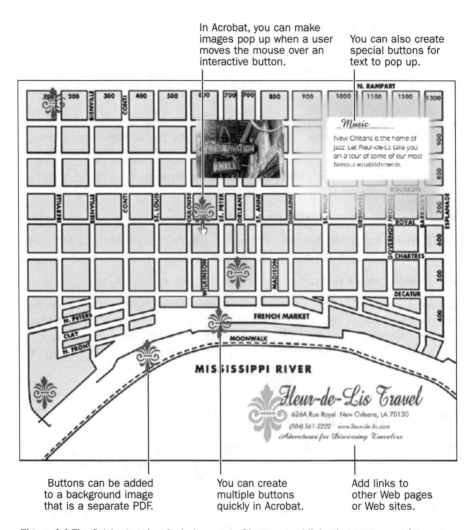

Buttons can be added to a background image that is a separate PDF.

You can create multiple buttons quickly in Acrobat.

Add links to other Web pages or Web sites.

Figure 4.1 *The finished project includes a set of buttons and links that a user can interact with to show images and text. Password security is used to protect the final document.*

To create her interactive map, Amanda needs

- A map image to use as a background for the project. The map must be sized correctly so that a user/viewer can see the whole map without having to scroll the page.

- A clear naming system. Amanda is working with a fair number of similar objects, and good design includes attention to the structure as well as the content of the work.

- Several copies of a button to serve as "hotspot" buttons on the map—that is, buttons that produce an effect in response to a user's mouse click.

- A number of photographic images to use for the pop-ups. To make the production process simpler, the images should share common dimensions.

- A number of text images to use for pop-ups that provide information on her agency's services, again using similar dimensions for simplicity and a unified appearance.

- A link from the map to the Fleur-de-Lis Web site.

- To make the finished project as small in size as possible because her users will be viewing the document online using either Acrobat or Adobe Reader.

- To apply simple security to protect the integrity of her project.

In the next sections of this chapter, you see how Amanda goes about building her interactive map, starting with the image preparation. If you don't plan to convert the images yourself in an image-editing program, skip ahead to the section "Converting Images in Acrobat." If you are working with Photoshop or another image editing program, read on.

Preparing the Images

The map uses a total of 19 images, including the background map image, six photo image pop-ups, six text image pop-ups, and an image of a fleur-de-lis, copies of which serve as the buttons users see and interact with. Images can be modified for use in Acrobat in any image-editing program. This section describes the different types of images used in the project and why the specific design choices are made. You can apply these principles regardless of the program you use to prepare them in.

 Download the **six JPEG image files** for the image pop-ups, which you alter in Photoshop or your image-editing program if you want. PDF versions of each image are also available for download so that you can see the converted format (filenames start with "**i_**"). Download the **six JPEG image files** for the text pop-ups. PDF versions of each image are also available for download so you can see the converted format (filenames start with "**t_**").

This is how Amanda prepares the images for the project:

- **Map image.** The map image is sized in Photoshop and converted to PDF in Acrobat. The goal is for viewers to see the entire map in the Acrobat or Adobe Reader window without having to scroll the page. Using a properly sized image looks more professional and doesn't inconvenience the viewers. In the sample project, the map is sized at approximately 6.5 x 5.5 inches. At this size the entire map can be displayed along with the default toolbars on the program browser window (**Figure 4.2**).

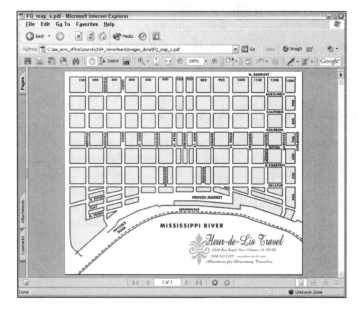

Figure 4.2 Make sure the document is sized correctly to view in a browser window without scrolling.

NOTE Acrobat's default toolbar arrangement uses two rows of toolbars, and the map could be larger and still visible in the program. But because Amanda's viewers will see the map through their Web browser, the map needs to be sized smaller than if it is viewed in Acrobat to account for the browser's toolbar height.

- **Text pop-ups.** The text pop-ups are created in Photoshop and sized uniformly to use for one of the rollover features. Using a uniform image size makes the job simpler because Amanda can create the set of six rollover buttons in Acrobat and then quickly substitute the appropriate text pop-up. The text pop-ups are converted to PDF in Photoshop, described in the bonus section for this chapter on the book's Web site entitled "Converting an Image to PDF in Photoshop."

- **Image pop-ups.** The image pop-ups are also created in Photoshop. Although the source images are different sizes, Amanda sets the size of the largest dimension (either height or width) to 2 inches for all of her images. The resizing contributes to a more uniform presentation and makes it simpler to use the images in the project's buttons. The image pop-ups can remain in their JPEG format.

- **Hotspot buttons.** The hotspot buttons that are visible on the map—those viewers click to see the pop-ups—are smaller versions of the Fleur-de-Lis logo. Amanda uses the image to create the first hotspot button and then copies the additional buttons in Acrobat. The button image is converted to PDF in Photoshop.

We won't be discussing image editing in Photoshop, but we'll see how to convert an image to PDF from within Acrobat itself.

Converting Images in Acrobat

Where you convert a document depends on the document type and your workflow. If you are working in a program that contains a PDF conversion function, like Photoshop or InDesign, you can convert the document directly from there. In fact, if you are working in Photoshop with PSD files, it is important to convert them from Photoshop because Acrobat doesn't have a conversion option for native PSD files; the same applies to InDesign documents.

You can create PDF documents from the source images in Acrobat. Acrobat includes preferences used for converting files of different formats to PDF; the conversion options vary according to the file format. Let's look at how to create the map PDF in Acrobat.

Follow these steps to begin the conversion process within Acrobat:

1. To view the preferences, choose Edit > Preferences (Acrobat > Preferences on a Mac) to open the Preferences dialog (**Figure 4.3**).

2. Click Convert To PDF in the categories column at the left of the dialog to display the Converting to PDF settings.

3. Click the file format you want to review from the list. In Figure 4.3, the TIFF file format is selected.

4. Read the current settings for the file format at the right of the dialog. The default conversion for TIFF files uses medium-quality JPEG compression for color; we'll change this option for this project.

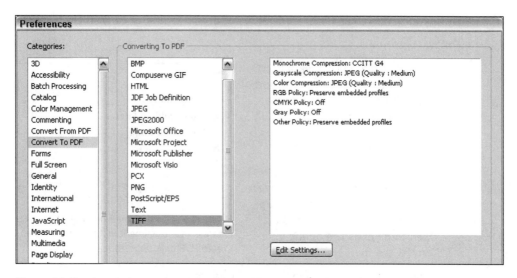

Figure 4.3 *Check and change the preferences before converting files to PDF in Acrobat.*

5. To modify the settings, click the Edit Settings button; the Adobe PDF Settings dialog opens (**Figure 4.4**).

6. Adjust the settings as desired. In Amanda's project, the converted image should be of high quality; click the Color pull-down arrow in the Compression options area of the dialog to open the list, and choose an alternate setting.

7. Click OK to close the dialog and return to the Preferences dialog; click OK to dismiss the Preferences dialog and return to Acrobat.

Once Preferences are changed in Acrobat, they remain that way until you change them again. If you can't recall all the settings you modified for a particular file format, click Default to restore the default range of settings.

Figure 4.4 *Modify the settings for a selected file type in this dialog.*

Download the **map.tif** file to use as the source image for the map. Download the **map.pdf** file if you want to see the PDF that is used for the background, where buttons and text will be added.

Once you have checked the conversion settings, it's time to convert the image.

Follow these steps:

1. Click the Create PDF task button to open its pull-down menu, and select From File (**Figure 4.5**). The Open dialog displays. If you can't see the task buttons, choose View > Task Buttons > Create PDF.

2. In the Open dialog, locate and select the file you want to convert to PDF. Amanda selects the map. tif file from her file folder. Click Open to dismiss the dialog and convert the file.

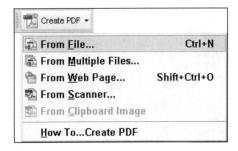

Figure 4.5 *Choose from a number of ways to create a PDF document in Acrobat from the Create PDF task button's menu.*

3. Choose File > Save to save the converted image PDF.

NOTE Task buttons are different from toolbars. On a toolbar, you see a collection of icons for commands that pertain to the same type of object, such as the Rectangle and Line tools on the Drawing Markups toolbar. Task buttons contain a number of functional options for performing a specific type of task, such as creating a PDF file or form.

Naming Project Content

Before starting the button-building process, it's important to take a few minutes to plan how the content will be named. Buttons are added using the default name "Button1" for the first button, with the number changing sequentially as additional buttons are added. Working with Acrobat's method for creating multiple copies of the same button complicates things even further by appending another number after the default number.

Although it is simple to keep track of three or four buttons in a project, when you are working with many buttons, as in this project, planning the naming structure for the buttons beforehand can save a lot of time in the long run.

For Amanda, the process starts with the text and image pop-up names. Amanda has used the content of the text pop-up and the content of the corresponding image prefaced with "t_" for text files and "i_" for image files. For example, the text image that describes Fleur-de-Lis Travel's mystery tour is named t_mystery.pdf; the corresponding image pop-up is named i_mystery.jpg. The three buttons for the mystery unit will be named

- **b_mystery**—for the hotspot button that contains the icon the user moves their pointer over to see the mystery text and image

- **t_mystery**—for the button that contains the text pop-up the user sees when the b_mystery button is active

- **i_mystery**—for the button that contains the image pop-up the user also sees when the b_mystery button is active

As you'll see later in this project, when actions are applied to the buttons, prefacing the button names with a letter divides the collection of button objects into categories that are much easier to sort through and makes troubleshooting any problems a lot easier.

The method you use for naming a series of objects in Acrobat is a matter of personal preference. Plan before you start. Use whatever naming structure you find understandable. Just be sure the names are useful in terms of keeping straight both the content and the relationships among the objects straight.

Drawing a Button

Now that the images are all prepared for the project, it's time to start the button-building process. A button is a form element—referred to as a *field*. In this project, however, we aren't using buttons for form building, like those used in Chapters 9 and 10. We'll use buttons here because of their ability to respond to users' mouse actions in interesting ways. The easiest way to approach button building is in batches. Amanda will draw and configure the first button and then add the rest.

Buttons commonly change appearance when you move the pointer over them, and they may change yet again when you click them. These changes are called *button states*. A button that uses Up, Over, and Down button states is a *three-state button*. The button states are named in reference to how they appear on the document:

- **Up**—before you interact with the button

- **Over**—when you mouse over the button

- **Down**—when you click the button

In the project, Amanda uses only the Up and Over button states. This means the buttons appear one way on the document when viewers see it, and another way when they mouse over the button. Nothing happens to the button's appearance when viewers click a button.

Acrobat includes four different button behaviors. The Push button behavior lets you configure different states for the buttons and is used in this project. The other button behaviors are None, which does nothing when users interact with it; Outline, which highlights the outline of the button when clicked; and Invert, which flashes the reverse of the button's color when clicked.

TIP Open and close toolbars as you are working in Acrobat to save time clicking through program menus. To quickly open a toolbar, right-click/Control-click the toolbar well and choose the toolbar from the menu; in this case, the Advanced Editing toolbar.

 Download the **button.pdf file** to create the button for the project.

The first buttons to add are the hotspot buttons that viewers can click to see the text and image pop-ups.

Follow these steps to draw the first button:

1. Choose Tools > Advanced Editing > Forms > Button Tool. Or click the Button tool ■ on the Advanced Editing toolbar; it is the Forms tool shown by default on the toolbar.

2. Drag a marquee on the page where you want to place the button (**Figure 4.6**). Release the mouse; the Button Properties dialog opens to the General tab. A button is named Button1 by default.

3. Name the button if you are using a custom naming system; the first button added to the sample project is the b_cruise button (**Figure 4.7**).

There is no right or wrong approach to which button to start with: Amanda started with this button because she intends to add each group of images to the buttons in alphabetical order.

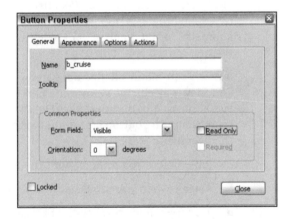

Figure 4.6 *Drag the Button tool to draw a marquee on the document where you want to place the button.*

Figure 4.7 *Name the button and choose other general characteristics in this pane of the dialog.*

NOTE In addition to naming the button and designing its appearance, you can also add a tooltip that displays when users move their pointers over the button on the page; in the project, it isn't necessary because the pop-ups will display information.

4. Select the Appearance tab, and define how the button will look by choosing colors for borders and backgrounds, as well as selecting font characteristics. Amanda's buttons don't use text or background colors. If you are starting with the program's default settings, you see both a border and background color in the color swatches. Click the Border Color color swatch and select No Color from the standard color palette; repeat with the Background Color.

NOTE If you want to use color for the borders or backgrounds, select one from the respective standard color palette. Or, you can click Other Color to open a Color dialog to choose a custom color. In **Figure 4.8**, the color options for the Background Color are shown.

5. Click the Options tab to display settings for defining the button's behavior and choosing its content (**Figure 4.9**).

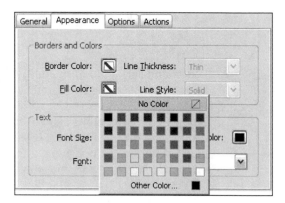

Figure 4.8 *Choose options to define the appearance of the button, including standard and custom colors for the background and borders.*

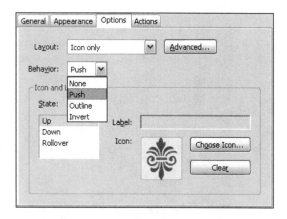

Figure 4.9 *Select characteristics for the button's content in the Options pane.*

6. Click the Layout pull-down arrow and choose Icon Only from the list. You can also choose different combinations of Label (which is text you type on the dialog) and Icon (an image) options from the list. In the project, you use an icon only. When you select an Icon option, the Advanced button is activated.

7. Click the Behavior pull-down arrow and choose Push from the list. A Push button is the only button you can construct in Acrobat that uses different configurable states. You need a three-state button to create the pop-ups.

8. Click Choose Icon to open the Select Icon dialog (**Figure 4.10**). Click Browse to display an Open dialog.

9. Locate and select the image or PDF file you want to use for the button, and click Open to dismiss the dialog and show a preview of the image in the Select Icon dialog. Click OK to dismiss the dialog; a thumbnail of the image displays on the Options pane of the Button Properties dialog, shown in Figure 4.9.

10. Click Close to close the Button Properties dialog and complete the button. The button and its content is shown on the document with a bounding box and the overlying button name (**Figure 4.11**).

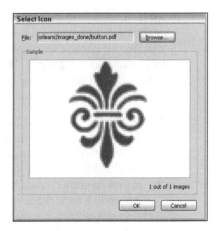

Figure 4.10 *The image you choose for the button is displayed in the dialog.*

Click the Hand tool 👆 on the Basic toolbar to deselect the Button tool. You can't see the finished button without its bounding box and overlying name when the Button tool is active.

Figure 4.11 *A button object shows the name and its bounding box as well as the content on the document.*

The Button Properties dialog also contains the Actions tab, used for setting different activities that occur when users interact with the button, such as opening a pop-up when a button is clicked. We'll add the actions after all the buttons are built.

Duplicating Buttons

There are two ways to create multiples of the same button in Acrobat. One method is to copy and paste the button; the other is to generate duplicates automatically using the Create Multiple Copies command. For Amanda's project, either method will work—let's use the simpler method, which is a shortcut method to copy and paste an object using shortcut keys.

BUTTON STATES

Acrobat's default button behavior is None, which is fine for some situations but not very attractive. Instead of configuring custom buttons like those used in this project, you can create simple buttons with a bit of pizzazz. Use the Outline behavior, which highlights the button's border when the button is clicked, or the Invert behavior, which reverses the dark and light colors in the button when clicked.

If you have worked with illustration or image-editing programs, you may have experimented with creating copies of objects using shortcut keys and dragging a new copy from the original on the file.

Follow these steps to duplicate buttons by dragging copies from the original button:

1. Click the Button tool on the Advanced Editing toolbar to select it; and then click the button on the document.

2. Press Ctrl/Command and drag the mouse away from the original button to create a second copy of the button. You'll note it has the same name as the original; it also has the same characteristics, including the hotspot button's fleur-de-lis image.

3. Repeat until you have the number of buttons required (in this case, six).

4. Double-click a button copy to open the Button Properties dialog.

5. Select the General tab and rename the button. The second button created in the project is named b_cuisine.

6. Click Close to dismiss the dialog and complete the button.

7. Rename the rest of the buttons; in the project the buttons are named b_history, b_music, b_mystery, and b_shop.

That's the first set of buttons complete! Now Amanda will work on the other buttons for her map.

Creating the Other Button Sets

It's a simple matter to create the other buttons as well. Instead of starting from scratch to build the set of six buttons containing the photo images and the set of six buttons containing the text images, Amanda will copy and paste one of the first set of hotspot buttons on the document and then work from there.

 Download the **map1.pdf** file to see the map now overlaid with buttons.

There's a trick to resizing the button correctly, as you see in the following steps as the text image buttons are created:

1. Click the Button tool on the Advanced Editing toolbar, and then click one of the hotspot buttons. It doesn't matter which button you select because they are all the same, and you'll modify it to use for the text image button.

2. Press Ctrl/Command and drag the mouse away from the button to create a new copy of the button. It has the same name as the original hotspot button.

3. Double-click the new button to open the Button Properties dialog.

4. Select the General tab and rename the button; the first text image button added to the project is named t_cruise.

5. Select the Options tab and click Choose Icon to select the image as described earlier in the "Drawing a Button" section.

6. On the Options tab, click the Advanced button to open the Icon Placement dialog (**Figure 4.12**). Click the When to Scale pull-down arrow and choose Never; click OK to dismiss the dialog and return to the Button Properties dialog.

7. Click Close to dismiss the dialog.

You'll see the button, but not much of its content. As you can see in **Figure 4.13**, the button's box on the right is too small. Drag a corner resize handle to increase the button's size until you see the whole text image of the pop-up.

Now make copies of the text pop-up button and change its icon as described in the "Duplicating Buttons" section. Because all text pop-ups are the same-sized images, you don't need to adjust the buttons' sizes. Repeat the same process for the image pop-ups, and adjust the button sizes as necessary.

You can try other advanced features to make sizing images a quicker process, depending on how you sized the original images. For example, in the Options tab of the Button Properties dialog, click Advanced to open the Icon Placement dialog. Choose Never from

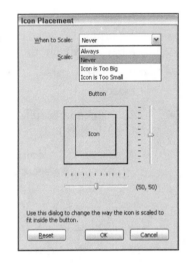

Figure 4.12 Select options to place button content precisely.

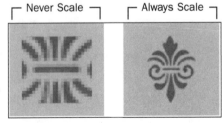

Figure 4.13 Using the custom settings, you see only a portion of the button icon's content.

Figure 4.14 You can use the Icon Placement options to size button images.

the When to Scale pull-down list to use the original sizes of the images regardless of the button's size (shown in the left image of **Figure 4.14**); choose Always to scale the image to fit within the bounding box, shown in the right image of Figure 4.14.

> **TIP** On the Icon Placement dialog, you can further customize the appearance of the button's icon. Options include scaling, proportional scaling, fitting to the bounds of the button's boundary box, or modifying the location of the icon in relation to the bounding box's edge.

In addition to the set of six hotspot buttons, Amanda's project now has six text pop-up buttons (with names beginning with "t_") and six image pop-up buttons (with names beginning with "i_").

As you can see, the final project has quite a collection of buttons (**Figure 4.15**)!

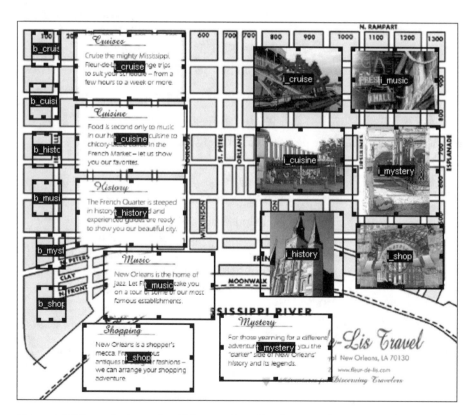

Figure 4.15 *The project contains 18 buttons, including 6 hotspot buttons and 12 image and text pop-ups.*

Adding Action to the Buttons

The final stage of button building is adding the actions. *Actions* are activities that are produced in the program in response to some event generated by the user, such as clicking a button or link, or by the program, such as displaying a page. Although you can add actions to individual buttons as you build them, there isn't much value to doing that in a project like this because you need to see the button names when configuring the actions—it's hard to select a name for a button that hasn't been built!

The only buttons that need actions attached are the six hotspot buttons. Acrobat contains a number of mouse actions that apply to buttons. Buttons can produce different actions based on where the pointer is in relation to the button or based on the mouse action itself. These mouse movements are called *triggers*.

As you'll see shortly, there are a number of mouse actions you can choose in the Button Properties dialog, listed in the Select Trigger pull-down menu on the Actions tab of the dialog (**Figure 4.16**). These triggers include

- **Mouse Up**—when the mouse button has been depressed and released
- **Mouse Down**—when the mouse button is depressed
- **Mouse Enter**—when the pointer moves over the button
- **Mouse Exit**—when the pointer moves away from the button area

NOTE There are other triggers used specifically for forms and media, such as the On Blur and On Focus triggers for form fields, and Page Visible/Invisible for media clips. Other document elements, such as pages, can also have triggers.

The most common button trigger is Mouse Up, and that is set as Acrobat's default trigger. The action is initiated when the user clicks a button with the mouse and then releases the button. Since Amanda's project uses images that appear and disappear in response to mouse actions, she'll use separate actions attached to two triggers—the Mouse Enter and Mouse Exit triggers. First you apply an action to the Mouse Enter trigger, and then you repeat the process for the Mouse Exit trigger. Each trigger is a separate type of interaction, so each needs its own action.

Follow these steps to add the actions to the first hotspot button, b_cruise:

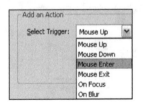

Figure 4.16 *Choose from one of several triggers that will initiate button actions.*

1. Double-click the button with the Button tool to open the Button Properties dialog, and then select the Actions tab.

2. To add the first action, click the Select Trigger pull-down arrow and choose Mouse Enter (the list is shown in Figure 4.16).

3. Click the Select Action pull-down arrow and choose Show/hide field (**Figure 4.17**).

4. Click the Add button—hidden beneath the pull-down list in Figure 4.17—and the Show/Hide a Field dialog shown in **Figure 4.18** opens.

5. Click the i_cruise field in the list, and click the Show radio button. Click OK to close the dialog and return to the Action tab of the Button Properties dialog.

6. Click the Select Trigger pull-down arrow again, and choose Mouse Enter again.

7. Click Add to open the Show/Hide Field dialog and choose the t_cruise field.

8. Click the Show radio button—which means the field will become visible when the user mouses over the button—and then click OK to close the dialog and return to the Actions tab of the Button Properties dialog.

Each time you add an action, make sure to check the trigger shown on the Actions tab. It defaults to Mouse Up, so you have to repeat the selection of the trigger each time you add another action.

9. Choose the Mouse Exit trigger from the Select Trigger pull-down list, and click Add to open the Show/Hide Field dialog.

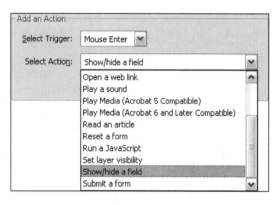

Figure 4.17 You can choose from a wide range of actions to apply to a button.

Figure 4.18 Select the field you want to show in response to the mouse action.

10. Select the i_cruise field; the Hide radio button is selected by default. Leave the default because you want the field to be hidden when the user mouses away from the button.

11. Click OK to close the Show/Hide Field dialog and return to the Actions tab of the Button Properties dialog.

12. Again, choose the Mouse Exit trigger from the Select Trigger pull-down list and click Add to open the Show/Hide Field dialog.

13. Select the t_cruise field, and leave the default Hide radio button selected.

14. Click OK to close the Show/Hide Field dialog and return to the Actions tab of the Button Properties dialog.

15. To check that the actions are all recorded, read the listing in the Actions section of the dialog. You see four actions—two Mouse Enter and two Mouse Exit actions (**Figure 4.19**).

16. Click Close to dismiss the Button Properties dialog.

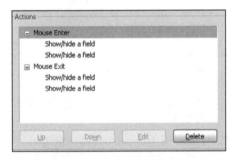

Figure 4.19 *Each hotspot button uses a set of four actions to show and hide its corresponding pop-up images.*

Repeat the entire process with the remaining hotspot buttons in the project. When you have finished, click the Hand tool on the Basic toolbar to test the buttons. If you prefer, you can test each button as you add it. Move the pointer over a hotspot button to show the image and its corresponding text; move the pointer away from a hotspot button and the images disappear (**Figure 4.20**).

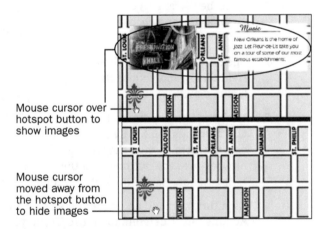

Mouse cursor over hotspot button to show images

Mouse cursor moved away from the hotspot button to hide images

Figure 4.20 *The images appear and disappear depending on the pointer's location on the document.*

Organizing the Button Layout

Acrobat includes several options for arranging objects on a document. In Amanda's project, the hotspot buttons need to be placed at corresponding locations on the map, and their image pop-ups are placed close to the hotspot button. Arrange these buttons by clicking them with the Button tool and dragging them to the appropriate locations.

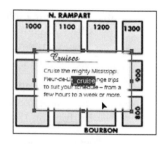

Figure 4.21 *Move one of the text fields to the desired location on the map.*

All the text pop-ups are displayed in the same location on the page, both vertically and horizontally. You can stack them manually at the appropriate spot, or you can use one of Acrobat's align features to do it for you. And instead of searching for all the fields on the document, select them easily in the Fields pane.

Follow these steps to select and align a set of fields:

1. Drag one button to the area where you would like the set of buttons stacked; in the project, the buttons will be stacked at the upper right of the map image (**Figure 4.21**).

2. Choose View > Navigation Tabs > Fields to open the Fields pane. If you like, you can drag this pane to dock it with the other Navigation Tabs at the left of the program window.

3. Ctrl-click/Command-click the buttons you want to align in the listing on the Fields pane (**Figure 4.22**). You see the different buttons listed on the pane; each set of buttons is prefaced by the letter and underscore, as described earlier in the "Naming Project Content" section, which makes it simple to find a particular group of buttons. Isn't that clever?

4. Right-click/Control-click the button you have correctly placed to open the shortcut menu. By clicking the button in the right location, you tell Acrobat where you want the remaining buttons placed.

5. Choose Align and an alignment option from the shortcut menu. You can choose from left, right, center, vertical, and horizontal alignment. The options you choose depends on where you placed the text images on your map.

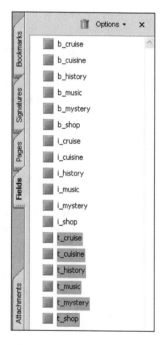

Figure 4.22 *Selecting the fields you want to arrange in the Fields pane saves time and confusion.*

6. Repeat the alignment process, choosing other Align and Center placement options until your set of buttons is stacked correctly, both horizontally and vertically.

    Again, the options you select will depend on where you originally placed the buttons on the map.

It doesn't matter in what order you stack the buttons, only one of the text pop-ups is shown on the document at a time. It also doesn't matter if the image pop-ups overlap one another or any of the hotspot buttons because they are only seen one at a time as well.

Working in the Fields pane can save a lot of time, particularly if you want to select a button that is within a stack of buttons. Instead of dragging other buttons out of the way to find the one you need, just click its name in the Fields pane.

PLACING CONTENT PRECISELY

Acrobat contains a number of placement tools you can use to place content in precise locations on a document page, including rulers, grids, and guide lines. You can choose the placement tools from the View menu. The default spacing for the grid that overlays the page is one-third inch squares, which can be customized in the program Preferences.

You can read about working with placement aids, and how to customize them, in Bonus Chapter 4 ("Creating an Interactive Catalog") on the book's Web site.

Modifying an Image in Acrobat

Now that the map is complete and tested, there are a few details to take care of. As Amanda works with the map, she realizes the text pop-ups would look better if there were some way to highlight the area on the map where the text consistently displays (the upper right of the map). She could reopen the document in her image-editing program, make changes, resave it as a PDF, and replace the page. Or she can save some time and work from within Acrobat to dynamically edit the document in her image-editing program and return the modified image to Acrobat—a process called round-trip editing.

Follow these steps in Acrobat to set preferences that specify an image-editing program:

1. Choose Edit > Preferences (Acrobat > Preferences on a Mac) to open the Preferences dialog.

2. Click TouchUp in the Categories column to display the TouchUp preferences.

3. Click the Choose Image Editor button to open a Choose Image Editor dialog.

4. Locate the program file you want to specify as the image editing program and click Open. The name of the program is listed on the Preferences dialog (**Figure 4.23**).

5. Click OK to close the Preferences dialog.

Download the **map2.pdf** file to see how the map looks after editing it and adding a Web link. If you have Photoshop, you can work along with your present copy of the project and do the round-trip editing yourself.

For some round-trip editing magic in Acrobat, follow these steps:

1. Click the pull-down arrow next to the visible TouchUp tool on the Advanced Editing toolbar if it is open, and choose the TouchUp Object tool ▣ from the pull-down options. Alternatively, you can choose Tools > Advanced Editing > TouchUp Object Tool.

2. Right-click/Control-click the document page with the TouchUp text tool to display the shortcut menu, and click Edit Image. If you are editing a particular image on a page, right-click/Control-click the image; in this case, the entire page comprises the image.

Figure 4.23 *Specify a program you want to use for editing images from Acrobat in the Preferences dialog.*

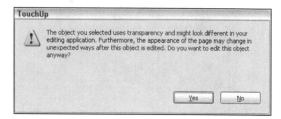

Figure 4.24 *Acrobat warns you if there are features of the document that may be altered after editing.*

3. Depending on the content of the image you intend to edit, a TouchUp dialog like that shown in **Figure 4.24** opens. Read the information—in this project the TouchUp dialog states that due to the document's transparency it may look different after editing.

If the transparency in the image is important, such as an image that overlays other content on the PDF file, you may want to click No and then modify the image through your image-editing program to control transparency.

4. In this case, click Yes to dismiss the dialog and launch the chosen image editing program.

5. The document opens with a temporary PDF filename. Make the desired changes, such as adding text, modifying image content, changing image colors, or as Amanda does, adding a yellow-to-white gradient to the area where the text images are shown on the map.

   If you add layers or vector data such as text, the document must be flattened by choosing Layers > Flatten Image in Photoshop.

6. Save and close the temporary document after making changes.

7. View the results in Acrobat. In this project, a gradient was added to the upper right of the map to serve as a background for the text pop-ups (Figure 4.25).

Figure 4.25 You can round-trip edit images from Acrobat, changing the image to add a gradient background.

Adding a Link to the Map

Links are one of Acrobat's features you can use to add navigation to a document. In the lower-right corner of the PDF containing her map, Amanda had placed her company's contact information, which includes text for a link to her Web site. Now she's going to add the link itself in Acrobat.

NOTE: You can read about transferring links from a source document to a PDF file in Chapter 5. Bonus Chapter 4 on the book's Web site shows you how to build a set of links using snapshot thumbnails of the project's pages. Bonus Chapter 1 on the book's Web site explains how to add a link to a bookmark.

To add the link to the map page, follow these steps:

1. Right-click/Control-click the toolbar well, and then select the Advanced Editing toolbar from the shortcut menu.

2. Click the Link tool  on the Advanced Editing toolbar and drag a marquee over the Web address on the map. Amanda's map includes her Web site address, www.fleur-de-lis.com.

3. Release the mouse to complete the marquee. The Create Link dialog opens (**Figure 4.26**).

4. Click the Link Type pull-down arrow and choose Invisible Rectangle (you don't want to see the link on the page).

5. Click the Highlight Style pull-down arrow and choose a highlight option. Amanda uses the Inset style.

6. Click the Open a web page radio button in the Link Action section of the dialog.

7. Click Next at the bottom of the dialog. The Edit URL dialog replaces the Create Link dialog.

8. Type the URL for the link. You must include the protocol, that is, the http prefix to the Web address (**Figure 4.27**). Amanda types `http://www.fleur-de-lis.com`

   The address used in the project is fictional—if you want to see the map in action, substitute the URL with a real Web address.

9. Click OK to close the dialog and finish the link.

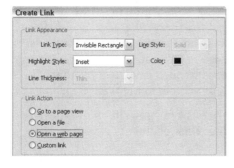

Figure 4.26 *Choose the link's appearance and action in the dialog.*

Figure 4.27 *Type the address for the Web link.*

10. To test the link, click the Hand tool on the Basic toolbar, and then click the link on the page. As the pointer is moved over the link's location, you see a Web hand icon, and the address is shown in a tooltip (**Figure 4.28**).

Figure 4.28 *The Web link shows the address in a tooltip.*

Now that Amanda has finished her map, she's ready to add the password security to protect her work.

DECREASING FILE SIZE

Before adding security and finishing the project, try a simple trick. Choose File > Save As, and resave the file as itself. Leave the name as is in the Save As dialog and click Save. A prompt asks if you want to overwrite the file; click Yes. If you have added or changed content, deleted and added objects, and so on, Acrobat maintains a record of all these changes that is stored in the document. Merely resaving the document as itself can decrease the file size dramatically. For example, my version of the sample project's document was more than 7 MB in size; after using the Save As command, the file size dropped to just under 1.3 MB—a dramatic saving.

Securing the Map

We've come to the end of the project as far as the design and construction goes. The final step is to add *encryption*, or security, to the map. Amanda worked long and hard to create an attractive presentation for her Web site, and it's a good idea to add a security policy to protect her work from users who might want to copy, print, or extract from the map.

There are several ways to add security, ranging from a simple password, to certificate encryption (described in Chapter 14), to server-based policies using third-party servers. In this case, Amanda will add a simple password to protect the document. The other forms of security are used for information exchange within a specified group of users and are not intended to protect content accessible to many anonymous users, such as visitors to her Web site.

You can work through several windows in Acrobat to apply different types of security. Let's follow the simple route and use the Document Properties dialog to add a simple password.

Follow these steps to apply security by way of a password:

1. Choose File > Document Properties to open the Document Properties dialog, and then select the Security tab.

2. Click the Security Method pull-down arrow and choose Password Security from the list (**Figure 4.29**). The Password Security-Settings dialog opens.

3. Choose "Acrobat 6.0 and higher" from the Compatibility pull-down list; a set of radio buttons become active.

4. Click the "Encrypt all document contents except metadata (Acrobat 6 and later compatible)" radio button.

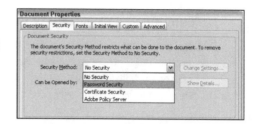

Figure 4.29 *Select the type of security to add to the document.*

5. Click "Use a password to restrict printing and editing of the document and its security settings." The Permissions Password field becomes active.

6. Type a password in the Permissions Password field. You can click the Printing Allowed and Changes Allowed pull-down arrows and select options from these lists; in this case, however, neither printing nor changes are allowed.

7. Click OK to close the dialog. A message displays describing the effect of third-party security products; click OK to dismiss the message.

8. A Confirm Permissions Password dialog opens; type the password in the Permissions Password field to verify the password and click OK. You return to the Document Properties dialog.

9. Click OK to close the Document Properties dialog. You see one more message dialog, this time telling you to save the document in order to save the security settings. Click OK to dismiss the message and return to the program.

Don't forget to save the document. And save it with an alternate name to make future work simpler. That is, if you save a copy of the original with security settings, you can use that on a Web page. If you need to make changes to the document, it's simpler to reuse the original and save it with security than it is to remove security, make changes, and then reapply security again.

Finally, to test the document, close it and then reopen it. You'll notice that many of the commands and tools are now inactive, based on the security settings selected. You won't be able to save or print the document, for example, nor can you use any of the editing tools. You'll also see a security icon at the lower left of the program window, indicating that security has been applied to the document. Move your pointer over the security icon to display a tooltip explaining the document's protection (**Figure 4.30**).

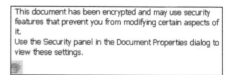

Figure 4.30 *A secure document displays an icon and messages on the program window.*

CHOOSING A COMPATIBILITY VERSION

You have to balance what you want to protect in a document against both its intended use and the likely audience. You can choose from Acrobat version 3.0 through version 7.0 compatibility: Each version has different security capabilities. In this project, using the Acrobat 6.0 compatibility option means that the document's content is encrypted but that its metadata (the information about the data the document contains) can still be accessed by search engines. This option is important for Amanda since her document is intended for online use on her commercial Web site.

Based on the versions of Acrobat Reader and Adobe Reader in use today, Acrobat 3.0–compatible documents can be viewed by the most users, Acrobat 7.0–compatible documents by the least number of viewers.

What Else Can She Do?

This brings Amanda's Acrobat adventure to a close. There are many ways she can enhance the presentation further. She might like to embed video or Flash movies into the map, like the Flash movie used in Chapter 5's project. She might decide to attach sound to play when the user opens the page (learn how to control page actions in Chapter 5 as well). Or, as an alternative, she might create buttons to control one or more pieces of music the user can listen to. She could also add more links from the map to other pages on her site or to other Web sites of interest to her users. She might also like to add a special link her users can click to send her e-mail directly from the map's page, using the same method as the e-mail bookmark used in the project that appears on the book's Web site in Bonus Chapter 1.

There's more she can do with the Mouse Enter and Mouse Exit triggers as well. For instance, she could use a faded version of the map in its own button that displays when the user moves his or her mouse over any of the hotspot buttons, or she could add other buttons that serve as backgrounds for the image pop-ups.

5

Creating Online Content in Acrobat

What if you need to create a large number of similar documents quickly? And what if you want to have those documents in a number of formats, including both PDF and HTML? Do you have to create the various file formats in a number of programs?

Fortunately, the answer to that last question is "No." Better yet, Acrobat 7 Professional lets you create numerous documents quickly using a template-like approach, and it gives you options for saving in a variety of formats, including HTML. Not only that, but Acrobat also offers some special features you can use to test how a document will look on a hand-held device. For a finishing touch, or to coordinate a document with the rest of your business documents and Web site, you can add a Flash movie or video file to any PDF document from within Acrobat 7 Professional, as you'll learn in this chapter.

The methods outlined in this chapter's project are among the simplest and quickest ways to build a set of uniform documents that can be repurposed for multiple uses. For example, rather than using links on the master Word document in Windows and then converting them, they can be added in Acrobat instead—and still produce the same results. The key to finding the best method is to keep your own workflow in mind as you experiment with the program.

Chuck Norris Real Estate

Chuck Norris ("No relation to the actor, but I'll fight to make the best deal for you!") is an ambitious young real estate agent and the proud owner of Chuck Norris Real Estate, a firm started by his father, Chuck Sr. (also no relation to the actor). Chuck Jr. realized that the nature of his business is becoming increasingly Web-based and mobile. Not content to use the "old" way of showing property listings—that is, by using pictures in the office window and carrying binders of information to home showings and open houses—he finally convinced Chuck Sr. they needed a company Web site, which was created a few years earlier. Now, Chuck Jr. would like to revisit how his prospective clients are using the information on his Web site and polish the appearance and functionality of his listing pages.

One thing he is concerned about is the appearance of his pages. In his business, appearances are important. He knows that sometimes a client will see a listing on his site and then print the page for reference. He has seen and worked with PDF documents, and he thinks they could be a logical way to give his clients printable information about his listings in a way that maintains the look of the document.

His other concern is mobility. Chuck has begun working extensively with a PDA (personal digital assistant) while on the road, and he finds it an extremely useful tool. He'd like to be able to have his listing information available on the PDA—which contains Adobe Reader—as well as the Web site.

Ideally, Chuck would like each listing available in both PDF and HTML formats, but he's not too keen on the potential workload involved. Chuck's listings originate as Word documents that he uses in the office. Some of the listings are prepared by his staff, while many are files he receives from his listing service. What he needs then is an efficient way of creating PDF and HTML documents for his listings from the source documents. Because presentation is important to him, Chuck also wants to add little touches like incorporating his spiffy new SWF (Shockwave Flash) logo (**Figure 5.1**).

Steps Involved in This Project

Time is a critical factor in Chuck's business. The real estate market is quite aggressive, and sales happen quickly. There have been times when his secretary is posting a Web page for a property at the same time he is closing a deal on it.

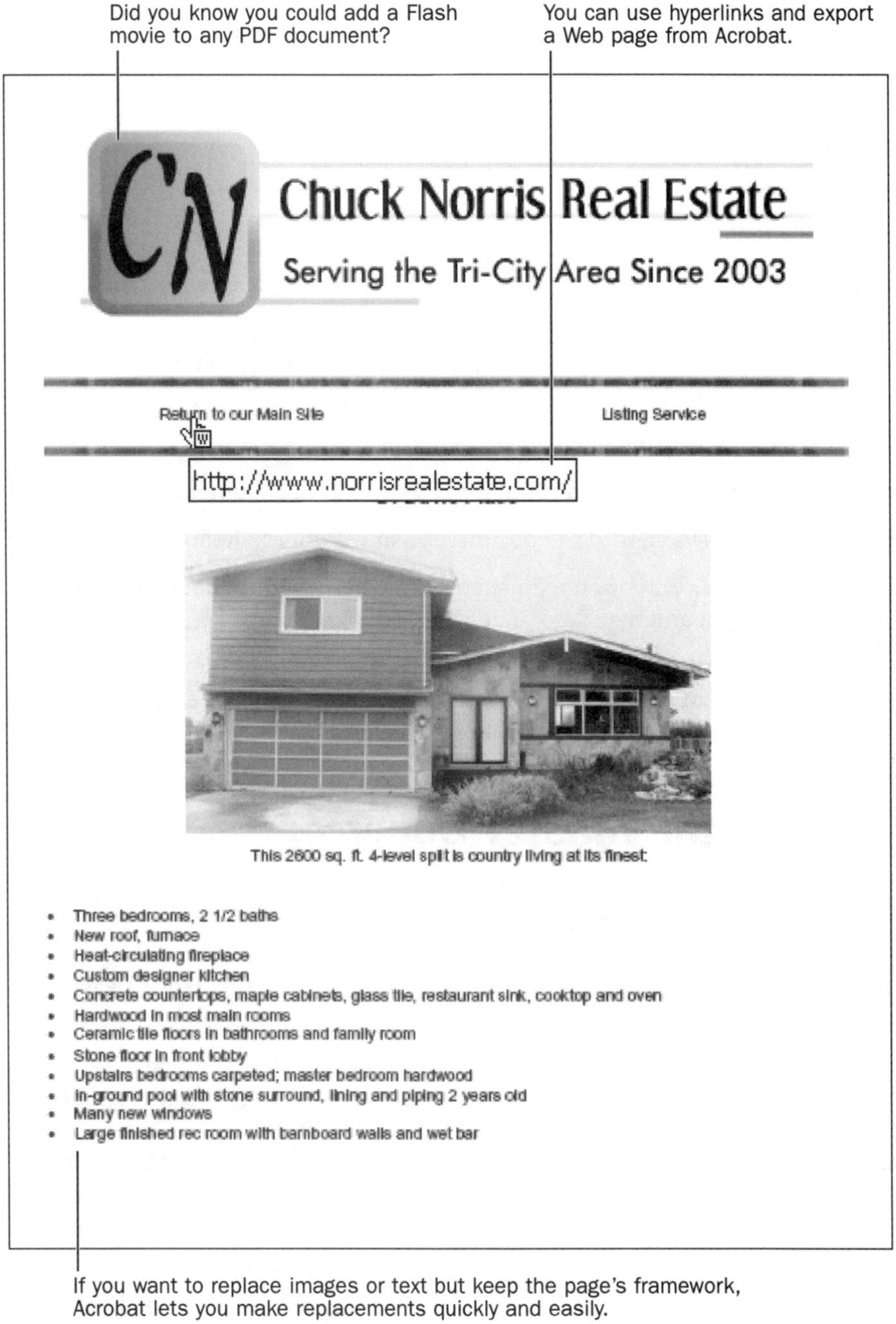

Did you know you could add a Flash movie to any PDF document?

You can use hyperlinks and export a Web page from Acrobat.

Chuck Norris Real Estate

Serving the Tri-City Area Since 2003

Return to our Main Site

Listing Service

http://www.norrisrealestate.com/

This 2600 sq. ft. 4-level split is country living at its finest.

- Three bedrooms, 2 1/2 baths
- New roof, furnace
- Heat-circulating fireplace
- Custom designer kitchen
- Concrete countertops, maple cabinets, glass tile, restaurant sink, cooktop and oven
- Hardwood in most main rooms
- Ceramic tile floors in bathrooms and family room
- Stone floor in front lobby
- Upstairs bedrooms carpeted; master bedroom hardwood
- In-ground pool with stone surround, lining and piping 2 years old
- Many new windows
- Large finished rec room with barnboard walls and wet bar

If you want to replace images or text but keep the page's framework, Acrobat lets you make replacements quickly and easily.

Figure 5.1 *The project includes elements created both in Microsoft Word and in Acrobat.*

Chuck realizes his basic problem is that he needs the same information in several formats:

- A Word document

- A PDF document

- A Web page

- A document he can read on his PDA

After exploring several options, Chuck and his staff decide to use Acrobat to manage a workflow that includes

- Creating a "master" document using a sample property listing in Word that includes two Web links, and then converting it to PDF

- Adding the company's Flash logo in Acrobat

- Exporting the Web page from Acrobat as an HTML document

- Testing the PDA view of the document using Acrobat's Reflow function

- Replacing the content on a finished page with new material to generate additional documents

The first stage in the project is creating a "master" PDF document from a Word document, one that allows him to use the same document for each property listing he needs to create in the future.

Building the Master Document

The first step of the project is to build a document to be used as a "master" document, which is essentially a PDF template. It's important to Chuck that the PDF property listings are built quickly and consistently. Using the master page concept, he can swap the content on the page using the Replace Pages command in Acrobat.

The master document begins as a Word file that includes small graphics serving as dividers on the page, Web links, and a sample listing placed in a table. Chuck saves the page as a DOC file and intends to swap images and text for additional listings as required. He could create a blank table with the graphic lines and links and save that as a template (DOT) file, but since Chuck doesn't like working with templates, swapping content is a better solution for him.

The document is converted using the PDFMaker in Word. Because Chuck intends to use the pages on his Web site, the conversion settings need changing (for more information, see the sidebar "Why the Smallest File Size Works

WHY THE SMALLEST FILE SIZE WORKS FOR THE WEB

Chuck intends the documents to be used online. The default Smallest File Size conversion option is tailor-made for this purpose:

- The PDF file is compressed.

- Any images on the page are *downsampled* (the number of pixels in the image is decreased, producing a smaller file) and the *resolution* (the number of pixels per inch) is decreased.

- The colors of all images are converted to a color system called sRGB, which is designed for onscreen viewing.

- The files are optimized for *byte serving* automatically, which means the document is downloaded to a user's Web browser on a page-by-page basis, resulting in faster page displays.

- Fonts are not embedded to save file size, which isn't a problem for Chuck because he doesn't need to use any custom fonts.

Chuck can use the same conversion setting throughout the project; when you choose configuration settings in the PDFMaker, they remain until you change them again.

for the Web"). Also, there are two links that Chuck plans to include—one to his Web site and one to his listing service. The links can be added either in Word or in Acrobat. In this project, they'll be added in Word (Windows).

Download three files—**master.doc, 24davis.jpg, and bar.jpg**—to work with the elements of the master document. Master.doc contains the source information, the 24davis.jpg file is an image used in the source file, and bar.jpg contains the horizontal graphic used in the table. Download the **master.pdf** to see the converted master document.

Follow these steps to create the PDF document from the Word document:

1. Choose Adobe PDF > Change Conversion Settings to open the Acrobat PDFMaker dialog.

2. On the Settings tab, click the Conversion Settings pull-down arrow and choose Smallest File Size from the list (**Figure 5.2**). The Smallest File Size option is ideal for Web and PDA use because it is the most compact conversion format.

3. Deselect all the Application Settings options except "Add links to Adobe PDF" and "Enable accessibility and reflow with Tagged PDF."

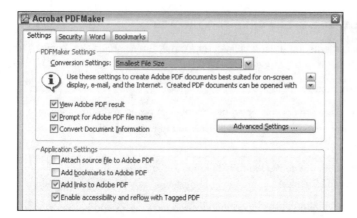

Figure 5.2 *Choose the conversion settings appropriate for online use of the document.*

Automatically, the page's Web links are converted and document tags are added to the PDF document, as required for the Web page. Document tags provide a structure for the document by defining each of the file's elements, such as headings, paragraphs, images, table rows and cells, and so on.

4.   Click OK to dismiss the dialog.

5.   Click Convert to Adobe PDF on the PDFMaker toolbar. The PDF document is created and saved with the name master.pdf.

Using Flash on the Master Document

Chuck wants to use his company logo on the listing pages. He has a Flash logo on his regular Web site and realizes it can also be used in the PDF document. It's much simpler to add the Flash file within Acrobat than it is to embed it in the Word document. There are two steps to placing a movie in a PDF document. First, the movie is inserted into the document using the Movie tool. Then, the settings are adjusted and customized according to how you plan to use the movie. In this project, the movie runs automatically when the viewer sees the page.

Download the **logo.swf** file, which is the Flash movie to be inserted into the document.

Follow these steps to add a movie to a PDF document:

1.   Click the Movie Tool 🔳 on the Advanced Editing toolbar, or you can select it by choosing Tools > Advanced Editing > Movie Tool.

2. Double-click the page where you want the upper left of the movie to be placed, or drag a marquee. Don't worry about the size of the marquee or its precise location because you can adjust the movie on the page. The Add Movie dialog opens (**Figure 5.3**).

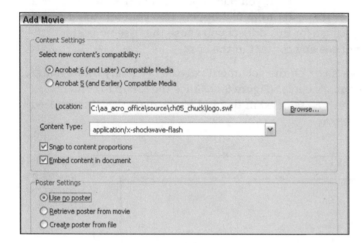

Figure 5.3 Select the movie file to use in the PDF document.

3. Click Acrobat 6 (and later) Compatible Media to access all the available options, including embedding, adding posters, and using Flash files.

4. Click Browse to locate the movie and select it. You see the file's location on the dialog, shown in Figure 5.3. Acrobat assigns a content type automatically when you select a file and determines the player needed to view the movie. You can select a different format from the Content Type pull-down list but may have difficulties playing the movie.

5. Leave the two additional options selected (they are selected by default). "Embed content in document" stores the movie file within the PDF file; "Snap to content proportions" maintains the movie's size in the document.

6. Choose a poster option—a *poster* is a still image that displays on the page when the movie isn't running.

- "Use no poster" shows the movie's background document, the option used in this project (shown in Figure 5.3).

- "Retrieve poster from movie" uses the first frame of the movie as a static image.

- "Create poster from file" lets you choose and use a different image for the poster. Click Browse to open a dialog and select the image. The file's location is listed on the dialog.

In Chuck's project, an action will be attached to the movie to make it play automatically when the page is displayed and no poster is needed, so select the "Use no poster" option.

7. Click OK to close the dialog and insert the movie. Acrobat draws a box the size of the movie on the page. If you had chosen either the "Retrieve poster from movie" or "Create poster from file" option, that content would appear in the box; but because for this project you chose the "Use no poster" option, you do not see any content in the box.

8. Position the movie's box on the document page as necessary by dragging it with the Movie tool's cursor (**Figure 5.4**). Since the "Snap to content proportions" option was selected in the Add Movie dialog, the box is sized correctly for the movie.

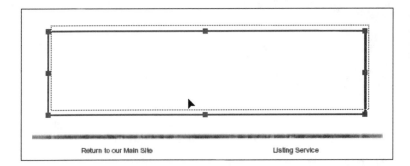

Return to our Main Site   Listing Service

Figure 5.4 Drag the movie's box to the correct position on the page.

9. Acrobat uses a Mouse Up action as the default *trigger* (see sidebar, "About Triggers and Events" for more information), or event that starts the movie playback. Click the Hand tool on the Basic toolbar, and then click the movie to play it on the page.

Customizing the Movie

Acrobat uses some default settings when it adds a movie to a document. Chuck wants to customize the appearance in a couple of ways. The default settings place a border around the movie, which he will remove because it detracts from the movie's appearance on the page. He also intends to add an action to make the movie play automatically.

ADDING A MOVIE TO A DOCUMENT

Movies can add a lot of interest, and in the case of the sample project, contribute to company branding. Be sure to plan ahead. When adding a movie to a PDF file, make sure the version of the Flash movie can be seen by most of your users—the most common version of the Flash player in use is version 6. An SWF6 movie is used for the sample project, which is compatible with Acrobat.

It's usually best to embed the movie in the document unless you know for certain that both the PDF file and the movie file can be accessed uniformly. For example, you may want to deselect the embedding option if you are using the document on a company intranet because you can make sure the PDF and movie files remain in the same folder location. For online use, however, it's much simpler and less likely to produce errors if you embed the movie.

Pay close attention to the file size as well: If your document is designed for distribution on a company intranet, the file size isn't nearly as much of an issue as in this project, where the content is intended to be viewed online. The Flash movie in the project is 12 KB in size, which is very quick to download as part of the PDF document.

A movie inserted into a PDF document can be modified in Acrobat through the Multimedia Properties dialog in three ways:

- You can create a number of versions of the movie, called *renditions*. Renditions are used when you want to distribute the movie to as wide an audience as possible, want to use both high- and low-quality versions, or want to use different renditions for different actions. The sample project uses a single rendition, which is the movie already selected.

- You can add actions that control how the movie functions.

- You can customize the appearance of the movie on the page.

Select the Movie tool on the Advanced Editing toolbar, and then double-click the movie on the page to open the Multimedia Properties dialog, which displays the Settings tab by default (**Figure 5.5**). The *annotation* is a name assigned by Acrobat to identify the object. You can type a description for an alternate text tag if you are creating an accessible document. In an accessible document, all visual content needs a text tag that describes what the image or movie contains so viewers using assistive devices like screen readers can understand the page's content. The default action on the dialog is a Mouse Up action, shown in the List Renditions for Event field. The embedded Flash movie is listed as the only rendition in Figure 5.5.

Instead of the default Mouse Up action, the project uses a Page Enter action, which means simply that the movie will play once the page displays. The action can be changed from either the Settings tabs or the Actions tab. When you choose an alternate trigger, you have to also choose a rendition to play in response to activating that trigger. That is, the rendition associated with the Mouse Up action isn't automatically applied to the Page Enter trigger.

 Download the **master_flash.pdf** file to experiment with customizing the movie on the page.

Follow these steps to change the trigger from the Settings tab:

1. Select the default Rendition from logo.swf for the Mouse Up trigger, and click the Remove Rendition button to delete it. You don't want the movie playing in response to a mouse click in the final document.

2. Click the List Renditions for Event pull-down arrow and choose Page Enter (**Figure 5.6**). The default rendition disappears from the Renditions field.

3. Click the Add Rendition button to open a pull-down menu and choose Using a File (**Figure 5.7**). The Select Multimedia File dialog opens (**Figure 5.8**).

Figure 5.5 *The default trigger for playing the movie is the Mouse Up action.*

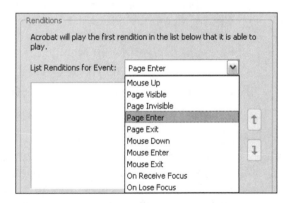

Figure 5.6 *Choose a trigger from the pull-down list on the Multimedia Properties dialog.*

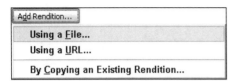

Figure 5.7 Select an option for locating a rendition of the movie.

Figure 5.8 Choose the movie you want to specify as a rendition.

4. Locate the movie file, and click Select to dismiss the dialog; the Add New Rendition Using a File dialog opens, showing you the selected file as well as the player used to run the movie.

5. Click OK to close the dialog and return to the Multimedia Properties dialog. The Renditions area of the Settings tab now lists Page Enter.

6. Select the Appearance tab. On this tab, you can specify whether to use a border for the movie as well as any border characteristics such as color and line type (**Figure 5.9**).

7. Click Close to dismiss the dialog and return to the document.

NOTE In the Add Rendition pull-down menu, you could also select By Copying an Existing Rendition, and then select the rendition already inserted in the file.

Figure 5.9 You can change the appearance of the movie's border.

ABOUT TRIGGERS AND EVENTS

A trigger is a user interaction or document activity that produces an event in a PDF document. For example, clicking a button is a trigger, and what happens when the button is clicked—such as opening another document or an e-mail window—is the event.

Acrobat includes a number of triggers that vary depending on the type of object you are working with. Media clips can be triggered by page events, such as the Page Enter trigger used in this project, whereas links and bookmarks can't.

The following triggers are available for media clips:

- **Page Visible.** Trigger occurs when the page containing the media clip is visible in the Document pane.

- **Page Invisible.** Trigger occurs when the page containing the media clip is not visible in the Document pane.

- **Page Enter.** Trigger occurs when the page containing the media clip is the current page.

- **Page Exit.** Trigger occurs when a user goes to a page other than the page containing the media clip.

- **Mouse Up.** Trigger occurs when the mouse button is released after a click.

- **Mouse Down.** Trigger occurs when the mouse button is clicked and held down.

- **Mouse Enter.** Trigger occurs when the pointer enters the movie's play area.

- **Mouse Exit.** Trigger occurs when the pointer leaves the movie's play area.

- **On Receive Focus.** Trigger occurs when a form field receives focus (becomes active), either through a mouse click or tabbing.

- **On Lose Focus.** Trigger occurs when a form field becomes inactive, either through a mouse click or tabbing to a different field.

NOTE To add more renditions of the movie, click Add Rendition to select the movie versions. Click Edit Rendition to open the Rendition Settings dialog to customize the renditions. Click the up and down arrows to reorder the list. Acrobat tries to play the first rendition in the list; if unsuccessful, it tries the second, and so on until the movie and player versions are compatible.

Save the file, and then close and reopen it. The Page Enter trigger starts the movie playing on the page (**Figure 5.10**). In the sample project, the document containing the Flash movie is renamed master_flash.pdf.

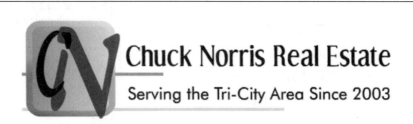

Figure 5.10 *Reopen the document to start the movie playback.*

Using the Pages on a PDA

Chuck would like to have the information about his listings available in a form that he can load onto his PDA and take with him. He thinks it's a cool idea and that it will appeal to his upwardly mobile clientele. Luckily, he can easily make the PDF documents for his property listings work on his PDA.

The screen on a PDA is extremely small, so zooming into the page to read the content makes it very difficult to figure out what part of the page is actually displayed—a problem known as *reflow*. If the document is tagged, as in Chuck's project, you can reflow the page to show the content more clearly. In either Acrobat or on your PDA (using Acrobat Reader), choose View > Reflow. You see how the page is interpreted by Acrobat's Reflow function (**Figure 5.11**). As you zoom in and out of the document pane, the text wraps to the next line automatically (**Figure 5.12**). In the figure, you can see the magnification is set at 300%.

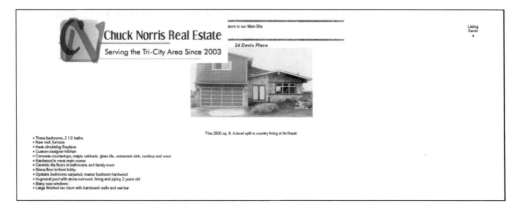

Figure 5.11 *Set the Reflow view to see how the page is interpreted.*

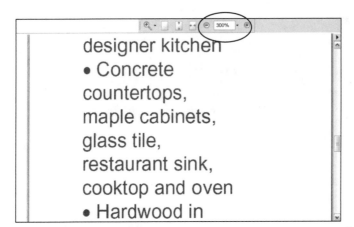

Figure 5.12 *The document flows automatically regardless of page size.*

Choose View > Reflow to deselect the function. Reflow isn't a permanent setting and you can't save the document in a Reflow view. Instead, it is intended to show you how the document can be viewed on other devices. If you are viewing a document using Reflow, the higher the magnification, the larger the size of the text and the fewer words on each line.

At this point, the entire PDF document is complete. Of course, Chuck wants to use more than one listing for his clients, and he can use the finished PDF document as a sort of template for the remaining property listings. You'll learn to do this in the "Replacing Pages" section later in this chapter. But first, Chuck wants to use the PDF document to create a page for his Web site.

Exporting a Web Page

Chuck would also like his new listing pages to be available on the Web site for users who don't want to open the PDF versions. To do this, he can export the HTML page directly from Acrobat, complete with images.

Acrobat can export content in two HTML formats as well as XML. Since Chuck wants a simple HTML page, he uses one of the HTML formats. The Flash movie won't be exported to the Web page, however, because it is an embedded component in the PDF only.

Follow these steps to export the Web page:

1. Choose File > Save As and select a file format option from the Save as type pull-down list (**Figure 5.13**). Choose either HTML 3.2 or HTML 4.01 with CSS 1.0 format (for more information on choosing the format, see the section

that follows, "Choosing the HTML Format.") Chuck uses the latter option for his project.

2. Click the Settings button—hidden beneath the pull-down list shown in Figure 5.13—to open the Settings dialog (**Figure 5.14**). Bookmarks and tags are generated automatically. If there are bookmarks in the document (a special type of link that connects a title to a page location), they are converted to links and placed at the start of the document.

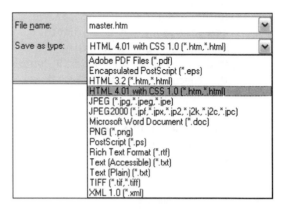

Figure 5.13 Choose an HTML format from the pull-down list.

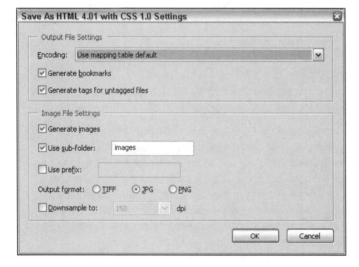

Figure 5.14 You can modify export settings if necessary.

3. Choose options in the Image File Settings pane. Acrobat creates a new sub-folder named "images"; rename the subfolder if you like. In Chuck's work-flow, using the same folder name for storing the images will save time. As each new PDF document is converted to HTML, the exported images can be stored in the same folder.

4. Click OK to close the Settings dialog and return to the Save As dialog, and then click OK to convert the file.

In the Explorer window (Finder window for Mac), you can see that the file's images are numbered and placed in their own folder (**Figure 5.15**). Note that there are only two images listed, although the document contains an image of a home as well as two horizontal graphics—Acrobat recognizes that there are two copies of the same horizontal graphics image and exports it only once.

NOTE How Acrobat interprets multiple copies of the same image depends on how they are added to the source Word file. In this case, the two copies of the same figure are recognized as copies of the same image.

Figure 5.15 *Acrobat generates images as well as the HTML page when exported.*

TROUBLESHOOTING

When you use Acrobat as a program for controlling input and output of different formats, occasionally you may find that you don't see anything on a Web page. Not a good situation! This problem can usually be traced back to the source Word document.

For example, if you use a text box in the Word document, the text in it isn't converted to PDF in the same way as regular text or text in a table. As a result, Acrobat doesn't recognize it as part of the document's structure. When you export the HTML page, anything within a text box is omitted. You can add the content to the structure tree in Acrobat by modifying the entire page's tags one by one, but that can be a laborious process. It's much simpler to rework the source document and try again. In the case of a text box, copy the text out of the text box and remove the text box structure. To align the text in a specific way, use a style in the source document.

Changing Preferences

If Chuck intends to export the PDF documents from Acrobat to use on his Web site on a regular basis, he may find that he repeatedly makes the same changes to the settings when he converts from PDF to an HTML format, such as using a prefix for image names or excluding bookmarks. If that's the case, he might want to change the program preferences.

To change preferences for documents you are converting from PDF in Acrobat, follow these steps:

1. Choose Edit > Preferences (Acrobat > Preferences on Mac) to open the Preferences dialog.

2. Click Convert from PDF in the Categories column, and select the HTML format from the list in the right pane (HTML 4.01 with CSS 1.0 for this project). The settings are listed on the dialog to the far right (**Figure 5.16**).

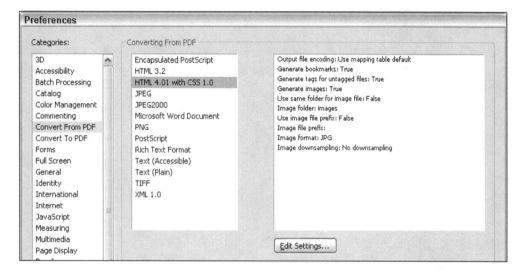

Figure 5.16 *Change the program preferences if you want to use other settings by default.*

3. Click Edit Settings to open the same Settings dialog as that shown in Figure 5.14. Make any desired changes, click OK, and then click OK again to dismiss the Preferences dialog.

Choosing the HTML Format

In this project, the HTML 4.01 with CSS 1.0 format is used to preserve the layout of the page. CSS stands for Cascading Style Sheet, which is a term that refers to special tags used in the HTML page (or in an attached page) that define what the content looks like. The other option, HTML 3.2, doesn't use CSS tags, so choosing this option might cause some of your content to display incorrectly. The table containing the listing information and created in the Word document was first converted to PDF using the PDFMaker, which maintains the style of the table. As Acrobat converts the document to a Web page, it also re-creates the custom styles used in the document, maintaining the document's appearance and layout.

NOTE Older browsers don't recognize CSS and won't display the chosen Web formatting correctly. Chuck decides to use the more modern approach because he thinks most of his customers are working with newer browsers that recognize the style sheet information.

You can see these custom styles from your Web browser. In Internet Explorer, choose View > Source to open a Notepad version of the page. You see the styles listed within the <head> tags of the HTML code (**Figure 5.17**).

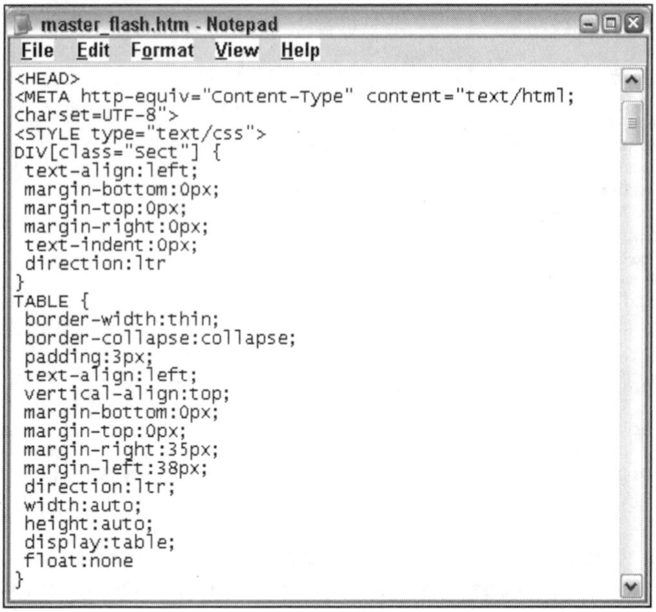

```
master_flash.htm - Notepad
File  Edit  Format  View  Help
<HEAD>
<META http-equiv="Content-Type" content="text/html;
charset=UTF-8">
<STYLE type="text/css">
DIV[class="Sect"] {
 text-align:left;
 margin-bottom:0px;
 margin-top:0px;
 margin-right:0px;
 text-indent:0px;
 direction:ltr
}
TABLE {
 border-width:thin;
 border-collapse:collapse;
 padding:3px;
 text-align:left;
 vertical-align:top;
 margin-bottom:0px;
 margin-top:0px;
 margin-right:35px;
 margin-left:38px;
 direction:ltr;
 width:auto;
 height:auto;
 display:table;
 float:none
}
```

Figure 5.17 Acrobat converts the page's styles to CSS styles incorporated into the Web page.

Replacing Pages

Chuck now has one page that is ready to go. He's created the PDF version of the property listings as well as an HTML page he can use on his Web site. Of course, he has more than one home to list, and he can use another of Acrobat's features to create both the PDF and HTML versions of the remaining documents.

You'll use Acrobat's Replace Page feature to slide the content for each property listing onto the PDF document page, replacing the text and images of the original page. Content you add in Acrobat—such as a comment, form field, or link—remains, regardless of the underlying page. In this project, that means that no matter which page is used to replace the original, the Flash movie remains.

So it's back to Word again. Using the Word master document, the image, and description of another property, you'll replace the one used for the original Word document. Then, you'll save the document with an identifying name (**Figure 5.18**). The example used in the project is named 18blackwood.doc, after the address of the property.

Identifying name is replaced   Image is replaced

Figure 5.18 *Replace the content on the master Word document for the next and subsequent property listings.*

Description copy is replaced   Image caption is replaced

Download **18blackwood.doc** if you want to try replacing a page in the master document. Download **18blackwood.jpg** if you want to try replacing an image in the master document. Download **18blackwood.pdf** to see the file in its converted state.

Convert the document to PDF using the Smallest File Size option (see earlier section, "Building the Master Document"). The resulting PDF (54 KB) is substantially smaller than the original Word document (145 KB).

To replace the page in Acrobat, follow these steps:

1. Open the document in which you want to replace the page—in this case, the master_flash.pdf document.

2. Choose Document > Replace Pages, and locate the file in the Select File With New Pages dialog. Click Select to dismiss the dialog and open the Replace Pages dialog (**Figure 5.19**).

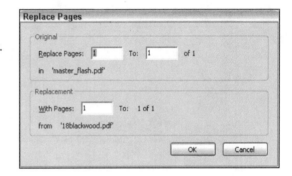

3. If there are multiple pages in both the original and replacement documents, type the page numbers in the fields. In this case, each document has only a single page, so the page numbers in Figure 5.19 are correct.

Figure 5.19 *Use the Replace Page feature to change the content on the page.*

4. Click OK to dismiss the dialog, and the underlying page content is changed. You see the content from the new listing's PDF document on the page, and the Flash movie remains on the page as well (**Figure 5.20**).

5. Save the document. The simplest naming convention for this project is to reuse the property's address as the PDF filename.

6. When you save the file reusing the original PDF document name, Acrobat asks if you want to replace the file. Click Yes in the message box to close the dialog and save the file.

NOTE After you save the file, you have to close it and reopen it in order for the Flash movie to start playing again.

Chuck can continue this process with all the new listings, swapping the content in the Word documents, creating PDF documents, and then replacing the pages in the master document before exporting the HTML versions.

Download **18blackwood_flash.pdf** to see the completed project.

What Else Could He Do?

Chuck's new system for creating the PDF property listing documents is complete. The goal was to devise a method for building uniform, compact PDF and HTML files for his new listings that can be generated quickly. He achieves this goal by using a simple Word document and a PDF document that acts like a template.

Chuck can add other content to the PDF documents as well, depending on how he would like to use the document. For example, he can add a button that lets a customer e-mail him for more information about a property (as described in

Bonus Chapter 1 on the Web site). He could also use another PDF document as an interface for displaying his listings documents. This interface PDF document might include a regional map with buttons that display the specific property's page when clicked, as described in Chapter 4's project.

6

Managing a
Print Job

There's no question that PDF files have greatly impacted the way we do business. And there is no doubt that they will continue to do so. Perhaps the area where the greatest and most obvious improvements have been made is printing.

In the not-so-distant past, for example, it could be very difficult to produce a professional product—such as an advertisement—without involving a third party, who would typeset it for you in the format required by the publication. It would be simply too time consuming learning all the various programs and too expensive to own them all, especially for a small business.

In the last few years, however, a number of standards have been developed that define specific characteristics and features to ensure that electronic content in a PDF document prints exactly as you intended, using all the correct fonts and colors, for example. This has given companies and individuals the ability to do their own layout and printing, saving them a lot of money and time.

What effect do such print standards have on you and your business? Now that you can control your documents and set them up for professional printing, does that mean your workload on the front end will suddenly be greater? Not at all!

As you'll see in this chapter, you can use a few different methods to prepare your prepress printing jobs. Using a regular Microsoft Word document, some specific print settings designed for prepress jobs, Acrobat 7 Professional, and Acrobat Distiller, you can create a file that complies with any number of print standards.

Big Bob's Furniture Emporium

This is a story about Big Bob McGee and a printing issue he is facing. Big Bob has been in the discount furniture business for 40 years and noticed that in the last few years his sales have been declining, due in large part to the discount chain furniture stores that have moved into town. Big Bob isn't going to take this lying down!

Big Bob decides that he needs to expand his advertising campaign, and maybe find a cheaper way of creating his ads as well. At the present time, his secretary, Sadie, types up the ads, which are then sent to various print publications where he pays for layout services. He already advertises quite heavily on local television, radio, and newspapers. He's now intending to blanket the city with advertisements in every vehicle he can find—from school yearbooks to community club newsletters and local magazines.

For the most part, he's not having any problems with his ad placement; everyone seems quite happy to take his advertising dollars. But he has run into a problem, and from a most unlikely source. He had been advertising for decades in a local magazine, which was recently bought out by a regional chain. Along with the new masthead, the chain brought in a new editor, and a new way of doing business.

Big Bob found an e-mail from the editorial office one morning in his in-box that said he had to submit his ads in a PDF/X-1a:2001-compliant format effective immediately, or pay conversion fees for modifying the files. Well, Big Bob didn't have a clue what the e-mail meant. To make things worse, his secretary, Sadie, was on vacation. Sadie always looked after that sort of thing. Before she left on her trip, she prepared his ads for the next few weeks and left them in a folder on her desktop.

After careful consideration, Big Bob did what any reasonable man in his position would do—he called a computer-literate relative; in this case, his niece, Dinah. Dinah said she would be willing to give it a try, and she reminded him that she was looking for a new TV. The two made a deal, and Dinah dropped in later that morning.

Dinah opened the Word document containing the "Halloween Special" ad (**Figure 6.1**). She was quite sure that there would be a simple way to handle

Figure 6.1 *Big Bob's advertisement starts life as a Word document.*

the task. She knew that Acrobat 7 contained a Preflight tool, used to evaluate a document and define its content in relation to specific printing standards (see the sidebar, "What Is Preflighting?"). She also knew that Acrobat produced PDF files that met the standards, so she would quickly be able to finish the job and have her new TV home in time for her favorite program!

Steps Involved in This Project

Dinah has no experience with creating standards-compliant documents in Word (or any other program for that matter). She starts off with an experiment. In this chapter, you'll see Dinah process the file in three different ways:

- First she'll use the Press Quality conversion setting in Word's PDF Maker and test the results in Acrobat using the Preflight tool. She doesn't use the correct conversion settings, and a raft of errors result.

- Next she'll print the document to a file and then convert it using Acrobat Distiller (a program used for converting documents from many programs).

Dinah is working with Microsoft Word, and printing to a file lets her use Acrobat Distiller for conversion.

- Finally, she'll try one more time using the PDFMaker in Word.

Although you can quickly and simply create a standards-compliant document using a PDFMaker in Acrobat 7 Professional, there are many instances where errors can be made. If you decide to follow along with Dinah's experiments, you'll see some of these mistakes in action.

To create the document in a format acceptable to the printer, Dinah has to

- Convert the source Word document to a PDF file
- In Acrobat, evaluate the document against the standard using the Preflight tool
- Analyze the results, and make any necessary changes or corrections to the document
- Produce the final PDF file, which will be ready for sending to the printer

Her first step is to convert the source document to a PDF file. Dinah decides she can work from Word using the PDFMaker, a plug-in installed in Microsoft Office programs when Acrobat is installed.

Method 1: Using Acrobat's Preflight Tool

Dinah thinks she can convert the document to PDF from within Word and then check it using Acrobat's Preflight tool. She reads through the ad first, looking for errors, and notices that Uncle Bob hasn't broken his habit of liberally sprinkling exclamation points throughout all his ads. "How can you expect your customers to get excited about buying our furniture if we don't look excited, too?" seems to be his motto. Well, she can't tell him how to write his ad but she can make it ready for printing. Let's see how she does this using the first method mentioned in the previous section: choosing the Press Quality setting when converting the Word document using the PDF Maker.

Converting the Source Document

Dinah first decides to change the conversion settings, remembering she'd noticed some press print conversion options listed in the Acrobat PDFMaker dialog. In general, if you choose the right settings for the right job, you will be successful. In this case, you'll see how terribly wrong things can go if you choose the wrong settings.

Download the original Word document named **bigbob_ad.doc** if you want to convert the original advertisement yourself.

Follow these steps to check and modify Adobe PDF conversion settings in Word:

1. In Word (Windows), choose Adobe PDF > Change Conversion Settings to open the Acrobat PDFMaker dialog. See the note below for making the conversion on a Mac.

2. Click the Conversion Settings pull-down arrow and choose Press Quality (**Figure 6.2**). This setting is used for files intended for printing presses, and Dinah thinks that it should work for the ad. She plans to check it in Acrobat after conversion to be sure.

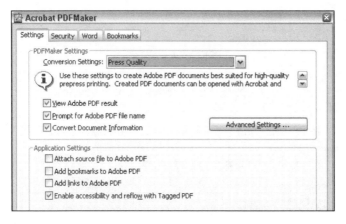

Figure 6.2 Dinah chooses the Press Quality setting before converting the document.

3. Deselect all the Application Settings check boxes except for "Enable accessibility and reflow with Tagged PDF." Using tags allows Acrobat to structure the document's content more readily (you can read more about tags in Chapter 8).

4. Click OK to close the dialog.

5. Click the Convert to Adobe PDF icon ⬚ on the PDFMaker toolbar. A Save Adobe PDF File As dialog opens, showing the PDF filename—the Word document name by default.

6. Click Save to close the dialog and process the file. Various dialogs display as Word's PDFMaker processes and converts the document.

7. Click Show Details (which toggles to Hide Details) on the dialog to expand the view to include descriptions of the conversion options you chose in the PDFMaker dialog as they are processed (**Figure 6.3**). The dialogs and progress bar displays close in Word, and the document opens in Acrobat.

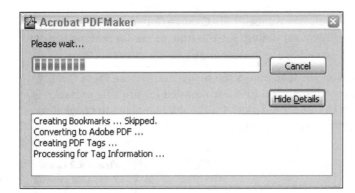

Figure 6.3 *The PDFMaker shows various dialogs and progress bars as the document is converted.*

NOTE Instead of providing an AdobePDF menu on the Mac, it uses the standard AdobePS printer that's installed by Acrobat. The AdobePS driver provides the necessary functionality (including picking the PDF/X setting) to all applications.

Dinah thinks that was pretty easy, and she is confident that her biggest concern for the day is deciding where to place her new TV. All that remains is to check the document in Acrobat, which is coming up next.

Preflighting the PDF File

Dinah is ready to test her document to see if it complies with the PDF/X standard. Remember that she chose what she thought were the correct settings. As you'll see in this section, her choices don't produce the effect she had hoped for!

There are many errors that can occur if the standards aren't met—you'll receive an error if any of the criteria listed in the sidebar "What Is Preflighting?" aren't met.

Download the original converted advertisement named **bigbob_ad.pdf** to test it using the Preflight tool.

WHAT IS PREFLIGHTING?

Print standards have been developed over the last few years to solve problems related to printing documents and to set criteria for graphic content exchange. The standards, called PDF/X, come in several similar forms, but each is important for ensuring that a document contains only the appropriate features, fonts, and formatting for graphic content exchange. Preflight, or preflighting, is a process that inspects the document's content to ensure that it contains only valid content that complies with the standards.

Acrobat 7 Professional offers the Preflight tool, used to analyze documents for print production, including PDF/X standards. It can also be used to evaluate other features of a document such as transparency (determining whether there are semitransparent objects in the document) and resolution (detecting the dots per inch—or dpi—of the document).

There are criteria that all PDF/X-compliant documents require that Acrobat's Preflight process detects automatically. These criteria specify that

- All fonts must be embedded in the source application. This means the information about the font is included in the document, ensuring that the fonts used in the output document matches those of the original document.

- Documents must use specific color spaces (methods of producing color). PDF/X-1a can use only CMYK and spot colors, or DeviceN color spaces. CMYK (Cyan-Magenta-Yellow-Black) color is used in four-color processing, like that seen in full-color books and magazines. Spot color refers to specific named colors, such as those found in color systems like PANTONE or FOCOLTONE. For instance, if you specify PANTONE 644C, you are specifying a particularly lovely shade of robin's egg blue. DeviceN color is an Adobe PostScript 3 color space that allows for specifying color components other than CMYK color. PDF/X-3 standards can also use RGB (Red-Green-Blue) color space using specific color profiles.

- Documents must contain information about the intended printing conditions. For instance, the PDF/X-1a:2001 standard defines an output-intent profile named U.S. Web Coated (SWOP).

- Bounding boxes, or coordinates that describe the location of the content in a document, must be specified.

The differences in the actual standards are based on the type of color used, the version of PostScript language each standard is based on, and what version of Acrobat is required to open the files. You can read about the various standards at the ISO Web site, www.iso.org, or at Adobe's Print Resource Center at http://studio.adobe.com/us/print/main.jsp.

Follow these steps to preflight the document:

1. In Acrobat, choose Tools > Print Production > Show Print Production Toolbar. The toolbar opens in the program window (**Figure 6.4**).

Trap
Presets
tool

Preflight
tool

Ink
Manager
tool

Figure 6.4 *Open the Print Production toolbar to easily access the tools.*

2. Drag the toolbar to dock with the other toolbars in the program, or you can leave it floating in the program window.

3. Click the Preflight tool on the Print Production toolbar.

4. The Preflight dialog opens, with the Profiles option automatically active; Acrobat loads the profiles from your hard drive, and you see them listed in the dialog. Profiles are created as part of the Acrobat 7 Professional installation process and are stored in the Acrobat installation files in your program files.

5. Scroll through the list of profiles and select the appropriate profile—in Dinah's project, the PDF/X-1a:2001 profile is required.

6. Read the description in the "Purpose of the selected Preflight profile" area of the dialog. The dialog reads, "Verifies whether the document is compliant with PDF/X-1a:2001" (**Figure 6.5**).

7. Notice that at the lower-left of the dialog, the PDF/X status is shown as "Not a PDF/X document."

8. Click Execute to start the evaluation process.

9. The dialog displays the Results pane automatically; the Results option is active at the top of the dialog.

10. Read the results of the evaluation (**Figure 6.6**). You can click the (+) to the left of some of the headings to display further information in an expanded view. In Figure 6.6, for example, the Preflight information listing is shown expanded, and the (+) has become a (−).

Wow! Dinah has some issues! It's clearly not the simple job she originally thought. But being the determined and diligent person she is, she decides to figure out what the results mean, and what to do about them.

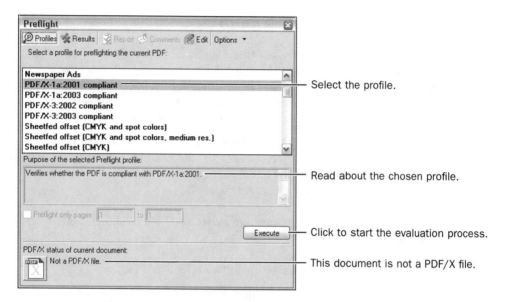

Select the profile.

Read about the chosen profile.

Click to start the evaluation process.

This document is not a PDF/X file.

Figure 6.5 *Test a document for compliance with standards or other features using the Preflight dialog.*

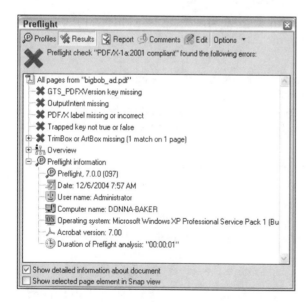

Figure 6.6 *When the Preflight process is complete, the evaluation is shown in the Results listing—Dinah's document has some problems!*

Interpreting Preflight Results

The Preflight results are displayed in the Preflight dialog and can be exported as a PDF document—it's handy to have a full document to read rather than a listing on a dialog, especially if you have a lengthy list of errors. You can include overview information and details. Dinah decides to create a report document to use as reference for working with the document.

Preflight reports can contain either an overview, or an overview and full details. In some files—for example, those with a lot of images—you may find a few errors that pertain to specific images. If you have the detailed report, it's easier to find the precise error messages.

 Download the original report named **bigbob_ad_report.pdf** to see Dinah's Preflight report results.

Follow these steps to save a Preflight results file:

1. Click the Report icon on the Preflight dialog to open a Save As dialog.

2. In the Save As dialog, name the report file. Or you can use the default name, which is the filename with "_report" appended to it.

3. Click the Save as type pull-down arrow and choose a format for the report. The default is PDF, which Dinah uses. You can also choose a text or XML file.

4. Next, choose a storage location. The default storage location is the folder containing the original PDF document; choose an alternate storage location if you wish. For this project, use the default location because it's simpler to keep track of both the original document and the report if they are in the same folder.

5. Choose the options for information to include in the report at the bottom of the dialog (**Figure 6.7**). You can choose to include an overview as well as details of the report.

   Dinah decides on both the overview and the details, which are the dialog's default selections. She also leaves the default display for the details, which is a transparent mask that displays on the document, highlighting any errors. Alternatively, she could choose to have the errors displayed as comments.

6. Click Save; the dialog closes, and the report document is saved and opens automatically in Acrobat.

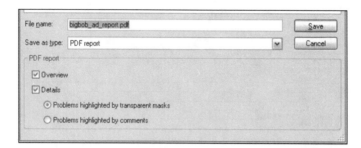

Figure 6.7 *Choose the type of information you want to include in the report document and how you would like it to be displayed.*

7. The Document Status dialog displays (**Figure 6.8**). The dialog states that the document contains both attachments and layers. Click Close to dismiss the dialog.

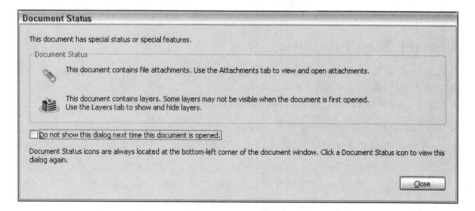

Figure 6.8 *The report document has special features which are described in the Document Status dialog.*

8. The document shows status icons at the lower left of the program window on the Status bar (**Figure 6.9**).

Now that the report is saved and open in Acrobat, Dinah can examine the errors in full detail.

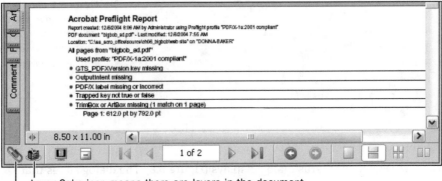

Layer Cake icon means there are layers in the document.
Paper Clip icon means there are attachments to the document.

Figure 6.9 *Icons are added to the bottom left of the program window on the Status bar.*

What the Report Contains

Take a look at how the program window looks with the report document displayed. **Figure 6.10** shows the various components; each of the following steps or components is shown by numbered callouts in the figure:

1. Click the (+) to the left of the "Preflight profile" label in the Layers pane (the + sign turns to a – sign) to display the two layers in the document.

2. Click the box to the left of the "All problems according to Preflight" layer to display the eye icon , meaning the layer is visible in the document.

    The second layer shows a transparent overlay of the problem areas of the document (described in Step 5 below); the transparency overlay was chosen in the Save As dialog in the previous set of steps.

3. Select the Attachments tab at the lower left of the program window to open the Attachments pane, which displays across the program window.

4. Look at the attachment and you see that the Press Quality.joboptions file is listed. This is the conversion settings option that you chose when you created the original PDF from Word.

5. The results of the report are shown on the first page of the document.

6. Any region of the document containing errors—be it a text block, image, or graphic—is shown by a red transparent overlay in the second page of the document. As you can see, the overlay covers the whole page—that's a lot of errors!

Step 1   Step 4   Step 5

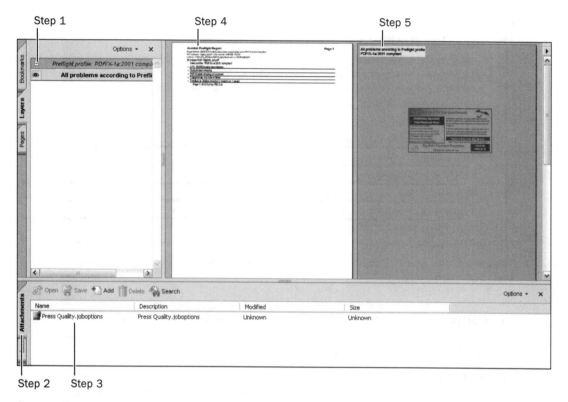

Step 2   Step 3

Step 1—Click (+) to the left of the Preflight profile.
Step 2—Select the Attachments tab.
Step 3—Note the .joboptions file is listed.
Step 4—Report results are listed on the document.
Step 5—The red overlay shows where the errors are—the whole page!

Figure 6.10 *The Report shows a number of components and information sources.*

Dinah heaves a heavy sigh and sets out on a quest for answers.

What the Results Mean

Using a variety of Internet and Acrobat resources (such as those listed in the "What Is Preflighting?" sidebar), Dinah discovers what the errors in the report mean (**Figure 6.11**). The errors in a Preflight results report will vary depending on the content in the document, the conversion settings used, and the standards you are trying to meet. Dinah's results are an example of what can go wrong when preflighting a document.

Acrobat Preflight Report

Report created: 12/6/2004 8:06 AM by Administrator using Preflight profile "PDF/X-1a:2001 compliant"

PDF document: "bigbob_ad.pdf" - Last modified: 12/6/2004 7:55 AM

Location: "C:\aa_acro_office\source\ch06_bigbob\web site" on "DONNA-BAKER"

All pages from "bigbob_ad.pdf"

    Used profile: "PDF/X-1a:2001 compliant"

- GTS_PDFXVersion key missing
- OutputIntent missing
- PDF/X label missing or incorrect
- Trapped key not true or false
- TrimBox or ArtBox missing (1 match on 1 page)
      Page 1: 612.0 pt by 792.0 pt

Figure 6.11 *The report's content lists the issues that prevent the document from complying with PDF/X standards.*

The top part of the report is self-explanatory. It contains the details of the file, where it is stored, the pages evaluated, and the profile used. As for the bulleted items, she finds that the following problems exist:

- **GTS_PDFXVersion key missing.** When a document is converted correctly, there is a notation made in the PostScript file that includes a version key, or reference to the file's PDF/X compliance.

- **OutputIntent missing.** The output intent matches the color characteristics of the PDF document with those of a printing device.

- **PDF/X label missing or incorrect.** When a document is converted correctly to a standards-compliant format, a label included in the PostScript file specifies its status.

- **Trapped key not true or false.** Trapping, or expanding colored objects on a page when printing to prevent gaps in the final printed document, must be specified as either on or off (see the sidebar "Understanding Trapping" for more information).

- **TrimBox or ArtBox missing (1 match on 1 page).** Using Acrobat, you can define several rectangular areas (or boxes) on a PDF page or preview those areas if they were already defined in a PDF file. A TrimBox defines the final trimmed size of a document and an ArtBox defines an area of a page and its position. For example, in the bigbob_ad.pdf document, the size of the ad is the TrimBox or ArtBox.

UNDERSTANDING TRAPPING

Documents printed by a commercial printer use more than one ink on the same page. Each ink prints separately and removes—or knocks out—any inks underneath so the colors aren't mixed incorrectly. The ink must be printed in alignment with the other inks so that no gaps are seen between the colors where the different inks meet. This alignment is called "in register."

Printing ink in register can be very difficult. To ensure results are satisfactory, you can use trapping, applied either in your source document (depending on the program used to create the source document) or in Acrobat. Trapping extends one object slightly so that it overlaps an object of another color. The most common form of trapping is spreading a light object into a dark object, maintaining the visual edge of the image or text (**Figure 6.12**).

In Acrobat 7 Professional, you can define trapping in a number of locations:

- Click Trap Presets ▣ on the Print Production toolbar to open the Trap Presets dialog, where you can edit, delete, or create new presets and assign presets to specific pages.

- Click Ink Manager ▲ on the Print Production toolbar to open the Ink Manager dialog where you can enter ink type, trap sequence, and neutral density.

- Choose File > Print > Advanced, and on the Advanced Print Setup dialog box you can specify trapping.

- Choose File > Document Properties > Advanced and specify whether an Adobe PDF file contains trapping information from the source application.

For complete information on trapping, see the Help files in Acrobat.

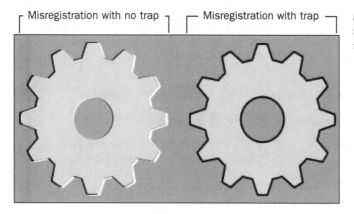

⌐ Misregistration with no trap ¬   ⌐ Misregistration with trap ¬

Figure 6.12 *Trapping is used to compensate for misregistration when colors are printed.*

Dinah decides that she is completely out of her depth, and she decides to hunt for another way to create the PDF document using the standards, rather than trying to resolve all these errors. Read about her continuing adventures in the next section.

Method 2: Using Acrobat Distiller

Dinah decides to return to the original Word document. She's sure she can find a method of creating the PDF document that doesn't produce errors. In fact, she thinks she can save the document and use it in Acrobat Distiller 7 to produce her document correctly. She still has her sights set on that new TV.

 Download the advertisement, **bigbob_ad.doc**, if you haven't downloaded it already and if you'd like to convert the document yourself using the method described in this section.

Acrobat Distiller 7 is a separate program installed as part of the Acrobat 7 installation process. It is used for converting PostScript (PS) and Encapsulated PostScript (EPS) files to PDF. PS and EPS files are produced in a range of programs, including illustration and publishing programs. Distiller can also convert another file format called PRN, which is a Windows-based version of a PostScript file generated by a specific group of print settings. Because Dinah's source document is in Word for Windows, she'll convert her file to a PRN file. If she were working on a Mac, the PDFMaker would automatically open Distiller, so she wouldn't need to create a PRN file.

Printing the Document to a File

Dinah decides to create a version of the advertisement's document printed to a file from Word. Printing a document to a file rather than to a printer will process the document just as for printing, but instead of printing a page, it saves the document in a different file format. For example, the default format for a Word document is DOC but when you print a Word document to a file it produces a PRN file.

Follow these steps to convert the source file to a PostScript PRN file:

1. Choose File > Print to open the Print dialog (**Figure 6.13**).

2. Click the Name pull-down arrow and choose Adobe PDF. This selection appears because when Acrobat is installed on your computer, a special printer driver is also installed.

3. Click the Print to file check box.

Figure 6.13 Choose Print settings to print the document to a file instead of a printer.

4. Click OK to dismiss the Print dialog; a Print to file dialog opens.

5. Name the file and choose a folder location in which to store the printed file.

You see the .prn extension is shown automatically in the Save as type field. The sample project's file is named bigbob_ad2.prn.

6. Click OK to close the save dialog and convert the file.

NOTE The document is printed using the settings normally used by the selected printer. For a PRN file to function correctly in Acrobat Distiller, you have to choose the Adobe PDF printer option because it applies the PostScript print commands to the file. If you leave your default printer selected, it will create a PRN file, but Distiller won't be able to use it.

What If There Are Errors?

Sadly, instead of creating the file, Dinah sees a message dialog (**Figure 6.14**). The dialog explains that a PostScript file must include fonts. Click OK to dismiss the dialog; you may also see a Windows Printing Error dialog; click OK again to close that dialog as well.

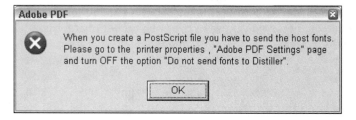

Figure 6.14 You have to send fonts to the printer, as described in the dialog.

The Adobe PDF dialog explains how to fix the situation, which is done by following these steps:

1. Choose File > Print to open the Print dialog. The Adobe PDF printer is still selected, as is the Print to file check box.

2. Click the Properties icon at the upper right of the Print dialog to open the Adobe PDF Document Properties dialog. The Adobe PDF Settings tab displays by default.

3. Click the "Do not send fonts to 'Adobe PDF'" check box to deselect it; the option is selected by default (**Figure 6.15**).

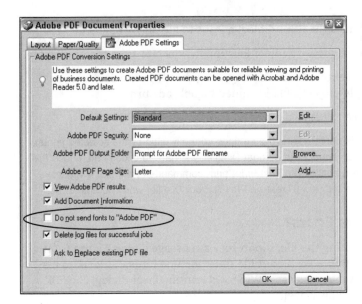

Figure 6.15 Modify the options to be sure the fonts are sent to the printer.

4. Click OK to close the dialog and return to the Print dialog.

5. Click OK on the Print dialog to dismiss the dialog and reopen the Print to file dialog again. The name you chose in the previous set of steps is already listed in the dialog.

6. Click the existing name in the dialog to select it, and click OK.

7. A message dialog asks if you want to replace the existing file; click Yes to dismiss the dialog and print the document to a file.

That's the first part of the job finished at last! Before closing the document and Word, Dinah reopens the Print dialog, chooses the default printer from the Name pull-down list, and deselects the Print to file check box. If she didn't, the settings would remain as is, and all documents printed from Word would produce PRN files instead of printed documents.

In the next section, Dinah works in Acrobat Distiller 7.

Creating the PDF File in Distiller

The next step is to convert the file in Acrobat Distiller to a PDF document. Acrobat Distiller is a separate program, listed in the Program Files. It is also available from within Acrobat 7 by choosing Advanced > Acrobat Distiller.

Download the document printed to a file, **bigbob_ad2.prn,** if you'd like to practice the Distiller conversion process.

Follow these steps to select and convert a PRN file to PDF:

1. If it's not already open, launch Distiller by choosing Advanced > Acrobat Distiller. It appears as a small window and has three menus (**Figure 6.16**).

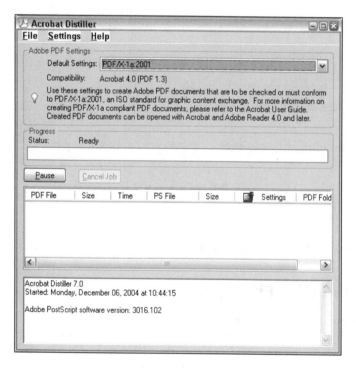

Figure 6.16 Acrobat Distiller 7 is a separate program from Acrobat.

2. Click the Default Settings pull-down arrow and choose PDF/X-1a:2001 from the list. Information about the conversion option is shown on the dialog.

3. Choose File > Open to display the Acrobat Distiller - Open PostScript File dialog. No files are listed in the upper part of the dialog.

4. Click the Files of type pull-down arrow and choose All Files (*). Now you see the bigbob_ad2.prn file is listed (**Figure 6.17**).

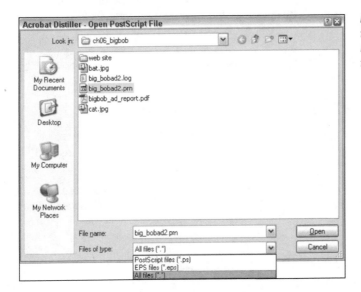

Figure 6.17 *To see the PRN file listed in the dialog, you need to change the default file type.*

5. Click the file to select it, and then click Open to dismiss the dialog and return to Distiller.

6. The file is processed, and the results are shown at the bottom of the Distiller dialog (**Figure 6.18**).

7. Close Distiller.

Finally, it's time to check the results again in Acrobat.

Preflighting the PDF File Again

Dinah takes a deep breath and opens the new and (hopefully) improved version of the advertisement's PDF document in Acrobat. The moment of truth is at hand. Is her job done for the day? Will she win the admiration of her Uncle Bob (and her new TV)? Read on for the exciting conclusion.

Download the converted PRN file, **bigbob_ad2.pdf,** if you'd like to test its standards compliance in Acrobat.

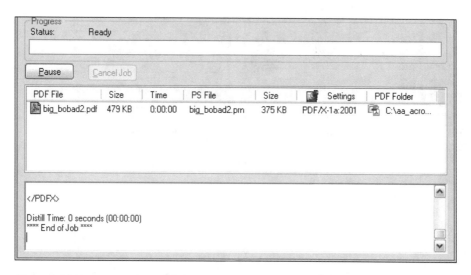

Figure 6.18 *The results of the file's processing are shown on the dialog.*

To preflight this version of the file, follow these steps:

1. Open the document in Acrobat. The file called bigbob_ad2.pdf is used for Dinah's project.

2. Click Preflight 🔎 on the Print Production toolbar, or choose Tools > Print Production > Preflight to open the Preflight dialog (**Figure 6.19**).

   At the lower-left of the dialog, you now see that the PDF/X status icon looks considerably different than it did in the first method. Instead of stating outright that the document isn't a PDF/X document, it instead states the status isn't verified. You also see a question mark overlaying the icon.

3. Click the PDF/X icon at the lower left of the dialog to test the document. You can also click the Execute button to run the evaluation.

4. The document is evaluated by the Preflight tool. Now you see the icon on the Preflight dialog has changed to a verified status (**Figure 6.20**).

To be sure she isn't missing anything, Dinah clicks the Results button at the top of the Preflight dialog to show the results of the evaluation (**Figure 6.21**). Yes, the document has met the standard!

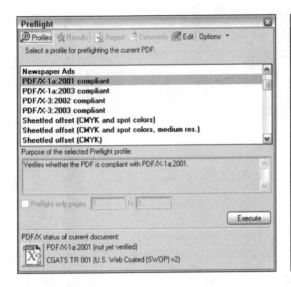

Figure 6.19 *The Preflight dialog shows the settings used in the document and that the PDF/X status needs to be verified.*

Figure 6.21 *You can check the details of the analysis in the Results pane.*

Figure 6.20 *Success at last! The document is verified.*

Method 3: Faster Document Conversions in Word

Dinah's job is finished. She is pleased with her efforts, but she has an additional thought. What if she could make it simpler still? She's a bit concerned about Sadie, Uncle Bob's secretary. Will she be able to produce the correctly formatted documents? On the other hand, Dinah could also use some new furniture, and if the process stays on the complex side, maybe she can make a few more deals with Uncle Bob.

But she decides to take the high road and investigate one last option. Dinah recalls that in the Acrobat Distiller dialog, she chose the PDF/X-1a:2001 settings from the Default Settings pull-down list. She knows that Acrobat installs the same conversion setting files in the PDFMaker as it does in Distiller. What if she could simply choose those same settings in Word? That would save printing to the file and then doing the conversion in Distiller.

To choose settings in Word and convert the document, follow these steps:

1. In Word, choose Adobe PDF > Change Conversion Settings dialog to open the Acrobat PDFMaker dialog.

2. Click the Conversion Settings pull-down arrow; the displayed Conversion Setting is the same Press Quality option Dinah chose for her first experiment. The options included in the pulldown list in the PDFMaker are the same as those in Distiller (**Figure 6.22**). Choose PDF/X-1a:2001 from the list.

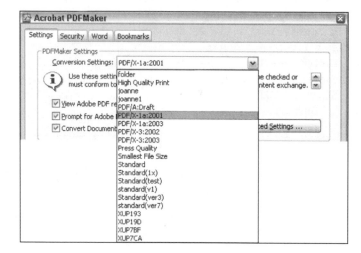

Figure 6.22 *The PDF/X standards conversion settings are in the PDFMaker's dialog.*

3. Click OK to close the dialog.

4. Click Convert to PDF ⊞ on the PDFMaker toolbar and save the file.

To be sure, Dinah confirms the validity of the document one last time in Acrobat. She is quite sure that Sadie will be able to follow the simple list of instructions to convert the documents but isn't so sure that she'll manage to confirm the documents' status in Acrobat. Before picking up her new TV, she decides to create a method for automatically testing the documents, called a Preflight Droplet.

Building a Preflight Droplet

A Preflight Droplet is a separate application you build from within Acrobat that is used to perform different Preflight tests. In effect, you create a separate mini program when you create a Droplet. You don't need to open Acrobat to preflight a file if you create a Droplet; instead all you need do is drag the file to the Droplet's icon to automatically process and test the file using the Preflight settings you chose when you created the Droplet. A Preflight Droplet can be stored on the desktop or added to the Start menu in Windows.

Before creating a Droplet, add folders to your hard drive to use for storing the results of the Preflight Droplet's processing. Dinah adds two folders to the desktop named PDF Files for Printer and PDF Files-Errors (**Figure 6.23**). It's simpler to create the folders before configuring the Droplet. When she creates the Droplet, she'll assign the PDF Files for Printer folder as the receiving folder when the Preflight test is correct and specify the PDF Files-Errors folder to receive a document that contains errors.

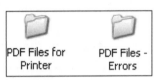

PDF Files for Printer   PDF Files - Errors

Figure 6.23 *Build folders to hold the processed documents before creating the Droplet.*

Follow these steps to construct the Preflight Droplet in Acrobat:

1. Choose Tools > Print Production > Preflight from the menu, or click the Preflight tool on the Print Production toolbar to open the Preflight dialog.

2. Click Options and choose Create Preflight Droplet from the menu (**Figure 6.24**).

3. The Preflight: Droplet Setup dialog opens (**Figure 6.25**).

4. Choose the profile you want from the "Run Preflight check using:" pull-down menu; if you have selected a profile before opening the dialog, it is automatically selected.

5. Click the On success check box and select the options for a successful test. You can move, copy, or create an alias of the document in a specified folder—in this project, the file itself will move to the PDF Files for Printer folder Dinah created earlier.

6. Click the Success folder button to open a Browse for Folder dialog (**Figure 6.26**). Select the folder to store the successfully processed files in—in this case, the PDF Files for Printer folder on the desktop.

Figure 6.24 *Creating a Preflight Droplet is one of the commands offered through the Preflight dialog.*

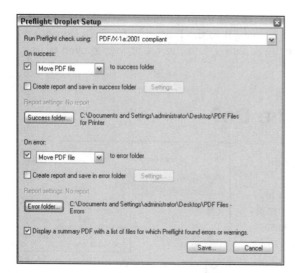

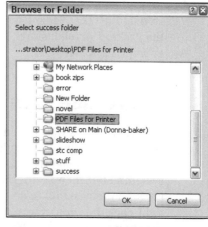

Figure 6.26 *Choose the folder created to store the processed documents.*

Figure 6.25 *Construct the Preflight Droplet in this dialog.*

7. Click OK to dismiss the dialog and return to the Preflight: Droplet Setup dialog. The chosen folder's name is now shown on the dialog.

8. Click the On error check box, and choose options for a test that generates errors. Again, you can move, copy, or create an alias, as well as generate reports (shown in Figure 6.25).

9. Click the Error folder button and choose the folder to store documents containing errors. Dinah selects the "PDF Files-Errors" folder.

10. Click Save, and the Save Droplet as dialog opens. Choose a location to store the Droplet, and click Save to close the dialog and create the Droplet. In Dinah's project, the Droplet is stored on the desktop along with the two folders for convenience **(Figure 6.27)**.

Figure 6.27 *The Preflight Droplet displays its own icon on the desktop.*

NOTE There are also options for creating reports and storing them, as described in the "What the Report Contains" section earlier in the chapter. In the project, Dinah decides not to create report files because she's concerned that the similarly named files might confuse Sadie. She doesn't want her sending the report instead of the ad to the publisher by mistake.

Now when a PDF document needs Preflight testing against the PDF/X-1a:2001 standard, all that Sadie has to do is drag it to the Preflight Droplet's icon on the desktop. Acrobat starts, the file is tested, and the file is then moved to its appropriate folder.

What Else Can She Do?

Because Dinah is working on a Windows computer, she could add the Preflight Droplet right to the system's Start menu rather than leaving it on the desktop. To do so, simply right-click the Droplet icon to open the shortcut menu and choose Pin to Start menu. Later, when a new document is ready for testing, all Sadie has to do is drag the document to the Start button ![Start], hold it until the Start menu displays, and then drop the file on the Droplet item to start the test (**Figure 6.28**).

Dinah decides to leave the Droplet's icon on the desktop with the folders to make it simpler for the secretary to understand the process. Besides, she's got a date with her new TV remote!

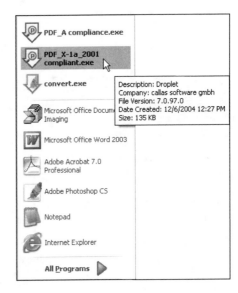

Figure 6.28 *The Preflight Droplet can be included in the system's Start menu.*

7

Managing E-mail Using Acrobat

One of the most common business tools—and for many of us one of the most difficult to organize and manage—is e-mail. Although you can use an e-mail program to organize threads and sort mail, it is still cumbersome. Then there is the question of how to store e-mail: Do you save all the important e-mail messages in folders? And what about their attachments? How do you organize and manage them? What if your administrator is telling you to delete e-mails because the server is too full? Is there a way to quickly organize and save e-mail without bogging down your server?

If these sound like questions you ask yourself often, then this chapter is for you. Acrobat 7 installs a PDFMaker in Microsoft Outlook (Windows) that you can use to automatically convert either single e-mails or folders of e-mails into PDF documents. The content of a converted folder is even displayed in Acrobat with a set of bookmarks that you can sort based on sender, date, and other criteria.

In Acrobat, you can use the new Organizer feature to keep track of your PDF documents. The Organizer lets you sort your e-mail (and other PDF documents) in a number of ways. You can even create virtual folders within Acrobat's Organizer to use for organizing and managing groups of files in collections.

You can embed attachments right in the e-mail and then transport them along with the PDF documents in a secure wrapper—sending the e-mail directly from within Acrobat—as you'll see in this chapter's project. You'll also see how your e-mail's recipients can save attachments from the PDF document, convert them to PDF, or extract them in their native file formats. Very handy features!

Sorting the (e)Mail

This is the story of Abby Taylor, a modern-day businesswoman with a modern-day problem. Abby is a successful sales agent for Taylor and Daughter, an office supply distributor. And yes, she is the daughter in said company. She conducts much of her business via e-mail—clarifying orders, discussing invoices, confirming shipping details, and so on. She often finds it difficult to keep track of the e-mail threads and attachments she has included with her correspondence, and she finds she spends a great deal of time sifting through e-mails for particular information.

She tried working with e-mail folders in Microsoft Outlook, creating folders with matching names on her hard drive for storing attached files, but found that was hard to keep track of. She finally resorted to printing every e-mail and attachment and sorting them by manufacturer, customer, or date.

Her other problem is making sure documents are seen by the right people. She sometimes has to send reminder letters and overdue statements, and she worries that someone other than the intended recipients might see the contents.

Abby decides to devise a system that will allow her to organize her e-mail content, keep track of her attachments, and send files to her customers that can be secured in a customized eEnvelope (**Figure 7.1**). And she can do this all through Acrobat.

Steps Involved in This Project

In many ways, this chapter is more a demonstration than an actual project because there is no final product. Instead, you'll see how Abby can handle her e-mail control issues using Acrobat.

To deal with her e-mails, she needs to do the following:

■   Devise a naming system for organizing customer and manufacturer e-mails. Abby decides to use a naming system similar to the one that she has tried with printed copies of all her correspondence.

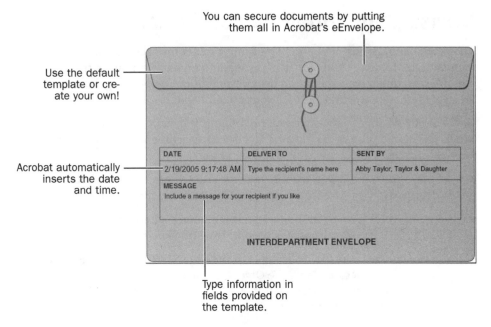

Figure 7.1 *You can create and use an eEnvelope to securely send your e-mails.*

- Convert her e-mails to PDF in Outlook. She can convert either a single e-mail or a folder of e-mails at one time; she can also append new e-mails to an existing PDF document.

- Create collections in Acrobat's Organizer to hold documents for particular clients and manufacturers.

- Apply a template in Acrobat for an eEnvelope (a secure wrapper for a document's content).

Abby decides to start by organizing the folders she has already constructed in her e-mail program, Microsoft Outlook. If you don't use Outlook as your e-mail client, you won't have a PDFMaker to work with to convert files or folders to PDF or append e-mails to existing PDF files. Instead, you can save the e-mails from your program as text files and then convert them to PDF from Acrobat. See the project details in Chapter 2 to learn about creating PDF files in Acrobat.

NOTE The e-mail files used in this project are generic—choose any number of e-mails from your own system and apply the processes described in this project.

Devising an E-mail Folder System

Abby organizes her business e-mail by using a folder for each company or manufacturer folders. There are as many ways to organize e-mail as there are e-mail users; unless you are bound by government or business regulations, find the method that works best for your e-mail habits.

However you go about your organization scheme, it is important to plan ahead. When you're intention is to convert e-mails and attachments in Outlook to PDF versions, here are a few ideas to keep in mind:

- Organize the e-mails you want to convert into folders. You can choose a folder and convert its entire content to PDF with one mouse click.

- Name the folders using an understandable name—when you convert the folder to PDF, the folder name is used as the PDF filename.

- You can create a series of collections in the Organizer that parallels your e-mail folder structure. Using the Organizer means you can access the folders' content directly from within Acrobat to prepare content for mailing, to do a search for specific terms, and so on.

NOTE If you are working with a different e-mail program, create the folders on your hard drive.

Abby decides to use the structure she has been working with in Outlook. In **Figure 7.2**, you can see she has two e-mail categories named "Manufacturers" and "Customers," each with separate folders for different companies.

She plans to convert the individual folders of e-mail to PDF files. As you'll see later in the chapter, she doesn't have to worry about the attachments—they can be included as part of the PDF files automatically.

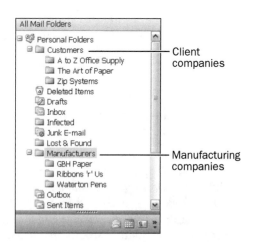

Figure 7.2 Abby has organized her e-mail into categories according to companies.

Converting Folders of E-mail to PDF

The simplest way to convert e-mails to PDF in Outlook is by using the Outlook PDFMaker, a menu and toolbar used for converting files to PDF that is installed in Outlook automatically as part of the Acrobat 7 installation process. When you specify conversion settings, the settings are used by default until you change them. For example, if Abby uses the View Adobe PDF Result option, the document opens in Acrobat each time she creates a new PDF file from an e-mail or a folder of e-mails. Before converting files, she takes a minute to check the conversion settings.

NOTE If you are working with a different e-mail program, convert the files to PDF from Acrobat; you can still use the conversion settings described in this section.

Adjusting Conversion Settings

Abby is taking some time today to build her PDF e-mail system. Before converting any files, she opens and modifies the conversion settings.

Follow these steps to adjust the settings:

1. In Outlook, choose Adobe PDF > Change Conversion Settings to open the Acrobat PDFMaker dialog (**Figure 7.3**).

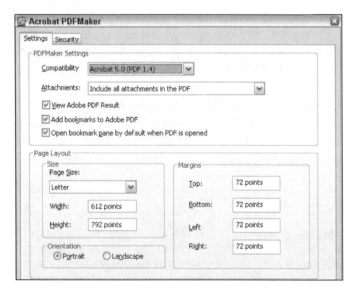

Figure 7.3 *Choose settings for conversion before creating PDF files from e-mails.*

2. On the Settings tab, choose options for conversion based on how you need to use the e-mails (see the next section for setting these options).

3. Select the Security tab and add the security settings you want.

4. Click OK to close the dialog.

> **TIP** If you add security—such as passwords—and then have to work with the document further in Acrobat, you have to enter the password before you can start working. Save yourself some time by adding security later in Acrobat, when you are finished with the documents.

Choosing Conversion Options

The default settings for converting e-mail in Outlook's PDFMaker are shown in Figure 8.3. By default, the PDFMaker uses the Acrobat 5 Compatibility option. If you leave the Acrobat 5 option, your recipients using Acrobat Reader version 5 and above, as well as Acrobat versions 5 and newer can view the content. Abby will use the default because she doesn't know that her viewers will all have the latest version of Acrobat or Adobe Reader.

You can choose to include attachments or not using options from the Attachments pull-down list. Because Abby wants her attachments included in the converted e-mails, she leaves the default option.

The next three check boxes pertain to how and when the converted document is displayed. Since Abby is converting batches of files and folders, she deselects the View Adobe PDF Results option to save time. Otherwise, each time she converts a folder, it opens in Acrobat. She intends to use the bookmarking process in Acrobat and leaves the two bookmark options checked—"Add bookmarks to Adobe PDF" and "Open bookmark pane by default when PDF is opened."

Abby also decides to leave the Page Layout options at their default settings. Using these options, her converted e-mails are shown on letter-sized pages with standard margins and a portrait orientation. With this basic page layout, Abby and her clients can easily print PDF versions of the e-mails.

Now it's time to convert the files. Drum roll, please!

Processing the Files

Converting folders of e-mails in Outlook to PDF is a simple one-click process. Abby has organized her content into folders, and now she decides to convert each client's or manufacturer's folder into a single PDF document.

Follow these steps to create the PDF:

1. Select the folder for conversion in the All Mail Folders listing in Outlook (the folders are shown in Figure 8.2).

2. On the PDFMaker toolbar, click the Convert selected folder to Adobe PDF 🖼 icon. The Save Adobe PDF File As dialog opens.

3. You'll see the name of the folder is shown as the PDF filename (**Figure 7.4**). Leave the default name or type an alternate name, and select a folder location. Abby organized her e-mails in folders earlier in the project, so she'll use the default names throughout.

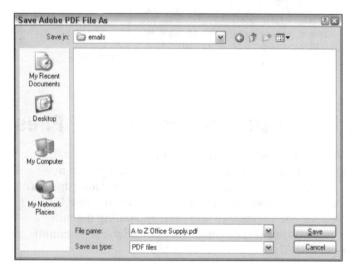

Figure 7.4 Choose a name and storage location for the file.

4. Click Save to dismiss the dialog.

5. The Creating Adobe PDF dialog opens (**Figure 7.5**), and you see a progress bar as the files are processed. The dialog includes the name of the mail folder. As each file is processed, the mail subject is shown on the dialog as well. When the PDF document is assembled, the dialog closes automatically.

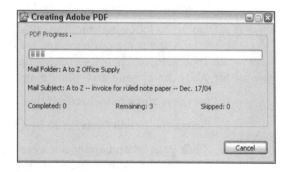

Figure 7.5 You see information about the file processing in this dialog.

6. Continue to process the remaining e-mail folders. In Abby's case, she is converting a set of six folders in total—three customer folders and three manufacturer folders. **Figure 7.6** shows all six folders have been processed.

It's simple to add additional content to an existing PDF version of your e-mail files in Outlook using another PDFMaker tool, as Abby discovers next.

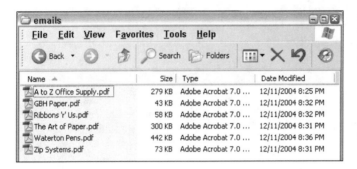

Figure 7.6 *Abby converts folders of e-mail from both clients and manufacturers to PDF documents.*

Appending E-mail Documents to PDF Files

Unless you are archiving e-mails for storage, managing a folder of e-mail on a specific thread or topic is an ongoing process, and the ability to add new content to an e-mail is an important element for successfully managing your e-mails. Rather than manually converting individual e-mails to a new PDF, opening the existing e-mail PDF in Acrobat, and then appending the new e-mail PDF to the file, Abby can use a PDFMaker tool in Outlook to automatically add new content to e-mails.

NOTE If you aren't working with Outlook, you will have to follow the manual conversion method described in the previous paragraph.

Although the following steps describe appending an e-mail to an existing PDF e-mail file, the same principle applies regardless of the content of the PDF you are appending to. That is, instead of appending an e-mail to another PDF e-mail file, Abby can append an e-mail to any PDF file she likes.

Follow these steps to include another e-mail in an existing PDF document:

1. Select the e-mail message to be appended to an existing PDF.

2. Click Convert and append selected messages to an existing Adobe PDF 📄. The Save Adobe PDF File As dialog opens (shown previously in Figure 8.4).

3. Select the file to which you want to append the new e-mail.

4. Click Open to dismiss the dialog and process the document.

It is certainly possible to convert a single e-mail to a PDF document in Outlook as well. Follow these steps to create the PDF:

1. Select the e-mail message in your e-mail program's folders.

2. Click Convert selected messages to Adobe PDF ▣ on the PDFMaker toolbar.

3. In the Save Adobe PDF File As dialog, shown in Figure 8.4, name the document and select its storage location. Click Save to dismiss the dialog and save the PDF document.

Once Abby has processed her e-mail messages, it's time to take a look at what she's produced in Acrobat.

Viewing Converted E-mail Documents

Remember earlier when Abby had selected her conversion settings and included the default option to add bookmarks to the PDF files? In this section, you'll see how Acrobat converts information from the e-mails, such as the sender or date, into bookmarks.

NOTE If you aren't working with Outlook but have used Acrobat's Binder feature (described in Chapter 2) to create PDF versions of your e-mail files, you'll find a single bookmark added to the binder for each e-mail in the file. You won't have the multiple bookmark arrangement described in this section.

Abby opens one of the converted e-mail folders in Acrobat. When the document opens, she sees both the first e-mail as well as the Bookmarks pane (**Figure 7.7**).

Bookmarks are arranged by Acrobat in four categories:

- Arranged by Date
- Arranged by Sender
- Arranged by Subject
- Personal Folders (which refers to the Outlook folder structure)

Use the bookmarks to locate a specific e-mail in a PDF. The same information derived from the e-mails is organized in the bookmarks in different ways. For example, if you remember the subject of an e-mail, click the (+) to the left of the Arranged by Subject bookmark heading to see the content listed alphabetically by subject line. If you remember the date (in the figure all e-mails have

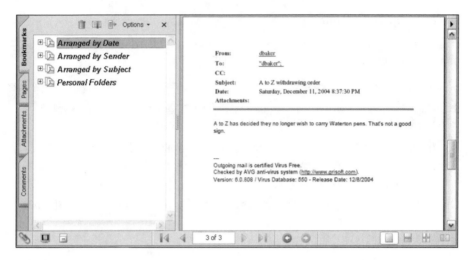

Figure 7.7 *Acrobat adds a set of bookmarks to the e-mail documents.*

the same date because they were created for this demonstration), click the (+) to the left of the Arranged by Date bookmark to see the content arranged chronologically.

NOTE You can read more about working with bookmarks in Chapter 2 and also in Bonus Chapter 1 on the book's Web site.

What if you can't remember the date and don't know the subject? Not to worry. You don't have to open all the bookmark categories—just use Acrobat's Search feature.

Searching E-mail PDFs

It is true that it takes a bit of time to construct a set of PDF documents from your e-mails. If you need to find information in those e-mails, however, you'll be glad you made the effort! Unlike searching e-mails in your e-mail program, which can be frustrating and imprecise, Acrobat's Search feature lets you find precise words or phrases in any number of e-mail PDF documents and files, regardless of the method used to create the files.

Because she often acts as an intermediary between her suppliers and her customers, Abby needs to find information in her e-mails on a regular basis. Let's follow through a search example as Abby looks for references to a particular part number.

Follow these steps to search one or more PDF e-mail files:

1. Click Search  on the File toolbar in Acrobat. The File toolbar is one of the default toolbars. If you have closed it, choose View > Toolbars > File to open it.

2. The Search PDF window opens at the right side of the program window. The window is locked to the right of the program window—you can widen the Search PDF window, but you can't collapse its width.

3. Type the search term you want to find in the "What word or phrase would you like to search for?" field on the dialog (**Figure 7.8**). Abby types in #3388.

4. Click one of two location radio buttons, either to search the current PDF document open in Acrobat or to search a location on your hard drive or server. In Abby's search, she's looking for all references to a particular part number in her e-mail folders, so she chooses the folder through the "All PDF Documents in" pull-down list.

5. Choose other criteria for searching if you wish, such as searching for whole words, using case-sensitive options, or searching bookmarks and comments.

6. Click Search in the Search PDF window.

7. The search is performed and the results displayed on the Search PDF window (**Figure 7.9**). You see the search term(s) listed, as well as the locations Acrobat searched.

Figure 7.8 Type the word or phrase you want to find in the dialog and specify the search location.

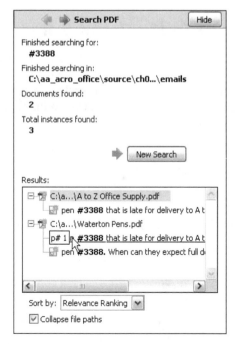

Figure 7.9 Results from a search are listed in the window by document name and page number.

8. In the Results area, click the (+) to the left of a document name to open its list of matches. If you move your pointer over a listing, you see the page number in a tooltip.

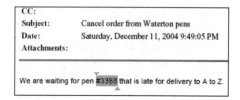

9. Click a results listing to display the document in Acrobat. The search result is highlighted in the document (**Figure 7.10**).

Figure 7.10 Acrobat highlights the search results in the document.

10. Click Hide to close the Search PDF window.

NOTE You can also perform advanced searches to specify other criteria for searching. Advanced searches are described in Chapter 12.

Abby is pleased with her progress so far. Next she'd like to experiment with Acrobat's Organizer to see if its features will take her one step closer to e-mail nirvana.

Organizing Files in Acrobat

Abby plans to build a folder structure in the Organizer, a super new feature in Acrobat 7. The folders you create in Acrobat, called *collections*, are virtual folders that are used within the program only; they have no impact on your system's file folders. You can add new collections, or add and remove files from those collections, without affecting your system folders in any way.

Follow these steps to name a collection and add new files in the Organizer:

1. Click the Organizer icon 🗂 on the File toolbar, or choose File > Organizer > Open Organizer. The Organizer opens in a separate window from Acrobat.

2. Acrobat includes three collections named collection 1, collection 2, and collection 3 by default; the collection list is part of the Files pane at the left of the Organizer window (**Figure 7.11**). You can drag the splitter bars between the frames to resize each frame as you are working.

3. Right-click/Control-click a collection name to show its shortcut menu (**Figure 7.12**). Click Rename Collection to activate the default name's text.

4. Type a name for the collection; in Abby's case, she names the first collection "manufacturers."

Categories pane lets you find files on your computer in a number of ways

Files pane shows a listing of the PDF files in a selected category

Pages pane shows you a preview of a selected file

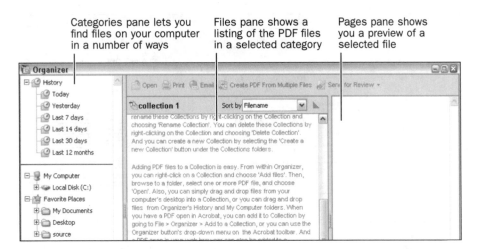

Figure 7.11 *The Organizer is a three-pane window you can use to manage PDF documents.*

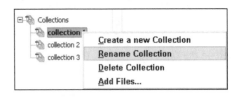

Figure 7.12 *Choose a command for working with collections from the shortcut menu.*

5. Right-click/Control-click the collection's name again, and choose Add Files from the shortcut menu to open the "Select files to add to your collection" dialog.

6. Locate and select the files you want to add to the collection, and click Add to dismiss the dialog; the files are added to the collection (**Figure 7.13**).

7. Repeat the process, naming collections and adding files. In Figure 8.13, both of Abby's collections have been added to the Organizer.

8. Close the Organizer when you are finished adding files.

Once Abby has her collections built, she can access her files either through the Organizer or through Acrobat. In Acrobat, she can click the pull-down arrow to the right of the Organizer button on the File menu to open a menu. Then she clicks Collections, the name of the collection, and the file she wants to view (**Figure 7.14**).

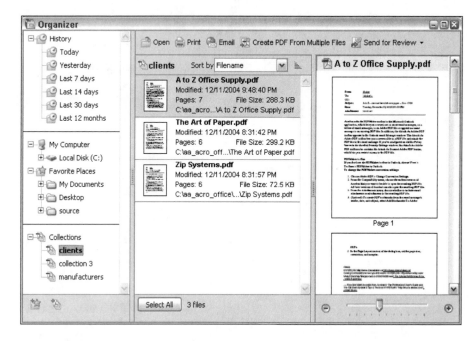

Figure 7.13 *Files added to the collection are listed on the Organizer window.*

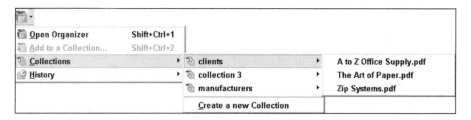

Figure 7.14 *Choose options from the Organizer's pull-down menu.*

Managing Collections

Once you have named your collections and added files to them, you can add more content or delete existing files as necessary. When you click a collection's name in the Categories pane, you have the following options:

- To remove a collection, choose Delete Collection from the shortcut menu; a confirmation dialog opens telling you that removing the collection will have no effect on the actual files on your computer.

- To add more files to a collection, choose Add Files from the shortcut menu, and select the new files in the "Select files to add to your collection" dialog.

- To rename the collection, choose Rename Collection from the shortcut menu to activate the text and type the new name.

You certainly aren't limited to three collections. You can add as many collections as you need for your particular project. Either choose Create a new Collection from the shortcut menu, or click the Create a new Collection button 🖻 at the lower left of the Organizer window.

In addition to working with collections, Abby can also access her files in other ways in the Organizer.

Other Organizer Options

The Categories pane of the Organizer allows Abby to find files in a number of ways. The more she works with the Organizer, the more familiar she becomes with its uses and how to integrate the options into her workflow.

In addition to the Collections category, described in the previous section, the Organizer includes the History, My Computer, and Favorite Places categories.

Using History Files

Acrobat's Organizer includes a History category, which stores information about all the files you have opened during a specific time frame, regardless of where they are stored on your computer. This can be handy if you recall you worked with a particular file last Tuesday, but can't remember its exact name. Any file you open in Acrobat, whether selected through the File > Open command, from a collection in the Organizer, or from your system's folders, is added to the History.

To work with the History, located in the Organizer's Categories pane, click a time frame from the History listing; a list of the PDF files you have opened during that period is displayed in the Files pane. To clear the listing for any point in time, click the option in the History listing—such as Yesterday—to display the content in the Files pane, and then click the Clear History button at the bottom of the Files pane.

NOTE Take care when clearing the History. Clearing a History setting such as Last Week also clears all History listings of shorter duration, such as Today or Yesterday.

The History contents are also available in the File menu. Choose File > History and one of the date options (**Figure 7.15**). The History command is conveniently listed above the last documents opened in the File menu.

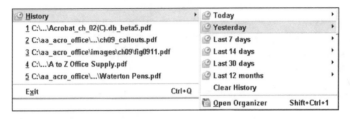

Figure 7.15 Acrobat arranges the documents you have opened in the History listings.

Figure 7.16 You can add folders to your Favorite Places for quick access in the Organizer window.

Defining Favorites

In the Organizer, right-click/Control-click the Favorite Places listing and click Add a Favorite Place, or click the Add a Favorite Place button 👑 at the lower left of the Organizer window. A Browse for Folder dialog opens. Locate the folder you want to add and click OK. The selected folder is added to the list (**Figure 7.16**).

Working with Organizer Content

There are other ways Abby can work with her files in the Organizer. She can find, sort files, and preview them in the Organizer window. She can also perform some actions on the files right from the Organizer.

Viewing and Sorting Documents

In the Files pane, Abby can view the content of a selected folder or collection. A regular PDF document shows a thumbnail; a document containing security shows only a PDF document icon (**Figure 7.17**). The files are listed in the Files pane in alphabetical order. You can sort the documents using many different methods. Click the Sort by pull-down arrow, and choose an option from the list (**Figure 7.18**).

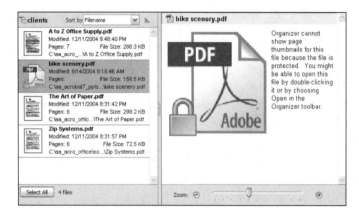

Figure 7.17 *A document containing security shows only an icon in the Files and Pages panes of the Organizer.*

When you select a file, it is shown in the Pages pane; you can zoom in or out of the document using the (+) and (–) buttons at the bottom of the pane, or drag the slider to show the file's content. You see scrollbars when the view is magnified, you select more than one document in the Files pane, or there are multiple pages in the document.

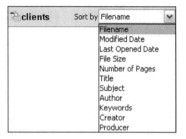

Figure 7.18 *You can sort documents in the Organizer in a number of different ways.*

Working with Files in the Organizer

The Organizer also contains a set of tools that Abby can use to work with PDF documents in Acrobat, as shown in **Figure 7.19**:

- Click Open to open selected file(s) in Acrobat.

- Click Print to print selected file(s).

- Click Email to open an e-mail window with the selected file(s) attached.

- Click Create PDF From Multiple Files to open Acrobat's Create PDF from Multiple Documents dialog (described in several chapters in the book, such as Chapter 2).

- Click Send for Review to initiate an e-mail review right from the Organizer window. You can read more about working with review cycles in Chapters 13 and 14.

Figure 7.19 *Perform a number of common document functions right from the Organizer window.*

Whether Abby is working in Acrobat or organizing and managing files in the Organizer, she is sure to save time in her work.

When she created the original PDF documents from e-mail folder contents, Abby chose to attach the source files to the PDF documents in the PDFMaker's settings. In the next section, you see how she and her clients can work with attachments in Acrobat.

Using PDF File Attachments

In Acrobat 7, Abby can attach files of any type to a PDF document so that the attachments are included with the PDF for storage or for e-mailing. The recipient can open the PDF file, and the attachments are included right along with the document—a simple fact that fills Abby with delight.

In her business, much of the exchange of information with both clients and manufacturers is conducted by e-mail. But attaching files to e-mails can be tricky business. Attachments are difficult to manage, and it's easy to forget to include an attachment when sending an e-mail. Or, attachments simply get "lost" on others' computers. By including the attachments with a PDF, there's no loss of information anywhere, and the recipient can always access the content directly from the PDF. If you move the PDF file on your hard drive, the attached files or pages automatically move with it, saving time in organizing and maintaining your files.

Displaying Attachments

Abby converted e-mails to PDF documents and included the attachments. **Figure 7.20** shows one of Abby's e-mails and its attachment information in the Attachments pane. She has an Excel spreadsheet attached to this particular e-mail. When her recipient opens the PDF file, they'll see the attachment listed in the document, provided she specifies that the document shows the attachment when it opens.

Information about the attachment   Attachments toolbar   Menu is also available from the Options menu

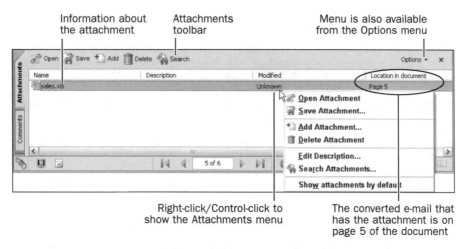

Right-click/Control-click to show the Attachments menu

The converted e-mail that has the attachment is on page 5 of the document

Figure 7.20 *Read about and work with file attachments in the Attachments pane.*

You can specify that attachments be seen when the PDF is opened in Acrobat by doing one of the following:

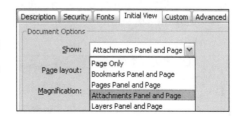

Figure 7.21 *You can specify that a document shows the Attachments pane automatically when it opens.*

- Click Options on the Attachments pane and choose "Show attachments by default."

- Choose File > Document Properties > Initial View. On the Initial View tab, choose Attachments Panel and Page from the Show pull-down list, shown in **Figure 7.21**.

Regardless of whether a document is attached when using a PDFMaker or added in Acrobat, the attachment is identified by a paperclip icon 📎 at the bottom left of the program window on the Status bar in Acrobat 7.

Abby can also add more information to an existing PDF in the form of attachments. Let's say she's having a problem with one of her suppliers' products. She can attach the e-mails outlining the problem to the e-mails she sends to the supplier. If she wants to extract just the pertinent information from an e-mail PDF, she can select the content, copy it to the system clipboard, and create a new PDF document from it to attach to her e-mail (see how to work with clipboard content in Chapter 2).

Adding More Attachments

Attachments can be added in two ways—either as attachments to the document itself or as comments attached to a particular location. Abby decides to try both methods.

To attach another document to the active PDF file from the Attachments pane, follow these steps:

1. Select the Attachments tab to display the Attachments pane across the bottom of the program window.

2. Click Add 🗐 on the Attachments pane toolbar to open the Add Attachment dialog.

3. Locate and select the file to be attached to the document.

4. Click Open to dismiss the dialog and add the attachment to the document's Attachments pane.

5. In the Attachments pane, the new attachment is listed as the Attachments tab in the Location in document column of the pane (**Figure 7.22**).

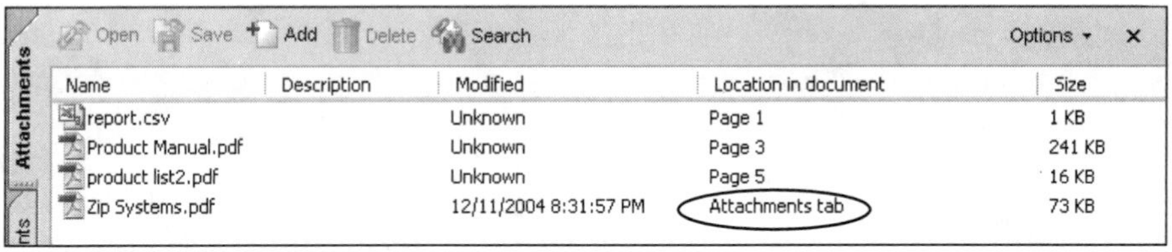

Figure 7.22 *You can attach a file to the active document.*

NOTE If the Attachments pane isn't open, you can click the Attach a File tool on the File toolbar.

Instead of attaching a file to the document at large, Abby can attach it to a specific location; this is referred to as attaching a file as a comment. As her viewers read the document, they see an icon indicating that there is a file attached. A document added in this way is a good method of notifying the users that there is additional information as they are reading.

To attach a file to a document in Acrobat as a form of comment, follow these steps:

1. Click the Attach a File as a Comment 🖉 tool on the File toolbar.

2. Move the pointer, which looks like a pushpin, over the document to where you want to display the icon indicating an attachment is embedded.

3. Click the document; the Add Attachment dialog opens.

4. Locate and select the file you want to attach. Click Select to close the dialog.

5. The File Attachment Properties dialog opens; if you like, choose an alternate icon, color, or opacity on the Appearance tab of the dialog (**Figure 7.23**).

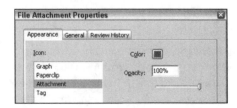

6. Select the General tab to display fields where you can modify the attachment's name, your name, and a description of the attachment. Abby's selections are shown in **Figure 7.24**.

Figure 7.23 You can customize the appearance of the attached file's icon.

7. Click Close to dismiss the dialog.

8. The Attachment icon is shown where you clicked on the page; move your pointer over the icon to see information about the attachment in a tooltip (**Figure 7.25**).

9. Save the document.

In the Attachments pane, the Location in document column shows the number of the page where you attached the file as a comment. Information added in the File Attachment Properties description is shown in the Description column of the Attachments pane (**Figure 7.26**).

Figure 7.24 Customize the text used in the attached file's comment box.

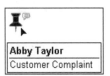

Figure 7.25 Information added to the properties shows on the page as a tooltip.

Figure 7.26 Descriptions added in the File Attachment Properties dialog are shown in the Attachments pane.

USING ATTACHMENTS IN OLDER VERSIONS OF ACROBAT

The attachments to Abby's PDF files can also be accessed by those working with versions 5 and 6 of Acrobat, as long as you've specified that attachments be seen when the PDF is opened, using one of the two methods described earlier in this section.

When a user opens the document using Acrobat 5 or 6, an information dialog displays that explains the file contains attachments you can view in the program. Click OK to close the dialog, and then choose Document > File Attachments to open the File Attachments dialog (**Figure 8.27**). You'll see the attachments listed according to their locations. Document file attachments are listed first, followed by those attached using the Attach a File as a Comment tool.

Click the name of a file in the dialog to view its details. You can use the buttons at the bottom of the dialog—Open, Import, Export, and Delete—to work with the attachments.

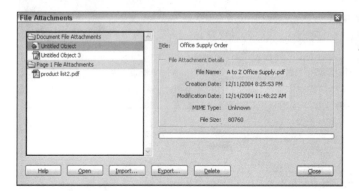

Figure 7.27 The attachments are listed in the File Attachments dialog in Acrobat versions 5 and 6.

There are a few other things you can do with a PDF file's attachments as well, as you'll see in the next section.

Other Attachment Activities

Aside from adding more attachments in Acrobat, there are several other activities Abby can experiment with. She can

- Add descriptions
- Open the attachments or convert the attachments
- Export the attachment from Acrobat
- Save, delete, or search attachments

Adding Descriptions

If you add an attachment as a comment and enter text in the File Attachment Properties dialog, that text is seen as a description in the Attachments pane (as shown in Figure 8.26).

Add a description to any attachment in a document by following these steps:

1. Select the attachment in the Attachments pane.

2. Choose Edit Description from the pane's Options menu.

3. In the Edit Attachment Description dialog, type the text you want to use for the description (**Figure 7.28**).

4. Click OK to close the dialog and add the description to the file's listing.

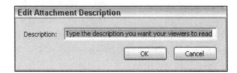

Figure 7.28 Add text describing the content of an attachment in this dialog.

Opening Attachments

To open an attachment, double-click a listing in the Attachments pane, click Open 📎 on the Attachments toolbar, or choose the command from the Options menu. A PDF file opens automatically. If the attachment is another file format, you see a warning dialog that describes the hazards of opening documents that might contain macros, viruses, or other possible problem makers. Click Open to open the document, or click Do Not Open to stop the process and close the dialog.

Saving the Attachments

Click Save 💾 on the Attachments toolbar or from the Options menu to save the attachment as a separate file. In the Save Attachment dialog, choose the storage location for the file. The file uses the name shown in the Attachments pane (which you can change). Click Save to close the dialog and save the file.

Deleting the Attachments

Click Delete to delete an attachment 🗑. Be careful when deleting attachments! If you delete an attachment, it's not in your system's Recycling Bin in case you need to restore it—it's removed completely from the document. If you delete an attachment and change your mind, choose Edit > Undo to restore the attachment to the file.

Searching the Attachments

You can also click Search 🔍 to open the Search PDF window and search the contents of the attached files. The Search PDF window provides you with a Search Attachments button automatically. Type the word or phrase you want to find in the attachments, and then click Search Attachments. The results are listed for both the PDF document you are working with and its attachments.

Abby is quite pleased with the extra functionality she has discovered in Acrobat 7. She is sure it is going to make document management a little simpler for her and her customers and suppliers. She has one worry, though, and that is about the documents' security. If she could just find a way to make sure the information attached to an e-mail will be seen by only the right people... (cue the dream sequence music).

Securing File Attachments

Needless to say, Acrobat has the answer to Abby's concerns, and she's not dreaming! Acrobat 7 Professional contains a new feature called an eEnvelope, used as a secure wrapper for a document and its attachments. An eEnvelope is the digital equivalent of a courier-delivered package—the courier cycles into your office, waits for a signature, and then hands over the package. Acrobat can do much the same thing, without leaving any tire treads in your lobby. eEnvelopes even look like envelopes!

Encryption using an eEnvelope doesn't modify the file attachments in any way. Just like a courier package, once you "break" the seal on the document—that is, once your recipient extracts the file attachments and saves them—the files are no longer protected.

Abby can send an e-mail to her customer, attach an invoice, embed the attachment in an eEnvelope, encrypt the eEnvelope using a password or certificate security method, and then e-mail it. Only the person with rights to open the eEnvelope can see the content. Which of course means that Abby has to inform her e-mail recipient of the password needed to use to open the attached files.

NOTE You can read more about encryption in Chapter 14.

Acrobat 7 Professional includes a set of three default eEnvelope templates, which are simply PDF files with an image and a few form fields, as you see in the next section. Instead of using one of the defaults, Abby could also create her own custom template. Read how to create and use a custom template in this chapter's bonus material on the book's Web site.

Using an eEnvelope in Acrobat

The default templates for eEnvelopes are interesting and serve a useful purpose (**Figure 7.29**). There's no doubt in a recipient's mind what the file is when they open it and see the envelope.

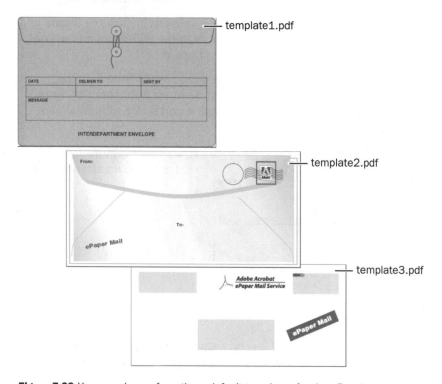

template1.pdf

template2.pdf

template3.pdf

Figure 7.29 *You can choose from three default templates for the eEnvelope.*

Download **abby_template.pdf** if you'd like to try creating your own template using the information in the bonus material for this chapter on the book's Web site. You can also download **abbyt.pdf**, which is the finished custom template. The original template file used in the project is the **template3.pdf** file, located on your hard drive. Or if you prefer, you can download a copy of the **template3.pdf** file.

You can work with an eEnvelope from within Acrobat. If you have access to Adobe LiveCycle Policy Server, a separate server product, you can also work from Outlook; this method is described in the sidebar "Adding an eEnvelope from Outlook" later in this chapter.

Abby is going to use one of the default templates to send a secure e-mail. Then she's going to complete the envelope manually.

Using the Wizard

Apply an eEnvelope using a wizard in Acrobat by following these steps:

1. Choose Document > Security > Secure PDF Delivery, or click the Secure task button 🔒 and choose the command from the pull-down menu. The five-step Creating Secure eEnvelope wizard opens.

2. In the first pane of the wizard, select the documents to attach to the PDF. Any attachments existing in the document are automatically listed (**Figure 7.34**). Click "Add file to send" to locate and select additional files, and then click Next.

Figure 7.34 *Specify the files you want to send in the eEnvelope dialog.*

If you add a file by mistake, you can click "Remove selected file(s)" to delete it from the list.

3. The second step of the wizard displays. Choose a template from the list (**Figure 7.35**). Abby selects the default template, named template1.pdf. Click Next.

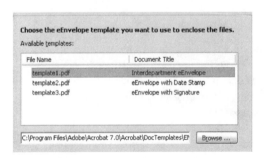

Figure 7.35 *Select a template to use for the eEnvelope's appearance.*

4. Select a delivery method option for sending the file. You can complete and e-mail the eEnvelope manually or automatically. Click Next.

The default option is to complete the template automatically, although you usually select the manual option to add the text in the fields. Use the automatic method if you have built a custom template that doesn't need any customization added.

5. On the next pane of the wizard, used to specify a security policy, click Show All Policies to display the list of policies (**Figure 7.36**).

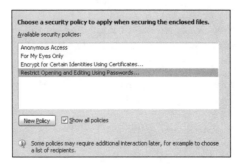

Figure 7.36 Select a security policy to use for the eEnvelope.

6. Select a policy to use for the eEnvelope. Abby decides to use the default password policy named Restrict Opening and Editing Using Passwords. Click Next.

7. The final pane of the dialog shows a list of the options you have selected in the other panes. Click Finished to close the dialog.

8. Because Abby chose to use a password for protecting the document earlier, the eEnvelope's wizard is replaced by the Password Security - Settings dialog (**Figure 7.37**).

Figure 7.37 The options available depend on the version of Acrobat you choose in the Compatibility setting.

9. Choose an option from the Compatibility pull-down list (see the sidebar "Encryption Options" for more information). Abby chooses an Acrobat 6-compatibility option because she's not sure if her recipients have the newest versions of Acrobat or Adobe Reader.

10. Select the document components you'd like to protect. Abby uses the "Encrypt all document contents" option.

11. Type a password in the File Attachment Open Password field.

12. Click OK to close the dialog and display a confirmation dialog. Retype the password and click OK to dismiss the confirmation and finish the wizard.

13. The final step depends on the delivery option selected in the wizard. If you chose to send the eEnvelope, enter your recipient's e-mail address in the e-mail dialog that opens, and click Send to send it on its way.

Abby's template requires her to enter her recipient's name on the field, so she'll do that next.

Finishing the Secure Package

Since Abby chose to complete the wizard manually, once the Creating Secure eEnvelope wizard closes, the template opens in Acrobat. The files she's attached are listed in the eEnvelope's Attachments pane.

To finish the eEnvelope and send it, follow these steps:

1. Click the envelope.sender field on the template and type the sender's name or e-mail address. Abby types Abby Taylor, Taylor & Daughter.

2. Click the envelope.recipient field on the template and type to add the recipient's name. Add a message in the envelope.message field, if you like.

3. Choose File > Save to save the file and apply the security settings.

   You don't have to add the date in the envelope.date field manually. When you use a template having a date field, the date is inserted in the field automatically as soon as you save the file (**Figure 7.38**).

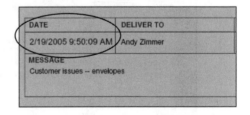

4. Open your e-mail program, and attach the PDF file to a new message addressed to your recipient; send the e-mail.

Figure 7.38 *The completed eEnvelope also displays the date and time.*

When the recipient clicks to open the attachment, they can open the eEnvelope only if they type the correct password in the Password dialog that displays.

Abby's managed to tame her unruly e-mails. But there are a few more things she might consider at a later time.

ADDING AN eENVELOPE FROM OUTLOOK

An eEnvelope can be created from Outlook when you are ready to send an e-mail, if you have access to Adobe LiveCycle Policy Server, a separate server product used by enterprise-level organizations.

Follow these steps to send a secured PDF file:

1. In Outlook, open a new e-mail message window.

2. Click Attach as Secured Adobe PDF on the Standard toolbar to open the Attach as Secured Adobe PDF dialog.

3. Choose the file you want to send through the dialog, and then select a security option (**Figure 8.39**). You can either restrict opening to the names listed in the To, Cc, and Bcc fields of the e-mail or select a policy.

4. Click OK to close the dialog. The document attachment to the e-mail displays as usual, but (secured) appears in the attachment's name (**Figure 8.40**).

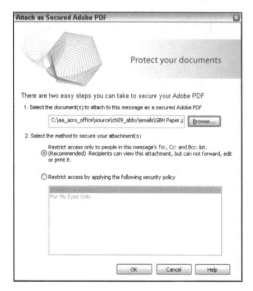

Figure 7.39 *Choose a security option to apply through Outlook.*

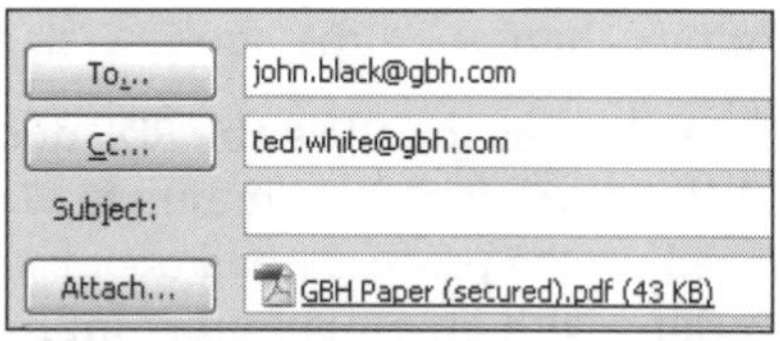

Figure 7.40 *The attachment is identified as secured right in the e-mail.*

ENCRYPTION OPTIONS

In the Password Security - Settings dialog, Abby has three choices based on what version of Acrobat she wants the file to be compatible with. Each of Acrobat 5, 6, and 7 have different encryption capabilities:

- Acrobat 5 encrypts the entire document and its attachments

- Acrobat 6 encrypts all content except for metadata, which is advanced information about the document's content. (You can read about metadata in Chapter 11 and in Acrobat's Help files.)

- Acrobat 7 encrypts only the attachments

The option you choose depends on what version of Acrobat your recipients are working with, as well as your security requirements. You can read more about encryption and security policies in Chapter 14.

What Else Can She Do?

There are other feats of Acrobat wizardry Abby might want to look at in the future, depending on how she likes her new e-mail management system. For example, if she finds it useful for managing a lot of material in addition to her e-mails, she could consider using the files as an archive of sorts.

She can convert or attach other business documents to e-mail threads for further reference or include other files in a number of additional folders. That way, the content is readily accessible through Acrobat, and she can search through attachments as well as PDF files to locate content easily.

Abby can create and use a custom template for the eEnvelope (**Figure 7.41**). Instead of using one of the preconfigured templates, she can save time filling in fields as well as giving her work a more custom look by building her own template. You can learn how Abby builds a custom template in the bonus material for this chapter on the book's Web site.

If she decides to follow the PDF document management route and to convert a large number of documents to PDF files, she could use a batch sequence to speed up the process (read about using batch scripts in Chapter 12). If you are working with an e-mail program rather than Outlook, consider using the batch sequence process in Chapter 12 to save yourself time when converting large numbers of files.

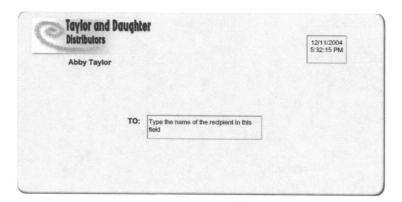

Figure 7.41 *Abby can build and save her own custom eEnvelope template.*

Abby might also consider creating an index for her documents, especially if she uses the Search feature frequently. That way, she can search through hundreds of documents more quickly than she would by searching selected documents. You can read about indexing in Chapter 12 as well.

8

Making Accessible Documents in Acrobat

Governments all over the world have introduced key legislation, such as Section 508 of the Rehabilitation Act in the United States, requiring that electronic and information technology be accessible to people with disabilities. With such importance now placed on accessibility in technology, it shouldn't come as a surprise that Acrobat 7 Professional contains many options, testing routines, tools, and wizards for making content in your PDF files accessible to people with visual or motor impairments who work with screen readers and other assistive devices. An accessible PDF document can be read in Acrobat 7 or Adobe Reader 7, as well as in earlier versions of the programs.

A whole world lies hidden within a PDF file, and you'll explore that new frontier in this chapter. For example, you'll learn several ways to apply and modify document tags—key elements of accessible PDF files. You'll see how to work with and change the reading order in a file. This is important for those who use screen readers to move through a page. You will also see how to define and use articles, which are structures added to a file to control navigation.

Acrobat contains testing features that range from high-contrast color schemes, to reading the page aloud, to tests that evaluate the accessibility status of a file. You'll see how to use these features and interpret the results. It's all quite easy to do, and you'll make many people's lives a lot easier if you create files that are truly accessible.

Lend a Helping Hand

Diane Lerner is the executive director of a local community organization called Helping Hands Community Information Services. The organization serves as a clearinghouse of sorts, providing information to the public as well as health and social service professionals. Helping Hands offers brochures, information sheets, and other printed material about the programs, as well as community resources available to those with mental and physical challenges.

In the past couple of years, Helping Hands has launched a Web site that displays information the organization has compiled from their resources in one easy-to-use online resource. The organization has received some very positive feedback from its users.

But many clients have told Diane they find it difficult to make their way through the organization's Web site because they are working with screen readers and other assistive devices, and the Helping Hands Web site hasn't been configured for accessible use. Diane has also learned that many users prefer to download pertinent information that they can access offline.

Diane decides that a useful way to both present the information to her clients and enhance the usability of the material is to provide PDF versions of the organization's information and the Web site's content. She also knows that Acrobat can produce accessible documents, and so she's willing to invest the time and effort to create material that's useful and accessible for her clients.

Diane is also aware that many of her clients use screen readers and other devices, and she is sure she can test the documents' usability in Acrobat before uploading the PDF files to her Web site.

Steps Involved in This Project

Diane plans to test a source document from one of her resources, and she'll convert some of her Web site content to see how easily it can be used in accessible PDF format (**Figure 8.1**). Finally, she'd like to see if a newsletter can be appropriately used by various assistive devices as well. She hopes to conduct

Specify how a user reads the text and images using Acrobat's Reading Order feature.

Acrobat can add tags to the file, identifying tables or headings, that work like tags on a Web page.

Use articles to easily define how your viewers read the page, even if it has a complex layout.

Give Yourself a Helping Hand

HELPING HANDS

Volume 3, Issue 1

10 January 2005

Icy streets and heavy snows make for treacherous travel

Staying Safe in Cold Weather

Winter is upon us. Take care when traveling on icy streets. This month's product reviews cover some new products designed to help you make your way through the ice and snow. Take a look on Page 3 to read about a line of ice spikes for canes and walkers that many of our consumers have found very helpful.

Persistent Developmental Delay

"Pervasive developmental disorders" is a term used to describe disorders, such as autism.

Whether a child is diagnosed with PDD or autism is a matter of scale. A diagnosis is made on the basis of a collection of 12 symptoms that are displayed by the child. These symptoms pertain to behavior, social interaction, and communication.

If a child displays similar behaviors but doesn't meet the criteria for autism, they may be diagnosed as Pervasive Developmental Disorder-NOS (PDD not otherwise specified), which is better known as PDD.

Children with both PDD and autism can vary dramatically in their abilities, behaviors, and intelligence.

Many children have a limited range of interests, and repetitive play skills, often accompanied by inappropriate social responses.

Often these children respond to sensory stimulation such as light, sound, fabric, or food in unusual or exaggerated ways.

Some children do not speak at all, or have only limited or repetitive language. Those with more advanced language often restrict their conversation to a small range of topics, and have a difficult time expressing abstract ideas like emotions.

Is There a Difference?

The term "PDD" has caused confusion for both parents and professionals due to the similarity of the behaviors in people with either autism or PDD. Both children with autism and PDD require similar education and treatment plans.

The causes of autism and PDD are unknown, but may relate to neurological damage or biochemical imbalance. Neither disorder is caused by psychological factors.

Autism and PDD Problems:

- COMMUNICATION ISSUES: UNDERSTANDING AND USING LANGUAGE
- DIFFICULTY RELATING TO PEOPLE, OBJECTS, AND EVENTS
- UNUSUAL PLAY BEHAVIOR
- DIFFICULTY IN CHANGING ROUTINE OR SURROUNDINGS
- REPETITIVE BEHAVIOR OR BODY MOVEMENTS

Inside this issue:

Use the Read Out Loud feature to listen to your file rather than reading it!

Test to see how a file looks for users working with high-contrast color schemes. What you see is not always what you get!

Figure 8.1 *Accessibility features can be added to any file in Acrobat.*

her experiments (in her office, not a dank and gloomy basement laboratory) and present the results at the next meeting of the organization's board of directors.

To complete her project and create content for accessible PDF files, Diane needs to

- Test her PDF files for basic accessibility features

- Convert a Web page to PDF and append it to an existing file

- Check the accessibility status of the documents using Acrobat's accessibility checking features

- Make any necessary repairs to her documents in Acrobat according to the files' Accessibility Reports

- Test and configure the file's reading order

- Try the Read Out Loud feature, which simulates a screen reader program

- Add *articles*—defined paths for readers to follow through a document— to a newsletter to create custom viewing

- Check how the pages look in a high-contrast color scheme

- Write a read-me file that users can access to learn how to use Acrobat and Adobe Reader's Accessibility Setup Assistant to configure the programs to work with their assistive devices

Diane has never experimented with accessible PDF files before. She definitely thinks it is worth the effort, especially considering her users and their needs. The first step in her project is to test the accessibility status of her converted Microsoft Word file, and then add tags to the document.

Testing and Tagging a File

Tags are a primary component of accessible documents. A tagged document contains a collection of tags, similar to those used in a Web page's HTML code, defining relationships among elements in the document, such as tables, lists, images, headings, and text. Like HTML tags in a Web page, you can't see document tags—they are part of the document's information.

Diane's first task is to test the accessibility status and tags of the health_tips.pdf file. She didn't create the PDF file, so she's not sure of whether the document is tagged or not.

Download **health_tips.pdf** to see the original PDF file Diane will work with. You can download the file **health_tips1.pdf** to work with the tagged version of the document.

Performing a Quick Check

There is a quick method for checking accessibility called, simply enough, Quick Check.

Follow these steps to evaluate a file's accessibility status:

1. Choose Advanced > Accessibility > Quick Check.

2. Acrobat displays the results of the check in a dialog. The Quick Check results indicate that Diane's document isn't structured, meaning it has no tags that define its contents.

3. Click OK to close the dialog.

Diane sees that the document isn't tagged, which is fine because she can add them. It's simple to add tags in Acrobat. Really.

Adding Tags in Acrobat

Tagging can be done in a source document if you are using a program that has a PDFMaker, or within Acrobat. Acrobat infers the structure of the document from its content and creates a suite of tags.

Follow these steps to add the tags:

1. To check for tags, choose View > Navigation Tabs > Tags to open the Tags pane. Sure enough—the Tags pane shows the file has "No Tags available" (**Figure 8.2**).

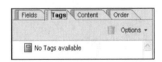

Figure 8.2 *Opening the Tags pane shows that the document isn't tagged.*

2. Click the Options button on the Tags pane to open its menu, and choose Add Tags to Document. Acrobat processes the file.

3. In the Tags pane, a new label replaces the No Tags available label seen earlier. Now the pane shows a Tags label, with a (+) to the left of the label (**Figure 8.3**).

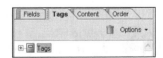

Figure 8.3 *After adding tags, the label in the Tags pane changes.*

4. Save the document with its set of tags. The project's file is saved as health_tips1.pdf.

Now that the document is tagged, Diane can check through the list of tags to be sure her document's tags match the content.

Working with Tags

The list of tags is collapsed within what is known as the *root tag*, named Tags. Click the (+) to the left of the label to open the hierarchy. The tags in the document are arranged below the root tag. Each tag also has a (+) to the left of its name; click to display the document content that is defined by the tag (**Figure 8.4**).

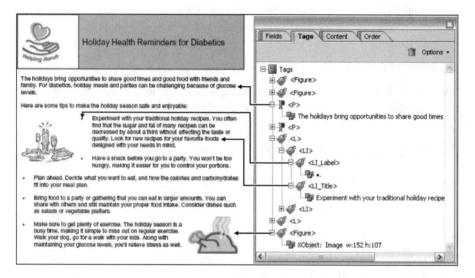

Figure 8.4 *The document's tags are listed in the Tags pane, and each tag shows the content it describes.*

If you look at the tags in the Tags pane, you'll see various icons to the left of the tags' names. The icons indicate the type of tag, which can range from paragraphs ⚑ to tables ⊞; many tags display the default Tag icon ⬧.

When you add tags to a document, Acrobat displays an Add Tags Report in the How To window to the right of the Document pane of the program window (**Figure 8.5**). The Add Tags Report for the health_tips.pdf file shows that there are three figures in the document that don't have alternate text, a requirement for an accessible document. You'll come back to alternate text later in the chapter in the "Adding Alternate Text" section. For now, click Hide to close the Add Tags Report.

The next step is for Diane to add another page to the existing file. She's going to append one of her Web site's pages to test that as well.

Appending a Web Page to a PDF File

Diane can append a Web page to an existing document using an advanced feature in Acrobat. She'll also review the tags and delete those she doesn't want.

NOTE Chapter 2 discusses converting a Web page to PDF using the Create PDF task button function.

Download **hh_home.htm** and **helping_hands.jpg** to use for the Web page conversion steps in this section.

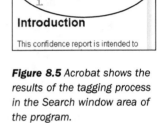

Figure 8.5 Acrobat shows the results of the tagging process in the Search window area of the program.

Adding the Page

Since Diane already has the PDF version of the first file open in Acrobat, she'll just convert and add the Web page from Acrobat.

Follow these steps to perform the conversion and add a page in Acrobat:

1. Choose Advanced > Web Capture > Append Web Page to open the Add to PDF from Web Page dialog.

2. Click Browse to open a dialog. Find and select the file for conversion; in the project, the file is named hh_home.htm. The filename is listed in the URL field on the dialog (**Figure 8.6**).

3. Click Settings to open the Web Page Conversion Settings dialog.

Figure 8.6 The Web page chosen for conversion is shown on the dialog.

4. Click the Create PDF tags check box (**Figure 8.7**). This way Diane won't have to add the tags again manually, as she did for the first document.

    The other settings are selected by default; these include adding bookmarks, creating headers and footers on each page using information from the Web page, and saving a refresh command.

5. Click OK to close the dialog and return to the Add to PDF from Web Page dialog.

6. Click Create. The dialog closes, and Acrobat processes the Web page.

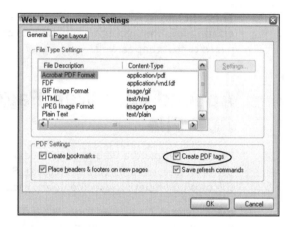

Figure 8.7 *You can specify that tags are added to the Web page when it is converted to PDF.*

7. The PDF version of the Web page opens in Acrobat, appended to the health_tips1.pdf file.

8. Save the file. The project uses the name hh1.pdf for the document composed of both the Web page and the original PDF file.

Reviewing the New Tags

If Diane checks in the Tags pane again, she'll see that there are additional tags that Acrobat added when the Web page was converted to PDF (**Figure 8.8**).

To check what a specific tag refers to, follow these steps in the Tags pane:

1. Click the tag you want to identify in the document.

2. Click the Options button on the Tags pane to open its menu, and choose Highlight Content.

3. The tag's content is shown on the document, highlighted by gray bounding boxes. In Figure 8.8, the <P> tag identifying the first paragraph in the Web page is selected, and in the document you can see the paragraph (below the logo table) is framed by a bounding box.

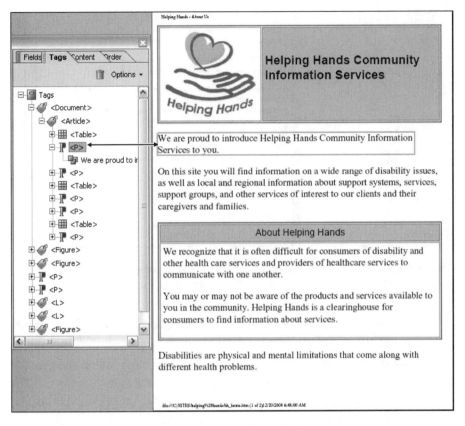

Figure 8.8 *The converted Web page's tags are added to the Tags pane.*

Deleting Extra Tags

Diane notices that at the very end of the converted Web page, there is an extra tag (**Figure 8.9**). The tag was converted from the Web page, which had an extra carriage return at the end of the document. Acrobat recognizes the carriage return as a new paragraph, even though it has no content.

As you'll see later in the chapter in the section "Reading Order," Acrobat will attempt to read the paragraph, even though it doesn't contain any content. Talk about a stubborn program!

You can remove unnecessary tags from the document by following these steps:

1. Click the tag you'd like to delete in the Tags pane.

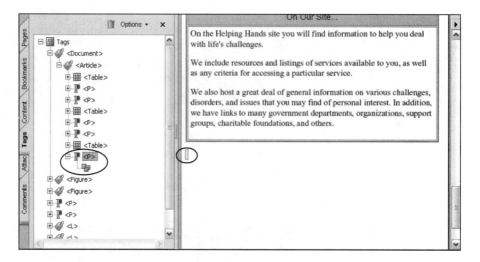

Figure 8.9 *Blank lines in the source document are defined as paragraph tags, even if they have no content.*

If you select the tag, it is deleted; if you select its content, only the content of the tag is removed and the tag itself remains.

2. Choose Options > Highlight Content from the Tags pane menu. The content on the document is shown with a gray bounding box.

In the project, you see a bounding box on the line following the last table on the converted Web page (shown in Figure 9.9).

3. Press Delete/Backspace on the keyboard, or choose Options > Delete Tag from the Tags pane to remove the tag from the document.

4. Save the file.

NOTE If you remove a tag and then change your mind, you can't undo the command. Choose File > Revert to return to the previously saved version of the document—a good reason to save your file before starting a new process!

Now that Diane has the two files combined and the tags are checked, she'll check the accessibility status of the file.

Running an Accessibility Status Check

Acrobat offers two ways to test a document's accessibility status. Diane used the Quick Check method when she started with the first document, which checks the document for tags. Now she'll use the Full Check process, which allows her to choose a range of testing options to evaluate the combined file and create a report.

If you created and tagged your own files, continue with your document in this section. If you prefer, download **hh1.pdf** to start from this point. The file after checking and repairing is named **hh2.pdf**; this version of the file and its report file, named **hh2.html**, are also available for download.

Running a Full Check

Follow these steps to evaluate the document's accessibility status:

1. Choose Advanced > Accessibility > Full Check.

   If the document isn't tagged, a message displays telling you to tag the document first and then run the Full Check. Since Diane's document is already tagged, the Accessibility Full Check dialog opens. The options used in the project are shown in **Figure 8.10**.

2. Select Report and Comment Options. By default, the Create Accessibility Report check box is selected.

3. Click Browse to define a storage location for the report.

   Depending on your workflow, the simplest location to store the report files is with your source documents. If you are doing other activities with the files, such as running batch sequences, or working with a large number of files, create a separate folder for the reports.

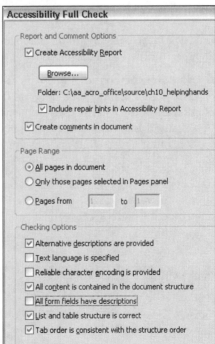

Figure 8.10 *Choose options for evaluating the document's accessibility status.*

4. The "Include repair hints in Accessibility Report" option is checked by default. Unless you are familiar with modifying page structures, leave this option selected to help you make repairs.

5. To show the results in the document itself as well as the report, click "Create comments in document."

6. Choose a Page Range. You can select the visible page, a specified range, or the entire document. Diane wants to check all pages.

7. Select checking options. All the options on the dialog are selected by default.

    Deselect options depending on the content of your document. For instance, you don't need to include checking that all form fields have descriptions if your document has no form fields. You can check for options such as alternative descriptions, text language, encoding, form field descriptions, list and table structures, and content inclusion.

8. Click Start Checking to dismiss the dialog and run the evaluation.

9. An Adobe Acrobat dialog opens and lists the problems in the document that prevent it from being fully accessible (**Figure 8.11**). Diane's document contains four figures that are missing alternate text.

10. Click OK to dismiss the information dialog; the results are shown in the How To window (**Figure 8.12**).

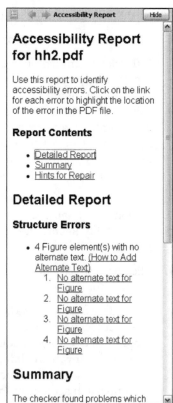

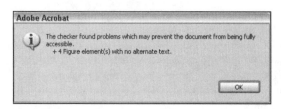

Figure 8.11 You see the results of the evaluation listed briefly in a dialog.

Figure 8.12 The full report is displayed in the How To window.

There aren't too many errors in Diane's document—just a few related to the images in the file.

Interpreting the Results

Acrobat creates an Accessibility Report as an HTML file, which is stored on your computer in the folder you select in the Accessibility Full Check dialog. When you first run the evaluation, the report is shown in Acrobat.

If you close the report by clicking the Hide button (close the window button on a Mac) on the Accessibility Report window, you can easily reopen it at any time. Choose Advanced > Accessibility > Open Accessibility Report. Locate and select the file in the dialog that opens. The report again displays in the How To window, or if you prefer, you can open the report in a Web browser.

Since the report is an HTML file, it contains hyperlinks that you can click for more information. The Report Contents section of the file, shown in **Figure 8.13**, has a list of three links you can follow for more information:

Accessibility Report for hh1.pdf

Use this report to identify accessibility errors. Click on the link for each error to highlight the location of the error in the PDF file.

Report Contents

- Detailed Report
- Summary
- Hints for Repair

- **Detailed Report**—lists the specific errors

- **Summary**—provides a recap of the information that the Accessibility Full Check displays in the Adobe Acrobat dialog prior to displaying the full report (shown in Figure 8.10)

Figure 8.13 *Links in the report let you move from section to section.*

- **Hints for Repair**—describes the methods you can use to make repairs to the document

To see a specific error to be repaired on the document, click one of the links in the Accessibility Report. The error is highlighted in the document (**Figure 8.14**).

Speaking of repairs, Diane's next step is to add the alternate text to the file.

Adding Alternate Text

Viewers using devices such as screen readers have the contents of the document read aloud. If there are non text elements in the document such as images, the screen reader can't interpret the objects, and the user misses out on some of your information. One of the most common errors in creating accessible content is omitting a text description of objects such as images. Fortunately, it's also one of the easiest errors to correct. You can attach alternate text to these

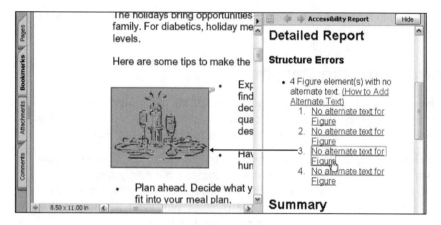

Figure 8.14 *Acrobat highlights a selected error on the page.*

objects to make them readable. The good thing is that although a picture tells a thousand words, you don't need nearly that many to use as alternate text! Alternate text for Diane's figures should describe the contents of the image, such as "Copy of the Helping Hands logo used next to the page title."

In the settings Diane chose for the Accessibility Full Check, she specified that Acrobat include comments in the document identifying the errors. Move the pointer over the comment icon next to one of the images to display the comment (**Figure 8.15**). The comment's text explains how the alternate text is used by people working with assistive devices.

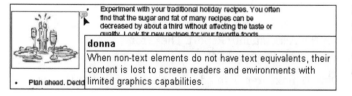

Figure 8.15 *If you choose the option before running the Full Check, the errors are shown in comments on the document page.*

NOTE   To read more about using comments, see Chapters 11, 13, and 14.

Correcting Document Problems

There are several ways you can work in Acrobat to correct alternate text errors. In the Tags pane, you can open the tags to find the specific listing for the image, and then choose Properties from the Options menu on the Tags pane. You can also add alternate text through the TouchUp Reading Order dialog, described in the sidebar "Making More Reading Order Changes" later in the chapter.

Alternatively (and to save a bit of time), rather than scrolling through a long list of tags, use the TouchUp Object tool to select the object instead.

Follow these steps to select and correct an image's content:

1. Choose Tools > Advanced Editing > TouchUp Object tool 🔲▾.

2. Right-click/Control-click the first image in the document with the tool to select the image and open the shortcut menu.

If you have a lot of repairs to make in a file, instead of scrolling through the document looking for them, select the link in the Accessibility Report to highlight the content in the document. In Diane's document, it's simple to find the error locations.

3. Choose Properties from the shortcut menu to open the TouchUp Properties dialog.

4. Select the Tags tab and type the descriptive text in the Alternate Text field (**Figure 8.16**).

Figure 8.16 Add the alternate text in this dialog.

5. Click OK to dismiss the dialog.

6. Repeat the steps with the remaining images in the document—there are four images in all.

7. Save the file; the project's file is saved as hh2.pdf.

Diane is pleased with her progress so far. She realizes she can make many of her current files accessible without much difficulty.

Removing Comments from the File

Before she continues, though, she has to remove the comments from the document because they no longer apply and certainly aren't needed in the finished product.

Follow these steps to remove the comments:

1. Select the Comments tab in the Navigation pane at the left of the program window to open the Comments pane (**Figure 8.17**).

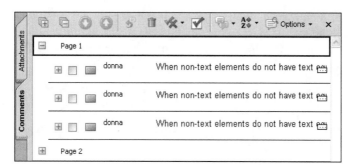

Figure 8.17 *Select the comments for deletion in the Comments pane.*

2. Click the Page 1 listing in the Comments pane.

    Don't click an individual comment as that selects just the single comment; selecting the page lets you delete all the comments from the page with one mouse click.

3. Click Delete 🗑 on the Comments toolbar to remove all the comments from Page 1.

4. Click the Page 2 listing in the Comments pane, and click Delete again on the Comments toolbar.

5. Click the Comments tab again to close the pane.

Diane decides not to include the comments option in the Accessibility Full Check dialog (shown in Figure 8.10) going forward with her project. She finds it simple enough to use the links from the Accessibility Report to highlight content that needs correction, and she'll save time if she doesn't have to remove comments.

NOTE Instead of removing the comments manually, you can remove them through the PDF Optimizer, which you can read about in Bonus Chapter 4 on the book's Web site.

Way back in the beginning stages of the project, Diane ran an Accessibility Quick Check on a file. The results are shown in the dialog in Figure 8.3 and explain that the document's *reading order*, the sequence in which the document is processed by screen readers or Acrobat's Read Out Loud feature, may not be correct because the document wasn't tagged at that point. Well, now that the file is tagged and accessibility errors are corrected, Diane will check the reading order as the final step in making sure the file is usable for her clients.

Reading Order

Acrobat 7 Professional contains a set of TouchUp tools; Diane will use the TouchUp Reading Order tool to check how the file is read. Acrobat interprets the layout of a page and decides which part of the document is read first, which is read second, and so on.

Often the reading order is fine, following the correct path through the page's content. Other times, some elements may be out of place, which can make it confusing for someone who is listening to the content on your page rather than reading it. The goal is to make the reading order as straightforward as possible. Once she's looked through the entire document, Diane will make any necessary changes to the reading order.

NOTE One way to test the importance of a proper reading order is to use Acrobat's Read Out Loud feature for yourself, described in the upcoming "Read Aloud to Me" section. If you test a page that has elements out of place, you'll soon realize how difficult it is to keep track of what you are listening to.

Checking the Reading Order

Acrobat determines the reading order on a page-by-page basis, showing you discrete blocks of content and listing the order numerically. Diane will check the reading order of her document first, before she reorders anything.

DIGGING FOR ARTIFACTS

No, you haven't opened an Indiana Jones novel by mistake—or a paper on an archaeological dig! Acrobat defines all the content in a document, whether or not it actually belongs. An item that it can't classify as a container, text, path (such as a table borders), or image is known as an artifact, which is a type of object that isn't read by a screen reader or by the Read Out Loud feature (more on this feature in the "Read Aloud to Me" section).

You can seek and destroy (or modify!) artifacts through the Content pane. There are several examples of artifacts in the sample project because Acrobat added headers and footers to the Web pages during their conversion. The Content pane shows the objects that make up the PDF document arranged in a hierarchy. It also includes at least one page, a set of annotations (or descriptions of content like comments or links) and the content objects for all the pages, listed in the order they appear on the page. You don't need a tagged document to see its content.

Follow these steps to identify artifacts in the sample project:

1. Choose View > Navigation Tabs > Content to display the Content tab, and click the (+) to the left of the hh2.pdf label to open the Content hierarchy.

2. Click the Page 2 label to open its list, and you'll see that the second item on the list after Annotations is named Container <Artifact> Helping Hands–About Us (**Figure 9.18**).

3. Click to open the Container's listing; you see the content is identified as Text ⓣ, and you can read the actual words held in the container—in this case the title of the Web page used in the project.

4. Right-click/Control-click the container to open the shortcut menu, and choose Highlight Content.

5. On the Document pane, the selected container's content is shown with a gray bounding box (**Figure 9.19**).

The second type of artifact in the sample project is the footer applied when the Web pages were converted (**Figure 9.20**).

To delete an artifact, choose Delete from the shortcut menu or the Options menu on the Content pane. Whether you leave the header and footer artifacts or delete them won't make a difference, as they aren't read by a screen reader. In the sample project, the artifacts are left in place.

To change the designation of the container, choose Properties in the shortcut menu (or from the Content pane's Options menu) to open the properties Content tab on the TouchUp Object dialog (**Figure 9.21**). Click the Container Tag pull-down arrow and choose an alternate container name.

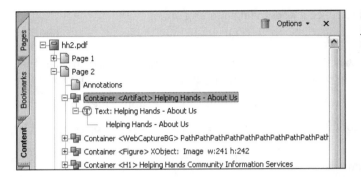

Figure 8.18 The elements of your document are shown in the Content pane.

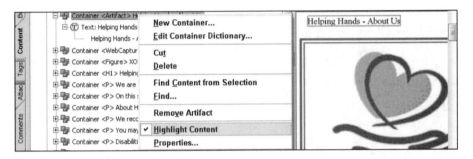

Figure 8.19 You can identify a selected container in the Document pane.

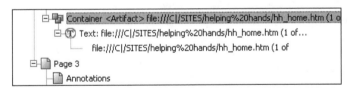

Figure 8.20 Footers added to the converted Web pages are also defined as *<Artifact>* containers.

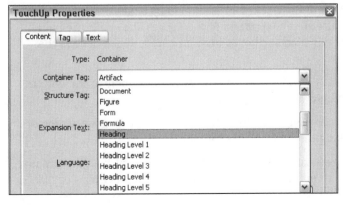

Figure 8.21 Choose an alternate container tag from the pull-down list.

Follow these steps to check a document's reading order:

1. Do one of the following:

    ■   Choose Advanced > Accessibility > TouchUp Reading Order to open the Reading Order dialog and activate the TouchUp Reading Order tool.

    ■   Choose Tools > Advanced Editing > TouchUp Reading Order Tool.

    ■   Select the tool from the Advanced Editing toolbar if it is open.

2. The default selections in the TouchUp Reading Order dialog and their effect on the document's appearance are shown in **Figure 8.22**.

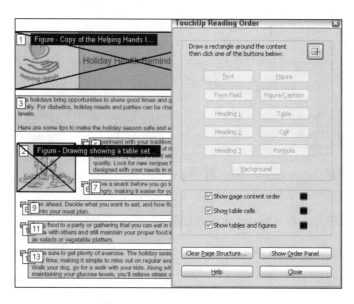

Figure 8.22 You can review the order in which content is read in a file.

You see the content of the document is framed by boxes of varying sizes. You also see the alternate text added to the figures shown on the page. Look at the order in which the boxes are numbered, which defines the reading sequence.

3. Drag the document's scrollbars or use the navigation tools at the bottom of the program window to display additional images.

4. Use the scrollbars or navigation tools to move through the pages of your document, checking the order of the content.

Overall, Diane is pleased with the reading order in the file, although there is one change she'd like to make on the first page of the document.

Modifying Reading Order

As seen in Figure 8.22, the reading order specifies that the table at the top of the page, containing the Helping Hands logo as well as the title of the information sheet, is read first. The second item read is the image of the dining table, followed by the introduction. Diane would like to reverse the order of the image and introductory text. Otherwise, when the page is read aloud, there's a description of the dining table before the user even knows what the page is talking about. That could be confusing!

Follow these steps to change the reading order:

1. Click the Show Order Panel button on the TouchUp Reading Order dialog to open the Order pane. You can also choose View > Navigation Tabs > Order to open the pane.

2. Drag the pane to dock it at the left of the program window with the other Navigation tabs if you like.

3. Click the hh2.pdf label in the Order pane to open its content, and then click the Page 1 label to open its list of items.

4. Look through the Page 1 listing in the Order pane and compare it to the document's reading order boxes shown in the document pane. You see the numbers correspond to the numbered boxes on the document page.

5. Click the object named [2] Image w:146 h:116 to select it. You see the corresponding figure's number box on the document page is also selected (**Figure 8.23**).

6. Drag the object downward below the introduction text object currently defined as number 3 in the Order pane. As you drag, you see a horizontal bar on the Order pane, which indicates where the object is moved when you release the mouse (**Figure 8.24**).

7. Release the mouse when the image object is positioned below the introductory text object.

8. Check the order again—now you see the figure is renumbered [3], both in the Order pane and on the page (**Figure 8.25**).

9. Close the TouchUp Reading Order dialog.

10. Save the file to preserve the changes. Diane's file is saved as hh3.pdf.

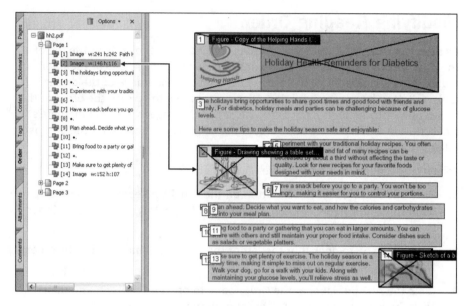

Figure 8.23 *The Order pane lists the document content by page; each page lists the objects in numerical order.*

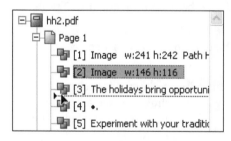

Figure 8.24 *You see where the object is moved as you drag it in the Order pane.*

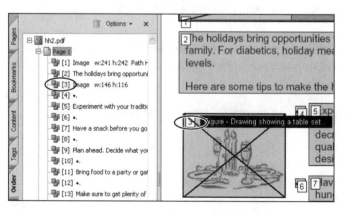

Figure 8.25 *Moving an object changes the reading order in both the Order and Document panes.*

So far so good! Diane thinks the process is pretty simple. Don't you agree? Come on now—you've had a glimpse into the world hidden inside an Acrobat PDF file, which not a lot of people can claim. Not only that, but if you've clicked through the menus in Acrobat 7 Professional and seen the many Navigation tabs listed, you must have wondered what they were used for—and now you know!

MAKING MORE READING ORDER CHANGES

Diane's file is quite straightforward in that there aren't columns, pull quotes, and so on that can make for a complex layout. Here's an example using the information sheet from the project after some of the reading order components were mercilessly stripped from the page.

If there is content that isn't included in the reading order, use the TouchUp Reading Order tool to modify the order manually by following these steps:

1. With the TouchUp Reading Order tool, draw a marquee around an area to be defined on the document. When you release the mouse, the content type buttons on the dialog become active.

2. Click a content type button to define the selected area; in the example, the Figure button is clicked (**Figure 8.26**).

3. The new component is added to the Order pane and numbered on the Document pane (**Figure 8.27**).

4. Continue with other changes as needed.

5. Close the TouchUp Reading Order dialog.

You can add alternate text to content while working with the TouchUp Reading Order tool, in addition to adding the alternate text in the TouchUp Object Properties dialog, described earlier in the chapter. With the TouchUp Reading Order tool, right-click/Control-click a figure on the page to display its shortcut menu, and choose Edit Alternate Text. Type the text in the Edit Alternate Text dialog and click OK (**Figure 8.28**). The dialog closes and the text is added to the file.

In some complex documents, it's simpler to remove the existing order altogether and start over. Save the document before you start in case you change your mind later. That way, you can simply choose File > Revert to return to the status of the document before your mad experiment.

Take a deep breath, and then click the Clear Page Structure button on the TouchUp Reading Order dialog. A confirmation dialog opens asking if you really want to do this. Click Yes to remove the reading order definitions, or select Cancel to cancel the command.

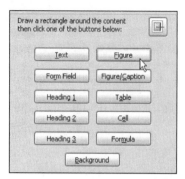

Figure 8.26 Click a button on the dialog to define the selected content.

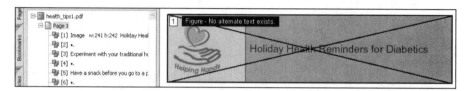

Figure 8.27 The new object is added to the page's Order list.

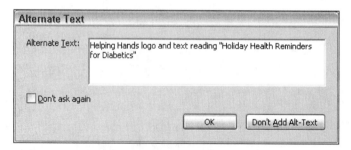

Figure 8.28 You can add alternate text to an image through the TouchUp Reading Order dialog.

In theory, the reading order of the file is perfect. Diane thinks it would be nice if she could test it in real life, but she doesn't have access to screen reader software. Acrobat to the rescue! She can test how the pages are read using the Read Out Loud feature.

Read Aloud to Me

Acrobat's Read Out Loud feature simulates some of the features of a full-blown screen reader program. Diane can test how her file is read right from Acrobat. Before testing the file, however, she'll set some preferences.

Download **hh3.pdf**, which is the file complete to this point, if you haven't been following along with the project; otherwise continue with your present file.

Reading Preferences

Diane needs to change her preferences before testing her file.

Follow these steps to check and change the Reading preferences:

1. Choose Edit > Preferences (Acrobat > Preferences on a Mac) to open the Preferences dialog.

2. Click the Reading category in the column at the left of the dialog to display the Reading preferences.

3. In the Read Out Loud Options section, choose a voice, pitch, and volume (**Figure 8.29**). In Windows, you can choose from several voices. Mac users can choose among numerous voices, including some that aren't even human—just the thing for listening to your favorite alien invasion tale!

4. Click the Read form fields check box to have text fields, check boxes, and radio buttons in fillable forms read aloud. Diane has no fields in her documents, so it doesn't matter whether this preference is selected or not.

5. Click OK to close the Preferences dialog and apply the settings.

SCREEN READER PREFERENCES

The Reading preferences include several options for screen readers. You can define whether you want the screen reader to read only the currently visible pages, the entire document, or the currently visible pages in a large document from the Page vs Document pull-down list. The default size for defining a document as large is 50 pages. Click the field and type a different number to change the definition of a large document.

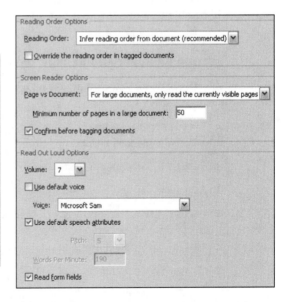

Figure 8.29 *Select characteristics for the Read Out Loud voice.*

NOTE If you need to make adjustments, you have to reopen the Preferences dialog because you can't modify settings in real time as you are listening.

Now that she's chosen a voice and its characteristics, Diane is ready to test the file.

Reading the File

Diane has modified and adjusted the tag structure and the reading order in her document, and now she'll test the page.

Start the reading process by following these steps:

1. Choose View > Read Out Loud, and select either Read This Page Only or Read To End of Document.

2. The reading starts. The process can be paused and resumed by choosing View > Read Out Loud > Pause / View > Read Out Loud > Resume.

   Diane can also control reading using shortcut keys—Ctrl-Shift-C to pause/resume.

3. When she has read enough, she can choose View > Read Out Loud > Stop, or use the Ctrl-Shift-E shortcut keys.

Success! The file reads as she intended, and her clients using screen readers will be able to move through her organization's material without difficulty.

SETTING UP KEYBOARD ACCESS ON A MAC

You can set up full keyboard access on a Mac using system-level preferences by following these steps:

1. Choose Apple > System Preferences > Keyboard & Mouse to open the Keyboard & Mouse Preferences dialog.

2. Select the Keyboard Shortcuts tab.

3. Select the Turn On Full Keyboard Access option at the bottom of the dialog.

4. Choose View > Universal Access; select either Enable Access For Assistive Devices to use installed screen reader devices or select Enable Text-To-Speech to use the Mac OS speech technology.

5. Choose System Preferences > Quit System Preferences.

When you open Acrobat in a Web browser, keyboard commands are mapped first to the Web browser. Some keyboard shortcuts may not be available for Acrobat, or may not be available until you shift the focus to the PDF document.

But what about people who use magnified screens to view content? Will they be able to see the content clearly and logically?

In the next section, Diane takes a look at a page from one of Helping Hands' newsletters, which are produced once a month. Diane would also like them accessible to her users, preferably without having to recreate them in a simple unstructured format. She can achieve this goal by using another Acrobat feature, called Articles.

Controlling a Document with Articles

Now Diane's attention shifts to another group of Helping Hand clients—those that work with magnified screens. Often people with impaired vision are able to read content on a screen by greatly magnifying the view.

NOTE Both Acrobat and Adobe Reader can display content at a high magnification that can still be read clearly using a process called reflow, which wraps text to the next line regardless of the page's magnification. You can read more about reflow in Chapter 5.

The problem with working at a high magnification is that it's difficult to define what you are looking at in the context of the entire document. **Figure 8.30** shows a part of Diane's newsletter PDF file at a high magnification. Although it's easy to read the letters, it isn't easy to determine what part of the page you are looking at.

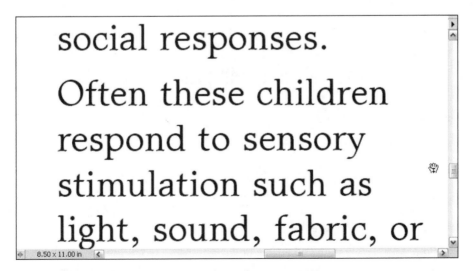

Figure 8.30 *Can you tell where you are on a page, or even what page you are viewing?*

Acrobat offers something called the Article tool, one of the Advanced Editing tools that you can use to define a reading path through a document. Articles are used to order how the text and graphics of a document are presented by a screen reader. Defining a reading path is especially useful if your file contains multiple columns, such as Diane's newsletter, or if content is carried over from one page to another, as often seen in magazines.

Download **hh_news.pdf** to see the original newsletter layout before articles are added to the page so that you can experiment with adding them yourself; if you'd like to see the newsletter PDF containing the articles, download **hh_news1.pdf**.

Adding the First Article Thread

Diane uses the Article tool to define article boxes on the page; a sequence of boxes are combined into an article thread.

Add the first article to the newsletter file by following these steps:

1. Choose Tools > Advanced Editing > Article Tool or click the Article tool ⬚ on the Advanced Editing toolbar if you have it open in Acrobat.

2. Click and drag a rectangular marquee; in the sample project the marquee is drawn around the newsletter's name. Release the mouse, and Acrobat draws the first article box, numbered 1-1 (**Figure 8.31**). The pointer changes to the Article pointer, also shown in Figure 8.31.

Figure 8.31 The Article tool automatically numbers the first box you draw.

3. Click and drag to add the second and subsequent boxes. In the sample project, there are five boxes for the content in the heading section of the newsletter. The sequence of boxes using the same article number is called an *article thread* (**Figure 8.32**).

    You don't have to add the article boxes according to the layout of the page—in the figure, you can see that only part of the background behind the text "Helping Hands" has been included in an article box. Acrobat numbers the articles consecutively.

Figure 8.32 Each time you use the tool, an additional box is added to the article thread.

NOTE You can add article boxes to a single article thread regardless of which page you are applying them to. Use the scrollbars or navigation tools to move the document to the correct page view, and drag a marquee for the new article box.

4. Press Enter/Return to stop the article drawing. The Article Properties dialog opens.

5. Type a name for the article in the Title field; the default name is "Untitled." The other information is optional (**Figure 8.33**).

6. Click OK to close the dialog.

Some documents have only one article; you can add as many as you need. In general terms, it makes sense to divide a file into a number of articles and name them logically to make them simpler for users to work with.

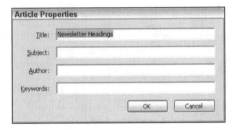

Figure 8.33 Type a descriptive name for the article thread in the dialog.

Finishing the Project's Articles

The newsletter file contains six articles. Diane will need to add the second and subsequent articles.

Follow these steps to add the remaining articles:

1. Click and drag with the Article tool to start the next article. Continue adding article boxes and article threads until all the content has been included in article boxes (**Figure 8.34**).

2. Select another tool to deselect the Article tool.

3. Save the document to preserve the articles; Diane's file is saved as hh_news1.pdf.

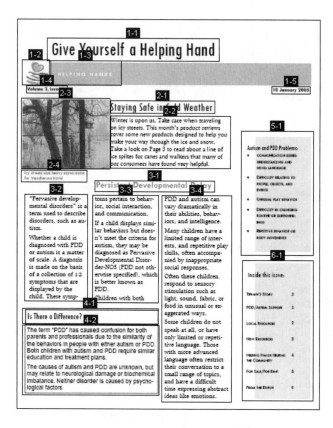

Figure 8.34 *You may have one or many articles in a file.*

Using articles lets your reader move through the document regardless of the magnification of the view, as you'll see in the next section.

Modifying Articles

Diane didn't make any errors in her article construction. Your results may vary. You can use any of the following methods to modify or adjust the articles as you are constructing them in your project:

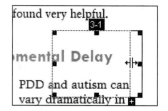

Figure 8.35 *Resize or move any article box on your document page.*

- Select an article box and drag the handles on its margins to resize it. You'll see the original size of the article box as well as the size it becomes when you release the mouse (**Figure 8.35**). You can also select an article box and drag it to another location on the page. An article box floats over the page and displays whatever page content shows within the box's margins.

- Right-click/Control-click the article to open the shortcut menu, and then choose either Box or Article to delete a single box or an entire article thread. If you delete a box, the remaining boxes in the article thread are renumbered; if you delete an article, the remaining articles are renumbered.

- To add a box to an article, click the article box displayed just before the point where you want to add one (for example, if you wanted to add a new box to a thread after the box numbered 4-1, you would just click box 4-1, as shown in **Figure 8.36**). Then, click the plus sign at the bottom of the selected box. A prompt dialog opens. Click OK and drag a marquee to create a new article box. The article thread is automatically renumbered (**Figure 8.37**).

Selected article box

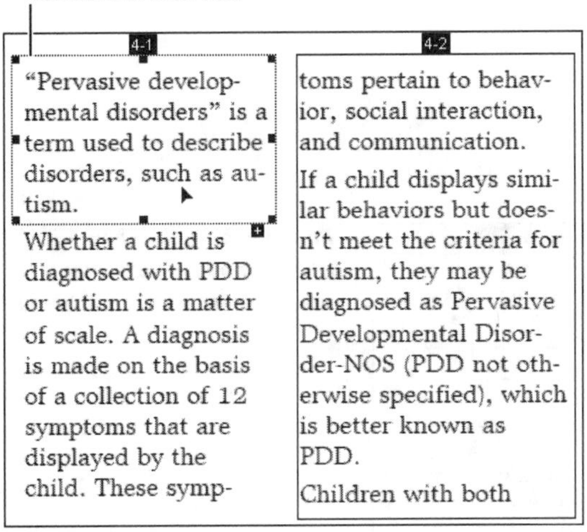

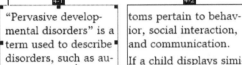

Figure 8.36 Select the article box you want to follow with a new article box.

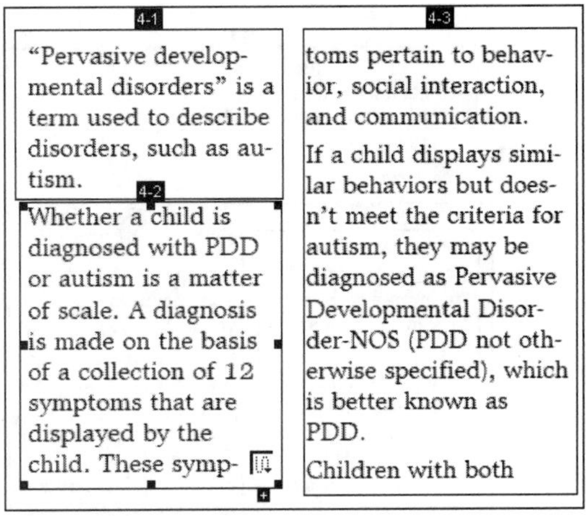

Figure 8.37 Adding article boxes to a thread renumbers the set of boxes automatically.

- To append an article thread to another article thread, click any article box in the article thread you want read first (**Figure 8.38**). Next, click the plus sign at the bottom of the article box. Ctrl-click/Option-click an article box from the article you want to be read next; you'll see the append article cursor appear. Release the mouse, and the two articles are combined into a single thread (**Figure 8.39**). The appended article boxes are numbered in sequence following those in the original article box.

Selected article box

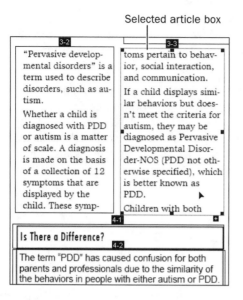

Figure 8.38 *Click any box in an article thread to tell Acrobat which article will have another article thread's boxes appended to it.*

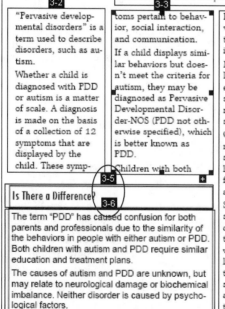

Figure 8.39 *Article boxes in an appended article thread are automatically renumbered.*

Reading Articles

Once the articles are added to the document, it's time for Diane to test them. You can read articles in both Acrobat and Adobe Reader using the Hand tool, keystroke combinations, or by working through the Articles pane.

Navigating Through a File Manually

Click the Hand tool or use keystrokes to read the article. The page zooms in and out automatically depending on the size of the article box being viewed. Click anywhere on the page—the pointer changes to the Follow Article pointer 🖑.

You can scroll through the page using the mouse wheel or dragging the Hand tool down the page.

To navigate through the article manually

- Press Enter/Return to go to the next page in the article.

- Shift-click/Shift-Return in the article to return to the previous page.

- Ctrl-click/Option-click in the article to go to the beginning.

The pointer changes to the End Article pointer 🖑 when you reach the end of the article. Click to return to the view displayed before you started reading the article thread.

Navigating Using the Articles Pane

If you prefer, you can also choose articles to read through the Articles pane (does it surprise you that Articles have their own pane? If you've read this far through the project, probably not!).

Follow these steps:

1. Choose View > Navigation Tabs > Articles to open the Articles pane.

2. Drag the tab to dock it with the other Navigation tabs at the left of the program window.

3. Double-click the article you want to read in the Articles pane's list. You see the icon before the article's title change to an arrow (**Figure 8.40**).

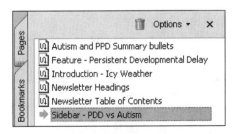

Figure 8.40 The article displayed in the Document pane shows an arrow in the Articles pane.

4. Read through the article in the Document pane; scroll using the Hand tool.

5. Double-click another article title to display another article in the Document pane.

Another success! Diane is nearly finished with her project. She wants to check one more simulation—for high-contrast color schemes—that she can set up in Acrobat.

Simulating High-Contrast Viewers

Diane would like to see how the file would look for users working with modified displays. You always see files in the colors used by a program, those set in your operating system, or custom colors used by the document's author. Modified displays are those that some users set in either their operating system or particular programs that allow them to see the content more clearly, often by using high-contrast colors.

Follow these steps to modify Acrobat to use custom colors and text visibility options:

1. Choose Edit > Preferences (Acrobat > Preferences on a Mac) and click the Accessibility category in the left column to display the Accessibility preferences.

2. In the Document Colors Options section select, the Replace Document Colors check box to activate the options (**Figure 8.41**).

3. Click the Use High-Contrast colors button, and choose a high-contrast color option from the pull-down menu, such as green or yellow text on black.

4. Click OK to close the Preferences dialog.

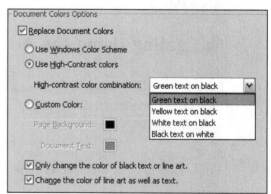

Figure 8.41 Choose alternate colors for the file display in the Preferences dialog.

Diane discovers an interesting problem, one that is commonly seen with high-contrast color schemes. In a section of the newsletter's page (shown in **Figure 8.42**), she sees that the text block at the right side of the figure is difficult to read. In the newsletter file, the text is black on a pale beige back-

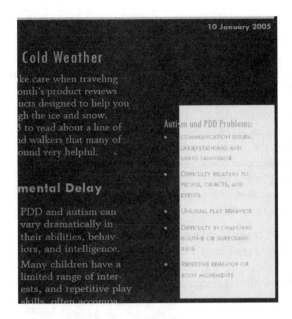

Figure 8.42 *Showing the newsletter in a high-contrast color scheme reveals a problem.*

ground, which looks quite attractive in a regular color scheme. Changing to a high-contrast scheme tells a different story. The light background and the light text used for high-contrast schemes are similar in color, which makes the text hard to read.

If Diane intends to provide accessible content, she's going to have to modify the newsletter's layout to prevent the contrast problem by removing the pale beige background from the text blocks. If she wants a way to make them stand out from the rest of the newsletter's text, she can frame them with a border that won't affect the contrast on the page.

Diane's had much success in her efforts. The last thing she wants to do

OTHER COLOR OPTIONS

Diane can choose other color options in the Preferences dialog, including Use Windows Color Scheme (in Windows), which uses a custom color scheme the user has set in the operating system. The third option is to use Custom Color. Click the option's check box, and then click the color swatches and choose custom colors. Only either custom colors or high-contrast colors can be chosen—selecting one toggles the other off.

She can also select line art and black text changes. If you don't want to change the color of text that is already colored, click "Only change the color of black text or line art;" to change the color of line art, click "Change the color of line art as well as text."

SCROLLING A DOCUMENT

Another feature Acrobat provides is automatic scrolling through a document, useful for viewers who find it physically difficult to use a mouse. Choose View > Automatic Scroll, or press Control/Command-Shift-H. The document starts scrolling from the position currently in the Document pane and stops when you reach the end.

Use the same keyboard shortcut to pause the scroll as well. Or you can click and hold the mouse button—as long as the button is depressed, the page stops. Release the button to restart the scrolling.

Press the Up or Down arrow key to increase or decrease the scroll speed, respectively. On a Mac, the functions are reversed. That is, the Up arrow decreases the scroll speed; the Down arrow increases speed. If you reduce the speed to 0, the text will start to scroll in reverse. You can also adjust speed using the number keys, with 0 the slowest and 9 supersonic speed. Put it in reverse by pressing the minus key on the keyboard or number pad; press Esc to stop the scrolling.

before finishing the project is to create a read-me file she can distribute to her users to help them work with PDF files more effectively.

Diane's Read-Me Instruction File

As a final step in preparing some sample documents to present to the Helping Hands board of directors in her quest to make accessible documents the norm for the organization, Diane decides to prepare a read-me file she can post on the organization's Web site. The file is intended to show users how they can set up Acrobat 7 and Adobe Reader 7 to more closely meet their needs using the Accessibility Setup Assistant, a wizard composed of a sequence of screens in a dialog used to configure a collection of program settings.

In earlier versions of Acrobat, many of the accessibility settings were available, but they were not easy to find because they were located in a number of different panels of the Preferences dialog. In version 7 of the programs, all these settings have come together into one wizard, which is much simpler to use.

 Download **hh_readme.pdf** if you'd like to read the original file showing the steps for using the Accessibility Setup Assistant.

Here is the content of Diane's read-me file:

Helping Hands

How to Use Acrobat 7 and Adobe Reader 7 Accessibility Features

Both Acrobat 7 and Adobe Reader 7 provide a wizard, which is a sequence of panes in a dialog used to set up the program for use with your screen reader or magnifier. The wizard has a set of five panes, called *screens*.

If you are working in Acrobat 7, choose Advanced > Accessibility > Setup Assistant; for those using Adobe Reader 7, choose Help > Accessibility Setup Assistant to open the Accessibility Setup Assistant. The wizard is the same in both Acrobat and Adobe Reader, with the exception of references to the program's name, which vary according to which program you are working in.

Follow these steps to set up the Accessibility Setup Assistant:

1. Open the wizard using the commands in either Acrobat 7 or Adobe Reader 7.

2. Choose the device you are working with on the first screen. You can select a screen reader, screen magnifier, or both.

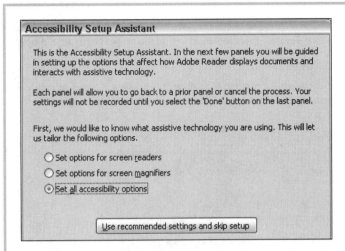

If you prefer, click "Use recommended settings and skip setup." The wizard closes and the program's preconfigured settings will be used.

3. If you want to choose settings yourself, click Next to show Screen 2.

4. On Screen 2, choose a high-contrast color scheme, a text smoothing option, and a default zoom for document viewing.

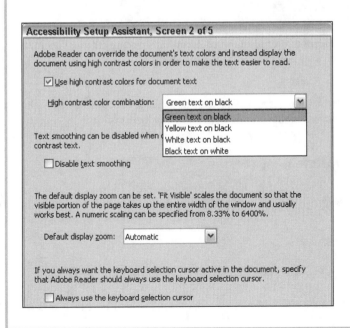

Depending on your device, you can check the "Always use the keyboard selection cursor" check box. Check your device's documentation to find the proper configuration option.

5. Click Next to show Screen 3.

6. On Screen 3, choose options for tagging. The default is to allow Acrobat or Adobe Reader to *infer*—or interpret—the reading order; you can also specify another option on the dialog.

Accessibility Setup Assistant, Screen 3 of 5

The reading order for documents that are not tagged can be set. With the recommended setting the reading order is inferred from the document and font, but you can set a specific reading order.

- ◉ Infer reading order from document (recommended)
- ○ Left-to-right, top-to-bottom reading order
- ○ Use reading order in raw print stream

For documents that have been tagged Adobe Reader can override the tagged order and use the reading order specified above. Normally this won't be needed.

- ☐ Override the reading order in tagged documents

Before adding tags to an untagged document Adobe Reader can prompt you to confirm the settings that will be used.

- ☑ Confirm before adding tags to documents

You can choose options to override a tagged document's reading order or confirm tagging before the program adds tags to an untagged document.

7. Click Next to show Screen 4.

8. On Screen 4, select an option for viewing large documents. Choose either the visible page or the entire document, or allow Acrobat or Adobe Reader to decide.

Accessibility Setup Assistant, Screen 4 of 5

Because large documents can take a long time to read, you can choose whether your assistive technology should access just the visible pages, the entire document, or whether Adobe Reader should decide which seems best for each document.

- ○ Deliver currently visible pages
- ○ Deliver the entire document at once
- ◉ Deliver all pages only for small documents

Maximum number of pages in a small document: 50

You can also define how large is large. Both Acrobat and Adobe Reader use 50 pages as the maximum size of a small document by default. To change this, click the field and type another document page size.

9. Click Next to show Screen 5.

10. On Screen 5, choose options for opening and saving documents. If you often read long documents, disable the document auto-save feature, which makes the document reload and begin reading again from the start of the document each time it is saved automatically.

Accessibility Setup Assistant, Screen 5 of 5

Auto-save might interfere with assistive technology software as it saves the document by causing the software to reload the document and restart reading from the beginning. This option lets you disable document auto-save.

☐ Disable document auto-save

When a document is reopened Adobe Reader can either open it at the first page or at the last viewed page.

☑ Reopen documents to the last viewed page

A PDF document opened from a web browser can be either opened in the browser or in Adobe Reader. Opening a document in Adobe Reader is recommended because opening in a browser can confuse assistive technology software.

☑ Display PDF documents in the web browser

If you often start and stop reading a document, click the "Reopen documents to the last viewed page" check box, which lets you pick up where you left off reading.

Choose whether to open a file in Acrobat or through a browser. You'll have to experiment with your assistive device to see if the browser creates any reading difficulties, which can occur with some devices. In that case, choose the option to open the PDF document in Acrobat or Adobe Reader.

11. Click Done to close the wizard and apply the settings.

Now that Diane has finished her experiments with accessibility features and processes in Acrobat, she's ready to face the board of directors. They'll be impressed!

What Else Can She Do?

Diane can set up a real production process for converting her files to accessible PDF documents as soon as she gets the board's go-ahead. Instead of converting each document and testing it, she can instead use a batch sequence and convert a whole folder of files at one time. You can read about batch sequences in Chapter 12.

Another consideration when preparing her files for conversion is to evaluate the layouts, as she did with the newsletter page, to see if there are any other issues when the files are viewed using high-contrast color schemes.

Converting and Updating a Simple Form

We all have experience with filling out forms—often in triplicate! Simply put, a form is a structured document used to collect information. A label describes the content you are to type in a form field, or you are offered choices from pull-down lists, radio buttons, and the like.

Acrobat 7 Professional lets you manage forms in different ways. You can start a form from scratch, adding and configuring the text and fields in Acrobat. Or you can convert an existing form to PDF and add the fields, using the original form as a background or template for the PDF-based form. Alternatively, if you are working in Windows, you can use Adobe Designer 7, a forms development and authoring tool that is included with Acrobat 7. You can learn more about using Adobe Designer in Bonus Chapter 3, "Constructing a Form Using Adobe Designer," on the book's Web site at www.donnabaker.ca/downloads.

Acrobat 7 Professional includes a set of Forms tools that you will use in this project to create an e-mail-based form for a deli. You'll start by modifying an existing form to make it usable as a PDF form. Then, you'll learn how to add some form fields and how to configure them. You'll also learn about designing and using a custom stamp, which is a type of Commenting tool, and how to quickly and simply change text on the form.

May I Take Your Order?

This is the story of Joe's Deli, a progressive little establishment that does a booming lunchtime trade. Joe Morton (famed owner of said establishment) has been looking for ways to expand his business and become more profitable. Alas, Joe can't physically expand his location because his deli is in the lower level of a heritage building in the financial district of a large city.

A few months ago Joe had the brilliant idea of offering a fax ordering option, and he printed menus for take-out and delivery orders that had been placed by phone. Now, he realizes that about one-third of his lunch business is from orders. He has hired additional kitchen staff, an order person, and delivery people to take care of the demand for his luscious pastrami—not to mention those big pickles.

Joe likes to make a few changes to keep his customers interested. Every morning, he decides which menu items are the daily special and writes them on the deli's menu board. He also scribbles the specials on a copy of his menu and then sends it to all the customers on his daily fax list. Customers who aren't on the daily fax list will often phone for the day's specials, and many drop in at the deli on their way to work to leave a lunch order.

Joe's girlfriend takes care of the menu. She created the original in Microsoft Publisher and updates it on a weekly basis. The problem is that she has to rebuild the file every week to include Joe's specials. Stacks of menus are then printed for the restaurant, and a copy of that newly created menu is faxed to customers, who fill it in and fax it back.

Joe needs an easier way to update and send his menu and let his customers know about the daily specials (**Figure 9.1**).

Steps Involved in This Project

A common requirement of working with forms is the ability to make changes. Using Acrobat, you can change content in a PDF form quite easily, which is especially useful when you want to change only one or two items or labels. Joe needs to do just that—he needs to change the specials listed on his e-mail menu on a daily basis.

For the most part, Joe can accomplish his goal using Acrobat. There are a few items to plan, but such careful consideration is going to result in a less hectic workday for his staff and better communication with his customers.

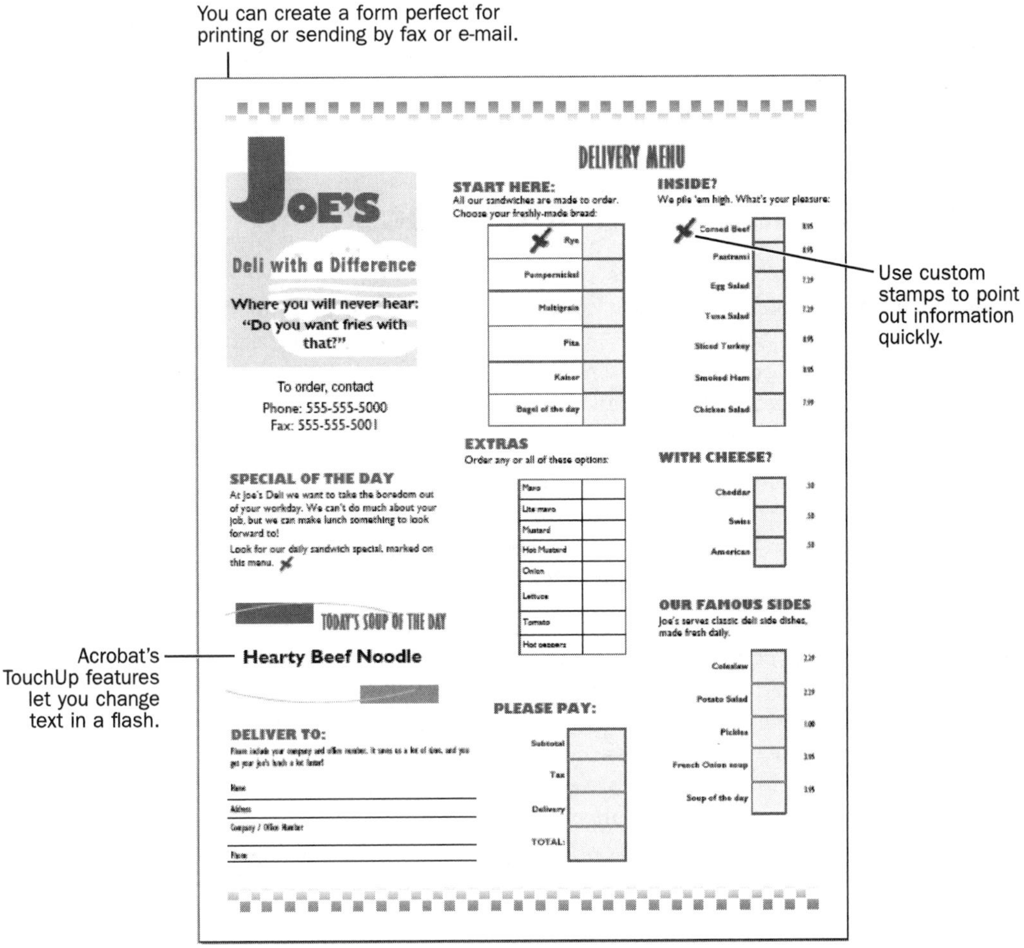

You can create a form perfect for printing or sending by fax or e-mail.

Figure 9.1 *Joe's Deli has a new, easy-to-update fax menu.*

This is what he needs:

- A source document that is designed for Acrobat use and can be updated both weekly and daily.

- A PDF document with a small file size so he can e-mail it to his customers without filling up their in-boxes.

- A PDF document that can be both read online and printed.

The first part of the project is to take a look at the source document and redesign it to use as an Acrobat-based form. Joe's girlfriend created the form in Microsoft Publisher, but the same principles apply to a form created in any program—from Word, to Photoshop, to Illustrator, to....

Redesigning the Source Document

Microsoft Publisher is a Windows program used for creating a wide variety of publications for desktop printing, commercial printing, e-mail distribution, or displaying on the Web. Acrobat 7 includes a PDFMaker for Microsoft Publisher 2003, that allows for simple conversion of a document to PDF with a single mouse click. But before we convert the menu, let's look at some ways to make it more useful in the long term.

Joe's menu is a basic two-fold takeout menu, with information about the business on the outside and the menu on the inside. It has special areas for customers to write their delivery information, including their fax numbers if they want the menu faxed to them (**Figure 9.2**).

This menu is well-designed and appropriate as a take-out menu for the restaurant. It isn't as convenient for customers who want to fax their orders because the menu is two-sided and they don't need most of the content on the reverse of the menu, such as the deli's location and marketing information, just to place a fax order. Rather than the two-sided menu Joe currently uses, it's a simple matter to duplicate portions of the existing menu and create a separate fax menu, a portion of which is shown in **Figure 9.3**.

The new menu is simpler for both Joe's staff and his customers for two main reasons:

- The menu is presented in simple framed tables; the frames make customers' choices easier to read and the preparation of orders easier for Joe's staff.

- The redesign makes it easier for the customer to calculate their costs and have the correct amount waiting at reception when the friendly delivery person arrives with their lunches.

If you have Microsoft Publisher, you can download **joe1.pub** and see the original document. You can also see the modified version of the publication before converting to PDF in **joe2.pub**. Download **joe2.pdf** to see the converted menu used in this project.

Figure 9.2 *Joe's customers write their delivery information on the menu, as well as their fax numbers if they want the menu faxed to them.*

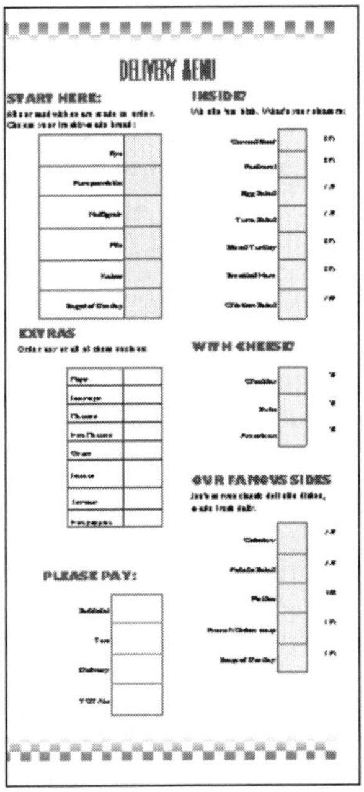

Figure 9.3 *The fax ordering menu is a simplified version of the original take-out menu.*

Converting the Source Document

Now that Joe's menu is redesigned, it's time to create the PDF version. As you've seen in earlier chapters, the PDFMaker is a set of tools that Acrobat installs into Microsoft Office programs in addition to a Main menu item called Adobe PDF (**Figure 9.4**). These tools make it easy to convert documents to PDF from within these applications, without having to open Acrobat. Acrobat 7 includes a PDFMaker for the first time for Microsoft Publisher.

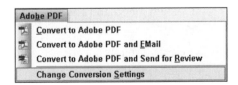

Figure 9.4 *The PDFMaker menu includes a number of commands.*

To convert a document in Microsoft Publisher, choose Adobe PDF > Change Conversion Settings to open the dialog (**Figure 9.5**). Unlike other programs, where the PDFMaker sets the Conversion Settings option to Standard settings by default, the default conversion setting in Publisher is Press Quality. Joe's menu isn't intended for high-end printing, and the resolution required for such printing results in a large file size, which Joe doesn't want (since one of Joe's primary goals is a small file size to avoid filling up his customers' e-mail in-boxes), so he needs to change to a lower-quality setting.

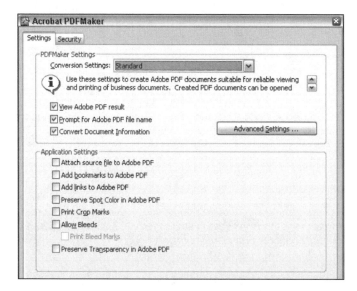

Figure 9.5 *Change the conversion settings to decrease the file size.*

On the Settings tab of the Conversion Settings dialog:

1. Click the Conversion Settings pull-down menu and choose Standard.

2. Deselect all the Application Settings options.

3. Click OK to close the dialog.

MORE ABOUT PUBLISHER'S CONVERSION SETTINGS

For a Publisher document, which can be used for high-end printing, you can select print-specific options such as bleeds, spot color, crop marks, and transparency options. PDF documents generated from Publisher files can also contain comments, tags, and bookmarks.

WHY JOE CHOOSES THE STANDARD CONVERSION SETTINGS

The PDFMaker includes another option called Smallest File Size, which is used for on-screen viewing of documents. That isn't the best choice for Joe because he uses distinctive fonts for his deli's printed material. Using the Smallest File Size option—although it may produce a slightly smaller file size—uses the fonts available from his customers' computers instead of embedding those used for the brochure design in the PDF itself. Depending on the customers' available fonts, the layout of the page may be significantly different from what he intended.

The PDFMaker also adds a toolbar to the program (**Figure 9.6**). Its buttons, from left to right, are

- **Convert to Adobe PDF** converts the active document to PDF using the preexisting conversion settings

- **Convert to Adobe PDF and EMail** converts the document and attaches the document to a blank e-mail message

- **Convert to Adobe PDF and Send for Review** converts the document to PDF and initiates an e-mail review cycle

Figure 9.6 Use the commands from the PDFMaker toolbar for easy, one-click file conversion.

Click Convert to PDF 📄 to start the process. The document is processed, using the default name and folder location for the PDF document. Click Save to save the PDF version of the menu.

Updating the Daily Specials Content

Joe's Deli offers daily specials. He decides every morning which of his sandwich creations will be on special for the day at a reduced price and marks his menu board. He also features a soup of the day. He has been in the habit of simply marking the daily sandwich special on his menu and scribbling in the soup of the day before faxing menus to customers in the morning.

Joe can keep to his routine and easily add the information to his new PDF menu. The sandwich special can be marked with a stamp, and he can use the TouchUp Text tool to add the soup-of-the-day information. Sounds pretty cool, eh? Let's see what he does.

CONVERSION OPTIONS

There are four basic types of PDF conversion that you use for most circumstances. In addition to these preconfigured options, you can create your own, either by modifying existing options or starting from scratch.

The four basic conversion settings are the following:

- Standard—the default set used for basic business document conversion and viewing. The Standard setting uses a printing resolution of 600 dpi.

- High Quality—used for high-quality output; prints to a higher image resolution but includes only a limited amount of coded information about the document's fonts. High Quality sets the printing resolution to 2400 dpi.

- Press Quality—used for high-end print production, such as image setters, and prints at a high resolution. All the information possible is added to the file. This setting includes all coded information about the fonts used in the document.

- Smallest File Size—creates the smallest file size possible; used for distributing content for the Web, e-mail, or onscreen viewing. Images are compressed and their resolution decreased. Fonts are not embedded.

"X" Marks the Specials—Stamp Tools

Joe draws a big "X" to identify the daily special on his deli's menu board. He can do the same thing by adding a stamp on his PDF menu before e-mailing it to his customers in the morning. Acrobat's Stamp tools are like old-fashioned ink stamps. Some of these stamps are dynamic—automatically adding a time or date to the stamp—but most are static.

To create a stamp, follow these steps:

1. With the PDF document open in Acrobat, choose Tools > Commenting > Show Commenting Toolbar.

   Save a few mouse clicks by opening the toolbar from the toolbar well. Right-click/Control-click the toolbar well to open the list of toolbars, and click Commenting.

2. First Joe looks at the basic stamps to see if there's one that will do the job. On the Commenting toolbar, click the Stamp tools pull-down arrow to open the menu shown in **Figure 9.7**.

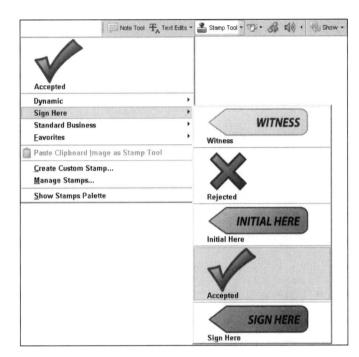

Figure 9.7 You can choose from a wide range of default stamps in Acrobat.

The upper three commands on the menu have submenus containing the stamp choices (Figure 9.7 shows the Sign Here options); the fourth option contains stamps you define as favorites. Joe decides on the checkmark stamp.

3. Click a stamp to select it. The pointer changes to resemble the comment's icon.

4. Click the document where you want to apply the stamp. In Joe's menu, the checkmark stamps are shown next to the day's special—corned beef on rye bread (**Figure 9.8**).

5. Joe also adds a stamp in the "Special of the Day" text block at the left of the page.

WHO ARE YOU?

If you haven't used the stamps or other processes that use digital identity information before, an Identity Setup dialog opens. Add additional identity information and click Complete to close the dialog and apply the stamp. If you want to change the identity information, choose Edit > Preferences/Acrobat > Preferences and click Identity in the left column of the dialog; modify the information in the identity fields, such as your name or organization.

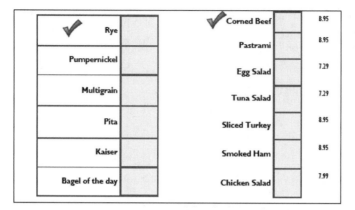

Figure 9.8 The checkmark stamp is used in the menu to show the daily special.

Custom Stamps

The stamps do the trick. It's easy for Joe's customers to see the special on the menu, but it would be nice if the stamp could look a little closer to the decorative "X" he scribbles on his menu board every morning.

 Download **dingbat.tif** if you would like to create Joe's custom stamp yourself.

To easily create a custom stamp in Acrobat:

1. Click the Stamp tools pull-down menu and choose Create Custom Stamp. The Select Image for Custom Stamp dialog opens.

2. Click Browse to find the file you want to use for the stamp, which can be in most common graphic formats, a PDF format, or a Word file. The Select dialog opens and displays the chosen file; click OK to close the dialog and return to the Create Stamp dialog.

3. Click the Category field and type a name for a new stamp category, or select one of the existing categories; then type a name for the stamp (**Figure 9.9**). Click OK.

4. To use the new stamp, click the Stamp tools pull-down arrow—you see the custom stamp category is listed with the program's categories. Click the new custom category to display its contents. In **Figure 9.10**, you see Joe's new custom stamp.

5. Click the stamp in the menu to select it, and then click the document page to apply the stamp.

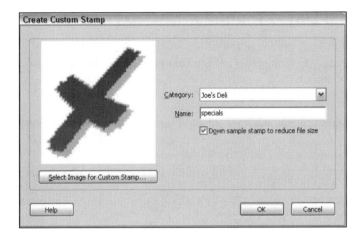

Figure 9.9 Name your custom stamp and assign it to a category, or create a new category.

Figure 9.10 Your custom stamp is available from the Stamps menu.

You don't have to open the menu to select a stamp to reuse it. Instead, move your pointer over the Stamp tool icon on the Commenting toolbar and click the icon, not the pull-down arrow. The last stamp you selected is active. If you close and reopen Acrobat, you have to select the stamp from the menu.

You can work with custom stamps in various ways. First, open the Stamp tool's pull-down menu and choose Manage Stamps to open the Manage Custom Stamps dialog. Then you can

- Select the stamp you want to remove and click Delete to remove a stamp

- Click Edit to reopen the Create Custom Stamp dialog (use this dialog if you want to rename the stamp, for example)

- Click Create to start building another custom stamp

Click Close to dismiss the dialog.

FINDING IMAGES FOR STAMPS

Here's a quick trick for creating images you can use for stamps: Look through your fonts. Several fonts display images rather than letters and numbers. The "X" image used for Joe's menu is actually the number "8" in the Zapf Dingbats font.

The Soup of the Day—Touching Up Text

Joe writes the soup of the day on his menu board—he can do the same thing in Acrobat using the TouchUp Text tool. This is a really slick way of making small changes in a document.

Follow these steps to make changes to text:

1. Choose Tools > Advanced Editing > Show TouchUp Toolbar (**Figure 9.11**).

   If you right-click/Control-click the toolbar well, the only option is the Advanced Editing toolbar. From there, the TouchUp tools are available as a sub-toolbar (this method saves you a step).

Figure 9.11 Use the TouchUp tools to modify content on a document; you can touch up text and other objects.

2. Click the TouchUp Text tool 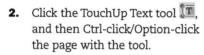, and then Ctrl-click/Option-click the page with the tool.

3. In the New Text Font dialog, select the font you want to use from the pull-down menu (**Figure 9.12**). It's easy to use a font that is contained in your document—when you open the pull-down menu, the fonts embedded in your document are listed at the top of the menu.

Figure 9.12 Choose a font in this dialog, and change the orientation of the text if you wish.

   For Joe's menu, the selected font is the bold version of Gill Sans MT, the font family used for much of the menu.

4. Click OK to close the dialog.

5. On the page, you see the default text label "New Text."

6. When you click the text with the TouchUp Text tool, you see a vertical I-beam cursor; type the replacement text (**Figure 9.13**).

Figure 9.13 Add new text to a PDF document using the TouchUp Text tool. Here you can also see the stamp used in the menu.

If you want to change some of the font characteristics, such as color or font size, follow these steps:

1. Right-click/Control-click the text with the TouchUp Text tool to open the shortcut menu.

2. Choose Properties from the shortcut menu to open the TouchUp Properties dialog (**Figure 9.14**).

3. Modify the text properties as desired.

4. Click Close to dismiss the dialog.

Don't worry if you don't place the text in the exact location you want it. You can move it using the TouchUp Object tool 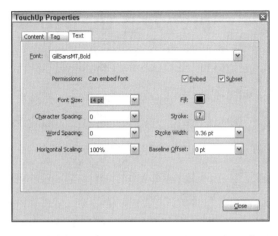 by following these steps:

1. Click the tool icon on the TouchUp toolbar to activate it.

2. Click the text. You see a bounding box surround the text block (**Figure 9.15**).

3. Drag the text to the perfect spot.

Figure 9.14 *Change the text properties—such as the font, size, or color—in the Properties dialog.*

Figure 9.15 *Adjust the text block's location on the page using the TouchUp Object tool.*

Making Changes Tomorrow

Now Joe's menu is ready to send to his customers. Whenever he wants to change the specials, all he has to do is open the menu PDF document in Acrobat and adjust the stamps and text.

Use the Hand tool on the Basic toolbar to drag the stamp to identify the day's special. Click the "soup of the day" text block with the TouchUp Text tool and select the existing text (**Figure 9.16**). Type the new name.

Figure 9.16 *Select the text for replacement using the TouchUp Text tool.*

Spreading the Word by E-mail

Joe's final task is to send his menu to his customers. He can e-mail it right from Acrobat. Choose File > Email to open your e-mail program; in Joe's case, a Microsoft Outlook window opens (**Figure 9.17**). The e-mail window is the same as that you see when you open a New window from Outlook, except the PDFMaker toolbar isn't available.

Click "To" to open the address book and select the customers' names. Hopefully Joe has created a distribution list containing his customers' names to simplify the process. The message's subject line is the file's name by default. Replace it with a descriptive subject such as Menu for Today, and include instructions or a message in the body of the e-mail. Click Send. It's that simple!

Figure 9.17 *Joe can e-mail the menu to his customers right from Acrobat.*

What Else Could He Do?

Joe has created a very usable form for his fax ordering service. There are many ways he could enhance his form to make it simpler for both his customers and his staff. For example, rather than having customers fill out, print, and fax back their orders, Joe could make the form *fillable*—that is, his customers would be able to type text directly into the form, which allows them to easily e-mail the orders back to him.

In addition to providing e-mail ordering, he could add calculations to the fields on the form to automatically process an order's cost, saving time for both his customers and staff. To save even more time for his customers, he could integrate features that allow the user to add information such as their name and address automatically at the click of a button.

In fact, these are such good ideas that the tale of Joe's Deli is continued in the next chapter. Will he successfully create the perfect form? Will the numbers all add up? Don't keep yourself in suspense. Quick—turn the page!

10

Making a Form Interactive

With Acrobat 7 Professional, you can create forms easily by using the Forms toolbar. Or, if you are working with Acrobat 7 Professional in Windows, you can use the new Adobe Designer, a complete forms design package that is installed as a separate program when you install Acrobat 7. You can learn how to work with Adobe Designer in Bonus Chapter 3, "Constructing a Form Using Adobe Designer," on the book's Web site (www.donnabaker.ca/downloads).

Whether you are working with Acrobat 7 Standard or Professional in either Windows or Mac, you can use the Forms tools to add a variety of form fields to a document. Not only that, you can configure form fields for a range of uses—from ordering a product to automatically e-mailing or printing a document. There are a number of Forms tools available in Acrobat, and this project uses all of them!

In particular, Acrobat 7 contains a very neat feature that you'll learn about in this chapter. Often, if you're using similar forms repeatedly, you find yourself typing in the same information—such as your name—over and over again. Using Acrobat, you can create a button that the user working in Acrobat can simply click to load files from their hard drives with, and automatically fill in some of the form fields on the document.

This chapter continues the story of Joe's Deli. In the previous chapter, Joe's take-out menu was transformed into a form that he could e-mail to customers and they could print, fill out, and fax it back. Now, Joe wants to take the process to the next level, constructing a form that allows his customers to add information directly to the form using Acrobat 4 or newer, which will save them having to manually enter information or print the form. Customers working with Adobe Reader can clear their entries from the form and e-mail their form data directly from the form, but they can't save or reload form data into the order form. Joe also wants to add calculations to fields to automatically compute order costs, sales tax, and other charges.

Joe's Deli, Part 2

Joe, featured in the previous chapter, runs a successful deli in a busy downtown location. The clientele of Joe's Deli is predominantly employees of financial and legal firms in the surrounding area.

Some months ago, Joe changed the way he delivers menus to his regular customers. Instead of faxing the menus daily, he created a PDF menu that he can easily update and then e-mail to his customers.

As a result of better and more convenient communication, Joe's delivery business has increased dramatically. He regularly hears from his patrons that they like the e-mail menu but would like to place their orders by e-mail as well, rather than having to print and fax their orders. Being the good businessman that he is, Joe decides to look into the matter.

Joe's present delivery form includes areas for his customers to manually check off the menu items they want to order and calculate their order totals. For every order, customers have to write or type the delivery information on the form—a tiresome chore for regular customers. Once the orders are received at Joe's Deli, his order taker has to calculate the order again. If the customer has ordered the daily special, a discount has to be deducted from the total. All that ciphering is almost automatic for Joe's long-time order taker, but not as quick for any other staff who may be involved.

Joe is planning a new method for ordering that uses the same form, but in a modified format (**Figure 10.1**). The form will include different types of form fields, such as radio buttons and check boxes, and will automatically calculate order costs, including sales tax and delivery. He also plans for several automated features on the form, adding a set of images he'll convert to buttons that customers can use to automatically load their delivery information onto the form if they are working in Acrobat, reset the form fields, and e-mail the form back to him.

EMAIL DELIVERY MENU

JOE'S

Deli with a Difference

Where you will never hear:
"Do you want fries with that?"

To order, contact
Phone: 555-555-5000
Fax: 555-555-5001

START HERE:
Choose your freshly-made bread:

Rye	
Pumpernickel	
Multigrain	
Pita	
Kaiser	
Bagel of the day	

INSIDE?
We pile 'em high. What's your pleasure:

Corned Beef	1.95	Sliced Turkey	2.95
Pastrami	1.50	Smoked Ham	2.29
Egg Salad	6.95	Chicken Salad	2.99
Tuna Salad	7.29		

$0.00

Click to select:

| ------- ▼ |

SPECIALS OF THE DAY
At Joe's Deli we want to take the boredom out of your workday. We can't do much about your job, but we can make lunch something to look forward to!

Click to order the sandwich of the day or soup of the day:

TODAY'S SPECIALS

| SOUP | | |
| SANDWICH | | |

OUR FAMOUS SIDES
Classic deli side dishes, made fresh. Type a quantity in the box:

Coleslaw	2.29
Potato Salad	2.29
Pickles	1.00
French Onion soup	3.95

Any special instructions?

WITH CHEESE ($.50)?
Click to select:

☐ American $0.00
☐ Cheddar
☐ Swiss

EXTRAS
Order any or all of these options:

alfalfa sprouts
hot mustard
ketchup
lettuce
lite mayo
mayo
mustard
onion
Spanish onion
tomato

PLEASE PAY:

DELIVER TO:
Please include your company and office number. It saves us a lot of time, and you get your Joe's lunch a lot faster!

Name
Address
Company   Office Number
Phone   Extension

Subtotal	0.00
Tax	0.00
Delivery	5.00
TOTAL:	$5.00

EASY ORDERING:

- Click each menu item you want to order.
- Fill in delivery information or load your file.
- Click "Email" to send.
- Click "Clear" to start again.

SAVE   LOAD   EMAIL   CLEAR

A. The basic content of the form is created in a simple document and converted to PDF. **B.** This type of form field lets the customer choose an option from a pull-down list. **C.** Add special fields in the form for the customer to click to select different items. **D.** You can create fields so that the user can add text like "Heavy on the pickles." **E.** Customers can add information automatically from a file they store on their hard drive. **F.** Tell Acrobat to automatically calculate fields. **G.** Special buttons are added so that a customer can easily e-mail, load information, or clear the form.

Figure 10.1 *The new Joe's Deli order form contains many automatic, user-friendly features.*

Steps Involved in This Project

Joe can use Acrobat's Forms tools to rework his delivery order form and provide the convenience his customers are asking for. The goal is to create a form that is easy for customers to use and one that automatically calculates order totals, including tax and delivery charges.

To make his new order form successful, Joe needs to do the following:

1. Make some simple modifications to the basic PDF order form he currently e-mails.

2. Add fields to the form to automatically calculate totals.

3. Add buttons to automate some of the processes, such as enabling his customers to e-mail their orders back to him with a single click of the mouse.

4. Include an automated process that allows his customers to have their delivery information automatically added to the order form at the click of a button—if they are working with Acrobat, not Adobe Reader.

The first step is to decide what he wants the new form to accomplish. The form he has been using had tables that customers used to order their lunches, and he plans to use Acrobat form fields instead.

Designing the Form's Function

Download **joe2.pdf** if you want to see the form in its current state before modifying it to use Acrobat's Forms tools. You can see how the original form's layout can be modified to make it simpler to use in this project, according to the list below.

On Joe's current delivery menu, food items are listed in a table that includes a field for customers to check off the items they want. Currently, Joe adds or adjusts a custom stamp on the order form every day before sending it, identifying the special of the day. He writes in text on the form to name the soup of the day (**Figure 10.2**).

SPECIAL OF THE DAY

At Joe's Deli we want to take the boredom out of your workday. We can't do much about your job, but we can make lunch something to look forward to!

Look for our daily sandwich special, marked on this menu.

TODAY'S SOUP OF THE DAY

Hearty Beef Noodle

Figure 10.2 Joe identifies the daily specials using a stamp and text on his PDF order form.

In order to redesign the form to function as he intends, Joe has to do the following:

- Add lists the customers can click to select items. Checkmarks and pull-down lists are familiar to his customers, so he'll use those that Acrobat offers.

- Convert the "Extras" table, which includes items such as lettuce and onion, to a list box, so a customer can choose a combination of items from the list.

- Adjust the prices of the fillings to reflect his actual prices, not the generic price point he had been using for convenience.

FORM DESIGN MUST-HAVES

While there is certainly no one right way to design a form, there are two concepts that you should keep in mind at all times. First, every design decision should focus on making it easier for your users to work with the form, such as offering prefilled fields or automatically selected options. Second, every field on a form should be designed to collect accurate information for you, such as using a list that allows users to select one or more condiments or prevents users from selecting more than one type of bread or filling. The changes to be made in Joe's form are designed to achieve these goals.

- Add a new listing to the form for the special of the day that the customer can choose by conveniently clicking a check box. If a customer selects either the soup of the day or the special of the day, the price needs to be automatically calculated.

- Add a comment box where the customer can type special instructions, like Easy on the onions.

- Add calculated fields for the subtotal, tax, delivery, and grand total.

- Add button labels for automating functions, including loading and exporting customer data, e-mailing the form, and clearing fields on the form.

How do these design plans get incorporated into the original menu? Let's look at how the form's structure is changed to meet the design requirements.

Modifying the Form's Source Document

It's often simpler to lay out labels, graphics, and other visual elements in the source document. Joe needs to modify the original form to make it simpler to add the form fields in Acrobat later.

Download **joe3_raw.pdf** to see the modified PDF form before any form fields are added.

By adjusting the form's layout in the following ways, Joe thinks (and rightly so!) that it will be easier to add the new form fields in Acrobat:

■ The Today's Specials block on the document is modified to give it the appearance of a fill-in form (**Figure 10.3**). Joe can still type the specials or use his custom stamp on the form before e-mailing it in the morning, but the addition of a form appearance makes it easier for customers to work with.

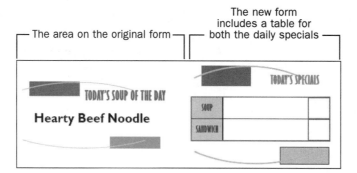

The area on the original form ⌐⌐ The new form includes a table for both the daily specials

Figure 10.3 *The daily specials are arranged into a form that a customer can click to order.*

■ The customer information area at the lower left of the form is reorganized to make it easier to add separate form fields for the telephone and office extension numbers, for example, by separating the labels on the form (**Figure 10.4**).

■ The condiments and extras listings are removed from the document, with only their headings remaining (**Figure 10.5**). Joe is going to add list box fields to the form later—customers can choose options from the list boxes and they save space on the form.

■ Customers will choose fillings from a combo box (a pull-down list); but they still need to see the prices, so the segment of the form containing the fillings list is arranged more efficiently, the prices are modified, and Joe includes a graphic element over which the sandwich cost is displayed when selected (**Figure 10.6**).

■ Four buttons are added to the lower right of the form, as well as a block of instructions for using them (**Figure 10.7**).

When the source document is ready, it is converted to PDF using the PDFMaker, as described in Chapter 10. To create the original form, Joe used Microsoft Publisher, which has a PDFMaker.

The original form lets customers write information on the lines

The new form will have separate form fields for each label

DELIVER TO:

Please include your company and office number. It saves us a lot of time, and you get your Joe's lunch a lot faster!

Name

Address

Company / Office Number

Phone

DELIVER TO:

Please include your company and office number. It saves us a lot of time, and you get your Joe's lunch a lot faster!

Name

Address

Company   Office Number

Phone   Extension

Figure 10.4 *Modifying the customer's information on the source form makes it simpler to add form fields in Acrobat.*

The original form lets customers check off their choices

The new form uses only the sections' headings

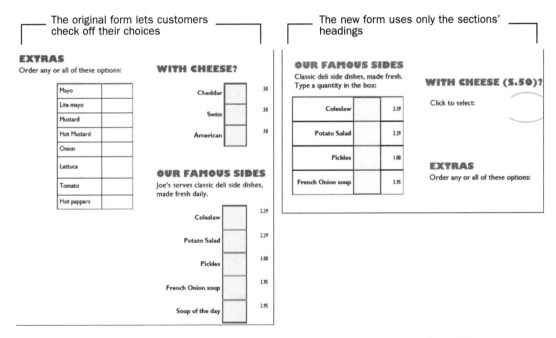

EXTRAS
Order any or all of these options:

Mayo	
Lite mayo	
Mustard	
Hot Mustard	
Onion	
Lettuce	
Tomato	
Hot peppers	

WITH CHEESE?

Cheddar		.50
Swiss		.50
American		.50

OUR FAMOUS SIDES
Joe's serves classic deli side dishes, made fresh daily.

Coleslaw		2.29
Potato Salad		2.29
Pickles		1.00
French Onion soup		3.95
Soup of the day		3.95

OUR FAMOUS SIDES
Classic deli side dishes, made fresh. Type a quantity in the box:

Coleslaw		2.29
Potato Salad		2.29
Pickles		1.00
French Onion soup		3.95

WITH CHEESE (S.50)?

Click to select:

EXTRAS
Order any or all of these options:

Figure 10.5 *The condiments and extras are changed for the new form because the choices will be offered in list boxes.*

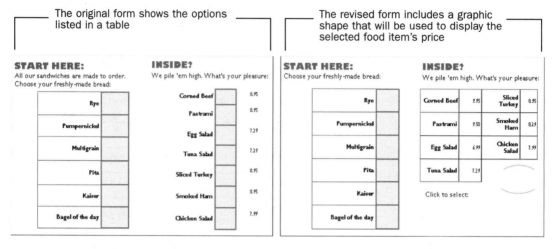

Figure 10.6 *The layout of the fillings table is changed to include space to insert a combo box listing customer's choices.*

Figure 10.7 *Button graphics are drawn in the source document to be used for automatic functions in Acrobat; adding ordering information explains how the form works.*

Form Elements—Things to Consider

Once the form is planned and the document is modified and converted to PDF, it's time to put the plan into action. Save yourself a lot of time when constructing a form in Acrobat by planning the processes.

Joe's form content has to answer three questions:

- Who—information about the customer

- What—what the customer wants to order

- How much—the subtotals and total cost of the order

Develop a Logical Naming Scheme

Before you click that Forms tool and draw your first form element, decide how you want to name the fields. It seems like a small detail, doesn't it? On the contrary, a logical naming structure makes your life much simpler in the long run:

- Using logical names lets others work with your form. If the names make sense, anyone who has to work with the form can understand immediately what a form field refers to.

- If you are having a troubleshooting problem with a form, it's much easier to check a form's content when you don't have to second-guess what you named a field.

- When you are assigning actions to form fields, Acrobat presents the available form fields listed in dialogs. It's much simpler to pick and choose fields when the names are self-evident!

- Acrobat offers automatic naming of form fields by appending numbers to the names. If you start with logical names, it's easy to understand automatic form field naming as well.

- Using a common prefix for groups of form fields makes it simpler to choose individual fields when you are working with field name lists.

APPROACHING CONSTRUCTION

Develop a system for approaching the job. In some cases, you may want to start with the more difficult or complex elements—such as list boxes—instead of simpler elements like buttons. Other times, particularly in long forms with numerous text boxes, you might find it easier to start at the top and work down.

I like to build all the form fields in a section of the form first. When you are satisfied with their structure, layout, and names, then you can go back to the start and add the actions, calculations, or JavaScript required for the form.

Regardless of the approach, consider the elements involved as well as how you like to work, and go from there. The goal is to make the job as efficient as possible with the least number of errors.

This chapter follows a little bit of both methods. To make it simpler to understand, you will build blocks of fields and apply some actions as you go along, adding calculations to a group of fields after their structure and function is complete.

Information Text Fields

An important area on Joe's form is the one that holds the information about the customer. Unless the correct delivery information is included, it's hard to deliver an order! These fields include the customer's name, address, and telephone number/extension. Text fields are used on the form to hold the customer information; the field names are prefaced with "c_." You'll see later how this naming system can be used for sorting and selecting form fields.

Follow these steps to add and configure the form's text fields:

1. Choose Tools > Advanced Editing > Show Forms Toolbar to display the entire toolbar (**Figure 10.8**).

   You can select individual tools from the program's menu, but because you are working with a group of tools, open the toolbar for easy access.

2. Click the Text Field tool  on the toolbar, and then drag a marquee on the document where you would like the field placed (**Figure 10.9**).

> **TIP** Careful naming of any fields you add to a project can be a real time-saver. In Chapter 4, for example, several button fields are added to the project, and organized into groups using prefixes. Joe follows the same process in this chapter, organizing groups of fields using prefixes.

Figure 10.8 Open the Forms toolbar to make it simpler to select different tools as you work on the form.

Figure 10.9 Draw a marquee on the page where you want to add the text field.

NOTE For all types of form fields, you draw a marquee with the appropriate tool on the document where you would like the field placed.

3. Release the mouse; the Text Field Properties dialog opens displaying the General tab (**Figure 10.10**).

4. Type c_name in the Name field.

5. Click the Required check box in the Common Properties section at the lower right of the dialog. In order for a customer to place an order, information must be provided in all the fields in the customer information area of the form. As mentioned earlier, it's hard to deliver to an unknown address!

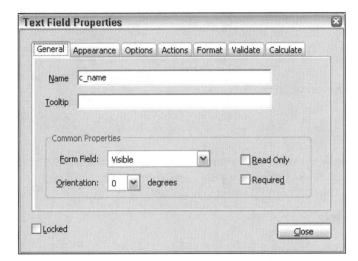

Figure 10.10 Name the field in the General tab of this dialog.

6. Select the Appearance tab. Make sure the Border and Fill settings are set to no color. If a color is showing on the color swatch, click it to open a small Color Picker, and select No Color to close the Color Picker and apply the color change.

7. Choose a font face and size. The project uses the default Helvetica font and generally a 9 pt size.

8. Click Close to dismiss the dialog and finish the field. That's one field down, and a hundred or so left to go!

NOTE You can only identify and select like types of fields. That is, if your form has several types of form fields, you can only work with one type at a time. When you click a tool on the Forms toolbar, all the fields created by that tool are identified by bounding boxes, and their names are displayed.

Creating Multiple Fields

There are a number of ways you can create multiple fields from a single field. In this part of the form, it's done by a simple copy-and-paste method.

Do the following to use the copy-and-paste method:

1. Click the field you want to copy with the Text Field tool. Its bounding box turns red and displays the name.

2. Ctrl-drag/Command-drag to create another copy of the field. Drop it on the Address line (**Figure 10.11**).

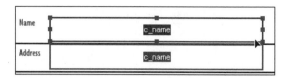

3. Repeat several times until all the fields are pasted. The project uses a total of six fields in the customer information area.

Figure 10.11 *Copy the field and drag it to its correct location on the form.*

Once the fields are copied, you have to rename them. Otherwise, you have several copies of the same field containing the same information.

Renaming Fields

Leave the original c_name field as is, and then follow these steps to rename the remaining fields:

1. Double-click a field to open the Text Field Properties dialog, which displays the General tab.

2. Click the "c_name" text, and change the text in the Name field.

3. Click Close to dismiss the dialog.

4. Repeat with the remaining fields.

In the form, the set of fields are named: c_name, c_address, c_officeno, c_company, c_phone, and c_phone2.

Now that you have fields, each with a unique name, the last step is to resize and organize the fields on the form to make the field sizes correspond with the layout of the form.

Resizing and Realigning Fields

Resize and realign the fields as appropriate. In Joe's project, for example, both the office number and telephone extension fields are much smaller than the other text fields.

Follow these simple steps to change the fields' size and alignment:

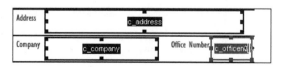

1. Drag a side handle on the first field you want to resize to decrease or increase the width (**Figure 10.12**).

Figure 10.12 *Resize a text field by dragging a side or corner handle.*

2. Ctrl-click/Command-click to select the other fields you want to change to the same dimensions.

3. Move your mouse over the field that is of the correct size, right-click/Control-click to display the shortcut menu and choose Size > Width to change the set of fields to the same width.

   In the same shortcut menu, you can also select both Height and Width to quickly resize several fields.

4. Acrobat offers ways to align and distribute fields on a form. Ctrl-click/Command-click to select the fields you want to adjust, and then right-click/Control-click to open the shortcut menu and choose the command (**Figure 10.13**).

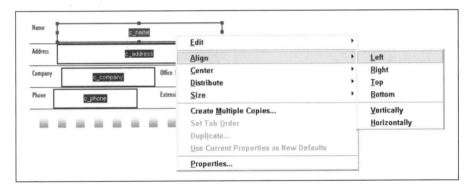

Figure 10.13 *Choose from a variety of alignment and distribution commands to organize and size your form fields.*

NOTE You can also move form fields in any direction using the arrow keys on the keyboard. Select the field or fields, and press the appropriate key to move the field(s).

Point It Out

When you have a group of fields selected and want to perform a single action, such as resizing them, you need to define one of the fields as an anchor. That is, Acrobat needs to know what you want to use as an example in order to configure the other fields to match. As you select fields you'll see that the bounding box of the field under your pointer changes from blue to red. The field with the red bounding box is the anchor. Make sure you right-click/Control-click to open the shortcut menu while your pointer is over the anchor field.

Adding Radio Buttons

The next section of the form to tackle is the list customers use to select a type of bread. A radio button list provides a set of options for the user to select from; as one option is selected, the others are deselected. There is a trick to using radio buttons in this way, which you'll learn in this section.

Follow these steps to add and configure the first radio button field:

1. Click the Radio Button tool ⊙ on the Forms toolbar.

2. Drag a small marquee to indicate the size of the button, and release the mouse. The Radio Button dialog opens and displays the General tab.

3. Type a name in the Name field. Joe used the name "bread" for obvious reasons. Don't add an identifying suffix to the field's name, such as those added in the customer information fields.

4. Select the Appearance tab and choose border, fill, and text characteristics if you like.

5. Select the Options tab. On this tab, you choose the type of button appearance and set the export value, which differentiates the fields from one another (**Figure 10.14**).

6. Click the Button Style pull-down arrow and choose an option from the list. In the project, the Check style is used.

7. Type a name for the field's contents in the Export Value field. Here, "rye" is the name used to differentiate it from other bread choices.

8. Click Close to close the dialog and complete the field.

Once the first field is created to your satisfaction, it's easy to add the others. Use the method described in the previous section, "Creating Multiple Fields," and create a set of six radio buttons.

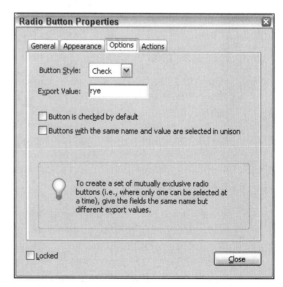

Figure 10.14 *Choose an option for the radio button's appearance, and set its value.*

The final step for the radio buttons is to change the values. When you copy-and-paste the set of fields, each uses the same characteristics, and the fields all have the same value. Double-click each field to open the Radio Button Properties dialog, and type new text in the Export Value field on the Options tab.

Whenever working with forms, it is always a good idea to test as you go along. Click the Hand tool 🖐 on the Basic toolbar. Click through the set of radio buttons. You see only one button is active at a time (**Figure 10.15**). Click another button, and the previously selected button is deselected.

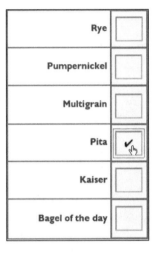

Figure 10.15 A customer can make only one selection in the radio button field.

WHY NOT JUST USE THE CHECK BOX TOOL?

The answer is actually pretty simple. It's easier to use radio buttons than a series of check boxes. The goal of this part of the form is for a customer to choose a type of bread, and only one type. By changing the values for each button, you can easily create a group of mutually exclusive fields. That is, if a customer chooses one option, all other options are deselected. You can also use check box fields drawn with the Check Box tool, but then you have to add actions to each field to deselect the other fields. The two daily specials are created using check boxes because of their planned design. If a customer chooses a special, any other sandwich order is deselected.

Working in the Fields Pane

Let's take a short break from form field building and look at how Acrobat can display your fields. Choose View > Navigation Tabs > Fields to open the Fields pane. You can drag to dock it in the Navigation pane or leave it floating in the program window.

All the fields added to your form are listed in the pane (**Figure 10.16**). You see the type of form field and its name. Look at the set of fields used for the bread radio buttons. Each is named "bread," and Acrobat has appended # and a number following the field's name, although on the document and in the properties, the fields don't have a unique name. The numbers correspond to the radio buttons' export values. For example, the listing for bread#0 has the export value of "Rye," bread#3 has the export value of "Pita," and so on.

Using the Fields pane is a great time-saver if you are building a form with a lot of form fields. Rather than scrolling through a document and then selecting first the appropriate tool and then the field or fields, you can simply select them in the listing in the pane. Right-click/control-click the field's name in the pane to open a small shortcut menu that allows you to rename or delete the field on the form, or open its Properties dialog.

Click Options at the top of the Fields pane to display its menu. The pane's menu contains the same commands for configuring, modifying, and creating forms as those available by choosing Advanced > Forms from the Main program menu.

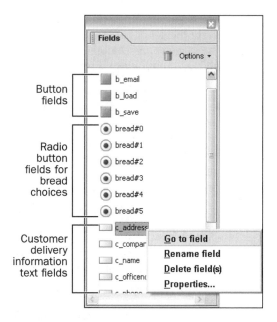

Figure 10.16 *Manipulate the fields in your document from the Fields pane.*

MAKING COMMON CHANGES

Suppose you add a collection of fields, such as several radio buttons, and realize you should have changed the border or the fill. Do you have to open the Properties dialog for each field separately and make the changes? Not at all. Select the fields on the document, or in the Fields pane if you have it open, and then right-click/Control-click to open the shortcut menu and choose Properties. The appropriate Properties dialog opens, and options that can be modified for the group of fields are active. You can't change the name of a group of fields, for example, but you can change an action or a font.

Make the change and click Close to apply the modifications to all the selected fields. This only works with fields of one type, so if you are using a particular shade of red in your document for framing fields, for instance, you have to select all the text fields and change them, then all the radio button fields, and so on.

If you want to make changes to different types of fields at the same time, use the TouchUp Object tool. Select the tool from the Advanced Editing toolbar, and click to select the fields you want to change. Then right-click/Control-click and choose Properties from the shortcut menu to open the dialog and make changes.

You can also select a group of fields and then make changes in the Properties Bar if it is open. To open the toolbar, right-click/Control-click the toolbar well and choose Properties Bar. The toolbar's contents vary according to the field selected (**Figure 10.17**). You can make common changes in properties such as fonts or colors on the toolbar, or click More to open the Properties dialog.

Figure 10.17 Common properties for a form field are shown on the Properties Bar, and the properties displayed change depending on the selected object.

Building a Combo Box

Now let's get back to form building. Next up, it's time to create the special kind of list called a combo box. A combo box field is like a pull-down list. You add the items to the list as you construct the field. Each item has a unique export value—in this case, the price of the item (**Figure 10.18**). The export values are important in Joe's form because they are used to calculate the price of the items.

His menu uses two combo boxes, in fact—one for the sandwich fillings and one for the cheeses.

Follow these steps to draw and configure the combo box for the sandwich fillings:

1. Click the Combo Box tool on the Forms toolbar, and draw a marquee on the document for the field. Don't worry about the precise size and location; you can adjust that later. Release the mouse, and the Combo Box Properties dialog opens.

2. On the General tab, name the field. In the sample project, the field is named "fill" (**Figure 10.19**).

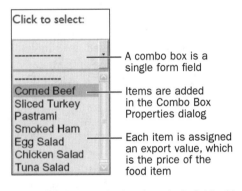

Figure 10.18 A combo box is a single field, with multiple items included, each having a unique export value.

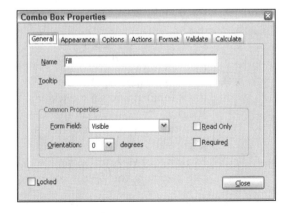

Figure 10.19 Name the combo box in the Properties dialog.

3. Select the Appearance tab, and set the border, filling, and text options for the field.

4. Select the Options tab. Type the name of the sandwich in the Item field, and then type its price in the Export Value field. Click Add to add the item to the Item List. Continue with the remaining sandwich types (**Figure 10.20**).

5. Add one more item to the Item List—a set of dashed lines having an Export Value of 0. Make sure this blank line is selected on the Item List to be used as the default.

Acrobat uses the selected item in the Item List as a default. If you use a blank entry with a value of 0, the sandwich cost is automatically changed to $0.00 when the form is cleared, which is the desired action.

6. Click Close to dismiss the dialog.

7. Adjust the location and size of the field on the document.

8. Click the Hand tool on the Basic toolbar, and then click the pull-down arrow on the field to display the list of items (**Figure 10.21**). Click through the list; you see you can only click one choice in this field.

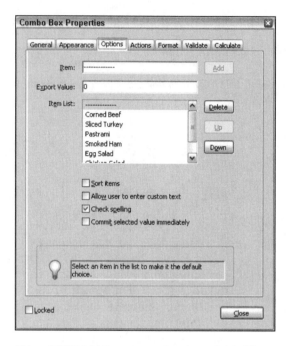

Figure 10.20 *Add the names of each sandwich filling and enter its price as the export value.*

Figure 10.21 *The items added to the combo box are shown in the field's pull-down list.*

Storing the Value

The combo box for the sandwich fillings includes a list of items, each having a unique name and an export value. When a customer chooses a selection in the combo box field named "fill," the item is identified, and its export value is determined based on the value you entered when building the form field. For example, the corned beef sandwich has an export value of 9.95; the egg salad sandwich has an export value of 7.29. It's very important to note that the prices for the sandwiches were changed to reflect Joe's actual costs. Each sandwich now has a unique price, which is important to the transmittal of the form data. If there are multiple items having the same export value, Acrobat doesn't know which sandwich item to assign the value to when the form data is later imported into Acrobat. If two or more of the sandwiches had the same price, Joe would have to build a set of check boxes to accurately price the items. OK so far?

A combo box is used for selecting an item from a list, but it isn't used for any sort of calculation. For that, you need to use a text field. Acrobat let's you choose an option in one field and then, using a calculation, transfer that value to another field. Sounds complicated, but really it isn't.

To create a text field used to store a selection a customer makes from the combo box, follow these steps:

1. Select the Text Field tool and draw a marquee on the document. Release the mouse to finish the marquee, and open the Text Field Properties dialog.

2. On the General tab, name the field; the sample project's field is named p_fill, meaning "price of the fill." Click Read Only—you want customers to see the value, but you don't want them to be able to change the field's contents.

3. Configure the text box's appearance however you like in the Appearance tab.

4. On the Format tab, click the "Select format category" pull-down arrow and choose Number. It is very important that you set any calculated field to a number format so Acrobat recognizes the content as numerical and performs the calculations. The default options on the Format tab also include two decimal places, which is fine for this field since it is displaying currency. If you like, choose a currency symbol on this tab as well (**Figure 10.22**).

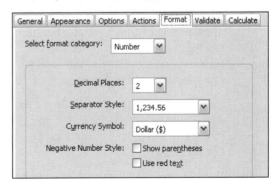

Figure 10.22 *Choose the characteristics for the numbers you want to display in the field.*

5. On the Calculate tab, click the "Value is the" radio button to activate it, and choose "sum (+)" from the pull-down list if it isn't selected by default (**Figure 10.23**).

6. Click Pick to open the Field Selection dialog (**Figure 10.24**). Scroll through the list to find the fill field, and click its check box to select it. Click OK to close the Field Selection dialog.

You see how the fields are arranged in groups based on the naming applied throughout the project.

7. Click Close to dismiss the Text Field Properties dialog.

To check that all the values are correct, click the Hand tool on the Basic toolbar, and then choose an item from the sandwich fillings' combo box. When you click another field or press Enter/Return on the keyboard, the value of the selection is automatically transferred to the field. If there are errors, check in the Combo Box Properties dialog that you have assigned correct prices to the items' export values on the Options tab.

Click the p_fill field with the Hand tool to try to select the text; the content of the field should be locked. If you can select the text, reopen the Text Field Properties dialog and make sure you clicked the Read Only check box on the General tab.

You use this value later when calculating the total cost of the customer's food order.

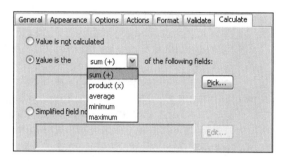

Figure 10.23 Choose a calculation option on this tab.

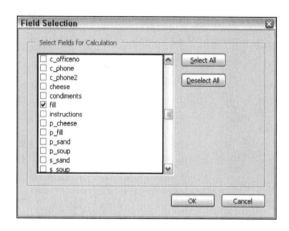

Figure 10.24 Select the field you want to use for the calculation.

Say "Cheese, Please"

The cheese options available to Joe's customers are listed as a set of three check boxes. Joe's customers can choose more than one piece of cheese for their sandwich if they like. The field for the cheese orders is named—you guessed it—"cheese." On the menu, each cheese option is $0.50. Joe adds the first check box, then adds and modifies copies, and finally adds text labels. He could have added a table in his source document, like that used for the bread selections, but wasn't sure how he was going to list the cheese selections.

Joe is adding one check box and then creating copies. Follow these steps to add the first check box:

1. Click the Check Box tool ☑ on the Forms toolbar to select it.

2. Draw a marquee on the document where you want to place the check box; release the mouse to complete the field and open the Check Box Properties dialog.

3. On the General tab, name the field. The project's field is named cheese1.

4. On the Appearance tab, choose a border and colors for the check box as well as a text size; Joe uses the default values.

5. On the Options tab, select the check appearance from the Check Box Style pull-down menu. Joe uses the default check mark.

6. Type the price of a cheese selection—.50—in the Export Value field. The export value is going to be transferred into a text field to use for calculating the cost of the customer's order.

7. Click Close to close the dialog and complete the field.

8. With the cheese1 field selected on the page, choose Edit > Copy, and then Edit > Paste twice to add two more copies of the field.

9. Double-click each of the new fields to open their Properties dialogs and change the name; Joe renames the fields cheese2 and cheese3. The export values can remain the same—that is, .50.

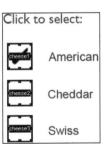

Joe didn't add text in his source document to use for labeling the cheese selections. Instead, he uses the TouchUp Text tool to add a label. He adds the labels "American," "Cheddar," and "Swiss" to correspond with the fields cheese1 through cheese3 (**Figure 10.25**).

NOTE For more information on working with the TouchUp Text tool, refer to Joe's earlier project in Chapter 9.

Figure 10.25 *Add check boxes and text labels for the cheese options.*

Storing Another Value

Since the cheese options are selected by check boxes, you need a calculated text field to store the value. Follow the earlier steps for constructing the text field. This time, name the field p_cheese, meaning "price of the cheese." Select the Calculate tab of the Text Field Properties dialog, and click Pick. The Field Selection dialog opens, which is where you choose the cheese1, cheese2, and cheese3 check box fields.

When a customer clicks one of the cheese option check boxes, the value is shown in the graphic area on the form designed to frame the cost of the product; if the customer selects two check boxes, you see the total in the field (**Figure 10.26**).

Because it is a read-only field, customers can see the value but can't change it.

Figure 10.26 *The text field shows the value for one or more cheese selections.*

Creating a List Box

A list box is a single field that shows a list of items that the user can select. Like a combo box field, a list box has a Properties dialog in which you add the items. Unlike a combo box field, however, a list box allows the user to select more than one item.

In Joe's project, customers can choose from a variety of condiments regardless of the type of sandwich they order, including the special. The list box is added to the Extras section on the form and allows customers to select one or more items. These items are added to a single list box field (**Figure 10.27**).

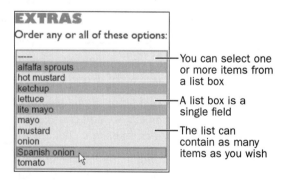

You can select one or more items from a list box

A list box is a single field

The list can contain as many items as you wish

Follow these steps to add a list box:

1. Click the List Box tool ▦ on the Forms toolbar, and drag a marquee on the document where you want to place the box. Don't

Figure 10.27 *The Extras list box field contains a list of condiments and toppings.*

worry about the precise size or location of the list box now, as you can adjust those later. Release the mouse; the List Box Properties dialog opens.

2. On the General tab, name the list box. The project's field is named "condiments."

3. Type some text in the Tooltip field to direct the customer if you want. A tooltip is a good option for this list box so that customers know they have more than one option (**Figure 10.28**).

4. Select the Appearance tab. Choose appropriate border and fill colors, and set the font size (**Figure 10.29**). Using the Auto size for the font may result in a text size too large for the list box space on the form.

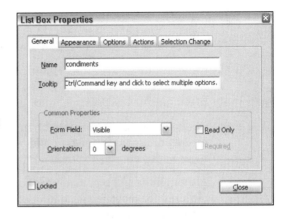

Figure 10.28 Name the list box and add a tooltip for customer information.

5. Select the Options tab. On this tab you add the actual content for the list (**Figure 10.30**). Type a condiment name in the Item field, and click the Add button to move the label into the Item List.

When an item is added to the list, the Add button is disabled, as shown in Figure 11.30. Typing a new item reactivates the button.

6. Continue adding items until the list is complete.

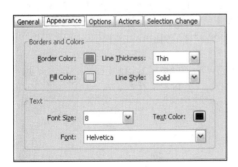

Figure 10.29 Choose colors for the list box that coordinate with the rest of the form.

Figure 10.30 Add and configure items for the list box in this tab of the dialog.

7. Organize the list. Click "Sort items" to reorder the list alphabetically; if you want to reorder it manually, select an item in the Item List and then click Up or Down to move it within the list.

8. Click "Multiple selection." Joe wants his customers to be able to select both hot mustard and mustard, if they want (although personally he thinks that's mustard-overkill).

9. Add a blank item to the list, or an entry such as "No options," or as in the sample project's combo box, add a set of dashes, which allows the customer to select no options for their sandwich if they prefer.

   Although the list box isn't used for calculations and a blank item isn't required for resetting a calculation, it is important to include it in the list box for the customers' benefit.

10. Click one of the items on the list to make it the default selection; the project uses the set of dashes as the default (**Figure 10.31**). This means when a customer views the form, one of the items is already highlighted. If you don't select an item, the first one on the list is selected automatically.

11. Click Close to dismiss the dialog and finish the list box.

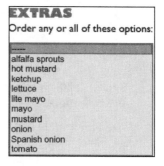

Figure 10.31 *The first item in the list box is selected by default.*

Click the Hand tool on the Basic toolbar and test the list box. You should see the item you selected as the default selection highlighted on the list box. Click the options to see that they select correctly; Ctrl-click/Command-click to select multiple options (**Figure 10.32**). If you can't select multiple items, reopen the List Box Properties dialog and make sure you checked the Multiple selection option on the Options tab.

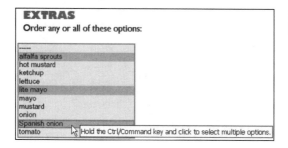

Figure 10.32 *Test the finished list box on the form.*

WHEN SHOULD YOU USE TOOLTIPS?

The short answer is whenever they make it easier for users to work with the form, such as providing a specific instruction that may be different from regular click and type actions. The tooltip in this section is a good example because customers may want to order several condiments but not realize they can select multiple items (the tooltip is shown in Figure 10.32).

Some people use tooltips for everything; others don't use them at all. Somewhere between the two extremes is probably best for general use. However, if you are designing an accessible form—one that is used by a person working with a screen reader or other assistive device—it's important to add a full range of tooltips to make the form understandable to the screen reader device.

Adding a Text Field for Special Instructions

A text field added to a document in Acrobat can be used for a range of purposes, such as typing text, showing calculations, or entering values. A text field can be blank, or as you see in this section, it can have default text added to it that gives the user instructions on how to use the field.

In the sample project, Joe wants to offer a way for his customers to make special requests, such as "Easy on the mustard" or "Heavy on the onions," so the form needs one more text field where they can enter any special instructions.

Follow these steps to add in a single text field for special instructions:

1. Click the Text Field tool and draw a marquee on the document. Release the mouse, and the Text Field Properties dialog opens.

2. On the General tab, name the field and type some text for a tooltip.

3. Select the Appearance tab, and choose colors and a font to coordinate with the rest of the form.

4. Select the Options tab and type some default text that shows the customer the purpose of the field (**Figure 10.33**).

5. Click Close to dismiss the dialog and finish the field.

TIP If you prefer, you can add a label for the field in the source program, or add one in Acrobat using the TouchUp Text tool. To avoid cluttering the design of the form in this project, the default text is used in the field instead.

6. Click the Hand tool on the Basic toolbar and test the field. You can click the text to select it and type alternate instructions (**Figure 10.34**).

Building a Set of Calculated Text Fields

Text fields can be used to perform calculations as well as to receive the results of calculations. You construct calculated text fields in the same way as shown earlier in the chapter, but some of the settings in the Properties dialog are specific to calculated form fields, as you see in this section.

There are other areas on the form where customers can make choices. A set of text fields are required for the side dishes. Depending on how hungry your customers are, they may want to order more than one side dish. How does this translate to the form design?

Figure 10.33 *Instead of having a text label on the form for a single field, you can add a tooltip that displays when the user moves their pointer over the field.*

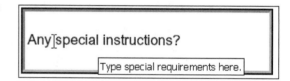

Figure 10.34 *The customer can add instructions or requests in this text field.*

Instead of using radio buttons, a combo box, or a list box, the best way to handle several items that can each be selected—in multiple numbers—is to offer the user a text field they can type a number into. For example, an especially hungry customer may want two orders of potato salad and one of coleslaw. Joe is too clever a businessman to pass up an opportunity like that!

To create a set of text fields to perform calculations, follow these steps:

1. Use the Text Field tool to draw a field, as you did in previous sections. The Text Field Properties dialog opens.

2. On the General tab of the dialog, name the field using a generic name. Since the set of fields is used for customers to choose side dishes, the name for the field in this project is "side_xxx;" in a later step, the "xxx" is replaced by the name of each side dish.

3. On the Appearance tab, deselect any border or fill colors—the form's table is already colored—and choose a font size and style.

4. On the Options tab, choose an alignment from the pull-down list. You can also set other features here, such as line wrapping or restricting the number of characters allowed (**Figure 10.35**).

5. On the Format tab, choose Number from the "Select format category" pull-down list (**Figure 10.36**). Also on this tab, you can choose decimal places or currency symbols; the sample project uses 0 decimal places for this set of fields, because you can't order 0.25 of a sandwich.

6. Click Close to dismiss the dialog and finish the text field.

7. Copy and paste the other three fields required to complete the set of four side dish order fields. In each case, change the name of the field to match the item, as in side_slaw (**Figure 10.37**).

8. Click the Hand tool on the Basic toolbar, click a side dish's field to make it active and type some text.

You can type or delete text, as well as enter numbers, in more than one of the fields. If you can't, reopen the Text Field Properties dialog and make sure Read Only is deselected on the General tab.

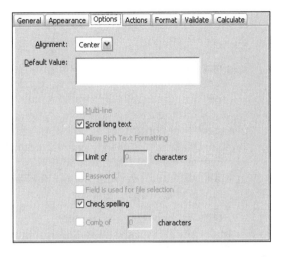

Figure 10.35 *Text field options include alignment and line characteristics.*

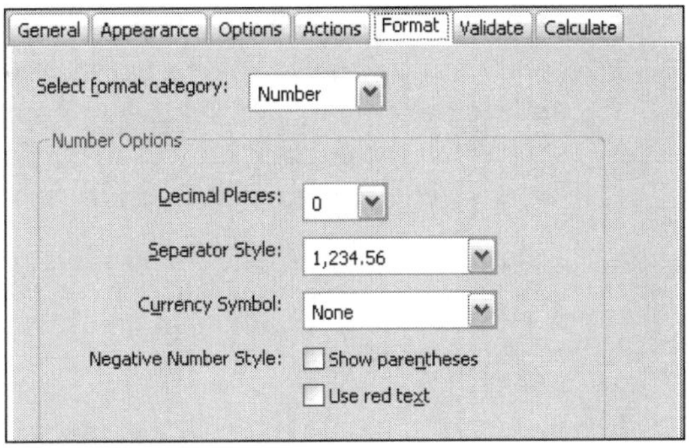

Figure 10.36 *Choose the numerical options on the Format tab.*

Duplicating Fields Automatically

Customers can select three pickles or two orders of coleslaw if they like. The cost of each side dish ordered must to be stored in the form for Acrobat to use to calculate the total order cost; this is accomplished through another set of text fields. These fields are quite different in that they are hidden from view in the final form. Although the customer can't see them, they are certainly valid fields, and used for calculations.

NOTE Although the fields are hidden in the final form, they aren't specified as hidden at this time. Once the form is finished and tested, you'll select and modify the fields' appearance—much simpler than trying to test the form's calculations when you can't see some of the fields!

Acrobat includes a handy feature that lets you create multiples of fields rather than adding and naming a batch of fields. You'll understand why the suggestion was made earlier to leave a generic name for the side dish fields.

Follow these steps to create multiples of fields:

1. Select the four side dish fields using the Text Field tool.

2. Right-click/Control-click to open the shortcut menu, and then choose Create Multiple Copies to open the dialog shown in **Figure 10.38**.

3. The default setting for fields copied both across and down is two fields. Change the values to create the number of fields required. In the project, for a set of four fields vertically, the "Copy selected fields down" field is set to 4, and the "Copy selected fields across" field is set to 1. The values include the original form field—you can't use a value less than 1.

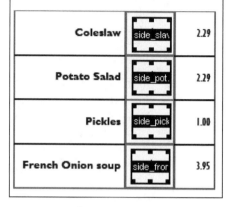

Figure 10.37 Add four fields the customer can use to select side dishes.

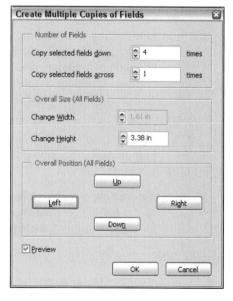

Figure 10.38 Quickly add and distribute a set of fields using this dialog.

4. Adjust the fields' distribution by clicking the up or down arrow in the Change Height field. This is an extremely cool feature, and it can save a lot of time when working with many form fields. If the copies extend both horizontally and vertically, you can adjust both height and width between the fields.

5. Adjust the position of the group of fields if necessary by clicking the appropriate Up/Down/Left/Right buttons.

6. Click OK to close the dialog and complete the fields.

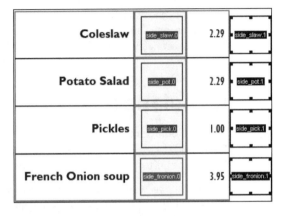

Figure 10.39 *The fields are automatically given sequentially numbered names.*

The fields on the document are renumbered automatically. Each field has a number appended to it, both the original four fields as well as the copies of the fields. For example, the original field named side_slaw is now named side_slaw.0, and its duplicate is named side_slaw.1. You can see the numbering for the fields in **Figure 10.39**. Numbering starts at 0 rather than 1, so if you have a set of four fields, they are numbered from 0 to 3, not from 1 to 4.

The original field isn't really gone—Acrobat builds a subset of the field name. If you check in the Fields pane, you see each field name has a (+) to the left of the listing. Click the (+) to view the nested fields (**Figure 10.40**). The automatic field duplication process produces numbered field names. Whether you change these names to more meaningful names depends on whether you can understand which field is which. It's simple to differentiate the group of fields based on the numbering (used to apply calculations, coming up next), so leaving the automatic numbering will work well in this case.

Figure 10.40 *Acrobat places the automatically numbered fields as subsets of your original field.*

> **PLACING FIELDS**
>
> The four fields added in this section are used for calculating the costs of the side dishes. Their location on the form doesn't really matter as they are eventually hidden from view. However, when you place them as shown in Figure 10.39, the fields are close enough to the originals so that you can understand which part of the form they belong to, and you can also see the side dish costs in the table—important for scripting and testing the fields.

Calculating Costs

Some calculations can be done entirely within the Properties dialog of a form field. In other cases, you need to use JavaScript, which is written in the JavaScript Editor, accessed through the Properties dialog.

There are two ways to calculate the cost of the side dishes ordered in Joe's form—the simple way uses a bit of JavaScript, which is the method Joe opts for. If you're uncomfortable with JavaScript (and you're not alone!), there is a less simple, but equally effective way of adding a set of fields to hold each dish's cost. The nonscripted method adds more fields to the form and requires just a bit more work. You can read how to calculate costs without using any JavaScript in the sidebar "Non-Scripted Calculations" at the end of this section.

Download **joe_javascript.txt** if you want to try the JavaScript in the project but aren't comfortable writing the script yourself. This is a text file that you can copy the scripts from and paste into the JavaScript Editor, as described in the following steps.

Scripting the First Field

Joe's not afraid of a little scripting, so he opts for the JavaScript method.

NOTE In the project, the fields have no borders or background color. These appearance settings are fine if you're among those who can't be bothered adding borders to fields that are to be hidden. On the other hand, you may feel more comfortable adding a border to differentiate the fields more clearly.

Follow these steps to add the first calculation:

1. With the Text Field tool, double-click the first copied field (in the project, this is the side_slaw.1 field) to open the Text Field Properties dialog.

2. Click the Format tab and click the Decimal Places pull-down arrow. Choose 2. The fields are copies of the side dish text entry fields, where the Decimal Place was set to 0 because a customer can't order a fraction of a side dish. You need to use two decimal places to calculate currency.

3. Click the Calculate tab. Click the "Custom calculation script" radio button, and then click Edit (**Figure 10.41**). The JavaScript Editor dialog opens.

4. Type this script in the box, being careful to type the exact punctuation (**Figure 10.42**):

```
var a=this.getField("side_slaw.0")
event.value=a.value*2.29;
```

5. Copy the script before closing the dialog if you have other fields to calculate. In this project, you reuse the majority of the script for the other three side dishes, and rather than starting from scratch each time, you can just modify the pasted script.

6. Click OK to close the JavaScript Editor dialog. The script is transferred to the Calculate tab of the Text Field Properties dialog.

7. Click Close to dismiss the dialog.

Next, you have to repeat the steps for the remaining three side dishes.

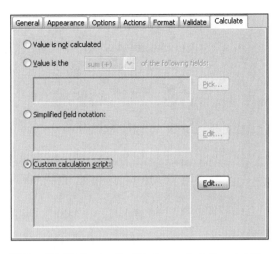

Figure 10.41 Choose the "Custom calculation script" option to add JavaScript to a field.

Figure 10.42 Type the custom script in the JavaScript Editor dialog.

HUH? WHAT DOES THAT SCRIPT MEAN?

Acrobat doesn't offer a way of automatically clicking or typing to use multiplication values in your fields. You have to actually write the script. Here's what the script means:

The first line says that you are naming a variable, "a"—a container to hold data—and states that the field is the side_slaw.0 field. This is the field in which the customers type the desired number of orders they want of a particular side dish, in this case, coleslaw.

The second line says that you want the script to do something, in this case, produce a value. Finally, you tell the program that you want the value of "a", the number the customer typed in the order field, and you want to multiply that value by 2.29, the price of the side dish.

Scripting the Other Side Dish Fields

The form contains a set of four side dishes. The first field is already scripted; now you have to repeat the process for the remaining fields. In each case, select the field for calculation (those ending in ".1"). Be sure to change the Decimal Places Setting to 2 on the Format tab of the Text Box Field Properties dialog.

The scripts used for each of the remaining three side dishes are slightly different from one another. That is, each is given a different variable name, references a different field, and with the exception of the coleslaw and potato salad, has a different value for multiplication. The side dishes, their field names, and the scripts are listed in Table 10.1. For reference, the script described in the first field's set of steps is included in the table.

Table 10.1 Scripts for Side Dish Fields

SIDE	FIELD NAME	CALCULATED FIELD NAME	REQUIRED SCRIPT
Coleslaw	side_slaw.0	side_slaw.1	var a=this.getField("side_slaw.0") event.value=a.value*2.29;
Potato salad	side_pot.0	side_pot.1	var b=this.getField("side_pot.0") event.value=b.value*2.29;
Pickle	side_pick.0	side_pick.1	var c=this.getField("side_pick.0") event.value=c.value*1.00;
French onion soup	side_fronion.0	side_fronion.1	var d=this.getField("side_fronion.0") event.value=d.value*3.95;

A QUICK WAY TO MODIFY FIELDS

You can't change the formatting of a group of fields from the Properties Bar—you have to open the Text Field Properties dialog by double-clicking a field. Make the changes on the first field, and then, instead of closing the dialog and reopening it to modify the next and subsequent fields, just click the field on the form. Automatically, the dialog shows the settings for the selected field, and you can repeat the changes (**Figure 10.43**).

If you move the Text Field Properties dialog to line up with the fields on your form, you can always see the field that is selected. When you are finished—and before you close the dialog—make one last check. Click each field in sequence and make sure the settings are correct.

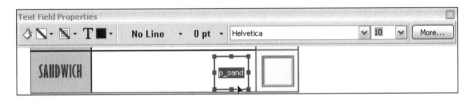

Figure 10.43 *The Text Field Properties dialog bar shows properties for any field you select on the form.*

Testing the Calculated Fields

Now you see the reason not to initially hide a batch of fields that should be hidden in the final form. Click the Hand tool on the Basic toolbar to deselect the fields. Now type values in the side dish text fields. As you click out of each field, the value of the script is calculated and displayed in the set of fields to the right of the side dish table (**Figure 10.44**).

Use multiple values in the amount fields to make sure your multiplication works correctly. Check that you have changed the decimal places on the Format tab. If you find your numbers don't look right, or they don't change, check the scripts. A common error is to use a variable (var = x) in the first line of the script and then forget to change the x.value in the second line of the script to match.

Coleslaw	1	2.29	2.29
Potato Salad	3	2.29	6.87
Pickles	3	1.00	3.00
French Onion soup	2	3.95	7.90

Figure 10.44 *Test the calculated fields to be sure the scripts are correct.*

NONSCRIPTED CALCULATIONS

As mentioned earlier, there's a way to get around adding custom JavaScript and still produce the necessary calculations. Instead of adding one set of fields, you add two—the extra fields hold a default value, which is the cost of the item.

Here's a quick example using a dummy field named "item":

1. Draw a marquee on the form using the Text Field tool, and release the mouse to open the Text Field Properties dialog. Name the field—this example uses the name "item."

2. On the Format tab, choose Number from the Select format category pull-down list, and set the decimal places to 0. Click Close to dismiss the dialog.

3. Right-click/Control-click the field to open the shortcut menu, and choose Create Multiple Copies.

4. In the Create Multiple Copies of Fields dialog, shown in Figure 10.38, set the "Copy fields down" value to 1 and the "Copy fields across" value to 3; click OK to close the dialog. You have three fields respectively named item.0, item.1, and item.2 (**Figure 10.45**).

5. Double-click the item.1 field to open the Text Field Properties dialog.

6. On the General tab, select Hidden from the Form Field pull-down list.

7. Select the Format tab and change the decimal places to 2. This field holds a currency value; the Number format is already chosen because the field is a duplicate of the original item field.

8. Click the item.2 field on the document to display the Text Field Properties dialog for that field. Change the decimal places to 2 again on the Format tab. There isn't a flaw in the program. When you select another field, the Properties dialog shows properties of that field.

9. Select the Calculate tab and click the "Value is the" radio button. Click the pull-down arrow and choose "product (x)" (**Figure 10.46**).

10. Click Pick to open the Field Selection dialog. Click the check boxes for both the item.0 and the item.1 fields, and then click OK to close the dialog. The two fields are listed on the Calculate tab.

11. Click OK to dismiss the dialog.

Now click the Hand tool and type a number in the first field, item.0, as well as the price for the item in the second field, item.1. You see the product of the two fields in the item.2 field (**Figure 10.47**).

The outcome is the same. The only difference between the two methods is that you use an additional set of fields. If you have prices that change frequently, it may be simpler to use this method rather than modifying the JavaScript for each field.

Now back to our regularly scheduled form programming.

Figure 10.45 Use the create Multiple Copies feature to add two additional fields to the document.

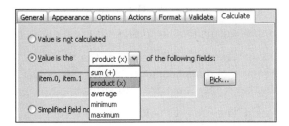

Figure 10.46 Choose the "product (x)" option from the pull-down list.

Figure 10.47 Type amounts and values in the fields to show the result of the calculation.

Adding and Configuring Check Boxes for the Specials

Joe's Deli has daily soup and sandwich specials. In the design of the form shown at the start of this chapter, we saw that Joe intends to type the names of the specials on the form, since he chooses the special every morning based on available ingredients (**Figure 10.48**).

When a customer orders the sandwich special, that's it—the special is ordered, and the sandwich options for breads and fillings should be deselected. But the customer can still

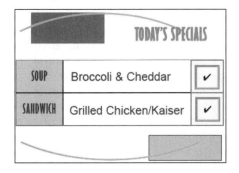

Figure 10.48 The daily specials are added to the form each day.

order the soup special or side dishes—Joe's far too astute a businessman to pass up those sales! On the other hand, if a customer orders the soup special, they should still be able to order anything else from the menu they wish.

Choosing the Soup Special

The two specials have check box fields for the customer to select. The soup special is simpler to program than the sandwich special—all you need to do is add a check box field; in the next section, you also add a calculated text field.

Follow these steps to add and configure a check box for the soup special:

1. Click the Check Box tool ☑ on the Forms toolbar to select it.

2. Draw a marquee on the document where you want to place the check box for the soup special; it can be moved and resized later. Release the mouse to finish the field's marquee and open the Check Box Properties dialog.

3. On the General tab, name the field. The project's field is named s_soup.

4. On the Appearance tab, choose a border and colors for the check box as well as a text size. The size of text you choose determines the size of the checkmark.

5. On the Options tab, select the check appearance from the Check Box Style pull-down menu. Joe uses the default check mark.

6. Type the price of the soup special—3.50—in the Export Value field (**Figure 10.49**). The export value is going to be transferred into a text field to use for calculating the cost of the customer's order.

7. Click Close to close the dialog and complete the field.

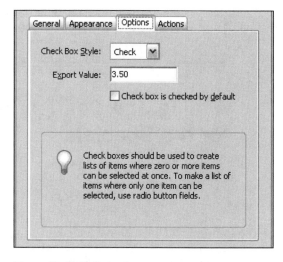

Figure 10.49 *Type the soup special's price in the Export Value field in the dialog.*

The Sandwich Special

Creating the field for the sandwich special is a bit more complex than that for the soup special because you need the form to react when a customer clicks the field. When a customer orders the sandwich of the day, that should be the only allowed sandwich selection on the form. That is, if the sandwich special's check mark is clicked, any choices made available in the bread, filling, or cheese lists should be automatically deselected. You can perform this forms wizardry using actions.

Joe is going to need to copy and paste the check box and place it in the form location for the customer to select the daily sandwich special.

Make these modifications using the Check Box Properties dialog:

1. Double-click the field to open the Check Box Properties dialog, or click More on the Properties Bar if it is open.

2. Rename the field on the General tab. In Joe's project, the field is named s_sand, meaning special sandwich—easy to remember!

3. On the Options tab, change the Export Value to 7.49, which is the price Joe charges for the sandwich of the day.

4. Select the Actions tab.

Here's where it gets interesting...

Assigning Actions to the Check Box

One of the form field actions allows you to specify what happens with other fields when one field is selected. You want the bread, cheese, and fill fields to be deselected when the customer clicks the sandwich special's check box. The actions used in this project produce changes in other fields on the document in response to a customer interacting with the fields. An action or activity that initiates an action or change elsewhere in the document is called a trigger. You can read more about triggers and actions in Chapters 4 and 5.

To create this action, follow these steps:

1. Select the Actions tab. The Select Trigger field shows a Mouse Up trigger by default (**Figure 10.50**). Since you want the customer's order form to reset itself after they click the sandwich special's check box, you can leave the default trigger. When the customer clicks the field and releases the mouse, the action occurs.

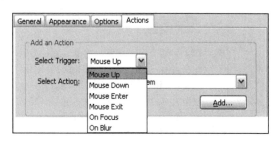

Figure 10.50 Use the Mouse Up trigger for the sandwich special's check box.

2. Click the Select Action pull-down arrow and choose Reset a form (**Figure 10.51**).

3. Click the Add button, shown in Figure 11.50. The Reset a Form dialog opens, and all the fields in the form are listed and selected by default.

4. Click Deselect All to clear the checkmarks beside the names of each field in the dialog's list.

   You only want five fields selected, and it's much quicker to select a few fields than it is to deselect many.

5. Click the proper fields to select the bread, cheese, and fill fields (**Figure 10.52**). Since the fields are listed in alphabetical order, it's easy to find the ones to select. You'll notice that because the selected bread and fill fields are combo boxes, you only have to select five fields in all—much simpler than choosing a field for each item.

6. Click OK to dismiss the dialog, returning you to the Text Field Properties dialog. You see the action is added to the Mouse Up action listing in the Actions portion of the dialog (**Figure 10.53**).

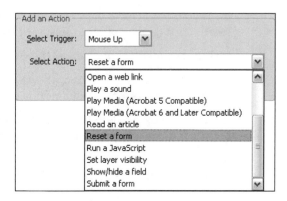

Figure 10.51 The Reset a Form action allows you to pick fields that are affected by the action.

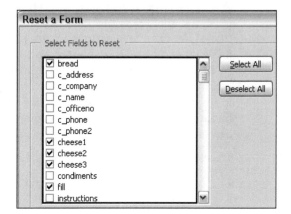

Figure 10.52 Specify the fields to be automatically deselected on the form.

NOTE If you want to check or edit the list, click the name of the action on the dialog to activate the Edit and Delete buttons.

7. Click Close to close the dialog and apply the action to the field.

Be sure to test the specials fields after adding them. Clicking the soup special check box should have no impact on the other fields on the form, but clicking the sandwich special check box should deselect the bread, filling, and cheese options on the form. If it doesn't, check the action you added to the field to be sure the Mouse Up trigger is selected and that the appropriate fields to be reset are selected.

Adding Hidden Text Fields

The specials are chosen using a check box, but Acrobat can't calculate a check box, so you need a pair of text fields to hold the values. These two fields will later be hidden. Like you did in the side dish part of the form, leave the fields visible until the form is complete for ease of testing.

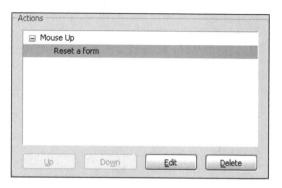

Figure 10.53 *The trigger and its action are listed on the dialog.*

Follow these steps to create the hidden text field (which holds the soup special's value in this project):

1. With the Text Field tool, draw a marquee for a text field and release the mouse to complete the marquee and open the Text Field Properties dialog.

2. Name the field. The sample project's field is named p_soup for "price of the soup" (not pea soup!).

3. Select the Format tab; choose the Number format, and leave the default 2 decimal places.

4. Select the Calculate tab, and then click the "Value is the" radio button. Leave the default "sum (+)" option selected.

5. Click Pick to open the Field Selection dialog, and choose the s_soup field. Click OK to close the dialog.

6. The selected field is shown on the Calculate tab (**Figure 10.54**). Click Close to dismiss the dialog.

General	Appearance	Options	Actions	Format	Validate	Calculate

○ Value is not calculated

◉ Value is the   sum (+) ▾   of the following fields:

s_soup   [Pick...]

Figure 10.54 *The export value entered in the special's Check Box Properties dialog will be converted to a number using the sum calculation.*

You also need a hidden field for the sandwich special. Create another text field, and then follow the same six steps. This time name the field p_sand for the "price of the sandwich" (described in Step 2). In Step 5, select the s_sand field in the Field Selection dialog.

To test the fields, click the Hand tool and then click each check box. When you click the soup special check box, you should see 3.50 appear in the p_soup field; similarly, clicking the sandwich special check box should show 7.49 in the p_sand field (**Figure 10.55**). You'll note in the figure that the two fields are placed in the areas where Joe will identify the specials. Because these are hidden fields, their locations don't matter, so Joe can leave them as is.

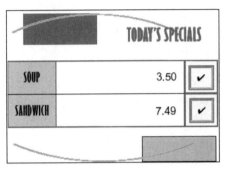

Figure 10.55 *Test the two check boxes to make sure the calculations work correctly.*

Final Form Field Fixes

If a customer clicks the sandwich special check box, choices made in the bread, cheese, and fill fields are automatically deselected. At this stage in the form's development, the reverse condition is not true. That is, if the customer selects the sandwich special, and then has a change of heart and clicks bread, cheese, or filling options, the sandwich special isn't automatically deselected. Deselecting the fields wasn't included earlier in the chapter when these fields were created because the fields for the specials weren't part of the form yet.

Acrobat offers two form field-specific actions called On Blur and On Focus. When a customer clicks a field to type a number, the program's activity moves to, or focuses on the selected field. When the customer clicks another field, the first field is said to be blurred, meaning it is no longer the active field. Before going on to the fields that calculate the order totals, you have to add actions to the bread, cheese, and fill fields so the sandwich special is deselected if the customer later decides to custom-build a lunch order instead of choosing the special. You'll use the On Blur action for this.

To use the On Blur action, follow these steps:

1. Open the field's Properties dialog.

2. On the Actions tab, click the Select Trigger pull-down arrow and choose On Focus.

3. Click the Reset a Form option from the Select Action pull-down list.

4. Click Add to open the Reset a Form dialog. Click Deselect All to clear the checkmarks.

5. Scroll through the list and check the p_sand and s_sand fields. You want to clear both the price and the checkmarks so the price of the sandwich isn't added to the order total by mistake.

6. Click OK to close the dialog; and then click Close to dismiss the Properties dialog.

Use the same steps to apply the field reset to the bread radio buttons, the fillings combo box, and the cheeses check boxes. You don't have to worry about the text fields associated with the filling and cheese selections; when the special is ordered, the filling and cheese options are deselected, and the fields pass a value of 0 to the text fields, which keeps the calculations of the total order correct.

Click the various combinations of fields to be sure the check box and price fields for the sandwich special are cleared when you click a bread radio button or select the pull-down arrows on either the fillings or cheeses combo boxes. If you find you can't make the fields automatically deselect, reopen the Properties dialog for that field, and be sure that you selected the correct fields in the Reset a Form dialog and that you have selected the correct trigger on the Actions tab.

ITEMS TO CHECK AT THIS STAGE OF THE FORM'S DEVELOPMENT

The next-to-final part of form development is the total-cost calculations, and you want the form to be working perfectly before you start adding calculations. Why? Because if you start working with numerous calculated fields and then decide you should have named a set of fields differently, for example, you will add time and unnecessary headache to your calculation process.

Make sure that all forms to be calculated are

- Named correctly. You can use a mixture of automatic and custom naming, as done in this project. Be sure you are comfortable with the names.

- Defined as numbers in the Format tab of the Text Field Properties dialog. Also make sure that all currency fields have decimal places.

- Text fields. Without using complex JavaScript, only text fields can be calculated.

Your Total Is...

Now for the calculation grand finale. At the bottom of the form, there is a small table used to show a customer the subtotal, tax, delivery, and grand total of the orders (**Figure 10.56**). The table needs four fields, each of which needs to be calculated; a couple of them need custom scripts.

Follow these steps to add and configure the first field, the subtotal field:

1. Use the Text Field tool and draw a marquee. Release the mouse to finish the marquee and open the Text Field Properties dialog:

2. On the General tab, name the field. Joe used total.0 as the name in the field. Select both the Read Only and Required check boxes (**Figure 10.57**). You don't want the customer to change the values, and you certainly need a total of the order shown on the form.

3. On the Options tab, click the Alignment pull-down arrow and choose Right.

4. On the Format tab, choose Number from the "select format category" pull-down list, and leave the default of 2 decimal places option.

5. Click Close to dismiss the dialog. You'll come back to the field's properties shortly.

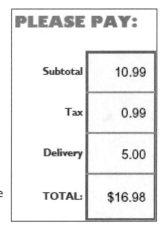

Figure 10.56 *The form includes a table that shows order costs.*

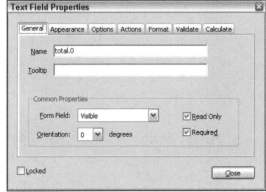

Figure 10.57 *Choose options specific to the totals fields.*

WHY NOT FINISH THE FIELD NOW?

I'm glad I asked. If you choose fields for calculation at this point, when you create the multiples of the fields, you have to then deselect the calculation options from all but the original field. It's far simpler to create the duplicates and then reopen the properties for the first field than it is to delete the calculations from the remaining fields. It's a personal choice, but you'll probably find it saves making time-consuming errors.

Next, create the other three fields following these steps:

1. Right-click/Control-click the total field to open the shortcut menu, and click Create Multiple Copies. The Create Multiple Copies of Fields dialog opens.

2. In the dialog, set the "Copy selected fields down" value to 4; set the "Copy selected fields across" value to 1.

3. Click OK to close the dialog.

Now on the form you see a set of four fields, named total.0 through total.3 (**Figure 10.58**).

This is what each of the four fields will do:

- total.0 adds the totals of the values for soup, sandwich, or sandwich special, cheese, and side dishes ordered.

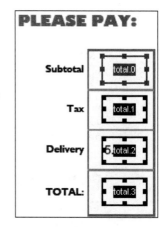

Figure 10.58 *Create a set of four fields by duplicating the first field.*

- total.1 multiplies the value of total.0 by a percentage to arrive at the sales tax.

- total.2 is a flat $5.00 delivery fee that is added to a text field.

- total.3 adds the total of the other three total fields.

Calculate the Subtotal

The four total fields are in place. Now return to the subtotal field.

Follow these steps to select the fields for calculating the subtotal:

1. Double-click the total.0 field to reopen the Text Field Properties dialog, and click the Calculate tab.

2. Click the "Value is the" radio button and leave the default "sum (+)" selection.

3. Click Pick to open the Field Selection dialog. Select the fields that contain calculated values (**Figure 10.59**).

   In the sample form, these are the four fields prefaced with "p_" (the price of the soup special, sandwich special, cheese,

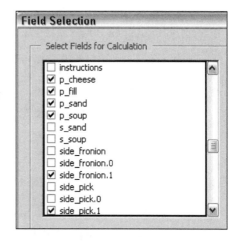

Figure 10.59 *Select all the fields that contain calculated values to use for the subtotal.*

and filling), as well as the calculated fields for the side dishes (for each side dish, these are the side_xxx.1 fields).

4. Click OK to close the Field Selection dialog. The chosen fields are listed on the Calculate tab.

5. Click Close to dismiss the dialog.

It doesn't matter to Acrobat whether there is content in a field or not. If there is no content, the value of 0 is added to the field's total.

Adding Sales Tax to the Order

The tax field—named total.1 in the sample project—calculates a percentage of the subtotal field. The calculation requires JavaScript.

Download **joe_javascript.txt** if you want to try the JavaScript in the project but aren't comfortable writing the script yourself. This is a text file that you can copy the scripts from and paste into the JavaScript Editor, as described in the following steps.

NOTE You can also experiment with a workaround using another field containing the value of the tax and then putting the value of tax into a third field, following the same method as that described earlier for the side dishes' fields in the sidebar, "Nonscripted Calculations."

Follow these steps to add the sales tax calculation to the total.1 field:

1. Double-click the total.1 field on the form to open the Text Field Properties dialog, and then select the Calculate tab.

2. Click the "Custom calculation script" radio button on the Calculate tab, and then click Edit to open the JavaScript Editor dialog.

3. Type this script (**Figure 10.60**):

```
var t1 =this.getField("total.0")
event.value=t1.value*0.09;
```

4. Click OK to close the JavaScript Editor dialog and return to the Text Field Properties dialog.

5. Click OK to dismiss the dialog.

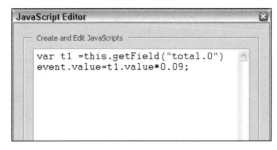

Figure 10.60 Write a script to calculate the tax as a percentage of the order's subtotal.

NOTE The script names a variable, t1 (after the name of the field itself, a simple way to keep track of variables), and says the value of the variable is the contents in total.0, the subtotal field. The second line of the script performs the calculation, which is to multiply the total shown in the subtotal field, total.0, by the tax rate—in this case, 9 percent.

Delivery Charges

Joe doesn't offer his customers free delivery. He charges a flat fee for delivery, and that is displayed in the total.2 field. Instead of using a calculation for this field, instead Joe can simply use a default value for the field. As it is already a read-only field, his customers can't change the default value.

Follow these steps to add the calculation to the total.2 field:

1. Double-click the field to open the Text Field Properties dialog, and click the Options tab.

2. In the Default value field, type 5.00, which is the fixed cost for delivering an order.

3. Click OK to dismiss the dialog.

The Grand Total

The final calculated field on the form is the grand total. Follow the same steps as those listed for the subtotal field, total.0. In the Field Selection dialog, choose the total.0, total.1, and total.2 fields.

To add a finishing touch to the totals, click the Currency Symbol pull-down arrow on the Format tab of the properties dialog, and choose Dollar ($). Now customers will see the totals on the form, the grand total displayed with a dollar sign (**Figure 10.61**).

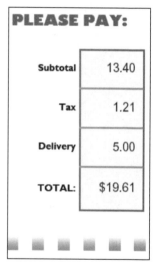

Figure 10.61 The grand total field displays a dollar sign as well as the total order cost.

Final Testing

There are still several button fields to work with, but they have no effect on how the form calculates or works. Before digging into these last few objects, test the form thoroughly by following these steps:

1. Test that all the fields work. Click through the fields and make sure that when you click a field, its appropriate action occurs. For example, if you

choose a filling, when you click another field (or press Enter or Return), the value of the choice should be shown on the p_fill field, and the prices in the total fields should change, with the exception of the delivery charge (the field named total.2).

2. Click all the fields you programmed to reset. For example, clicking the sandwich special check box should deselect bread, filling, and cheese options.

3. Check the field calculations. For example, make sure the tax field calculates correctly and that multiples of side dishes produce the correct value.

Troubleshooting Field Order Errors

If you notice that there is something wrong with how the fields seem to be filling, check the field order. In a form like this one, for example, the subtotal must be calculated before the tax, of course.

To check the field calculation order, and modify it if necessary, do the following:

1. Choose Advanced > Forms > Set Field Calculation Order to open the Calculated Fields dialog (**Figure 10.62**).

2. Click a field that is in the wrong order and click either the Up or Down button to move the field in the list. In Joe's form, the only fields that require a specific location are the three total fields— these fields should follow all the other fields in the form in the order shown in the figure. Remember that total.2 is simply a locked text field with a default value for the delivery charge. It doesn't matter which order a customer clicks the cheese and filling options.

3. Click OK to close the dialog. Test the form again.

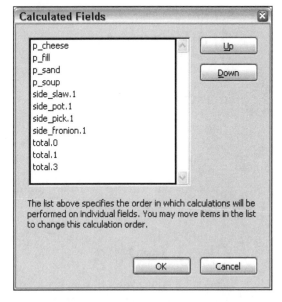

Figure 10.62 Modify the order in which the fields are calculated in this dialog.

Hiding Fields

After you have thoroughly tested your form and are sure it works correctly, that's a good time to hide the fields that don't need to be seen in the final form.

Follow these steps to hide the fields:

1. Ctrl-click/Command-click with the Text Field tool to select the fields to be hidden. These include the four side_xxx.1 fields, and the p_soup and p_sand fields.

2. Click More on the Properties Bar, or right-click/Control-click a field and choose Properties from the shortcut menu.

3. In the Common Properties area on the General tab, click the Form Field pull-down arrow and choose Hidden. Click Close to dismiss the dialog.

One last thing. Look at the fields carefully and tweak any size or alignment problems you discover.

Making the Form Easy to Use

Finally, the last part of the job is here. And to think, this is a simple form! At the bottom right of the sample form is a set of four graphic objects that we'll place buttons over (**Figure 10.63**). Buttons in Acrobat can be very complex and use different button states, or appearances, based on the mouse action. In this case, since the form already includes graphics for each element, we'll simply use buttons without any borders or fills and the default button state. You can read more about button states in Chapter 4.

Joe's hope, and his customers' request, is that ordering be a very simple task. Using FDF (File Data Format) files customers can automatically reorder food items and enter their contact information. In effect, unless there are special instructions, customers using Acrobat don't have to type anything on the form.

Some people are creatures of habit, and they're likely to order the same things on a regular basis. For this reason, all the data from the form fields are both exported from and imported into the form.

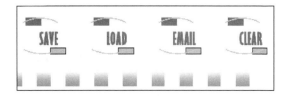

Figure 10.63 Place invisible buttons over the document's graphics for the customer's use.

NOTE You can achieve the same results using a set of links. Since this entire chapter is about forms, and buttons are a form type, let's go with buttons.

The four buttons are designed for these purposes:

- The **Save button** lets a customer save the information in a completed menu form as an FDF file that they can reuse at a later date—perhaps to order lunch tomorrow. All the fields on the form are exported to the saved file.

- The **Load button** loads the customer's FDF file into the form, automatically filling in the fields on the form.

- The **Email button** allows the customer to send Joe an order with a click of the mouse.

- The **Reset button** removes content from all the form fields except the customer's name, address, and telephone and extension numbers.

Saving the Information

The first graphic image on the form is the Save button. Follow these steps to configure a button field for the form:

1. Click the Button tool ▨ on the Forms toolbar, and then drag a marquee over the first graphic object on the form. Release the mouse to finish the marquee and open the Button Properties dialog.

2. Type a name for the field on the General tab. The sample project's field is named b_save. The "b_" naming convention keeps the buttons in a group in the Fields tab and makes it simpler to work with other field selection tasks on the form.

3. Although the instructions for each button are shown on the form just above the set of graphics, you may wish to add tooltips here as well.

4. Select the Appearance tab, and set the border and fill to no color.

5. Click Close to dismiss the dialog.

You return to this button again shortly, but first copy and paste three more buttons. Align and distribute the four buttons over the button graphics on the document.

TIP Once all the common properties are formatted for a set of fields, it's a good idea to duplicate or copy the rest of the fields and then start with the first one again to configure its special features, such as actions or calculations.

Saving the Form's Content

It is convenient for customers to be able to save their contact information and what they have ordered in a file on their hard drive that they can load into the form to fill the fields automatically. Give the customers the option to save their form data by adding an action to the Save button. The Save button will work only in Acrobat, not in Adobe Reader.

Download the sample FDF file named **joe3.fdf** if you want to see the data used in the project's example.

Follow these steps to add and then test the action for the Save button:

1. Double-click the b_save button with the Button tool to reopen the Button Properties dialog.

2. Select the Actions tab, and then click the Select Action pull-down arrow and choose "Execute a menu item" (**Figure 10.64**).

3. Click Add (hidden beneath the pull-down list in Figure 11.64) to open the Menu Item Selection dialog.

4. Choose File > Form Data > Export Data from Form. The command is listed on the dialog (**Figure 10.65**).

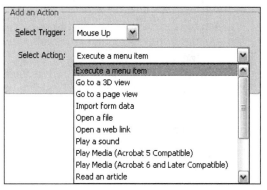

Figure 10.64 *Exporting form data requires using a menu action; select the option on the Actions tab.*

Figure 10.65 *Choose a menu item to use as an action in this dialog.*

5. Click OK to close the Menu Item Selection dialog. You see the action is added to the Actions tab list.

6. Click Close to dismiss the dialog.

TIP Make sure you store the file in a folder that makes sense. For some people, this is within the Acrobat installation folders, for others it may be a folder on the desktop named "Stuff."

To test the button, click the Hand tool and then click the button. The Export Form Data As dialog opens, showing the form's name with the .fdf extension; in the sample project, the file is named joe3.fdf. Change the name if you like, and choose a storage folder. Then click Save to close the dialog and save the file.

Bringing the Data Back

On to the second button—the Load button. This button is designed for the customer filling out the form using Acrobat, not Adobe Reader, to quickly load all the data back into the form so they can make changes as necessary or just reorder. There are actually two different ways to attach a load data file action. One is more practical than the other in this form. You'll see why as you read along.

Follow these steps to add an action to the Load button:

1. Double-click the button over the load graphic to open the Button Properties dialog.

2. On the General tab, rename the button. Joe's button is named b_load.

3. Select the Actions tab. Follow the same steps as you did for the b_Save button, except this time choose File > Form Data > Import Data to Form.

If you look through the Select Action pull-down list, you see an action named Import Form Data. That's not the best action to use in this case because it points to a specific FDF file in a specific location. You want the customers to be able to choose and use their own FDF files.

4. After selecting the action, click Close to dismiss the dialog.

5. Test the field. When you click the b_Load button with the Hand tool, the Select File Containing Form Data dialog opens. Customers can locate and select their own files from wherever they are stored on their computers.

6. Click Select to close the dialog, and note that the content exported from the form earlier is now loaded into the form fields.

E-mailing the Order In

The customer has to have an easy way to send their deli order. Although they can save the form and then attach it to an e-mail, search for Joe's e-mail address, type the address, and then send the e-mail, for some folks that takes longer than walking down the street to the deli and ordering in person.

The Email button automatically sends the form to Joe, regardless of whether the customer is working with Acrobat or Adobe Reader. For this button, you can use a menu action again or one of Acrobat's listed actions. Joes uses the preconfigured action in the project.

Follow these steps to create the Email button:

1. Double-click the button over the e-mail graphic to open the Button Properties dialog.

2. On the General tab, rename the field; Joe uses the name b_email.

3. Select the Actions tab, and then choose the "Submit a form" option from the Select Action pull-down list.

4. Click Add to open the Submit Form Selections dialog.

5. Click the "Enter a URL for this link" field and type the e-mail address prefaced with the mailto: tag (**Figure 10.66**).

THERE IS ANOTHER WAY

If you want your customers to have more control over the e-mail (along with more work), select the "Execute a menu item" action from the Select Action pull-down list, and choose File > Email from the Menu Item Selections dialog. When a customer clicks a button using this action, a blank e-mail dialog opens containing the PDF form, and they have to manually apply the address and then send the e-mail. Alternatively, a button can be programmed using a custom JavaScript to send an e-mail of the entire PDF document directly to Joe.

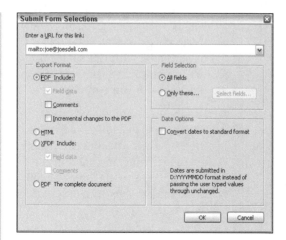

Figure 10.66 Type an e-mail address and the appropriate tag in this field.

6. Leave the remaining default options, and click OK to close the dialog and return to the Button Properties dialog.

7. Click Close to dismiss the Button Properties dialog.

Testing the E-mail

Once you've created the Email button, it's a good idea to test it out. Here's how that's done:

1. Click the Hand tool, and then click the b_email button. The Select Email Client dialog opens.

2. Choose the method you want to use to send the e-mail (**Figure 10.67**). The default option is your Desktop Email Application; choose another option if appropriate. Click OK to close the dialog.

3. The Send Data dialog opens next. From this dialog, you can click Print File if you want a paper copy of your order. Fortunately, you can also click the Don't Show Again check box, so you don't have to deal with this dialog in the future. Click Send Data File to proceed with the e-mail process.

4. Finally, an e-mail dialog opens. The message is addressed to Joe, the FDF file is attached, and there are instructions included in the body of the e-mail (**Figure 10.68**). Click Send to send the order on its way.

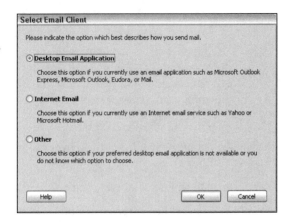

Figure 10.67 *Choose the e-mail method you want to use to send your order to Joe.*

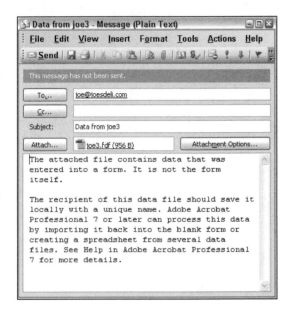

Figure 10.68 *The e-mail dialog is preaddressed, and the FDF file is attached automatically.*

What Happens at Joe's End

When Joe's staff receives an e-mail order, they can import the file directly into a blank form in Acrobat by clicking the Load button on the form or by double-clicking the attachment on the e-mail message. From there, the form can be printed, sent to the kitchen staff for filling, and stapled to the finished order, ready for delivery. Pretty slick, don't you think?

To preserve the integrity of the original form, it's best that Joe save the original using a different name.

Resetting the Contents

Joe adds one last feature to the form for his customers' convenience. A final button is added to reset, or clear, the fields. It's easy to change your mind when filling in a form, and it's annoying to have to search through to make changes manually. The Clear button resets the fields whether the form is being used in Acrobat or in Adobe Reader.

If the form contains a Clear button, you can exclude a customer's contact information from the reset list so the customer can simply select their order items again without having to type their name and contact information manually or reload form data again. It's a nice touch!

Follow these steps to configure the reset button:

1. Double-click the button over the clear graphic on the document with the Button tool to open the Button Properties dialog. Name the button—it is named b_clear in the project.

2. Select the Actions tab, and then click the Select Action pull-down arrow and choose "Reset a Form."

3. Click Add to open the Reset a Form dialog. By default, all the fields on the form are selected.

4. Deselect only those fields that hold customer contact information. In this project, these fields were prefaced with "c_," making them easy to select on the dialog.

5. Click OK to close the dialog, and then click Close to dismiss the Button Properties dialog.

6. Click the Hand tool, and then click the Clear button. You should see all the fields on the form except the customer's information reset (either cleared or set back to their default values).

Download **joe3.pdf** if you want to see the completed form as constructed in this project.

What Else Can He Do?

The sky is the limit when it comes to form design. Joe might like to further automate some of the features of his menu, offering wider ranges of options for different sandwiches, for example. It may be a good idea to add an automatic time and date field to the form so his kitchen staff can sequence the orders more precisely. He might want to add a document JavaScript that pops up a "Thank You for Ordering" message when a customer sends an e-mail, or plays a tune while the customer is deciding on an order—who said Muzak was the exclusive domain of elevators! If you can think it, Acrobat can probably provide it.

As Joe ponders his new form, he starts thinking about other aspects of his business, like customer feedback. Wouldn't it be cool if he could...

You guessed it! Joe is becoming hooked on Acrobat forms. Join him one more time in Bonus Chapter 3 on the book's Web site as he investigates Adobe Designer, Acrobat's integrated forms design program included in Acrobat 7 Professional for Windows.

11

Working with Technical Drawings

Acrobat 6 Professional was the first version of Acrobat that allowed you to work with layered technical drawings, created in either Microsoft Visio or AutoCAD. Continuing this trend for supporting technical and engineering information in PDF format, Acrobat 7 Professional offers additional tools and options, including a tool that enables you to convert metadata stored within a drawing so that you can view it in the PDF file. *Metadata* is embedded in the source program in Windows, either AutoCAD or Microsoft Visio, and can be read in Acrobat or Adobe Reader using the Object Data tool.

In this chapter, you'll see how a landscape architect shares a plan, created in Microsoft Visio, with a landscape contractor, who can use Adobe Reader 7 to read and work with the embedded data in the PDF file.

Acrobat 7 Professional includes a set of measuring tools the architect uses to identify perimeter, distance, and area in a drawing. Because his plan is drawn to scale, the architect uses the scale to interpret the measurements and then place them and other information in comments that are to be shared with the contractor.

Technical drawings, such as the plan used in this chapter's project, can also be protected using a security policy. Refer to the bonus material on the book's Web site (www.donnabaker.ca/downloads) to see how to create and use a digital signature. In addition, you'll learn how to exchange digital certificates with others, and how to read and extract information from a signature file.

The first part of this project, converting the Visio drawing to PDF, is exclusive to Windows; however, manipulating the drawing, signing it, and sending it for review can be done in either Windows or Mac OS.

That's the Plan

Tyler "Ty" Wilson is a landscape architect specializing in residential design and development. Although he typically works on large, multiple-dwelling projects, he is quite busy with projects for individual homeowners. Ty uses several programs to develop his landscape plans, often opting for Visio for small residential designs.

The project he is working with today is the backyard of the Taylor family, a lovely couple with two small children and a couple of big dogs. They want a kid-friendly backyard and a big fence to contain their mutts, who have a tendency to tour the neighborhood. Ty's contractor on this project is Syd.

Ty is looking for a way to communicate efficiently with Syd and the Taylors. For this and future projects, Ty would like to be able to build his plans and then distribute them as necessary in one format. Currently, he has to generate multiple versions of his drawings so they can be read by contractors and clients in their various reading programs. He also has to send lists of specs and requirements in e-mails separate from those with the plans attached. Ty would like to settle on one format that could easily be adopted by all, and he thinks PDF is the way to go.

He'd like to embed information about project components right in the PDF, and fortunately he can do that as well using Acrobat 7 Professional. He can also add measurements of different project elements as comments in the PDF document before sending it to his contractor. Ty would also like to enable his contractor to estimate project costs directly from the drawings. If he generates PDF versions of his drawings, he can enable commenting in the drawings that allow contractors to work directly with commenting tools on the PDF drawing, in either Acrobat 7 or Adobe Reader 7.

Ty's looking for an all-in-one solution. He wants a drawing that can be read easily, display metadata, be measured, commented on, and exchanged securely (**Figure 11.1**). He's got a lot to learn!

Use measuring tools to accurately measure content to a specified scale.

Work with custom information added in the source drawing.

Convert measurements to comments for future reference.

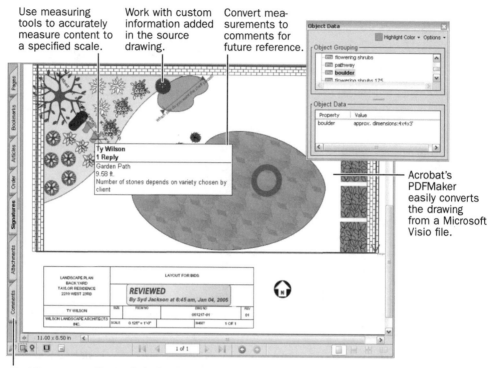

Acrobat's PDFMaker easily converts the drawing from a Microsoft Visio file.

Enabling commenting tools in Acrobat 7 Professional allows users with Adobe Reader to work with the drawing.

Figure 11.1 *Ty's drawing can be enabled and used for many purposes.*

NOTE Don't try this at home, kids! The drawing shown in Figure 11.1 is a composite image showing many different features used in this project. You can't work with all the tools and dialogs shown in this figure all at the same time.

Steps Involved in This Project

Ty has a number of steps to follow in this project. You know, of course, that it will all work out in the end! Ty needs to

- Convert his Visio drawing to PDF and enable the embedded data that he includes in the drawing for viewing by his contractor

- Add measurements as comments in the PDF drawing for his contractor to use for estimating costs

- Enable the drawing to be used by Syd, who works with Adobe Reader 7, and then e-mail the file to him

- Syd will then use the Commenting and Object Data tools in Adobe Reader 7 to work with the drawing

- As a final touch, Syd will add a dynamic stamp to the document that places his name and the date on the file before sending just the comment data back to Ty

- Ty will receive the comment data and add it to his copy of the drawing

Ty's first step is to convert his Visio drawing.

Converting the Drawing

The PDFMaker that Acrobat 7 installs automatically in Visio has the ability to convert multi-layered Visio drawings to PDF, maintaining the layers as individual PDF layers. (You can read about using a layered document in Bonus Chapter 2 on the book's Web site.) In Ty's drawing, however, maintaining the individual layers isn't important for his purpose, so he's going to export the PDF as a single layer.

There are two parts to the conversion process: First, Ty has to choose conversion settings according to his drawing's use, and then he has to convert the drawing.

 If you use Microsoft Visio and would like to convert the source file yourself, download **taylor_project.vsd.**

Choosing Conversion Settings

As previously mentioned, Ty doesn't need separate layers for his drawings, so he'll flatten the drawing to a single layer.

Follow these steps to choose conversion settings for the drawing:

1. In Visio, choose Adobe PDF > Change Conversion Settings to open the Acrobat PDFMaker dialog.

2. Click the Conversion Settings pull-down arrow and choose Standard if it isn't shown by default.

   Ty would like the option to print the plan as well as view it onscreen, and the Standard setting allows him to do both.

3. In the Application Settings portion of the dialog, leave the "Include Visio custom properties as object data" in the Adobe PDF option selected, as well as its subselection, "Exclude Visio objects with no custom data."

    In Ty's project, whether he deselects the exclusion option or not makes no difference in the exported drawing because all objects have custom data.

4. Click OK to close the dialog.

Once the conversion settings are chosen, Ty can create the PDF version of the drawing.

Performing the Conversion

Follow these steps to work through the Visio PDFMaker's dialogs and convert the drawing to PDF:

1. Click the Convert to Adobe PDF icon ![icon] on the PDFMaker toolbar, or choose Adobe PDF > Convert to PDF to open the first pane of the dialog.

2. The conversion settings option to include custom properties (object data), which is shown again in the first pane of the dialog. Leave the check box selected and click Continue.

3. Choose the layering option for the page; the default, Flatten all layers, is used in Ty's project (**Figure 11.2**). Click Continue.

4. A confirmation pane opens describing your layer choices (**Figure 11.3**). Click Convert to PDF.

5. A Save Adobe PDF File As dialog opens, using the Visio document's name and folder location by default. If you like, change the name and choose an alternate storage location. Ty uses the default, and his drawing is saved as taylor_project.pdf.

6. Click Save to dismiss the dialog and convert the drawing.

Now that Ty's drawing is converted, he can open it in Acrobat and get to work.

Figure 11.2 Select how the layers are handled in the PDF file.

Figure 11.3 The PDFMaker confirms your layer choices.

Viewing the Document Status

When the PDF file is opened in Acrobat, a Document Status dialog displays (**Figure 11.4**). The dialog describes the special features in the document—in this case, the object data. Click Close to dismiss the dialog. You see the Object Data icon displayed on the Status bar across the bottom of the program window. When Ty moves his pointer over the Object Data icon, a tooltip displays basic information about using the Object Data tool (**Figure 11.5**).

Ty's first task is to add some measurements in Acrobat. (By the way, he can also add measurements in the Visio drawing, but that program isn't the subject of this book!)

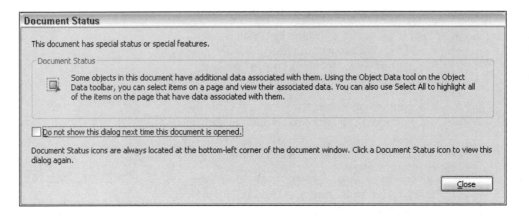

Figure 11.4 *The document's object data comprise a special status item, as described in the dialog.*

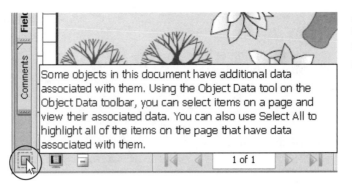

Figure 11.5 *Acrobat displays the Object Data icon and tooltips at the bottom of the program window.*

Measuring Objects

Acrobat 7 Professional includes several tools you can use to measure elements on a page, such as the distance between two columns of text, or the space between two objects in a PDF drawing. If you are working with a scaled drawing, as Ty is in his project, you'll even be able to assign a scale. (You can choose from a number of values, such as pixels, inches, or even miles!) If you add annotations to the measurements, the values are converted to comments in the PDF file. For more information on working with comments in general, see Chapters 13 and 14.

Download **taylor_project.pdf** if you'd like to practice adding measurements to the drawing. Ty is adding several measurements to the drawing, and if you prefer to see the drawing complete with his measurements, download **taylor_project_M.pdf**.

To open the Measuring toolbar, choose Tools > Measuring > Show Measuring Toolbar (**Figure 11.6**). Since Ty is working with all the tools, it's simpler to open the toolbar. He could also right-click/Control-click the toolbar well at the top of the program window and click Measuring to open the toolbar.

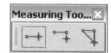

Figure 11.6 *Acrobat 7 Professional includes a set of measuring tools.*

Ty is adding several measurements in the drawing that will help Syd, his contractor, prepare his estimates. The three tools on the toolbar measure distance, perimeter, and area, and Ty uses all three in the drawing. First up, he'll measure distance.

Measuring Distance on a Drawing

Ty uses the Distance tool to measure the distance between two discrete points on the plan. He wants to measure the length of a path in the planting bed and use that measurement as well as text in a comment.

Follow these steps to perform the measurement:

1. Zoom into the drawing at a magnification that clearly shows the content you want to measure. The magnification level depends on the drawing's content and the area you want to view.

2. Click the Distance tool  on the Measuring toolbar; the pointer changes to crosshairs, and the Distance Tool dialog displays (**Figure 11.7**).

3. The drawing's scale is ⅛"=1', which is set using the decimal equivalent in the dialog (0.125 in = 1 ft). Type 0.125 in the Scale Ratio field. Leave the default inch value.

4. Click the pull-down arrow for the second scale ratio value, which defaults at 1 inch, and select "ft" from the pull-down list.

Figure 11.7 Choose scale settings for the tool in the dialog.

5. Click the Measurement Markup check box to activate the annotation field, which also saves the measurement as a comment. Type text in the field to represent the measurement—Ty types Garden Path. In the drawing, the length of the garden path is being measured.

6. Click the location for the first point on the drawing; in Ty's drawing, the first point is placed next to the garden bench.

7. Drag to the second point; in the drawing, the second point is clicked at the edge of the planting bed (**Figure 11.8**).

8. Click the mouse again to complete the measurement. A line is added to the page complete with end arrows. The Markup Annotation and the length of the line are shown on the page as well (**Figure 11.9**).

Figure 11.8 Place the start and end points with the tool.

NOTE To stop the drawing process, select another tool from any toolbar or press the Esc key on your keyboard.

Ty has added the length of the garden path to the drawing. Later, before sending it to Syd, his contractor, he'll add more information to the measurement's comment. Next, he's going to measure the perimeter of the garden.

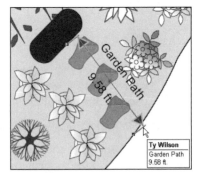

Figure 11.9 The drawing shows the measured area as well as a label and the distance.

Measuring the Perimeter of an Object

Ty's plan calls for a brick wall around three sides of the garden. He has included object data describing the wall (as you'll see in the "Viewing Object Data" section), but he wants to have the measurement added to the drawing as well. Because he already set the scale ratio in the previous section, Ty doesn't need to enter it again. When he uses another tool, the ratio is automatically set, saving time when working with the drawing.

Follow these steps to measure an object's perimeter:

1. Zoom in or out of the Document pane to display the area for measuring. In the project, the brick wall surrounds the drawing area.

2. Click the Perimeter tool ⊹ on the Measuring toolbar; the pointer changes to crosshairs, and the Perimeter Tool dialog displays.

3. Type a new Measurement Markup Annotation in the field; Ty types `Brick Wall Exterior Dimensions` (**Figure 11.10**).

4. Click the point where the measurement is to start; in Ty's project, the first point is set at the lower-left edge of the brick wall.

    As you move the mouse and click, the values being measured are displayed on the Perimeter Tool dialog; the Distance, Perimeter, and Angle settings are shown in Figure 11.12.

5. Click the location for the next point; in the project, this is the upper-left edge of the brick wall.

    To limit, or *constrain*, the segments to straight lines as you draw, hold the Shift key as you drag and click the mouse.

6. Add the remaining two points at the upper right and lower right of the brick wall.

7. Click the mouse again to complete the measurement.

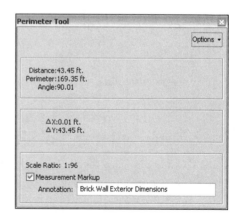

Figure 11.10 *The annotation and measurements are shown in the dialog.*

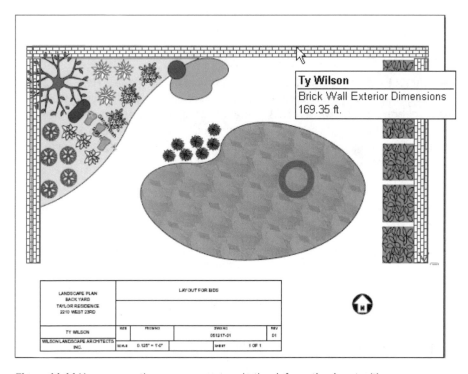

Ty Wilson
Brick Wall Exterior Dimensions
169.35 ft.

Figure 11.11 *You can see the measurement and other information in a tooltip.*

8. Click the Hand tool or another tool on any toolbar and move the pointer over the perimeter line added to the drawing. You see Ty's name, the annotation, and the measured perimeter in a tooltip (**Figure 11.11**).

Two down and one to go. Ty also wants to determine the area of the patio. He can measure the area using—you guessed it—the Area tool.

Determining the Size of an Area

Finally, Ty wants to measure the large flagstone patio the Taylors want in their backyard. He can use the Area tool to define the size of the patio, which Syd can then use to estimate material costs for constructing the patio.

Follow these steps to define an area on a drawing:

1. Display the region to be measured on the Document pane. Zoom in or out as necessary to show the entire region.

2. Choose the Area tool from the Measuring toolbar.

A circle displays when the tool
is over the original point.

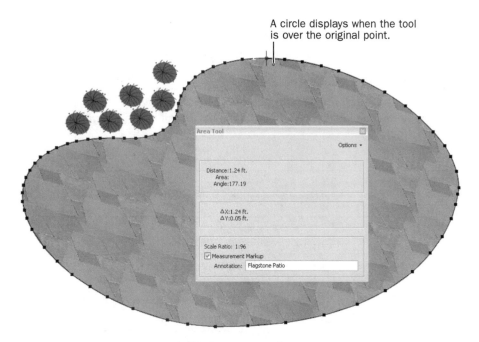

Figure 11.12 *Draw points around a shape to measure its area.*

3. Type an annotation in the Area Tool dialog. Ty types Flagstone Patio for his
drawing.

4. With the tool, click a series of points along the perimeter that defines
what you want to measure. Since Ty is following a curved shape, that's a
fair number of points added to the drawing (about 70 points in all).

5. When you return to the first point added to the area, you see a circle
below the crosshairs, which means the shape is closed (**Figure 11.12**). Click
the first point again to complete the area.

Ty has finished adding measurements to the drawing, which were added to the
PDF file as comments. He'd like to add some more information to those comments; that's coming up in the next section.

Modifying Annotations

When Ty added the measurements to his drawing, he clicked the Measurement
Markup check box on the tool's dialog and typed text in the Annotation field.
Acrobat converts the text and measurement to a comment. Comments can be

viewed by moving the pointer over a measured area and viewing the content in a tooltip, like that seen in Figure 11.11, for example. Ty can also work with the comments in the Comments pane, one of Acrobat's Navigation tabs.

To view the comments and add information, follow these steps:

1. Select the Comments tab at the left of the program window; the Comments pane is displayed across the bottom of the program window (**Figure 11.13**).

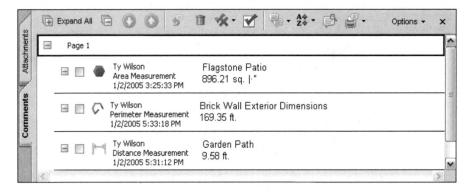

Figure 11.13 The measurement comments are listed in the Comments pane.

2. Click Expand All on the toolbar at the top of the Comments tab to open all three comments in the page.

   You can also click the (+) to the left of each comment, which toggles to (–), as shown in the figure, indicating the comment is expanded.

3. Click the comment text to activate the text field. The text includes both the annotation typed in the tool's dialog as well as the measurement.

4. Type additional text in the comment field as required. Ty adds more information about all the measured areas (**Figure 11.14**).

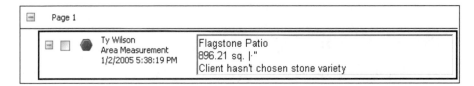

Figure 11.14 You can add more text to a comment in the Comments pane.

5. Move the pointer over a measured area on the drawing; you see the additional text shown in the tooltip (**Figure 11.15**).

6. Click in a measured area on the drawing with the Hand tool to see the text shown in a pop-up box (**Figure 11.16**).

7. To close the Comments pane, select the Comments tab again.

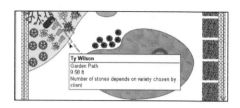

Figure 11.15 Additional text displays in the measured area's tooltip.

Save the file. The version of Ty's drawing used to this point in the project is saved as taylor_project_M.pdf ("M" for "measured").

All Ty has left to do is to enable the file to be used with Adobe Reader and then e-mail it to Syd.

If you'd like to experiment with Ty's file in Adobe Reader 7, download **taylor_project_E.pdf** from the Web site. This version of the file has been enabled for use in Adobe Reader 7.

Enabling the File for Use in Adobe Reader

First Ty has to enable the file to be used by Syd, who uses Adobe Reader, not Acrobat.

Follow these steps to prepare the file:

1. Choose Comments > Enable for Commenting in Adobe Reader. A Save As dialog opens.

2. Save the file with an alternate name; the project is saved as taylor_project_E.pdf ("E" for "enabled," get it?).

Figure 11.16 The Comment's popup box shows the text from the Comments pane.

Before e-mailing the drawing, take a look at the lower left of the program window. You see a new icon on the Status bar . This icon means that the document has been enabled for use in Adobe Reader.

E-mailing the Drawing

Finally, Ty sends the file to Syd.

Follow these steps to e-mail a PDF file from Acrobat:

1. Open the document you want to send in Acrobat. Ty is sending the taylor_project_E.pdf file.

2. Choose File > Email to open an e-mail message window. The e-mail uses filename as the subject line and includes the open **Figure 11.17**).

3. Enter the recipient's e-mail address, and send the file.

That's all there is to it! Ty is finished for the day.

Now we'll turn to Syd's tasks. He's going to work with the drawing's embedded data and comments. Since Ty enabled the document's Commenting features, Syd can work in Adobe Reader 7.

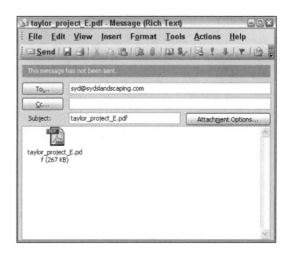

Figure 11.17 *The open PDF file is included as an attachment to the e-mail.*

Opening the Drawing in Adobe Reader

Syd saves the e-mailed PDF file and then opens it in Adobe Reader. When the file opens, a Document Bar displays above the Document window stating that the document is enabled for use in Adobe Reader (**Figure 11.18**). Click Hide to close the Document Bar and save screen space.

NOTE If the document had been distributed using Acrobat's Review features, a How To window would also display. Read about using the review process in Chapters 13 and 14.

Now that Syd has seen the lay of the land, so to speak, he's ready to dig into the drawing and see what he can uncover. OK, maybe that's a cheesy metaphor—but he is a landscaper, after all.

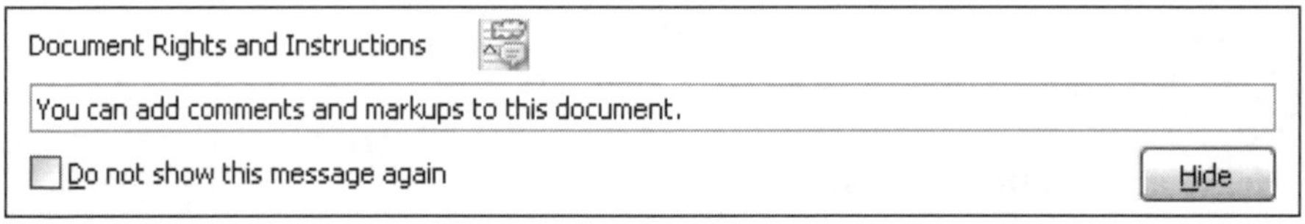

> Document Rights and Instructions
>
> You can add comments and markups to this document.
>
> ☐ Do not show this message again   Hide

Figure 11.18 *Because Ty enabled the document in Acrobat 7 Professional, Syd can use the Commenting tools in Adobe Reader.*

Viewing Object Data

When Ty created his drawing in Visio, he included custom properties for the objects and groups of objects in the drawing. This information contains details about specific parts of the project, such as types of plants he'd like to use, details about the structures that need building, and so on. In the section "Converting the Drawing," you saw Ty include these custom properties and how Acrobat obliged by converting them to object data.

Displaying Object Data

Acrobat 7 Professional and Adobe Reader 7 offer the Object Data tool, which can be used to identify and examine data embedded in the PDF file's source file as custom properties. The Object Data tool—the single tool on the Object Data toolbar—is automatically enabled in this project because the file contains the appropriate type of objects.

Follow these steps to examine Object Data in a project file:

1. Open the Object Data toolbar by choosing Tools > Object Data > Show Object Data Toolbar in Adobe Reader 7.

2. Choose the Object Data tool  from the toolbar, or select it from the Tools menu.

   When you mouse over an object on a drawing that contains metadata, the pointer changes to crosshairs (**Figure 11.19**).

3. Double-click the object to select it—the first click selects all the objects with data on the drawing and the second click selects just the object below the crosshairs. The Object Data dialog opens, and the contents of the embedded data are shown in the dialog (**Figure 11.20**).

   As you can see in the figure, the drawing contains a large number of objects that include data. Click through the objects in the drawing to see the data.

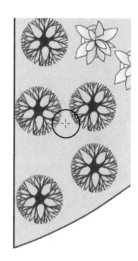

Figure 11.19 The Object Data tool displays crosshairs when moved over objects containing metadata.

Figure 11.20 Information about the selected object is shown in the dialog. The Property and Value custom data were added in the source program.

4. To work with the drawing's data, click the Options button on the Object Data dialog and select different functions, such as zooming to the selected object, counting similar objects, or copying the content to the clipboard.

Fun with Objects

Here are some experiments you can try with the drawing's object data:

■ Click the Highlight Color pull-down arrow on the Object Data dialog to open a color picker, and choose another color for the highlighting identifying a selected object.

■ Choose the object Rectangle.4 from the list, and then click the Options pull-down arrow and choose Count. The Adobe Reader dialog opens, listing the number of objects having the same data associations. In this case, the brick walls are each separate rectangles; together they make up the wall, and each contains the same object data.

■ Select an object from the Object Data dialog, and then choose Zoom to Selection from the Options menu on the dialog. You see the drawing resets itself in the Document pane to display the selected object (**Figure 11.21**).

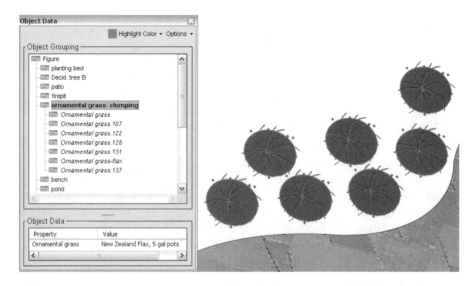

Figure 11.21 Use the Zoom to Selection option to quickly reset the drawing in the program window.

- Click through several of the listings in the Object Data dialog, and you see they expand and contract automatically. If an object was built as a group, when you click its name, the component elements are listed; clicking another object in the dialog collapses the group automatically. The ornamental grasses shown in Figure 11.21 are an example.

- To go back to an object you have previously viewed, choose Previous View from the Options menu on the Object Data dialog.

Enough fooling around—Syd's got work to do! In the next section, you'll see how he uses a combination of Commenting tools and Object Data information to add his content to the drawing.

Adding Comments to the Drawing

There are a few things that Syd needs to add to the drawing. For example, he has to ask Ty to clarify some details before he can complete his cost estimates. He'll respond to one of Ty's comments and add two comments of his own.

If you'd like to see the content Syd added to the drawing, download **taylor_project_syd.pdf** from the Web site. Otherwise, you can experiment with the version of the file you have opened in Adobe Reader (or Acrobat).

Responding to Comments

Rather than littering a page with a great number of new comments, you can simply reply to an existing comment.

Follow these steps to add a comment response:

1. Select the Comments tab at the left of the program window to display the Comments pane across the program window.

2. Select the comment you'd like to respond to.

3. Click Reply on the Comments pane toolbar; a Reply row is added to the Comments pane (**Figure 11.22**).

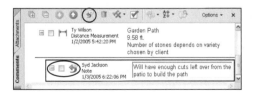

Figure 11.22 *Reply to a comment rather than adding a separate comment to the drawing.*

4. Type the text for your response. Syd types: `Will have enough cuts left over from the patio to build the path.`

When Ty receives the comments back from Syd, he'll see his response.

Using Object Data Information in a Comment

Syd wants to ask Ty a question about one of the plant selections and decides to copy the property and value from the object data into a new comment.

Follow these steps to use the object's metadata:

1. Click the Object Data tool to select it, and then click the object on the drawing to open the Object Data dialog.

    Syd wants to inquire about the shrub hedge at the right of the garden, called "shrubs" in the Object Data dialog (**Figure 11.23**).

2. Click the text under Property and Value in the Object Data area at the bottom of the dialog to select it.

3. Click the Options pull-down arrow, and choose Copy Data to Clipboard.

4. Close the Object Data dialog.

5. Choose Tools > Commenting > Note Tool. If you prefer, choose Tools > Commenting > Show Commenting Toolbar to open the toolbar on the program window, and then click the Note tool.

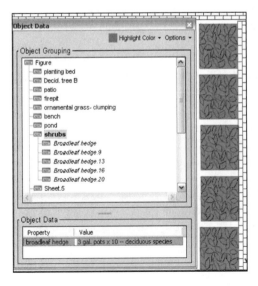

Figure 11.23 Select the object on the drawing to have it automatically selected in the Object Data dialog.

6. Click the drawing with the Note tool where you'd like to place the comment. Syd clicks over the sketch of the shrubs.

7. A note box opens; choose Edit > Paste or use the shortcut keys Ctrl/Command-V to paste the copied object data into the comment.

8. Type additional text for the comment (**Figure 11.24**).

When Ty reviews the drawing, he'll be able to see immediately what Syd is referring to without having to use the Object Data tool.

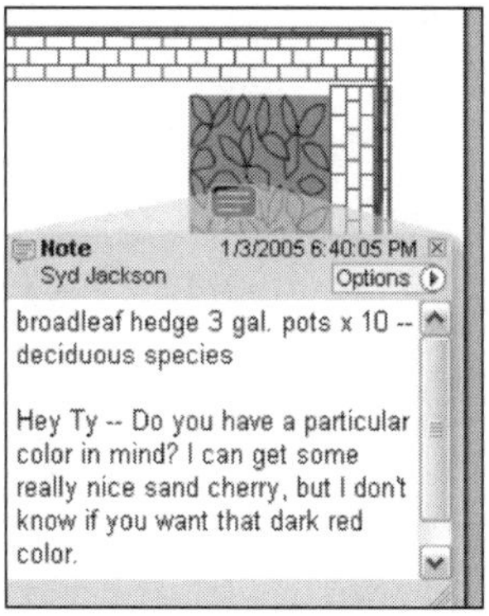

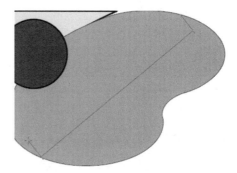

Figure 11.24 *You can use both pasted text and new text in a comment.*

Using Dimension Comments

The third comment Syd adds to the drawing uses the Dimensioning tool, available on the Drawing Markups toolbar and one of the specialized Commenting tools. The Dimensioning tool lets Syd add a line with two endpoints to the drawing.

Follow these steps to add a Dimensioning comment to the file:

1. Choose Tools > Drawing Markups > Dimensioning. If you prefer, choose Tools > Commenting > Show Drawing Markups Toolbar to open the toolbar on the program window, and then click the Dimensioning tool ⊡.

2. Click the drawing where you want to place the first point on the line, drag to where you'd like the end point, and click again (**Figure 11.25**).

3. Release the mouse to complete the line; you'll see an active cursor where text can be typed for a comment.

4. Type the comment, then press Esc on the keyboard or select another tool to finish the comment.

Figure 11.25 *Use the Dimensioning tool to draw a measured comment line on a file.*

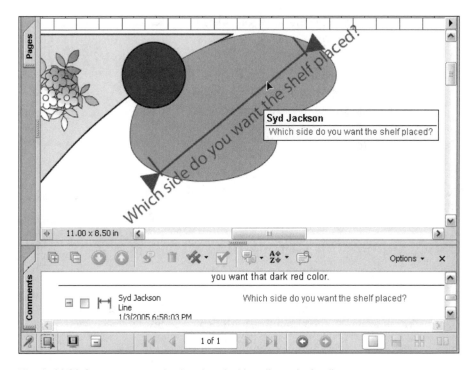

Figure 11.26 *Comments can also be placed with a dimensioning line.*

5. Move the pointer over the line. You'll see that the text has been added in a tooltip in addition to being added on the drawing and in the Comments pane (**Figure 11.26**).

In the real world, it's very likely that many, many more comments would be added to the drawing. In the name of expediency (and mindful of your boredom threshold!), this concludes the addition of comments in this project.

Next Syd's going to add a dynamic stamp comment before sending it back to Ty.

Adding a Dynamic Comment

The final phase of this epic journey is for Syd to add a dynamic stamp showing the date and time before he sends it back to Ty. One group of Commenting tools is called Stamp tools, and they do indeed work like old-fashioned ink stamps. Of course, since they are digital, the stamps can be made dynamic. That is, they can include a name and date stamp with the graphic image of a stamp. Syd uses one of Acrobat's dynamic stamps for the drawing.

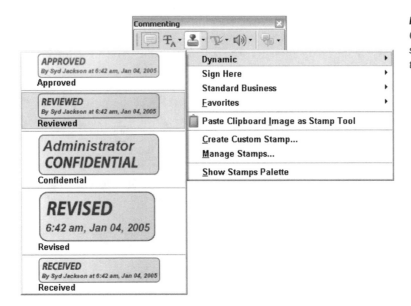

Figure 11.27
Choose a dynamic stamp from the toolbar's menu.

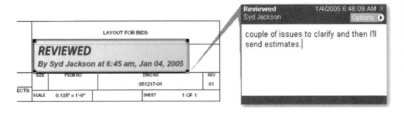

Figure 11.28 *Click the page to apply the stamp. You can add text in a comment box as well.*

Follow these steps to add a Dynamic stamp to the drawing:

1. Choose Tools > Commenting > Show Commenting Toolbar to open the toolbar. If you like, you can drag it to dock with the other toolbars at the top of the program window if you like.

2. Click the Stamp tool pull-down arrow to open its menu, and click Dynamic > Reviewed (**Figure 11.27**). The stamp becomes active.

3. Move the stamp over the page and click the location where you'd like it placed. The stamp is placed on the page, and a comment box opens.

4. Type any additional information in the comment box, if needed (**Figure 11.28**).

5. Save the file one last time to preserve the comments added to the drawing.

Syd's final task is to send the comments back to Ty. He could use the same method Ty used—that is, e-mail the entire PDF file—or he can send just the comments back, which he decides to try. What could it hurt? He's getting into this digital communication thing.

Sending Comments

Syd decides to send just the comments back to Ty. As you'll see in this section, comments can be exported as an FDF file, which is a very small file. In this project, the comments file is 11 KB, whereas the entire drawing is about 350KB. Sending and receiving comments is a very efficient way to exchange information.

 Download **taylor_project_syd.fdf** if you'd like to work with Syd's comments, or try exporting your own.

To send just the comments from a file, follow these steps in Adobe Reader:

1. Choose Document > Comments > Export Comments to open the Export Comments dialog.

2. Adobe Reader uses the filename and its storage location by default. In this case, the file is named taylor_project_syd.fdf.

3. Click Save to dismiss the dialog and save the comments' file.

4. To send the comments file, Syd opens an e-mail window, addresses it to Ty, and then attaches the taylor_project_syd.fdf file.

Integrating Comments

Down the road, Ty receives the e-mail from Syd in his in-box. Syd saved a copy of the file and sent just the comments back to Ty. The comments' file is named taylor_project_syd.fdf, and Ty doesn't have a copy of the drawing with that name. Not to worry—he can integrate the comments into any of his copies of the plan.

In this case, he'll use the taylor_project_E.pdf file because that was the version of the plan he mailed to Syd.

When he receives the e-mail, he can do one of the following:

■ Double-click the attachment in the e-mail message to open Acrobat.

- Save the attachment on his hard drive, and then open his last version of the file and import the comments into it.

Let's look at both of these options, starting with the e-mail attachment.

NOTE There are no Web files for this section. The comments file, **taylor_project_syd.fdf**, is on the Web site, and you can integrate it into any of the other versions of the drawing.

Integrating Comments from an E-mail Window

The first option is to work from the e-mail window. If Ty doesn't have Acrobat already open, it's simpler to open the file directly.

Follow these steps to integrate comments into an alternate document:

1. Double-click the attachment in the e-mail message.

2. Acrobat opens and searches for the file. When it isn't found, which of course is the case as Syd has the only copy using his name in the file name, the dialog shown in **Figure 11.29** displays.

3. Click Yes to dismiss the dialog; a Select File Containing Form dialog opens. Because the comments are stored in an FDF file, Acrobat defines the content as a form.

4. Choose the file you want to integrate the comments into, and click Select. Ty uses the taylor_project_E.pdf file.

5. The dialog closes, the chosen file opens, and the comments are imported into the document.

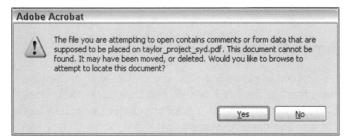

Figure 11.29 Acrobat tries to integrate the comments into the document, but the attempt failed.

Comment including
copied object data

Reviewed stamp
comment

Dimensioning
tool comment

Reply to Ty's original comment

Figure 11.30 *The integrated comments are displayed in the Comments pane.*

6. Select the Comments tab at the left of the program window to open the Comments pane. You'll see Syd's comments are added to the file (**Figure 11.30**).

7. Save the file with the additional comments.

If Ty already has the drawing open in Acrobat, he can work from within the program to incorporate the comments.

Importing Comments in Acrobat

Suppose that Ty doesn't want to work with the file immediately when he receives Syd's e-mail with the attached FDF file. He can save the e-mail attachment to his hard drive like any other type of e-mail attachment and then later add the comments right into the open document.

Follow these steps to import comments into an open document:

1. In Acrobat, choose Comments > Import Comments from the main program menu; the Import Comments dialog opens.

2. Locate and select the FDF file, and click Select.

3. The dialog closes, and a confirmation dialog opens, explaining that you are importing comments from a different version of the document.

4. Click Yes to dismiss the dialog and load the comments into the open document.

5. Save the file with the additional comments.

Which option you use is a matter of timing and workflow. If you have the document open, work from there; if not, work from the e-mail program. Of course, in the end the results are the same.

What Else Can Ty and Syd Do?

If Ty decided to distribute the drawing to a number of contractors—for example, if he wanted to request bids from several people—he could use Acrobat's review process. In that way, he could control the distribution and follow the reviewing and comment-gathering processes through Acrobat's Tracker feature. You can read how to set up a formal review and use the Tracker in Chapter 13.

In Ty's work, the integrity of the drawing is important, and he can't allow his drawings to be modified for professional and legal reasons. Ty could use digital signatures and certify the drawing, as described in Chapter 14's project. He could take it a step further and create a custom signature appearance, like that shown in **Figure 11.31**. The bonus material on the Web site for this chapter shows you how to create a custom signature, examine a signature, extract a certificate from an existing signature, and how to exchange digital certificates with others.

As an alternative to using certificates, Ty could enclose the drawing in an eEnvelope for secure transmission to his contractor, as discussed in Chapter 7. He could even create and use a custom eEnvelope template, as described in the bonus material for Chapter 7 (on the book's Web site).

He might also like to add programmed fields to the drawing that would allow his contractors to click a button and return the comments to him automatically by e-mail. You can read how to use that process in Chapter 10.

Figure 11.31 *Check out the bonus material on this book's Web site to see how Ty creates a custom signature for certifying his drawing.*

If he had access to a Reader Extensions Server (an Adobe Enterprise product), he could also enable the drawings for signatures that could be applied in Adobe Reader. Since he's not an enterprise sort of guy, he's comfortable with the method he's set up. By the same token, if Syd were working with Acrobat 7 instead of Adobe Reader, Ty wouldn't have to enable the drawing for use in Adobe Reader and could add a signature field for Syd's signature when he finished working with the drawing. Read about using signatures in Chapter 14.

On Syd's part, he can export the data from the drawing's object data to a file. He could, for example, create a table of the plants required by the landscape plan and use that as the basis for costing. To do this, he'd copy the object data from the appropriate objects (as he did for the comment) and then paste them into a document or spreadsheet.

If Syd were feeling particularly artsy, he might want to create a custom stamp to use on the drawing when he'd finished reviewing it. You can read about custom stamps in Chapter 9.

12

Assembling
a Library

Suppose you have thousands of historical documents that have been converted to PDF for safekeeping and storage, and suppose further that you need to search for specific information in those files regularly. Although you can hunt for content in the whole collection by using Acrobat's Search feature, the search process can be quite lengthy, as you can imagine. Repeatedly having to choose search terms and then waiting isn't anyone's idea of a good time. Now suppose there was a way to shorten that waiting time considerably. Wouldn't that be a good thing? Nod your head in agreement, and read on.

One way of managing documents using Acrobat 7 Professional is through its Catalog feature. *Cataloging* is the process of assembling a collection of documents and indexing it to create a formal catalog. Using PDF documents as the basis for maintaining and storing collections of business-critical and historical documents allows you to do full-text searches of content with the two search functions that are part of the Acrobat program and Adobe Reader. You can use both the Find and Search features, as you'll see in this chapter.

The ARWU

The Amalgamated Retail Workers Union (ARWU) is a trade union organization representing several thousand workers employed in a variety of retail settings. Over the past several years, as its membership has continued to grow, the union's management decided it was in their best long-term interests to invest in hardware, software, and training for their staff to improve the way they handle union business—specifically, arbitration cases—on their members' behalf.

It's important for the union's industrial relations officers (IROs) to be able to access pertinent information—whether from past arbitrations and rulings or from other legal and union sources—that they can use to prepare cases.

It's often a difficult process. The IROs hunt through binders of historical documents that the union has maintained over the years and then make photocopies of any material that may be relevant. Once they search historical material, they move to regional and federal rulings—also stored in binders—that contain case law and other information they receive by subscription from a national service, again photocopying what they need.

As is bound to happen, material that might be relevant to a case sometimes isn't available—for instance, a fellow IRO may have taken pages from a binder to use for a short while, intending to return the material to the storage folders, but forgetting to do so. And even when the information is available, the process of sorting through the binders is labor intensive and time consuming, not to mention a bit haphazard. The IROs may or may not become aware of all the pertinent documents, and if they do, they may not be able to find them.

The Internet adds another layer of opportunity—and an additional nest of potential problems. The ARWU can access information from around the world that can help them in representing their members' interests, if they know where to look. Once an IRO finds a relevant document, he has to copy or download the file and then print it to use in the case preparation.

In walks our case-study hero. Henry Dickens is a progressive kind of guy. As a senior IRO in the ARWU, he has embraced the technology that the organization uses to manage many aspects of its operation, including the membership and operational databases. Henry recognizes that there is a significant problem regarding his fellow IROs accessing the information they need when they need it, and he has been encouraged by the union's management to explore solutions to the problem.

Henry believes the IROs' problems would be solved if they found a way to do the following:

- Effectively archive and store the organization's information to preserve the content.

- Manage their information in a way that allows staff to easily access it, without wasting time searching for missing documents.

- Organize and maintain content from outside the organization that is used for preparing their cases, including both subscription documents and information gathered from Internet sources.

- Maintain the collection to prevent lost or missing documents.

Steps Involved in This Project

After considering and dismissing a number of options as too costly—having their documents captured by their database developer—or too inefficient—having copies made of all documents for each IRO—Henry decides the simplest and most effective way to handle the situation is to use PDF documents.

NOTE At roughly this point in nearly every chapter you see a lovely image of the finished project. In this case, there's not much to show. The project is a functional one, and the only thing you could see is a list of index and database files, or possibly a Search PDF window—not the most scintillating visuals.

Henry plans to build a PDF catalog that contains

- Documents converted from newer internal documents and rulings

- Documents scanned from historical records

- Documents converted from Web pages

Henry learns that their legal subscription service offers PDF versions of its material at a lower cost than their present paper-based subscription, and they can use the PDF documents in the archive. Using a PDF subscription saves not only money, but also time, because the documents can be used in the collection without much processing.

This is what he needs to do to complete his cataloging project:

- Locate the source documents in Microsoft Word for the most recent cases and convert them to PDF.

- Scan historical documents and convert them to searchable PDF format in Acrobat.

- Convert selected Web page material to PDF.

- Create a searchable index.

- Apply a password to the documents in the collection that prevents users from changing the content.

The first step in the process is to convert the Word documents stored on hard drives all over the office to PDF. In reality, the first step would be to gather all those Word files together in one location, but this is a book about Acrobat, not office management, so we'll assume that task has been done.

Converting Word Documents for the Collection

The simplest part of Henry's task is to convert all the available text documents, which the organization has been storing both digitally and on paper. Withe the help of two office assistants, the many files the union has generated over the years are assembled in one folder location. Instead of opening all the files in Word and using the PDFMaker to convert the files, Henry can work from the desktop after checking settings in Word. Using Word's PDFMaker, he can add features like links, bookmarks, and tags to the documents. The only require-ment for this project is that its structure be tagged.

NOTE When Acrobat 7 is installed on your computer, part of the installation process includes menus and a toolbar that are also installed in Microsoft Office programs, includ-ing Word. These menus and toolbar are called the PDFMaker.

Tags describe the content of the document. For example, an image tag is used to describe the actual image included in a document; a paragraph tag describes the actual content of a paragraph of text, and so on. Acrobat's cata-loging process is a functional process that indexes the content of the docu-ment and stores that information in a database. You can read more about tags in Chapter 8.

To modify Word's PDFMaker settings, choose Adobe PDF > Change Conversion Settings from the Main menu to open the Acrobat PDFMaker dialog (**Figure 12.1**).

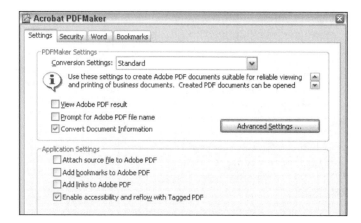

Figure 12.1 Check the PDFMaker settings before converting Word documents.

On the Settings tab, shown by default when the dialog opens, choose these settings:

■ Click the Conversion Settings pull-down arrow and choose Standard. The documents don't need to be converted for high-quality printing, but Henry thinks users should have an option to print the documents if they wish, so he chooses the Standard settings rather than the Smallest File Size option. For more on the different Conversion Setting options, see the sidebar "Conversion Options" in Chapter 9.

■ Deselect "View Adobe PDF result" and "Prompt for Adobe PDF file name." Because Henry intends to convert a large number of files simultaneously and use the document's existing names for their PDF filenames as well, deselecting these options saves a lot of time.

■ In the Application Settings area of the dialog, deselect all options except "Enable accessibility and reflow with Tagged PDF." The documents were created by a number of different people using a number of templates, and he doesn't need bookmarks for any individual file's contents, nor does he need links or the source files attached.

Click OK to close the Acrobat PDFMaker dialog. Now Henry is ready for the conversions.

Follow these steps to convert a batch of documents:

1. Open the Windows Explorer window and create a new folder.

2. Drag the source Word documents to the folder.

3. Select all the files. Then right-click/Control-click to open the shortcut menu and click Convert to Adobe PDF (**Figure 12.2**).

    The Save Adobe PDF File As dialog opens and shows the document's name. Since you have a new folder for the set of files you are converting, you don't need to select a folder location for each file.

4. Click Save to dismiss the dialog. The Adobe PDF Status dialog opens (**Figure 12.3**). As each file is processed, you see a progress bar that stays open until the entire batch of files is converted.

That was a quick task!

Scanning in Acrobat

One part of the collection Henry is compiling is made up of historical documents that are available only as printed pages. Instead of rekeying the documents, they can be scanned into Acrobat. Acrobat works with your scanner software directly, opening its scan dialog from within Acrobat. Any scanner that is properly configured for your computer can be used with Acrobat.

NOTE In this section, you see how to work with single documents. For a large project, you might want to investigate working with dedicated scanning software or automatic scanning using high-speed scanners.

Follow these steps to scan a document into Acrobat:

1. Click the Create PDF task button to display the menu, and click From Scanner to open the Create PDF File from Scanner dialog (**Figure 12.4**).

2. Select your scanner from the Scanner pull-down list—any scanners you have configured for your system are shown on the list.

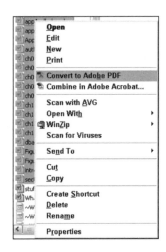

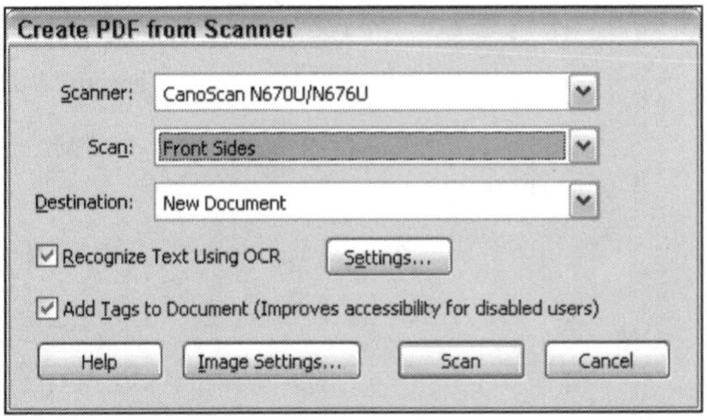

Figure 12.2 Use the shortcut menu to convert a batch of documents quickly.

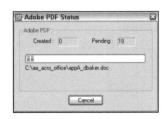

Figure 12.3 You can track the progress of the file conversion process in this dialog.

Figure 12.4 Choose settings before scanning a document into Acrobat.

3. Choose Front Sides or Both Sides from the Scan pull-down list. If you have two-sided documents and you have a duplex scanner—that is, one that can scan both sides of a document—choose the Both Sides option; otherwise, leave the default Front Sides option selected.

4. Specify a destination for the scanned page. If you have open documents, Acrobat offers a choice between a new document and appending the scan to the active open document. In Henry's case, the documents are scanned as separate files.

5. Make sure the Recognize Text Using OCR check box is selected. If it is not, then select it.

   The default option is to use the OCR (Optical Character Recognition) process to create a searchable document, meaning the content of the document is converted to words and images that you can then use with Search and Find features.

> **TIP** The dialog also includes an Add Tags to Document option. For the most part, you will always want to include this option for any document converted to PDF. It doesn't add appreciably to the file size, and it allows for more accurate manipulation of the content, such as changing or modifying content. Although you can add tags from within Acrobat, it's quicker in a big project to choose the option before scanning.

6. Click Scan to start the conversion process. Acrobat opens your scanner's dialog. Follow your scanner's instructions and start the scan.

7. When the page has been scanned, you see the Acrobat Scan dialog (**Figure 12.5**). Continue with more pages as required; click Done to dismiss the dialog and end the scan.

Figure 12.5 Control the scanning process from Acrobat.

8. Choose File > Save to save the PDF document.

Most of Henry's documents are relatively short. If he were working with very large documents—hundreds of pages each—he would want to break each document into logical chunks, such as individual chapters, and save each as a separate file. Acrobat's indexes work much faster with shorter files.

ONE DOCUMENT OR MANY?

If you are scanning in Acrobat, decide beforehand how you want to handle the documents. Some people prefer to scan the whole project as one document and then extract pages into separate documents; others prefer to scan and save each document as it is finished. The amount of work involved is likely the same for both methods, so which one you choose just depends on your personal preference.

Working with a Scanned Document

PDF files created by scanning documents using older versions of Acrobat or from programs such as Photoshop create image PDFs, which means you can read and print the document, but the text isn't captured—that is, it isn't converted to letters. Instead, the document contains an image of the text. Because image PDFs are not searchable—you can't search for specific words or phrases, for example—you'll want to make sure to take advantage of Acrobat's OCR (optical character recognition) feature.

Acrobat uses the OCR process to capture text in two ways; you need to choose which option you prefer before scanning. In the Create PDF from Scanner dialog, click the Settings button to open the Recognize Text - Settings dialog (**Figure 12.6**).

Click the PDF Output Style pull-down menu and choose from two options:

Figure 12.6 *Choose a language, conversion option, and image downsampling value before scanning.*

- **Searchable Image** keeps the foreground of the page intact and places the searchable text behind the image. You'll find this option produces output closest to the original because Acrobat doesn't change the appearance of the document's letters.

- **Formatted Text & Graphics** rebuilds the entire page, converting the content into text, fonts, and graphics. This option can often result in substituted fonts and characters that are different in appearance from the original text of the document.

IS IT AN IMAGE, OR IS IT TEXT?

If you open a document and aren't sure if it contains images and text or an image of the page, click the page with the Select tool ⌶ Select on the Basic toolbar. If you see the flashing vertical bar cursor and can drag the Select tool to highlight content, the page contains text; if you click a text area on the document and the entire page is selected, you have an image PDF (**Figure 12.7**).

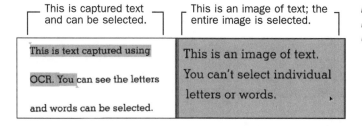

This is captured text and can be selected.

This is an image of text; the entire image is selected.

This is text captured using OCR. You can see the letters and words can be selected.

This is an image of text. You can't select individual letters or words.

Figure 12.7 *You can tell if text is an image or captured text using the Select tool.*

If you choose the Searchable Image option, results can vary depending on the quality of the source document. Plan ahead, and check your scanner settings carefully. Scan black-and-white images at 200–600 dpi, with 300 dpi an optimal resolution; scan grayscale images (made up of shades of gray only) or color images at 200–400 dpi. Acrobat needs a minimum of 144 dpi to perform OCR. If your scan is outside the range, you see a warning message and the scan won't proceed.

Not all fonts and colors scan well. It's best to capture text in black and white, and a font of about 12 points is the optimal size. If your document contains text with smaller point sizes, you can successfully scan it an a higher resolutions, such as 600 dpi. Scanning with a higher resolution produces a larger file but you won't have to rekey the document before converting it. Colored or decorative fonts are difficult for the program to recognize and can lead to search and indexing errors.

However, if you use the Formatted Text & Graphics option, Acrobat actually replaces the text in the document with letters and numbers and also captures the images. In some cases, the content of the page appears different because Acrobat has assigned different fonts to the document (**Figure 12.8**). Some content may be unrecognizable; characters the program is unable to decipher are called *suspects*. Acrobat contains a method for evaluating a converted bitmap on a suspect-by-suspect basis; the clearer the original document, the less work you have to correct its content.

When converting a big project like Henry's, try to use the Searchable Image conversion option, if possible. It will make your final PDF cleaner and easier to read.

(4)   In the event the Publis
fundamental that a sat
right to deem the Man
pursuant to Paragraph

2.   **(c)**   Although the Publis
the **Work's** accuracy and complete

Figure 12.8 *The text in a converted document may display several different fonts.*

Converting Web Pages to PDF

The last components for the library are some Web pages. Henry and his colleagues usually save Web pages of information to use in building cases. They can easily convert entire Web pages, or even just selected content from a Web page, to PDF right from Internet Explorer.

Converting an Entire Web Page

A one-button PDFMaker is installed in Internet Explorer when you install Acrobat 7. This makes doing the conversion a simple task for anyone who wants to view and work with Web pages in a manageable way.

Here's how to use the PDFMaker to convert the Web page:

1. Display the Web page you want to convert.

    If the Web page includes frames, all the content is flattened into one PDF document page.

2. Click the PDFMaker's pull-down arrow to display its menu, and choose Convert Web Page to PDF (**Figure 12.9**). The Convert Web Page to Adobe PDF dialog opens. The dialog uses the page's title as the name by default.

Figure 12.9 *Choose commands from Internet Explorer's PDFMaker.*

3. Rename the file as necessary, and choose a storage location.

4. Click Save to convert the Web page.

Henry realizes that in some cases he doesn't want all the accessory material for the Web pages, such as navigation or ads. For these pages, he can convert only the portion of the page he wants.

TIP You can also right-click the page to display a shortcut menu that includes the Convert to PDF and Convert to Existing PDF commands.

Follow these steps to convert only a portion of the Web page:

1. Click the page (with the mouse) where you want to start the selection, and then drag to select the content for conversion to PDF.

2. Click the PDFMaker's pull-down arrow and choose Convert Web Page to PDF, or right-click to open the shortcut menu shown in **Figure 12.10**. You see the options include conversion and appending commands.

3. In the Convert Web Page to Adobe PDF dialog, select the two options in the "Adobe PDF Conversion options" area at the bottom of the dialog (**Figure 12.11**).

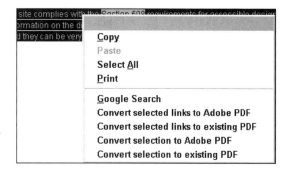

Figure 12.10 You can add selected content to an existing PDF document or create a new document.

Figure 12.11 Selected content on a Web page activates additional savings options.

4. Click Save to convert and save the Web page as a PDF document.

SAVING CONVERSION TIME

The PDFMaker also includes some preferences, all of which are selected by default. Click the PDFMaker's pull-down arrow, and choose Preferences to open a small dialog. The available preferences include:

- Open the document in Acrobat after conversion

- Ask for confirmation before deleting a PDF document

- Ask for confirmation before adding pages to a PDF document

- Warn before adding pages to a PDF document that has been modified

When working on a big conversion project, you might want to deselect the options to streamline your conversion process.

Attaching Pages

The PDFMaker includes several other commands for attaching the PDF of the Web page to an existing PDF document. Choose the command and then select the document to which you want to append the Web page. Click Save to convert the Web page and append it to the end of the selected document.

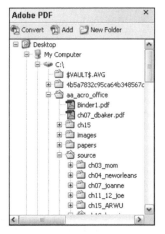

USING THE ADOBE PDF EXPLORER BAR

The Adobe PDF Explorer Bar is a pane that opens at the left of the Web browser window and can also be used to attach pages (**Figure 12.12**). You can select documents from this pane for attaching converted Web pages to existing PDFs, or select files to open from the Explorer Bar.

If you open a PDF document from the Explorer Bar, the document is displayed in Adobe Reader in the Web browser. If the Explorer Bar is displayed when you close your Web browser, it is open the next time you open the Web browser.

Figure 12.12 *You can use the Adobe PDF Explorer Bar to locate files on your computer.*

Designing an Index

Converting the documents to PDF is only the first stage of Henry's project. He also plans to create an index using Acrobat's Catalog feature. Aw c'mon now, this is the fun part! The benefit of using an index rather than Acrobat's Search feature is speed. When you are working with hundreds of documents, building an index and including it with the documents it indexes will make searching much quicker.

Before creating the index, Henry has to do some planning. He and his assistants have stored the converted documents in a single folder in a drive location that is accessible to all the IROs. As the index is generated, Acrobat adds indexing files and folders in the same folder location on the hard drive. Keeping all the content together prevents errors.

Acrobat's indexing feature can handle up to 500 case-sensitive stop words. Stop words are common words—such as "and" or "the"—that can be excluded from the index. Excluding stop words can produce a slightly smaller index, but creating a list of words to exclude can be confusing to the index's users. For instance, the phrase "all the people," if used as a search term, won't produce any results if "the" is a stop word that has been excluded. Henry and the gang decide not to use stop words.

OFFERING USERS MORE OPTIONS

You can also use custom terms to describe a document, including subjects and keywords. These words can then be used as search terms when searching the document collection. Subjects and keywords can be interchangeable, although a document has only one subject. Confused yet? Here's an example: Suppose you are assembling a collection of documents about dogs. The title of a document might be "Bowser's Big Day." That is fine as a title, but almost useless when searching for the document in a collection—unless you are looking for Bowser! If you included a subject, or classification, such as "veterinarian visit," your users would find the document by using "veterinarian" as a subject search term.

Using the same example, you could assemble a number of keywords, such as "doctor," "animal hospital," "checkup," and "vaccinations." If the user then searches for one of these keywords using the Keywords option in the Search PDF window, they again would see the document in the search results.

Be sure to differentiate the type of words you are using and explain them to your index users. Define a word as a subject or a keyword—not both—for best results. If you search using a keyword term and have used the same term as a subject in some documents, your search results will be inaccurate. For example, searching for a keyword string such as "floral arrangement" when the term was specified as a subject, won't return the desired results.

Henry plans to create a read-me file so users can work with the index more effectively. The read-me file is a list of instructions that describe how the index is designed and ways users can work with it to produce the most accurate results.

As a last step, he also plans to add a "Confidential" watermark to the pages and protect the content with a password. Instead of making the changes to each document manually, he will work with a batch sequence.

PDF/A STANDARD

PDF/A is an emerging international standard for archiving documents using PDF. It is designed to preserve documents for long-term storage and maintain their usability without depending on external technologies, code, or other factors. For example, Acrobat 7 allows you to embed Flash movies in a PDF document. According to the standard, because a Flash movie depends on an external technology (a Flash player), the document isn't considered compliant with the standard. The PDF/A standard is being used worldwide by governments and other organizations to preserve document collections in as simple a format as possible. That way, if you want to view a document in twenty years, you don't have to hunt through dusty digital archives looking for some old media player to view the content or drive a hundred miles to get a password from a retired government employee.

To comply with the PDF/A standard, the document must meet the following criteria:

- It can include only text, raster images, and vector objects

- It can't include scripts

- It must have all fonts embedded

- It can't contain security options such as passwords or other types of encryption

Henry's document collection doesn't comply with the standard as he is using passwords to protect the content.

Building and Applying an Index

Now that Henry has made all his design decisions and has assembled his documents in the proper, shared folder he's using to store the collection and index, he's ready to build it. And when he's done, there will be a happy group of IROs there to thank him.

Follow these steps to configure the index:

1. Choose Advanced > Catalog to open the Catalog dialog.

2. Click New Index. The New Index Definition dialog opens. Add information to the dialog to name and describe the index, and select the folders you want to include, as well as any you want to exclude (**Figure 12.13**).

3. Click Options to customize the index by adding or removing content from the index (**Figure 12.14**).

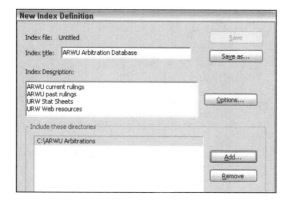

Figure 12.13 *Select the files and write descriptions for your index.*

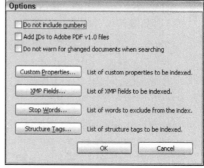

Figure 12.14 *Customize the index using specific features in this dialog.*

4. Click OK to close the Options dialog and return to the New Index Definition dialog.

5. Click Build to open the Save Index File dialog. Name the index file, and save it with the document collection.

6. Click Save to dismiss both the Save dialog and the New Index Definition dialog. The index is created and the results appear in the Build dialog.

7. Click Close to dismiss the Build dialog.

The index creates its own subfolder and files, including the index.pdx file (the index's database file) and a log file. Don't delete or move any of the indexing folders or files or you will corrupt the index.

Setting Preferences

For Henry, building an index is a one-shot deal—his normal workday won't include creating and manipulating indexes on a regular basis. On the other hand, his assistants, who will maintain the index, may want to set preferences in Acrobat that are applied automatically to any new index that is built.

To do so, choose Edit > Preferences (or Acrobat > Preferences on a Mac) and click Catalog in the categories pane at the left of the dialog to show the Catalog preferences. The Catalog preferences include the same options as those used to customize the index shown in Figure 12.13, as well as several other options, such as creating a log file or forcing an ISO standard (**Figure 12.15**).

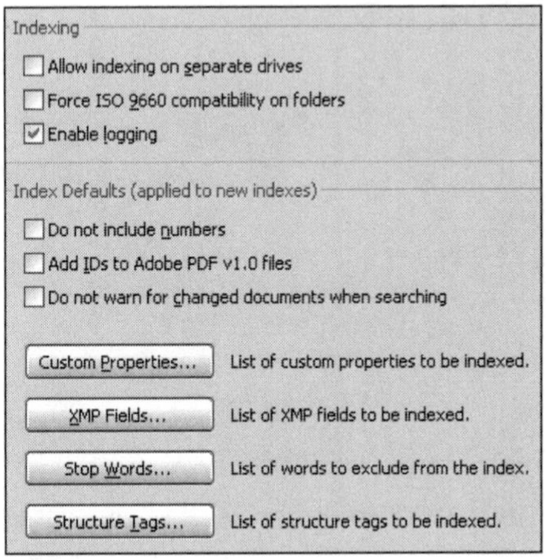

If you intend an index to be used cross-platform, you might want to choose "Force ISO 9660 compatibility on folders." This option applies the ISO standard document-naming process automatically to filenames to comply with MS-DOS filenames, which are names of less than eight digits with no spaces. This preference renames the files themselves, but you'll have to rename folders manually to comply with the standard.

Figure 12.15 You can set preferences that apply options to new indexes automatically.

Most of these preferences are self-explanatory and include things like choosing drive locations for storing the index files and excluding numbers from new indexes.

Maintaining an Index

The Catalog feature has to be rerun whenever changes are made to the contents of the documents in the index. This includes adding new documents, making changes to existing documents, and moving or renaming documents. If documents in your collection are changed in any of these ways, you have to rebuild the index because it no longer points to the content accurately. In Henry's project, the content of existing documents isn't changed, but new documents are added on a regular basis. Therefore to maintain an accurate index, he needs to rerun the Catalog feature whenever new documents are added.

To maintain the index, follow these steps:

1. Choose Advanced > Catalog to open the Catalog dialog.

2. Click Open Index and select the index's PDX (Catalog Index File) file from the indexing folder.

3. Click Open to dismiss the dialog and open the New Index Definition dialog, which is the same one as that shown in Figure 12.13.

4. The buttons at the bottom of the dialog are active when you open an existing index. Click Rebuild to repair and reconfigure the index; to delete an existing index, click Purge.

CHOOSE YOUR OPTIONS

You can customize your index in a number of ways using the Options dialog, shown in Figure 12.14:

- Click the "Do not include numbers" check box if you want to omit numbers from the index. Use this option if your indexed documents contain a lot of numerical information that isn't likely to be searched, because including the numbers adds to the search time.

- Click the "Add IDs to Adobe PDF v1.0 files" check box if you are working with very old PDF files; unless you have files created with Acrobat versions 1 or 2, you don't need to select this option.

- Click the "Do not warn for changed documents when searching" check box to prevent viewing a warning dialog.

- Click the Custom Properties button to open a dialog that lets you specify custom document properties to include in an index. The custom properties are then included as a search option in the Search PDF window. Custom properties, such as those used in Microsoft Office files can be included in an index.

- Click the XMP Fields button to open a dialog that lets you select custom XMP (Extensible Metadata Platform) fields, which are indexed and included as a search option in the Search PDF window. XMP fields are imported XML content that can be included with a document's contents.

- Click the Stop Words button to open a dialog in which you can specify words to exclude from the index—stop words are described in the "Designing an Index" section.

- Click the Structure Tags button to open a dialog to choose tags that can be used in searching. For example, you might want to use <image> to search for images in a document collection.

Testing the Index

Once the index is created, it's time to test it using Acrobat's Search function. You can perform simple searches in a single document using the Find toolbar (**Figure 12.16**). Choose View > Toolbars > Find, or right-click/Control-click the toolbar well and click Find. Type a search term in the field, and click Previous or Next to move the document to the next occurrence of the word, which is highlighted on the page. Click the Find pull-down arrow to open a list of additional search criteria.

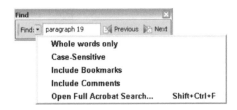

Figure 12.16 *Use the Find toolbar to locate content in a single document.*

Use the Search PDF window for searching a document collection. Henry intends to include a read-me file with the collection so his colleagues know how to use the index. A read-me file is a set of instructions that accompanies many products, such as software, databases, programs, and other computer content. Using a read-me file is a conventional way of providing additional information to users; the very name of the file says it all.

This is what the ARWU read-me file contains:

Working with the ARWU Arbitrations Index

The new ARWU Arbitrations Index allows you to search the contents of all our current and historical documents and reports. You can also access the ARWU stat sheets as well as information from the ARWU Web site. To preserve the integrity of our indexed documents, we have added a password to each document that prevents changes to the contents.

Follow these steps to work with the index:

1. Open Acrobat or Adobe Reader.

2. Click the Search button on the File toolbar to open the Search PDF window at the right of the program window.

3. Click Use Advanced Search Options at the bottom of the Search PDF window to show the advanced settings.

4. Click the Look In pull-down arrow and choose Select Index.

5. In the Index selection dialog, click Add to open a dialog for locating the index file. You'll find the index in the ARWU Arbitrations folder on the shared drive. Select the ARWU Arbitrations.pdx file and click Open.

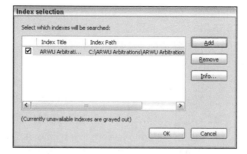

6. The dialog closes, and you see the index listed on the Index selection dialog.

7. Click OK to close the dialog. In the Search PDF window, the Look In field now displays "Currently Selected Indexes."

Now you're ready to search the collection. Once you have attached the index to a document, you will see it attached each time you open the file.

Here are some tips for setting up your search:

- Type the word or words you want to find in the first field. You can't search using wildcards such as (*) or (?).

- Click the "Return results containing" pull-down arrow and choose an option for tailoring the search. You can choose to match all the words, the exact phrase, or some of the words, or you can use a Boolean query.

- You can use up to three additional search parameters to customize the search further. Use the pull-down lists below the "Use these additional criteria" label. Click the left pull-down menu to display a list of options. Select the search option. Type a search term in the field, and then click the right pull-down arrow and select a modifier. A check mark displays in the check box to the left of the criteria's fields. Be careful using additional search criteria because the returned results must contain all the additional search criteria. Click the criteria's checkmark to deselect it if you have narrowed your search too much.

After typing in your search term(s), click the Search button to perform the search. Acrobat will search all the documents in our index. The filenames and locations are shown in the Results area pane of the Search PDF window.

The names of the files are collapsed—click the (–) to the left of the filename to open the list of matches. Move your pointer over a listing to display information about the match. When you click a result, the document is loaded into Acrobat or Adobe Reader, and you see the search results highlighted on the document page.

You can also sort by other criteria than the filename. To reorder the results, click the pull-down arrow below the Results area of the Search PDF window and choose to sort by modification date, location, or relevance ranking.

More Handy Tips

If you are doing a lot of searching, try using some of the shortcut keys for faster reviewing of your search results. Once you have finished conducting the search and opened the first document, you can use these shortcuts:

- Press F3 to jump to the next hit.

- Press Ctrl/Command-] to go to the next document; press Ctrl/Command-[to go to the previous document.

- When you are using results in a particular document, press Ctrl/Command-G to go to the next result; press Ctrl/Command-Shift-G to go to the previous result.

Another tip for customizing searches is to set Search Preferences—good for you power-searchers. Choose Edit > Preferences (or Acrobat > Preferences on a Mac) and click Search in the Categories pane of the Preferences dialog. Then select the options that will work best for you.

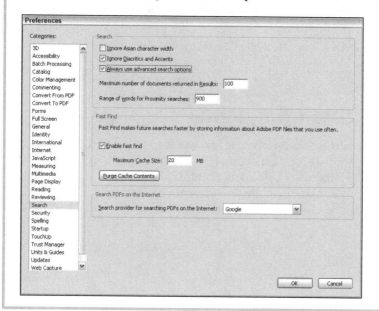

- Some documents contain diacritics or accents. Select the Ignore Diacritics and Accents option to find terms whether or not they include an accent or diacritic mark; you don't have to add the diacritics or accents in the Search PDF window to perform the search.

- Click the "Always use advanced search option" to automatically open the advanced settings on the Search PDF window, which allows you to search our index or use custom search terms such as the keywords.

- We have indexed several hundred documents. When you are searching, note how long it takes to get search results. You might want to change the "Maximum number of documents returned in Results" preference. The default is 100; to search our entire collection you might want to change the value to 800 to be sure to search all our documents, although that could make the search longer to perform.

- You can use Proximity searches to find words within a certain range of one another. The default is set at 900 words. You might like to experiment with this number to get more accurate results. If you use a Proximity search, you need to select the "Match Exact word or phrase" option from the "Return results containing" pull-down arrow on the advanced search PDF window. Type two or more words to search for in the documents. Any occurrence of the search terms within 900 words of one other is returned. For example, the words "arbitration award" are returned whether the words are next to one another or separated by 899 other words.

- Use the Fast Find preference to cache the returns from your searches, or store them in a temporary storage location as completed searches. You can specify the size of the cache, which defaults at 20 MB. Using a cache makes searching faster, as Acrobat checks the cache first to see if a specific search has been conducted previously.

When you are finished, click OK to close the Preferences dialog.

Using a Batch Sequence

As a final step, Henry's document collection needs to be protected. He wants to add a watermark reading "Confidential" to the document. But his collection numbers in the thousands of pages and hundreds of documents. Do he and his assistants have to open each document manually, and then add the watermark to each document? Not on your life! Those tasks alone could add days to the project.

Thanks to Acrobat 7 Professional, Henry can create and apply a batch sequence to all the files that will automatically make the changes to the documents with a couple of mouse clicks. All he has to do is make four decisions before building a batch sequence:

- Which commands he needs to run and their details

- Which files to use

- Where to store his finished files

- What format to use for the finished files.

Acrobat includes eight default batch processes, including some for common tasks such as removing attachments, opening a number of files, or printing chosen files, and you can easily write your own custom sequence. You don't need to have documents open in Acrobat to apply a batch sequence to them.

When you create a batch sequence, many of the commands you choose must be configured, as you'll see in Henry's example. Before the batch sequence's configuration is complete, he has to choose settings in the respective dialogs for Acrobat to apply when the batch sequence is run. For example, Acrobat can't read his mind and choose settings for the watermark; he has to specify the details in the Add Watermark & Background dialog.

Follow these steps to configure a batch sequence:

1. Choose Advanced > Batch Processing to open the Batch Sequences dialog.

2. Click the New Sequence icon. A small dialog opens to name the sequence; type the name and click OK. Use a meaningful name for the sequence—Henry's batch sequence is called "arbitrations."

   The Edit Batch Sequence-arbitrations dialog opens.

3. Click the Select Commands button to open the Edit Sequence dialog (**Figure 12.17**).

Figure 12.17 *Add and configure commands for the batch sequence.*

4. Click an arrow to open the category of action, such as Document, in the column at the left of the dialog.

5. Select a command, and then click Add to move the command to the list at the right of the dialog. In the sample project, the Add Watermark & Background command is selected in the left column and added to the list in the right column. If you add multiple commands, you can reorder them by clicking the Move Up and Move Down buttons, or delete an action by clicking Remove.

6. Click the arrow to the left of a command to see its contents.

Now that Henry has chosen the commands he wants to use in the batch sequence, he has to specify the settings Acrobat will use when the batch sequence runs.

MAKE IT INTERACTIVE

If you want to configure each document separately, such as adding custom Document properties, click the Interactive Mode button ☐ which is the depressed gray box at the far left edge of the list of command names (at the right of the Edit Sequence dialog). The button then displays a gray-and-white icon ☐ in the gray box.

When you run the batch sequence, Acrobat prompts you for settings for the actions—the prompts depend on the action you are using in the batch sequence. For example, if you are adding a watermark and want it to be different in each file that the batch sequence is modifying, when the batch sequence is running, it stops processing and opens the Add Watermark & Background dialog for each individual document so you can configure the settings accordingly. In Henry's project, he wants the batch sequence to run independently, so he uses the same settings throughout.

Adding the Watermark

Henry wants to automatically apply a watermark to each page. He wants a text watermark that can be seen on the pages but doesn't print.

Follow these steps to configure the watermark:

1. From the Edit Sequence dialog, click the Add Watermark & Background command in the right column of the dialog, and then click Edit to open the Add Watermark & Background dialog (**Figure 12.18**).

2. In the Type area of the dialog, click Add a Watermark and deselect the "Show when printing" option.

3. Click From text in the Source area of the dialog. Type the text in the field, and then choose a font, font size, color, and paragraph alignment from the appropriate pull-down lists.

4. In the Position and Appearance area of the dialog, specify the alignment for the text on the page, and indicate preferences in the Scale, Rotation, and Opacity options. In Henry's project, the text is aligned vertically 0.5 inches from the bottom of the page, and the Opacity is set to 20%.

5. View the page preview on the dialog. If there are open documents when you create a batch sequence, you see the first page of the document in the Preview area. As you make changes to the watermark, they are shown in the preview.

6. Select a Page Range. By default, All Pages is selected.

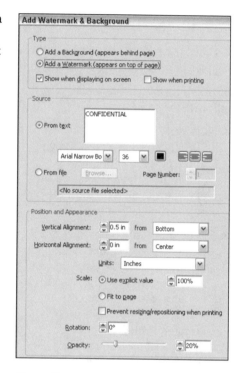

Figure 12.18 *You can add a watermark to each page of a document using a batch sequence.*

7. Click OK to close the dialog and return to the Edit Sequence dialog.

When the batch sequence runs, each document automatically has the same watermark applied to it.

Finishing the Batch Sequence

It's been a long journey through the land of document collections and index-ing, but our hero Henry is coming to the end of the road at last.

To finish the batch sequence, follow these steps:

1. Click OK to close the Edit Sequence dialog, returning you to the Edit Batch Sequences - arbitration dialog. You see the two commands are now listed on the dialog (**Figure 12.19**).

2. Click the "Run commands on" pull-down arrow, and choose an option from the list for run-ning the command based on the project's requirements. In this case, Henry chooses the Selected Folder option and then clicks Browse to select the ARWU Arbitrations folder. The name of the folder is dis-played on the dialog.

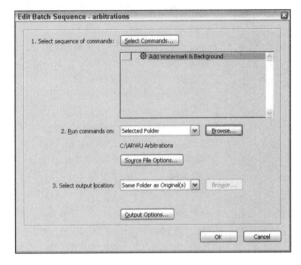

Figure 12.19 *The configured command is added to the dialog.*

NOTE After applying the batch sequence to the present catalog contents, Henry may want to revise the folder location if he uses a storage folder to hold new material on an interim basis before adding it to the catalog.

3. Click the Select output location pull-down arrow and choose an option for storing the processed files. In this case, since the files are staying in the same folder, Henry leaves the default.

TIP If you want to make a distinc-tion between processed files and the originals, click Output options. Here you can choose custom names, whether to overwrite an existing file, as well as choosing an output for-mat—any type of file you can convert to PDF can be included in a batch sequence, such as text, Microsoft Office files, or images.

4. Click OK to close the Edit Batch Sequence - arbitrations dialog, returning you at last to the original Batch Sequences dialog. You see the new sequence is added to the list (**Figure 12.20**).

5. If Henry is ready to run the batch sequence, he can click Run Sequence on the Batch Sequences dialog. If not, he can click Close to dismiss the dialog.

Figure 12.20 *The completed batch sequence is available for use.*

At a later time, when he's ready to run the batch, Henry can reopen the Batch Sequence dialog, select the new sequence, and then click Run Sequence.

Maintaining the Catalog

Henry's job is finished. The ARWU will find the cataloged documents much simpler to work with. The union should also realize savings in time and photocopying costs, and no one will have to search in vain for documents that are sitting on someone's desk.

It's important to maintain the index's database too. The ARWU receives regular material from its parent organization as well as other sources that the IROs use for preparing cases. To add the content to the database, it may be simpler to add the new files to a separate temporary storage folder first, and then apply the batch sequence. This way Acrobat won't rerun the batch sequence on files that are already processed.

Once the new files have their watermark and security added, they can be moved to the catalog folder, and included in the index. If Henry chooses a temporary folder to process the files, he has to change the batch sequence's selected folder to that of the temporary storage folder. Once files are added to the index's folder, the index needs rebuilding; he should set a schedule for rebuilds according to how often material is added.

What Else Can He Do?

After working with the index for a while, Henry should get feedback from his colleagues as to how they are using the index and if it is meeting their needs. There are a few things that he may want to change over time. For example, the users may find it useful to have keyword searching, which can be added to the documents through the Document Properties dialog.

The IROs might also want to add security to their document collection to protect its contents. In that case, Henry can reopen the Batch Sequences dialog, select his custom batch sequence, and click Edit Sequence to reopen the series of dialogs. In the Edit Sequence dialog, he can select the Security command and then click Edit to open the Password Security - Settings dialog, and choose passwords. You can read about password security in Chapter 4. To apply the password settings, he has to rerun the batch sequence.

13

Communicating with Comments

One of the biggest challenges businesses, both large and small, have to face is managing information. Whether you are in the entertainment business or work for a software company, you use documents as your standard means of conveying information. Managing and controlling what goes into your documents can be a daunting task, especially when many people are involved in communicating and tracking the information. Fortunately, Acrobat 7 can handle many document-related tasks. One of its strongest features (made even stronger in the current release of the program) is its built-in process for managing document reviews.

A *review* is a system in which one member of a team controls and manages the distribution of a document using Acrobat 7 Professional. The reviewers are invited to participate and given copies of the document. They are also granted rights to use a set of tools to add a wide range of comments to the document, including graphic, text, and editing comments. The automated reviewing process then returns the comment data from the document to the originator of the review cycle.

Once the review is complete, the comment data can be used in a number of ways for revising the original content. You could use Acrobat's TouchUp tools, for example, to make small changes to text or add additional lines of text, and so on. Or, as in the project in this chapter, you can export the comments from Acrobat 7 Professional directly into the source Microsoft Word document (in Windows) to make more extensive corrections.

In previous versions of Acrobat, only people working with the full version of Acrobat could participate in reviews. Now Acrobat 7 Professional allows the originator of the review to enable PDF documents for commenting by anyone working with the free Adobe Reader 7, expanding the ability to work with comments to millions of additional users.

You can use either Windows or Mac versions of Acrobat 7 for starting, conducting, and analyzing results of the review. The final part of the project, which describes how to export the comments into the source Word document, is a Windows-only feature.

Lemming Systems

"Where we lead—the rest must follow" is the motto of a progressive little software company called Lemming Systems, the brainchild of Stanford Lemming. Lemming specializes in building custom databases for corporate clients in the manufacturing industry. As part of the total service package, Lemming creates customized specifications and user manuals for all its clients. Creating these masterworks is the purview of Brad Wilson, the subject of this chapter.

Brad admits he really likes his job, but there's one caveat to that statement. Although he enjoys the creative process and takes pride in the finished product, he often finds it difficult, confusing, and downright irritating to receive comments on drafts of the documents he prepares.

Brad has ongoing issues concerning document control and feedback. A bottleneck in his workflow occurs every time he has to circulate a document for review. Although there are only a few key people in the organization who have to evaluate and comment on his work, it takes days or even weeks to have the reviews returned to him.

Brad's present method of generating feedback is haphazard at best. He and his assistant, Sherry, build a draft based on specifications he receives from the developers and other key personnel. Then he prints and distributes copies of the draft for review. After a few e-mail reminders, some in-person cajoling, and the occasional mild threat, the drafts are returned with notes. After deciphering the returned drafts and their collections of scribbles and arrows, Brad and Sherry collate the information and integrate the comments into the next draft.

Brad has learned that there are reasons why his reviews aren't ready for him on time. For some people, it is that they don't look at the contents of their in-boxes regularly and often don't notice when a new document arrives. For others, it is simply the fact that they spend all their time using a keyboard and find writing notes by hand tedious and time consuming.

As early as Acrobat 5, Brad yearned for the ability to conduct reviews of his documents sans paper. Unfortunately, as head of the two-person technical documents department, he and his junior writer are the only members of the Lemming organization using the full version of Acrobat; all other employees work with Adobe Reader. Now he has just upgraded to Acrobat 7 Professional and imagine his surprise when he realizes that he can control and manage the review of his documents in an entirely new way!

Steps Involved in This Project

Brad has the perfect solution to his ongoing frustration. Instead of sending anyone paper documents, he is going to use Acrobat 7 Professional's Comment & Markup feature to handle the reviews digitally (**Figure 13.1**).

This is what he needs to do (you'll notice that nowhere in this list is the word *paper* mentioned):

- Convert his source Word document to PDF.

- Initiate the review, specifying control and management details, including enabling the document for reviewing by participants using Adobe Reader.

- Invite participants to the review.

- Receive and incorporate responses.

- Integrate the comments into the original Word source document.

- Repeat the process as necessary for further review and, ultimately, approval of the finished piece.

Converting the Source Document

Brad constructs most of his manual in Microsoft Word, and the specification sheets are built either as Word tables or as Excel spreadsheets that are then inserted into the Word document. The document also contains database design objects created in Visio. The first step in the process, once the draft is complete, is to convert it to PDF.

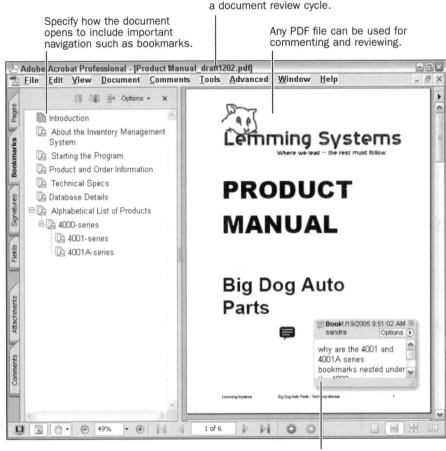

Figure 13.1 *Lemming Systems needs a way to manage workgroup input on business-critical documents.*

 If you'd like to convert the source file yourself, download **Product Manual.doc** from the Web site.

Working in Word, follow these steps to convert the document to PDF:

1. Choose Adobe PDF > Change Conversion Settings to open the Acrobat PDFMaker dialog. Select the Settings tab if it is not open by default.

2. Click the Conversion Settings pull-down arrow and choose Standard from the list.

Standard is the default setting used in the PDFMaker and will be active unless you've used other settings previously.

3. On the Application Settings area, choose these options:

- Add bookmarks to Adobe PDF

- Add links to Adobe PDF

- Enable accessibility and reflow with Tagged PDF

4. Select the Bookmarks tab and then click Convert Word Headings to Bookmarks. PDFMaker automatically selects the Heading 1 through Heading 9 options.

The sample project uses modified Word headings, and Brad wants bookmarks for the Heading 1 through Heading 3 headings—deselect those you don't want to convert (**Figure 13.2**).

5. Click OK to close the Acrobat PDFMaker dialog.

6. Click the Convert to Adobe PDF button 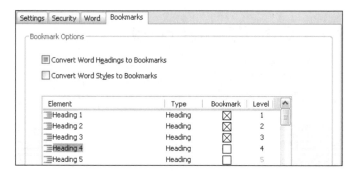 on the PDFMaker toolbar, or choose Adobe PDF > Convert to Adobe PDF.

The file is processed. As it is converted, several dialogs display showing the print and conversion processes. If the "Prompt for Adobe PDF file name" option

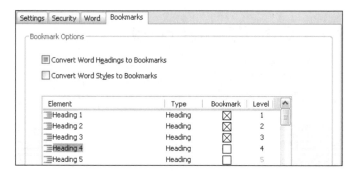

Figure 13.2 Select Headings to create PDF bookmarks automatically.

is selected on the Settings pane of the Acrobat PDFMaker dialog, a Save As dialog opens for you to specify the file's name and storage location—PDFMaker uses the Word document's name by default. Brad's project is saved as Product Manual.pdf.

WHY BRAD CHOOSES THESE SETTINGS

The settings chosen for the PDF document creation are used for specific purposes, either based on the intended use of the document, its content, or for further manipulation. Brad chose the following settings on the Adobe Acrobat PDFMaker dialog for his project:

- The Standard setting is the PDFMaker default settings. At the end of the commenting-and-markup cycle, Brad will use the High Quality Print option (along with the settings described in this section) to create the final PDF that he distributes to his client. The High Quality Print setting produces a document at a higher resolution than the Standard conversion option and also uses a higher resolution for color and grayscale images. The Standard setting, however, produces a smaller file size, useful for the distributing and commenting phase of the project.

- The "Add bookmarks to Adobe PDF" and "Convert Word Headings to Bookmarks" options are selected to generate the bookmarks for the manual automatically. Brad intends to send his customer a PDF copy of the finished manual as well as a printout.

- Some of the material in the package has links to content on the company's Web site and other external sources. Choosing the "Add links to Adobe PDF" option ports the links to the PDF document, again useful for the PDF version of the manual.

- "Enabling accessibility and reflow with Tagged PDF" is used in this case to make sure the edits can be integrated back into the original Word document correctly, as described later in the chapter.

Starting a Review Directly from Word

You can also start a comment-and-markup cycle directly from Word. Instead of choosing the Convert to Adobe PDF setting, click the Convert to Adobe PDF and Send for Review button 🖼 on the PDFMaker toolbar, or choose Adobe PDF > Convert to Adobe PDF and Send for Review from the PDFMaker added to Word's main menu. The file is processed, converted to PDF, and opened in Acrobat automatically, displaying the wizard you use for the review process.

Because Brad wants to check through the bookmark structure first before starting the review, he needs to convert the file to PDF and then check it out in Acrobat.

Checking the Document

Once Brad created the framework for his review, he's ready to start the review process after a quick check of the bookmarks. You can learn how to modify and reconfigure bookmarks in Chapter 2 and Bonus Chapter 1 on the book's Web site.

Open the document in Acrobat and select the Bookmarks tab to display the Bookmarks pane. You see the bookmarks arranged in a hierarchy, nested according to their respective heading designations in Word. That is, each Heading 1 is shown as a first-level bookmark, Heading 2's are nested within a first-level bookmark as second-level bookmarks, and so on (**Figure 13.3**). It isn't necessary to include bookmarking structures in a document intended for review, but it can be a useful feature. In Brad's project, using bookmarks lets those reviewers in particular areas quickly locate the content they want to review. The database manager, for instance, can click the database-related bookmarks to display pertinent content. Also, since Brad intends to start distributing a structured PDF document to his customers, he can show the reviewers how the bookmarks are defined, and they can add comments about the bookmarks as well.

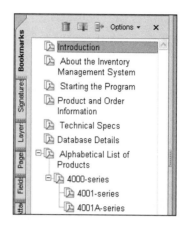

Figure 13.3 *Bookmarks are added to the PDF document and displayed in a hierarchy.*

TIP In the interest of saving time further along in the process, check your document one last time before starting a review. It takes you a few minutes, but saves having to deal with comments from every reviewer pointing out typos.

Specifying the Opening View

Brad wants his reviewers to check the document's bookmark structure along with the content; therefore, he wants to be sure the bookmarks are visible when the document opens. Acrobat allows you to save a setting in the file that defines what the viewer sees in the just-opened document.

Follow these steps to define the opening view:

1. Choose File > Document Properties to open the Document Properties dialog, and then select the Initial View tab.

2. Click the Show pull-down arrow, and choose Bookmarks Panel and Page from the list (**Figure 13.4**).

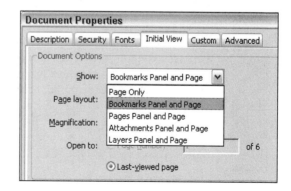

Figure 13.4 *Specify what you want the viewer to see when they open the document.*

3. Click OK to dismiss the dialog.

4. Save the file to save the specified opening view setting.

Initiating a Comment and Review Cycle

Start the review from the Task Buttons. If they aren't showing, choose View > Task Buttons > Send for Review to display the button on the toolbar. Click the Send for Review task button to display its menu, and choose Send by Email for Review (**Figure 13.5**). You can also choose several other options on the menu, including starting a Web-based review and using the Tracker, which is the interface for controlling a review.

Figure 13.5 Use the commands on the Send for Review task button to initiate and manage reviews.

The Send by Email for Review dialog opens. This is a three-pane wizard that guides you through the review design and initiation processes, which include

- Selecting the file

- Defining recipients and any special instructions

- Previewing and modifying the e-mail message that is sent to participants

Follow these steps to configure the review settings:

1. Click the pull-down arrow on the Getting Started: Initiating an Email-Based Review pane of the wizard, and choose the file you want to use for the review. If a document is open in Acrobat, its name is shown by default.

The first pane of the dialog describes the process. It explains that recipients receive tools and instructions along with the document and that management of the comments and document can be controlled; it also lists the software required to participate in the review.

2. Click Next to show the second pane of the wizard, Invite Reviewers.

3. Click Address Book to open your e-mail client's address book to select names. Alternatively, type the e-mail addresses in the dialog (**Figure 13.6**).

4. To customize the review and take advantage of Acrobat 7 Professional's new capabilities, click Customize Review Options to open the Review Options dialog (**Figure 13.7**).

5. Type the e-mail address, or click Address Book to open the Address Book dialog and select the name of the recipient of the review results. If your document's review requires Drawing Markup tools (a special toolbar in Acrobat used to add drawn comments such as boxes and arrows), click the "Display Drawing Markup Tools for this review" check box.

6. Click "Also allow users of Free Adobe Reader 7.0 to participate in this review" to enable the document's commenting features for those working in Adobe Reader 7.

7. Click OK to close the Review Options dialog and return to the wizard, and then click Next to display the third pane of the wizard.

8. Acrobat 7 includes a default e-mail message for reviewing. It explains the process the user must follow to use the document. Customize the e-mail message as necessary. For example, Brad can add "Complete the review and return comments by [date]" into the subject line or the body of the e-mail.

9. Click Send Invitation to send the document on its way. The Outgoing Message Notification dialog opens, explaining that the message has been given to your e-mail application.

10. Click OK to close the dialog; save some time in the future by clicking the "Don't show again" option to hide the dialog permanently.

That's one part of Brad's job done. The e-mail has been sent to his reviewers with the document attached. Let's see how the review works in Adobe Reader 7.

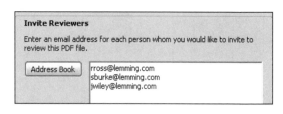

Figure 13.6 *Add the names of the recipients in this pane of the wizard.*

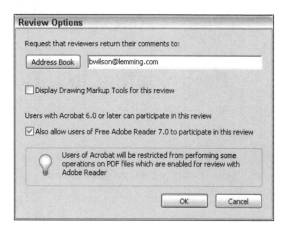

Figure 13.7 *You can customize the way in which e-mails are distributed, including enabling the commenting process for recipients who are using Adobe Reader 7.*

GRANTING USAGE RIGHTS

Only Acrobat 7 Professional has the capability to enable documents for Adobe Reader review-ing, and enabled commenting can only be done by e-mail. Acrobat also provides methods for browser-based reviews; for users to participate in a browser-based review using Adobe Reader, they must have access to Adobe server products, either Adobe Document Server or Adobe Reader Extensions Server.

Rights are granted on a document-by-document basis. That is, if you are working with Adobe Reader and can comment on one document, that doesn't mean you have the rights to comment on every document you open.

Participating in a Review

Brad has distributed the document to his reviewers, who receive the manual document as an attachment in their e-mail. The instructions for the review are contained in the body of the e-mail. When his reviewers open the attachment in Adobe Reader 7, the interface includes several components in addition to the document (**Figure 13.8**):

- The Bookmarks pane and the Document pane are shown as specified by Brad when he saved the document before starting the review.

- The Document Message Bar is shown above the two panes describing the document's commenting capabilities and summarizing what the reader has to do to participate in the review.

- The How To window displays at the right of the program window, and the information page, "Participate in an email-based review," is visible.

- The Commenting toolbar is open and overlays the program window.

To conduct the review, follow these steps:

1. Choose File > Save As to open a dialog. Define a location for the file and click Save.

2. Add comments to the document using the Commenting tools, as described in the next section.

3. Click Send Comments on the Commenting toolbar.

TIP For ease of use, you can drag the Commenting toolbar to the toolbar well at the top of the program window to dock it with the other Adobe Reader 7 toolbars.

4. Depending on the e-mail client configuration, there may be additional information dialogs displayed; follow the prompts to send the comments back to the review initiator.

Bookmarks pane   Document Message Bar   Document pane   How To window

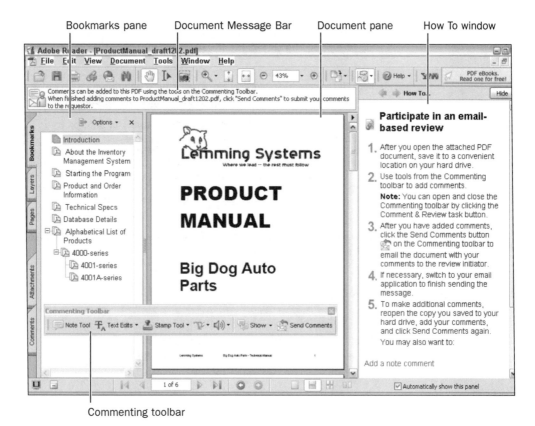

Commenting toolbar

Figure 13.8 *Recipients see the document as well as several other features in Adobe Reader 7.*

Using Commenting Tools

Acrobat 7 has a range of commenting options reviewers can access from the Commenting toolbar. You'll find pull-down menus and subtoolbars for tool groups, such as text edits and stamps.

Table 13.1 lists the tools on the Commenting toolbar, and describes what each tool is used for.

Table 13.1 Breakdown of tools on the Commenting Toolbar

TOOLBAR ICON	FUNCTION
	The Note tool lets you add notes to the document.
	Text Edit tools let you indicate text edits on a document. You can select several tools from the subtoolbar for specific types of edits.
	Stamp tools pull-down menu let you add a variety of stamps to a document, including custom and dynamic options.
	The Highlighting tools work like electronic versions of traditional highlighting pens or ink pens that cross out or underline text.
	Attach tools let you add either a file or a voice comment.
	Show tools let you access the Comments list, view comment content, and sort comments in a number of ways.

Adding a Comment

Comments are very easy to apply in Acrobat. First, choose the tool on the Commenting toolbar that you want to use, and then click the document or drag a marquee. Here's a brief summary of the various Commenting tools—Text Edit tools are covered in the next section:

- **Note tool.** Notes are generally used more than any other type of comment. Clicking the document with the Note tool opens a pop-up window. When you begin typing, text for the note is inserted (**Figure 13.9**). To save space on the document, click the close box in the pop-up window. You then see a small Note icon on the page; click the icon to open the pop-up window again.

Figure 13.9 Use the Note tool to add annotations to the document.

- **Highlighting tools.** These tools are a subtoolbar bar of the Commenting toolbar. Select a tool from the subtoolbar, and then drag it across the text you want to identify (**Figure 13.10**). To add text, double-click the highlight to open a pop-up window, and type the text in the window.

Figure 13.10 *Identify a particular passage on the document using a Highlighting tool.*

- **Stamp tools.** The Stamp tools are updated versions of old-fashioned ink stamps. Click the Stamp tools icon on the Commenting toolbar to open a set of menus and submenus (**Figure 13.11**). Some of the stamps are dynamic in that they add the date or time when you add the stamp to the document. You can also create custom stamps. Click the document where you want to apply the stamp. Like other types of stamps, double-click the stamp on the document to open a pop-up window to type text.

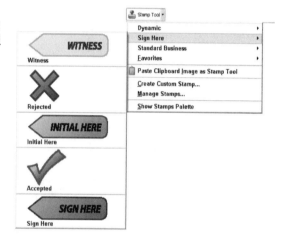

Figure 13.11 *Choose from one of the many available Stamp tools, or create your own custom stamps.*

- **Attach tools.** You can either attach a file or record an audio comment. Select an option from the Attach tools pull-down menu (**Figure 13.12**), click the document with the pointer, and then follow the prompts to find the file to attach or record the comment.

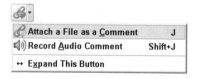

Figure 13.12 *You can also attach files or voice comments to a document.*

All comments you add to a document can be modified. You can change the appearance or color of icons, add a subject, and reposition comments on the document. To delete a comment, click it in the Comments list or on the Document pane and then press Delete.

Using Text Edit Tools

Brad is particularly interested in his reviewers using the Text Edit tools, because then he can integrate the changes directly into the source Word document. So he's going to give each reviewer a list of instructions for working with Text Edit tools. In a perfect world, all the comments intended for edits would be done with the Text Edit tools, but he is quite aware that for the first attempt, he will have to do some modification to the document's comment structure himself. Maybe in future reviews!

In an e-mail message to his reviewers, Brad explains how to use the Text Edit tools. His e-mail message contains the following information:

The Text Edit tools, a subset of the Commenting toolbar, work in the same way as writing comments on a printed page but are much more efficient.

Please follow these steps to use the tools to indicate changes you want made to the content of the document:

1. Click the Text Edits pull-down arrow to display the list of tools. If you have selected text on the page, the tools are all active. If you haven't selected any text, click the Text Edits pull-down arrow and click the Indicate Text Edits tool to activate the Text Select tool (used to insert, delete, or replace text).

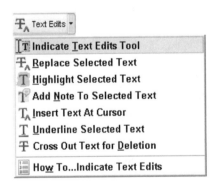

2. Click "How To...Indicate Text Edits" to open the How To window, which explains how to use the insert, delete, and replace text-editing options.

   If you are comfortable with the instructions, click the "Don't show again" check box (if it appears) to hide the dialog in future reviews.

3. Add your edits by doing one of the following:

- Click in the text of the document and type to insert text. On the document, you see an insertion caret icon, λ^{ir} and the text is placed in a pop-up comment box.

- Select the text to delete using the Text Select tool, and press Delete or Backspace on the keyboard. You see the text crossed-out on the document.

- Select the text with the Text Select tool and type new text to replace existing text. The text you type appears in a Replacement Text pop-up comment box, the selected text displays a strikethrough, and an insertion caret is shown at the end of the string of text you selected with the tool.

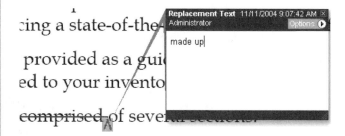

Comments added to edits are indicated by a small "A" above the selected text Th.

4. On the Commenting toolbar, click Send Comments to return the comments to me by e-mail.

Thank you. I look forward to receiving your feedback.

Working with the Select Tool

Brad didn't want to overload his reviewers with too much information on how to add comments. However, you can also approach the text-editing process in another way by using the Select tool ⯈ on the Basic toolbar, selecting the text and then applying one of the following Text Edit tools:

- **Replace Selected Text** replaces the selected text with typed text that is displayed in a pop-up comment box.

- **Highlight Selected Text** highlights the selected text.

- **Add Note To Selected Text** opens a comment box for you to add information about the text that is selected in the document.

- **Insert Text At Cursor** lets you type additional text, which is then placed in a pop-up comment box.

- **Underline Selected Text** places an underscore under the selected text.

- **Crossout Text for Deletion** adds a strikethrough to the selected text.

If you select text using the Select tool on the Basic toolbar, the Select icon displays on the page over the selected text. When you click the icon, the menu displays (**Figure 13.15**). You can choose a number of different comment types from the menu. Note that the menu doesn't contain the entire list of comment types; for some text editing, such as Crossout for Deletion, you have to use the Text Edit pull-down menu option.

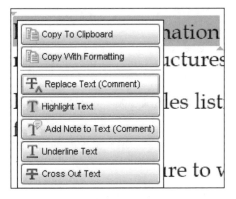

Figure 13.15 *You can choose comment types from the Select tool's menu.*

Returning and Integrating Comments

When your reviewers have finished commenting and marking up their copies of the document, returning them to the initiator is a simple process. Once the comments are returned to Brad, it's simple for him to add the comments back to his original PDF file as well.

Returning Comments

When the reviewers are finished with the file, they can send the comments back to Brad directly from the Adobe Reader program.

Follow these steps to return the comments from a review in Adobe Reader 7:

1. Click Send Comments on the Commenting toolbar. The dialog shown in **Figure 13.16** opens.

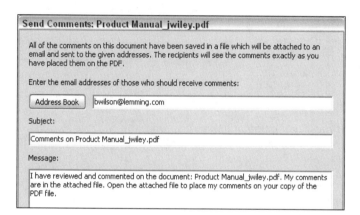

Figure 13.16 Acrobat automatically opens an e-mail dialog, complete with subject and message.

2. The dialog shows the return e-mail message, which is already addressed using the settings specified by Brad. Modify the text if you want to add your own message.

3. Click OK to send the comments on their way. The comments are sent as an FDF (File Data Format) file.

Next Brad integrates the comments into his original PDF file.

If you'd like to work with the comment files from Brad's reviewers, download **comments_john.fdf**, **comments_rick.fdf**, and **comments_sandra.fdf** from the Web site, and then add them to the PDF file from Acrobat (see the sidebar "Working from Acrobat" at the end of this section).

Integrating Comments

Brad can work from within Acrobat to import comments into his open PDF file, or he can work directly from the returned e-mail. He chooses to work from his e-mail program.

Follow these steps to open a file and integrate comments from an e-mail message:

1. Double-click the attachment to the e-mail; the dialog shown in **Figure 13.17** opens. Acrobat automatically recognizes the document as part of a review that is being tracked.

2. Click Yes to open the original document and integrate comments from the copy. You can also open the copy or cancel the import altogether by clicking the appropriate buttons.

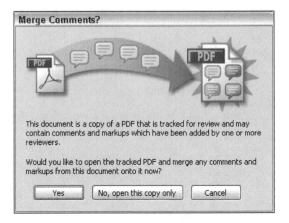

Figure 13.17 *Acrobat recognizes incoming documents as part of a tracked review and offers several options.*

3. An Adobe Acrobat message dialog opens saying that any comments from the copy have been integrated into the original; click OK to dismiss the dialog.

As Brad receives the replies from his reviewers, he can continue to integrate the comments into his original document while allowing his reviewers to maintain their own copies complete with their comments. Maintaining digital control of the process should help to resolve any issues that can arise when working with paper and trying to reconcile comments from different sources manually—handwritten comments are easier to miss or misinterpret than are those that are typewritten. Also, using the Acrobat review process is extremely time efficient.

Once Brad has received the comments and integrated them into his original document, he can save the document using a separate name. Using a distinctive name, such as appending the review date to the end of the original document's name makes it easier to track the progress of a project. He saves the file as Product Manual_draft1202.pdf.

WORKING FROM ACROBAT

Instead of opening the comments' files from the e-mail program, Brad can also work in Acrobat directly. Open the file, and then select the Comments tab to display the Comments pane. Click the Options button, and select Import Comments; then locate and select the comment file. Read more about working with comments from Acrobat in Chapters 11 and 14.

Managing the Review

In the "old" days, Brad would have to manually flip through the edits he received to see who had finished commenting and whose feedback was still outstanding. He would then have to send out e-mail "reminder" messages. Using Acrobat's Tracker and the Comments list, he can control the information from within Acrobat.

Opening the Tracker

Follow these steps to open the Tracker:

1. Choose View > Task Buttons > Comment & Markup to display the button if it isn't already displayed on the toolbars.

2. Click the pull-down arrow on the Comment & Markup task button and choose Tracker from the menu.

3. The Tracker opens as a separate window (**Figure 13.18**). You see the following review categories listed in the left frame of the window:

    ■ **My Reviews** lists any reviews that you have initiated and are managing.

    ■ **Participant Reviews** lists those reviews that you are participating in, but which are initiated by someone else.

    ■ **Offline Documents** lists any documents that are involved in Web-based reviews that have been used offline.

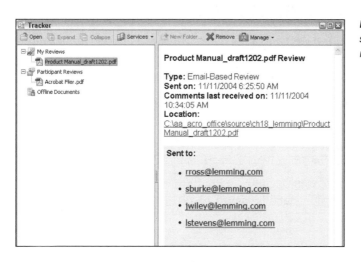

Figure 13.18 The Tracker shows information about reviews.

The right pane of the window shows the name of the selected review, the storage location of the original review document, and a list of the participants. The participant list is composed of active links; click a name to open an e-mail dialog addressed to the selected participant.

Managing the Review

The Tracker gives you several ways to manage communication with the review participants.

Click Manage on the Tracker toolbar to open the pull-down menu. From this menu, choose one of the following commands:

- **Email All Reviewers** opens an e-mail dialog preaddressed to the participant list. Add the message and send the e-mail.

- **Send Review Reminder** opens an e-mail dialog addressed to the participants. The message reminds them of the document that is to be reviewed, as well as a list of directions for reviewing.

- **Invite Additional Reviewers** opens the Send by Email for Review dialog. Follow the wizard to add more participants.

It's simple to keep track of a review having three or four participants; it's much more difficult to control a review with dozens of participants. But the Comments list makes the task easier by allowing you to sort comments in a number of useful ways.

Using the Comments List

Once comments are integrated into a document, they can be used and examined in a number of ways.

Follow these steps to work with comments in Acrobat:

1. Select the Comments tab at the left of the program window to display the Comments pane.

    Unlike most of Acrobat's navigation panes, the Comments pane displays horizontally under the Document pane and any open Navigation panes.

2. Comments imported into the original draft are arranged in the Comments list according to page by default (**Figure 13.19**).

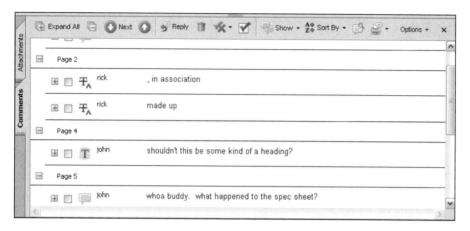

Figure 13.19 *By default, Acrobat arranges comments in a document according to page number.*

3. Click the Sort By button's pull-down arrow and choose a sort method (**Figure 13.20**). Brad chooses the Sort By Author option to reorder the list of comments.

4. The sorted list is collapsed; click the (+) to the left of a name to open the list of comments from a selected author (**Figure 13.21**).

Some of the comments in the document are simply text edits intended for reintegrating into the original Word document, while others pertain to aspects of the PDF document itself, specifically the bookmarks, which Brad asked the reviewers to evaluate. All the comments used in the sample project can be used in the source Word document, either as edits or comments.

Figure 13.20 *You can choose from among several ways to sort the contents of the Comments list.*

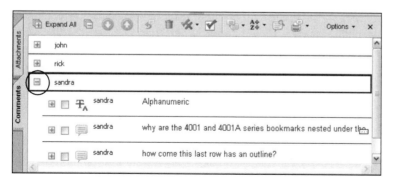

Figure 13.21 *Open and close reviewer's comments by clicking the (+) or (–) icon to the left of the name.*

Exporting Comments to a Word Document (Windows)

Earlier in the chapter, we tagged the document prior to conversion with the PDFMaker. You'll see why in this section.

If you have a tagged PDF created from a Word XP, or Word 2002 or later document, you can automatically integrate edits into the original document from Acrobat if the conversion was done using the PDFMaker in Windows—no manual corrections required!

Download **Product Manual_draft1.doc** if you'd like to see the Word document with the integrated comments. This file can be viewed in either Windows or Mac versions of Word; use this version of the file if you are working in Mac because there is no exporting function for comments in Mac OS. Use your own versions of the project files if you are working in Windows and want to follow along with the steps.

You can work from either Acrobat (using the Comments menu commands) or Word (using the Acrobat Comments menu commands). Decide which method to use based on your workflow. If you have just finished working with comments in Acrobat, continue to work from there; if you have the source document open in Word, use the Word commands.

The process involves two parts—first you decide what method to use for exporting the comments from the PDF file, and then you decide how you want the comments placed in the Word document.

> **TIP** Make a copy of the original Word document so you can import the comments into it. Integrating comments into a copy preserves the integrity of your original document and allows you to track the text-editing process.

Exporting the Comments

There's no difference in the comment export-import process whether you are starting from Acrobat or if you are working in Word. Brad has his PDF file open in Acrobat.

Follow these steps to export the comments from Acrobat to a Word document:

1.   Click the Comment & Markup task button's pull-down arrow to display its menu, and choose Export Comments > To Word, or click Comments on the menu and choose Export Comments > To Word.

2. Microsoft Word opens, and the Import Comments from Adobe Acrobat dialog opens, which describes the integration process. Click OK to close the dialog and start the import process.

You can select the Don't Show Again option at the lower left of the dialog once you are familiar with the process.

3. The Import Comments from Adobe Acrobat dialog opens (**Figure 13.22**). The name of the PDF file from which you are exporting appears in the top field. Click Browse and select the source Word document into which you want to integrate the comments. Brad's file is named Product Manual_draft1202.doc.

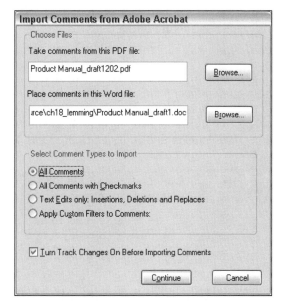

Figure 13.22 *Follow the dialog to select the comments for importing.*

4. Among the import options available, you can choose:

- **All Comments** to import the entire range of comments from Acrobat—the option chosen in the sample project.

- **All Comments with Checkmarks** if you used a personal commenting system in Acrobat using checkmarks to identify a subset of comments to import. You can see how checkmarks can be used in Chapter 14's project.

- **Text Edits only: Insertions, Deletions and Replaces** to restrict the imported comments to those created by the Text Edit tools.

- **Apply Custom Filters to Comments** to specify comment imports by author, type of comment, or comment status.

- **Turn Track Changes On Before Importing Comments** if you are using several versions of the document.

5. Click Continue to dismiss the dialog and process the comments.

6. The Successful Import dialog opens once the comments are processed. The dialog lists the number and types of comments and describes how to proceed.

If Acrobat can't evaluate the structure of the source document's tags, you may see an Unconfirmed Placement listing on the Successful Import dialog. Click the View List button to see a list of the comments that have unconfirmed placements. Acrobat adds the comments to the document where it thinks they belong.

7. Click Integrate Text Edits to start the edit integration process.

Next, Brad has to decide how to integrate the comments and edits into the Word document.

Integrating Edits and Comments into the Word Document

Once the comments are processed, you have more decisions to make about how to integrate the comments into the Word file.

Follow these steps to integrate the comments into the source Word document, continuing from the set of steps in the previous section:

1. The Adobe Acrobat Comments dialog opens when the Integrate Text Edits button is clicked on the Successful Import dialog. You see the number of comments that can be converted; the first comment available for integrating into the document is displayed and highlighted in the Word document (**Figure 13.23**).

2. Click Apply to make the edit and modify the text in the Word document.

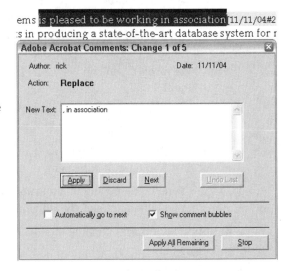

Figure 13.23 *Acrobat highlights the content identified by the imported comment in the document.*

3. Click Next in the Adobe Acrobat Comments dialog to continue with the next edit; repeat until you've finished all the edits.

If you don't want to use the edit, click Discard. If you have sorted the comments in Acrobat or are using a filter in Word, click Apply All to apply all the converted comments; click OK to agree to the process and dismiss the dialog. The comments are applied automatically to the Word document.

4. After processing is complete, you see the Text Integration Summary dialog that explains what has been done to the document. Click Done.

5. Check the document. The edits are applied and note comments are attached as Word comments throughout the document (**Figure 13.24**).

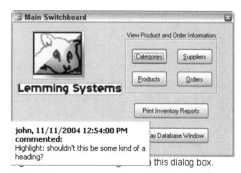

Figure 13.24 *Review the finished document and check the edits.*

COMMENT MIGRATION

You import comments into a PDF document only once. When you are working with multiple versions of a document, it is simpler to save numbered copies. In this way, each time you circulate a document for comments, you have a PDF document that can accept comments. You can also migrate comments, which is a secondary method of adding comments to a document.

Choose Comments > Migrate Comments to open the Migrate Comments dialog, and select both the document you are migrating comments from as well as the one you are migrating comments to.

The migration process searches a document and tries to place additional comments in the correct locations based on the document's tags. There may be placement discrepancies based on the differences between the two versions of the document, which you have to adjust manually.

Acrobat places migrated comments according to these principles:

■ Text comments applied to selected words display within the same words if they exist in the revised document; if the words are mismatched, the comments are placed on the first or last page of the document; if text is deleted, the edit is converted to a note.

■ Stamps, notes, and drawing markups are applied according to the original document's structure; if the page is deleted, the comment is placed on the last page of the revised document.

What Else Can He Do?

Brad has finished the first round of reviews and edits—without any paper—and has saved a lot of time in the process. The next phase of the review process is to create a new version of the PDF document and recirculate it to his participant list. When he has approval from all reviewers, his document is ready for printing.

There are many other Commenting features that he can use. He can, for example, use a checkmarking system in Acrobat's Comments list to sort the comments for export to the Word document, which can be very useful if there are a lot of comments in the document and not all of them need to be exported to Word. You can see how checkmarks are used for managing comments in Chapter 14.

Brad can also create comment documents in Acrobat, such as a comment summary that can be saved as a PDF document on its own (also described in Chapter 14), or he can export the comments to a text or FDF file.

14

Secure Reviewing and Reporting

Developing and communicating with business documents can be a very involved process, often requiring input gathered from many people, and over the course of several review cycles. How on earth do you manage to keep track of who's who and who is responsible for what? And how can the review process be controlled?

Many aspects of modern business require that the exchange of information that is secured in some way, whether that be a package the receptionist signs for on delivery or a briefcase cuffed to a courier's wrist. PDF documents are no different.

Chapter 11's project introduced you to the concept of digital signatures, including creating a Digital ID, exchanging certificates, and applying an initial signature to a document using a process called *certification* (discussed thoroughly in that chapter's bonus Web material). Chapter 13 described how to conduct a simple review process using Acrobat 7's Tracker feature to control the distribution of the files and collection of the feedback.

In this chapter, you'll combine the review process with secure document exchange. Whereas the project in Chapter 13 showed a simple review for users working with Adobe Reader, the project in this chapter is designed only for those using Adobe Acrobat 6 or 7—not Adobe Reader—because it includes working with digital signatures, a feature that's not included in a file that is enabled for those working with Adobe Reader.

In this project, you'll also learn how to do much more with comments: creating a comments summary from a set of reviews, generating different formats based on the file's content, and managing the list of comments using Acrobat's Checkmark feature. Then you'll discover how to add multiple signatures to the same document and uncover ways to examine document versions based on their contents at the time a signature is applied.

Sign Here, Please

Erin Crowley is a busy administrative assistant in a municipal government office. Part of her responsibility is the distribution and control of service tenders, which are documents that list the specifics for contracts being offered to the public for bidding. Drafts of tenders offered to service providers are created using government templates and then circulated to several key people in her department for input and review before the final tender is sent to the department's attorney for approval.

Today Erin is working with a janitorial service tender. The department's tender will be made available to companies interested in bidding on a janitorial contract. She's incorporated basic information from several key areas, such as property management, health and safety, and others, into the basic tender file. Erin's plan is to create a PDF from the tender file and then circulate it to the various players for their input. She'll ask the reviewers to comment on the information she's added to the boilerplate tender form.

Erin's colleagues have recently completed some Acrobat 7 Professional training sessions. Many of the management staff in Erin's office have started using Acrobat 7 and are getting into the Commenting tools. Some are finding the program useful for reviewing plans and other submitted materials, and a couple of the more adventurous among them have started using Acrobat for organizing their e-mail. They all learned how to create Digital IDs and exchanged them during their training sessions, but nobody's actually used one in real life yet!

NOTE See how to manage e-mail using Acrobat in Chapter 7; you can learn how to create and exchange Digital IDs in the bonus Web site material for Chapter 11's project.

Steps Involved in This Project

This is the first time Erin is tracking a review and using signatures in Acrobat 7. When the tender has been reviewed by all parties, Erin's going to process the comments using a Checkmark feature in Acrobat's Comments pane. She thinks the Checkmark feature will help her organize her work, and she'll print a report of the review she can use to incorporate changes into her draft. Finally, when the document is complete, she'll forward it to the reviewers again for signatures to acknowledge their acceptance of the finished wording before forwarding it to the attorney (**Figure 14.1**).

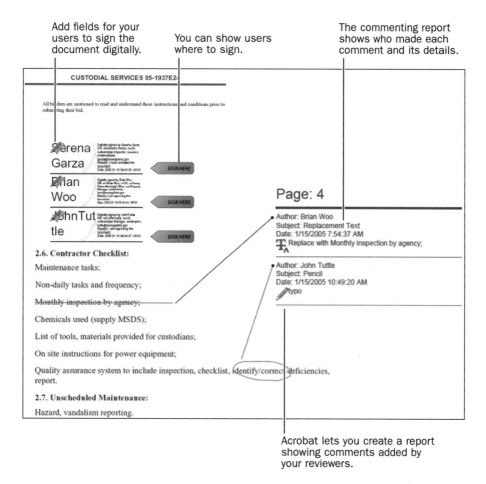

Figure 14.1 *Use Acrobat's features to manage content in your documents, such as changes made during a review, and signatures.*

To complete the project, Erin needs to

- Create the PDF version of the tender proposal from two other files
- Set up and conduct the review of the proposal

- Collect returned comments and integrate them into her copy of the file

- Process the comments in Acrobat

- Create and save a report on the comments

- Modify the original tender file to incorporate the changes

- Add a footer to the pages

- Add signature fields to the file and modify the opening page

- Circulate the document for final signatures

- Check the signed versions

Erin is going to start by converting the original tender file and a cover sheet to PDF. She'll work from within Acrobat.

NOTE Several chapters in the book have described how to work with the PDFMaker in Microsoft Word, such as Chapter 2 and Chapter 13.

Creating the Basic PDF Files

Instead of converting each document to PDF in Word and then combining them in Acrobat, Erin is working directly from Acrobat. She's going to check the PDFMaker settings and then convert and combine the files.

 If you'd like to convert Erin's documents yourself, download **tender.doc** and **tender_cover.doc** from the Web site. The combined PDF file is also on the Web site, named **custodial_tender.pdf**.

Checking Conversion Settings

In Acrobat, follow these steps to check the conversion settings:

1. Choose Edit > Preferences (Acrobat > Preferences) to open the Preferences dialog.

2. Click Convert to PDF in the Categories column to display the Converting to PDF options (**Figure 14.2**), and then click Microsoft Office in the Converting to PDF list to the right.

3. Click Edit Settings to open the "Adobe PDF Settings for supported documents" dialog (**Figure 14.3**).

4. Click the Adobe PDF Settings pull-down arrow and choose Standard. Erin plans to use the Standard settings because they provide both a small file size and an adequate resolution for printing.

5. Click the Adobe PDF Security pull-down arrow and choose None from the list. Erin doesn't need to add security, such as a password, to the document.

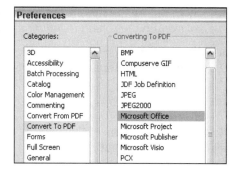

Figure 14.2 *You can specify file conversion settings from within Acrobat.*

6. Leave the Enable accessibility and reflow check box selected, and deselect the other options. Erin doesn't need any bookmarks or links in her converted tender proposal.

7. Click OK to close the dialog and return to the Preferences dialog; click OK again to dismiss the Preferences dialog.

Now that Erin has checked the settings, she'll convert the two documents to a single PDF file.

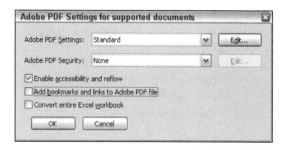

Figure 14.3 *Choose basic conversion settings in this dialog.*

Creating the PDF File

Erin is going to use Acrobat's Binder feature to create her file. You can read about using the feature in depth in Chapter 2, as well as Bonus Chapter 1 on the Web site.

Follow these steps to combine the files:

1. In Acrobat, click the Create PDF task button to open its menu, and then choose From Multiple Files to open the Create PDF From Multiple Documents dialog.

2. Click Browse to display the Open dialog, and then choose the files to add to the PDF file. Erin chooses contract.doc and contract_cover.doc.

3. Click Add to dismiss the Open dialog and list the files in the Files to Combine column on the Create PDF From Multiple Documents dialog.

4.   Click OK. The Create PDF From Multiple Documents dialog is replaced by Progress and Acrobat PDFMaker dialogs as the files are converted.

5.   When the files are converted, a Save As dialog opens. The file is named Binder1.pdf by default. Rename the file; Erin renames it custodial_tender. pdf.

6.   Click Save to dismiss the dialog and save the combined file.

Now that she's got the PDF version of the file, she's going to send it to her management group for commenting.

Starting the Review

Decide in advance how you want your users to access the file. If the recipients are mixed—that is, they are working with both Acrobat and Adobe Reader 6 or 7—you can use the default settings as you set up the review. But your reviewers need to know they can only comment if they have Acrobat or Adobe Reader 6 or 7. You don't have to remember this detail because Acrobat automatically includes the information in the e-mail it creates to invite participants to the review. Acrobat 7 Professional automatically enables a file to be commented on in Adobe Reader 7.

On the other hand, if the document contains signature fields, as Erin's will, enabling it for commenting in Adobe Reader 7 prevents the same document from being signed in Acrobat 7 due to the programming complexities involved.

Erin is distributing her document internally, and the recipients are all working with Acrobat 7, not Adobe Reader. She'll set up a review using the Tracker, but she'll modify some of its settings. You can read about using the Tracker for recipients working with Adobe Reader 7 in Chapter 13.

Follow these steps to set up a review for Acrobat 7 users:

1.   In Acrobat, click the Send for Review task button and choose Send by Email for Review to open the dialog, which is a three-pane wizard.

2.   In the first pane, click the Browse button and select the file you wish to send for review. If the file is open in Acrobat, it is automatically shown in the dialog's field. Erin is using the custodial_tender.pdf file.

3.   Click Next to display the second pane. Type the addresses of the review participants, or click Address Book to load your system's e-mail address book and then choose the recipients (**Figure 14.4**).

4.   Click Customize Review Options to open the Review Options dialog.

5. Type the return e-mail address in the field on the dialog (**Figure 14.5**). You can also click the Address Book button to open your system's address book and select a name.

6. Deselect the "Also allow users of Free Adobe Reader 7.0 to participate in this review" check box. Erin plans to use signature fields with the document later in the project, and unless this option is deselected, the fields won't be available for her recipients to sign.

7. Click OK to close the Review Options dialog, returning you to the Send by Email for Review wizard. Click Next to show the third pane of the wizard.

8. Read the default text for the review invitation and modify it if necessary. Erin leaves the default text.

9. Click Send Invitation to dismiss the dialog and send the invitations. Depending on your system's configuration, you'll see an Outgoing Message Notification, saying the invitation has been delivered to your e-mail client and will be sent according to your system's schedule.

10. Click OK to dismiss the dialog.

Now that Erin has sent the invitations, she's going to wait for the comments to return from her colleagues. They are sending her FDF (File Data Format) files containing their comments on the document.

NOTE Read more about FDF files and how they are used in a review in Chapters 11 and 13.

Figure 14.4 *List the addresses of those you want to invite to a document review.*

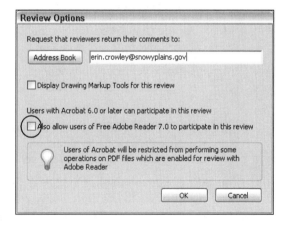

Figure 14.5 *Deselect the default enabling option to customize the document's options to use signatures in a reviewed file.*

Incorporating the Comments

Acrobat has the uncanny ability to keep track of files—which is a good thing because they can often be ornery devils, don't you think? When Erin receives the comments file via e-mail, double-clicking the file will automatically open the master PDF document, and Acrobat will ask if she wants to add the comments to the file. Isn't that handy?

Erin has received FDF files from her reviewers but wants to work within Acrobat, so she'll bring the comments back into her master PDF file. Erin is going to work in the Comments pane to do this.

 To work with the FDF comment files that Erin uses in the project, download **tender_serena.fdf**, **tender_brian.fdf**, and **tender_john.fdf**.

To incorporate the comments into a file, follow these steps:

1. Open the original file used for initiating the review in Acrobat. Erin's original file is named custodial_tender.pdf.

2. Select the Comments tab to display the Comments pane across the bottom of the program window.

3. Click the Options button on the Comments pane to open its menu, and choose Import Comments. The Import Comments dialog opens.

4. Select the comment files to import into the PDF file. Erin selects the tender_serena.fdf, tender_brian.fdf, and tender_john.fdf files.

5. An Adobe Acrobat dialog opens stating that all the comments in the reviewed file were placed in the original document—click OK to dismiss the dialog. You'll have to respond to the dialog three times because an information dialog opens for each imported FDF file.

6. Scroll through the list. You'll see there are a fair number of edits that Erin has to make to the draft. Many are simple, but there is also a new section that needs to be added to the end of the file, as can be seen in Serena Garza's note in **Figure 14.6**.

Next Erin has to decide how she's going to make the revisions. She saves the file before starting to edit the document; the file is saved as custodial_tender1.pdf.

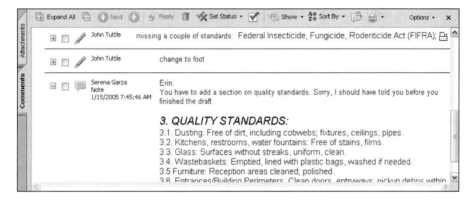

Figure 14.6 Erin reviews the edits she has to make in the Comments pane.

NOTE If the comments were generated in a different version of the file—for example, if the recipients saved a copy of the file and then added their comments and exported them to you, or if you resaved the file—Acrobat opens an information dialog that says the selected FDF file doesn't contain comments from the document you have open in Acrobat and asks if you want to import them anyway. Click Yes to dismiss the dialog and integrate the comments.

Making and Tracking Corrections

There are several ways Erin can approach her editing. She can make all the changes in Acrobat using the TouchUp Text tool, she can make all the changes in her source document and recreate the PDF file, or she can use a combination of the two methods. She's going for the combo today.

NOTE You can read how to export comments from Acrobat into a file's source Word document in Chapter 13.

Erin decides she'll make the changes on the PDF file using the TouchUp Text tool—with the exception of the additional section, which she'll add from another Word document. In earlier drafts of the tender form, she had included a section that was removed and now learns in the comments that it has to be put back in again. Ah, office life!

To finish this part of her task, she will make changes using the TouchUp Text tool and then track her progress using checkmarks.

If you'd like to use Erin's document complete with the comments and text revisions, download **custodial_tender1.pdf**; if you previously downloaded the comment files and integrated them into a copy of the tender file, continue working in your file.

Sorting the Comments

Erin decides the simplest way to approach dealing with the comments is to sort them first.

Follow these steps to sort the comments by author:

1.   Select the Comments tab to display the Comments pane across the bottom of the program window.

2.   On the Comments pane, choose Sort By > Author. You see the comments are sorted by names of the comment file authors.

     The comment listing is collapsed on the Comments pane. That is, only the names of the comment authors are shown, and the individual comments added by each author are hidden.

3.   Click the name of the first author on the list to display the list of comments. In Erin's document, the sorted comments show Brian Woo's comments first, which is fine as his are the simplest to deal with.

Now that the comments are sorted, Erin is going to use one of Acrobat's TouchUp tools to change the content in the document.

Touching Up Text

You can either select the tools from the program's menu or open the Advanced Editing toolbar. Since Erin is working in several areas of the document, it's simpler for her to open the toolbar.

Follow these steps to open the toolbar and change the first comment:

1.   Choose View > Toolbars > Advanced Editing to open the toolbar; drag it to dock in the toolbar well with the other toolbars.

2.   Click the visible TouchUp tool on the Advanced Editing toolbar to show the TouchUp tool subtoolbar. Click TouchUp Text 🔲 to select the tool.

3.   In the Comments pane, click the first comment. You'll see the document pane displays the comment on the page.

4. Click the error in the text with the TouchUp Text tool and type the replacement text. In Erin's project, the first correction from Brian's comments list is to change a value from 2,800 to 2,500 (**Figure 14.7**).

One correction down, and a whole lot more to go! To keep track of her edits, Erin is going to use the Comments pane's Checkmark feature.

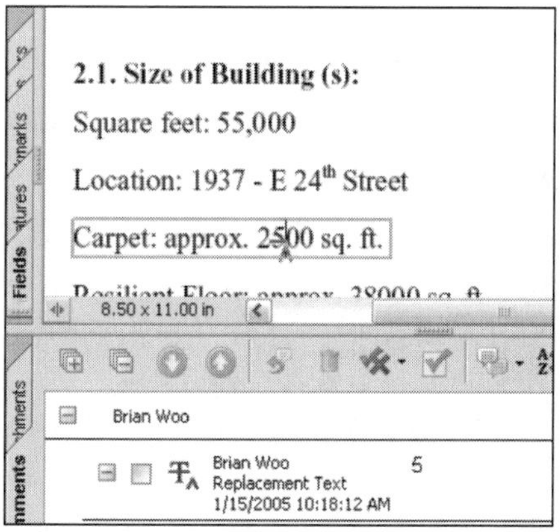

Tracking the Comments

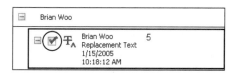

Figure 14.7 Using the TouchUp Text tool is a quick way to make simple changes in the file.

Erin's project isn't that difficult to manage, but since she anticipates working through Acrobat quite a bit in the future, she's developing a system to control and track her work. She's going to use the Checkmark feature included in the Comments pane.

Follow these steps to add a checkmark to a comment in the Comments pane:

1. Select the comment you want to apply the checkmark to.

2. Click the Checkmark icon ☑ on the Comments pane.

3. The first time you use the feature, an Adobe Acrobat information dialog opens explaining that the checkmarks are internal to your copy of the document only and aren't shared with others in the review. This, of course, is what Erin wants.

4. Click OK to dismiss the dialog. A checkmark is shown in the check box to the left of the comment's listing in the Comments pane (**Figure 14.8**).

Figure 14.8 You can use checkmarks to track comments you have worked with.

Erin continues through the project, replacing and making text changes to all but the "major" replacement, an entire section that needs to be added to the reviewed version of the project file.

To check your progress and make sure you haven't missed any comments, you can sort the comments based on checkmarks by following these steps:

1. Click Sort By on the Comments pane to open the pull-down list.

2. Choose Checkmark Status. The comments are resorted again, and this time there are two categories—Unmarked and Marked.

3. Click the Unmarked category to display the list. The only outstanding comment that Erin hasn't processed is the inserted text (**Figure 14.9**).

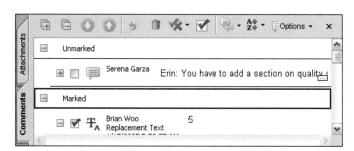

Figure 14.9 Sort the list based on checkmarks to review your progress.

4. Save the file. Erin's file is saved as custodial_tender1.pdf.

Next she's going to handle that text insertion problem using an inserted page, and then she'll add a footer to the document in Acrobat.

Inserting a Page

One of the comments Erin has to process requires her to add a huge block of text to the document. Although she could certainly add it to the file using the TouchUp Text tool in Acrobat 7 Professional, it would take far more time than it would to simply add another page to the document and then tweak the text.

Since Erin originally had this content in the tender document (a couple of draft cycles before the start of this project!), she's already got a copy of the file she can use. In Microsoft Word, she copies the page, pastes it to its own file, then saves it and creates a PDF using Word's PDFMaker.

Download **tender_extra.pdf** to insert the new page into the project file—**custodial_tender1.pdf**. If you'd like to see the file after the modifications are complete, download **custodial_tender2.pdf**.

Follow these steps to insert a page at the end of the custodial_tender1.pdf file:

1. Display the last page of the open file in the Document pane.

If you display the page before the location for the file being inserted, the page selections are loaded automatically into the Insert Pages dialog.

2. Choose Document > Insert Pages to open the Select File To Insert dialog. Choose the file to add to the open document; Erin selects the tender_extra.pdf file.

3. Click Select to dismiss the dialog and open the Insert Pages dialog. The dialog shows the name of the selected file. Since the final page of the file was displayed in the Document pane before starting the insertion process, the Location field shows the After selection (or you can choose it from the pull-down list). In addition, the page is preselected as page 5 of 5.

4. Click OK to dismiss the dialog and insert the page in the file.

5. Save the file. Erin's project is saved as custodial_tender2.pdf.

Now that the extra page is inserted, Erin is going to use Acrobat to add a footer to all the pages of the file.

Using Headers and Footers

Erin could have applied a footer in Acrobat prior to starting her review. Being the efficient person she is, she decided to wait until the review was done, just in case she needed to make significant changes to the draft—which of course is what happened. Now that she's got the entire document assembled, she's going to add the footer to the pages before circulating the file again for signatures.

NOTE Rather than adding footers in Acrobat, Erin could have imported them with her source document. If she had included the footer in the page she just converted and imported, the footer would have been added automatically to the page in the PDF file. In that case, she'd have to make any adjustments to the page numbering on the pages using the TouchUp Text tool.

Follow these steps to add a footer:

1. Choose Document > Add Headers & Footers to open the Add Headers & Footers dialog. Select the Footers tab.

The three footer content fields at the top of the dialog align content to the left, center, and right of the document page, respectively (**Figure 14.10**).

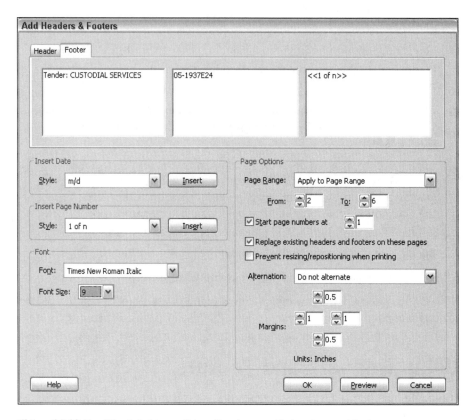

Figure 14.10 *Use this dialog to configure the document's headers and footers.*

2. For both the Insert Date and Insert Page Number sections, click the pull-down arrows and choose a style. Erin is adding a page number but not a date, and chooses the "1 of n" style from the Insert Page Number Style pull-down list.

3. Click the field where you want the content to be placed, and then click Insert to insert the selected page number to footer fields. Erin clicks the right-aligned field to place a page number in the right-hand corner of each page.

4. Click another content field to activate it and type text if you like. In the sample document, Erin adds Tender: CUSTODIAL SERVICES in the left-aligned field and 05-1937E24, which is the tender's control number, in the center-aligned field.

If you put text in a field and want to move it, select it and drag it to the appropriate field.

5. Click the Font pull-down arrow, and choose a font for the footers; click the Font Size pull-down arrow, and choose a font size. Erin uses Times New Roman Italic font in 9pt size.

6. Select Page Options as needed for the document. You can choose a page range, a custom number from which to start numbering pages, whether to replace existing headers/footers or prevent resizing/repositioning for printing, and whether to apply the footers to all or alternate (even or odd) pages.

For Erin's document, she chooses Apply to Page Range from the Page Range pull-down list and types 2 and 6 in the To and From page range field, respectively. Then she clicks the "Start page numbers at" check box and types 1. In this way, the cover page she added to the document isn't included in the page count, and won't have a footer.

7. Choose margin locations. Erin's project uses the Acrobat defaults. Click a margin's field and type a custom value, or use the up and down arrows to adjust the margin's value. The four Margins fields correspond to the top, bottom, left, and right margin values.

8. When the settings are complete, click Preview to open the dialog shown in **Figure 14.11**. Click the page arrows at the bottom of the dialog to view the footer on various pages of the document. You can't see the selected custom font due to the small size of the preview, but you can assess its location.

9. Click OK to close the Preview dialog and then click OK to close the Add Headers & Footers dialog.

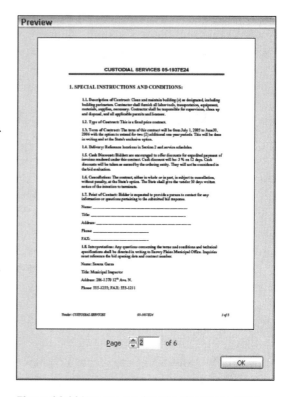

Figure 14.11 *You can preview the placement of the footers in this dialog.*

10. Check the location, content, font, and font size on the actual document pages (**Figure 14.12**). If you need to make adjustments, reopen the Add Headers & Footers dialog, make your changes, and click OK to close the dialog.

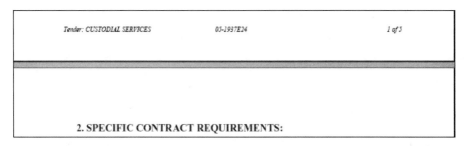

Tender: CUSTODIAL SERVICES　　　　*05-1937E24*　　　　*1 of 5*

2. SPECIFIC CONTRACT REQUIREMENTS:

Figure 14.12 *A unified footer is applied to the document using the specified settings.*

Erin reopens the Comments pane, and with a flourish she checks the final comment. Done! She's not taking any chances though. Now that she's processed the edits, she's going to keep a record of the comments before modifying the file for signatures.

Creating a Comments Summary

Erin's situation is quite common, isn't it? Sometimes it's difficult to second-guess your colleagues' intentions—or read their minds—regardless of how efficient you are at your job. Since Erin has had to take out and replace sections of the document a few times, she decides to create a comments summary PDF to record what changes she made and where—just in case.

Acrobat includes several varieties of comment summaries. The option you choose depends on personal preference as well as the structure of your document. A summary document is a separate document from both the master document and the comments.

Download **Comment Summary.pdf** to see the comments summary for Erin's file, or you can follow along to create your own.

Follow these steps to create a comments summary:

1. Select the Comments tab to display the Comments pane across the program window.

2. Click the Options button, and choose Summarize Comments from the pull-down menu to open the Summarize Options dialog (**Figure 14.13**).

3. Click an option to choose a layout.

The dialog offers four ways to create the summary; when you click a radio button, you see a small example of how the layout will appear. Erin chooses the "Document and comments with connector lines on single pages" radio button. Read more about the various options in the sidebar, "Choosing a Summary Option."

4. Click the Paper size pull-down arrow and choose an option. Erin uses the default Letter page size.

Figure 14.13 Choose options for the layout of the comments summary file.

5. Select an option from the Sort comments by pull-down list, or leave the default Page option selected, as Erin does. You can also sort the comments by author, date, or type of comment.

6. If you like, other options allow you to select the font size and choose whether to include the comments from the entire document or only those shown in the Document pane.

7. Click OK to dismiss the dialog.

8. Acrobat processes the document and creates the file, adding "Summary of Comments on" to the first heading of the page's content.

9. Save the comments summary file. You can use the default name—in the project, the file's default name is "Summary of Comments on CUSTODIAL SERVICES 05-1937E24.pdf"—or rename the file. Erin names her file Comment Summary.pdf.

When you look through the file, you'll see a listing of comments on each page beside the content, as well as connector lines showing where the comments are placed (**Figure 14.14**).

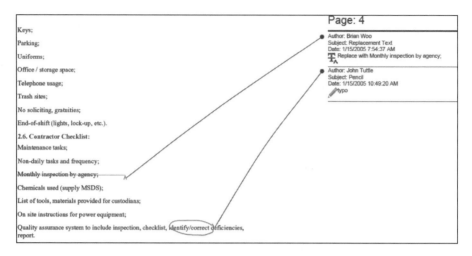

Figure 14.14 *The lines connect a comment's information to its location on the page.*

Automatically Creating a Summary

There is another way Erin can create the comments summary. In the Comments pane, click Print Comments > Create PDF of Comments Summary to automatically generate a summary file. The summary document includes separate comment pages, with each comment numbered and the corresponding numbers shown on the document's content page.

NOTE To print the summary directly, click the Print Comments button on the Comments pane, and choose Print Comments Summary.

Erin has the editing finished. It's time for some final tweaks—in accordance with her original plan—and then she'll send the final version to the reviewers again, this time for signing.

CHOOSING A SUMMARY OPTION

The format you select for creating your comments summary depends on the content and how you intend to use the PDF file. For example, since Erin wants a printed record of what she's done, using the option she selected places the comments and connector lines on the same page as the content when she prints the summary. If she planned to use it onscreen only, using one of the options that puts the content and the comments on separate pages is easier because you can view the pages side by side in Acrobat.

Use the connector line options if you are visually inclined (as Erin is); for the more numerically inclined, Acrobat 7 offers the "Document and comments with sequence numbers on separate pages" layout, which adds numbers to the page copy where the comments are located and also numbers the information about the comments. Regardless of the option selected, the point is to maintain a record of the document as well as the comments and where they are located.

Preparing the Document for Signing

Erin included a cover page for her tender document's review process that included "Draft1" on the page. After saving a copy of the file, she's going to remove that label and strip out the reviewers' comments,.

Saving a Copy

When a file is part of a tracked review, each time it is opened, Acrobat will show a dialog about the reviewing process. Erin's finished with that part of the project, and she doesn't want to keep responding to that dialog! Before getting the file ready for signing, she'll save it as a copy.

To separate a document from a tracked review, use the Save a Copy rather than the Save As command.

Follow these steps:

1. Choose File > Save a Copy. An information dialog opens explaining that using the command separates the file from the tracked review—which is the whole idea!

2. Click the Save a Copy button to dismiss the dialog and open a Save dialog.

3. Name the file and choose its storage location.

4. Click Save to dismiss the dialog and save a copy of the file. Erin's copied file is saved as CUSTODIAL 05-1937E24.pdf, which is the official name of the document (named according to the type of tender and its number).

Deleting the Draft Label

Now that she has the "separated" copy, Erin wants to delete the "Draft 1" label. Click the label on the cover page using either the TouchUp Text tool or the TouchUp Object tool selected from the Advanced Editing toolbar. Both tools produce the same outcome. If you use the TouchUp Object tool, select the object and press Delete on the keyboard; if you use the TouchUp Text tool, select the text and press Delete on the keyboard.

NOTE You can read more about working with the TouchUp Object tool in Chapter 8 as well as Bonus Chapter 4 on the book's Web site.

Deleting Comments

Erin doesn't need the comments in the copy of the document she's circulating for signatures. If she were involved in a large project with many review cycles and herds of comments, she could remove the comments as part of using the PDF Optimizer. Since the document is quite simple, as is the review, Erin will remove the comments manually.

Follow these steps to remove the comments:

1. Select the Comments tab to display the Comments pane.

2. Click the Collapse All icon 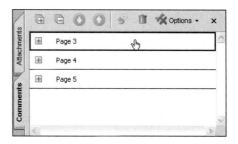 on the Comments pane to collapse the listings into their sorted headings.

NOTE To select all the comments in a single step, click any comment, and then press Ctrl-A/Command-A.

3. Click the first listing in the Comments pane, which is Page 3 in this project if you are using the default Sort By Page option. The selected listing is highlighted by a black border (**Figure 14.15**).

4. Click Delete on the keyboard or the trash can icon on the Comments pane. The page's comments are removed, and the next page's comments are highlighted.

Figure 14.15 *The selected comment group is highlighted on the Comments pane.*

5. Press Delete on the keyboard or click the trash can icon on the Comments pane two more times to remove the comments from the remaining pages.

6. Save the document.

Next Erin is going to add some stamps and signature fields for the reviewers to sign.

Placing Stamp Comments on the Page

Now that Erin has a stripped-down version of the file, she's going to add some stamps to it to show the reviewers where to sign the document to approve it. To set the stamps evenly on the page, she'll use Acrobat's gridlines. You can read more about working with and customizing gridlines in Bonus Chapter 4 on the book's Web site.

Preparing the Page View

Follow these steps to place the gridlines on and add the stamps to the page:

1. Display the cover page in the Document pane.

2. Choose View > Grid to display the gridlines on the page. The default grid placement uses ¼-inch squares.

Now Erin will add Sign Here stamps to the page.

Adding Stamp Instructions

Acrobat includes a wide variety of preconfigured stamps. Erin is going to use one of the Sign Here stamps to indicate to the reviewers where they have to sign. You can read more about using stamps in Chapter 11 and creating custom stamps in Chapter 9.

1. Choose Tools > Commenting to open the Commenting toolbar; drag it to dock it with the other toolbars in the toolbar well at the top of the program window.

2. Click the Stamp tool's pull-down arrow to open its menu, and choose Sign Here > Sign Here.

   The Sign Here stamps are a collection of common stamps you'd use on a document to point out common commenting options, such as signing or initialing (**Figure 14.16**).

3. The pointer changes to the stamp's image; click the page to place the stamp.

4. Click the Stamp tool on the Commenting toolbar again—not the pull-down arrow—to select the same Stamp tool again.

5. As you move the pointer away from the toolbar, you see the Sign Here stamp is active again (**Figure 14.17**).

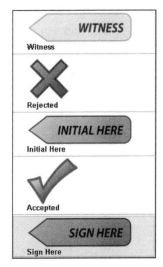

Figure 14.16 Erin adds stamps to show her reviewers where to sign the document.

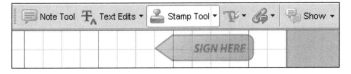

Figure 14.17 Clicking the Stamp tool activates the last tool selected.

6. Add one more copy of the stamp to the page, for a total of three Sign Here stamps.

Now that the stamps are placed, Erin is going to add signature fields. She's going to add the first field and then create duplicate copies automatically.

Adding Signature Fields

A signature field can be added when someone signs a document, or a signature can be placed into an existing signature field on a document. Since Erin's colleagues haven't worked with signatures before, she's going to give them fields to sign on the cover page of the document.

Adding the First Field

Follow these steps to add the first signature field to the cover page:

1. Click the Sign task button's pull-down arrow to open its menu, and choose Create a Blank Signature Field.

2. An Adobe Acrobat dialog opens saying that the Signature Field tool is selected and that you can draw a marquee to place the field. Click OK to dismiss the information dialog.

3. Drag a marquee on the page where you'd like to place the signature field, and release the mouse.

4. The Digital Signature Properties dialog opens; select the General tab.

5. The field is named Signature1 by default; click the text in the field and delete "1." Erin is using the automatic field duplication method, which automatically renumbers fields, as you'll see in the next section.

6. Click the Tooltip field and type text instructions. For the first signature field, Erin types Serena–please sign here (click to sign).

7. Click Close to dismiss the dialog and complete the field.

That's one signature field down, and two more to go. Erin could draw the second and third fields manually, but she'd like to try Acrobat's field-copying process.

Copying Fields

Rather than reselecting the tool and drawing additional fields, Erin is going to create multiple copies of the field automatically on the page.

NOTE You can use the same method to duplicate any type of field—see how Joe does it in Chapter 9 and how Amanda uses copies in Chapter 4.

Follow these steps to create multiple copies of a field:

1. Right-click/Control-click the field on the page to open the shortcut menu.

2. Choose Create Multiple Copies to open the Create Multiple Copies of Fields dialog.

Acrobat automatically adds copies to the page according to the values set in this dialog. The default values are 2 fields across and 2 fields down.

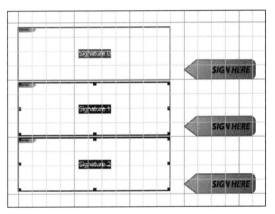

3. Reset the values according to how many copies you need. In her document, Erin needs a set of three fields in one column, and so she sets the "Copy selected fields down" value to 3 and the "Copy selected fields across value" to 1.

4. Click OK to close the dialog and add the copies of the fields. You'll see the fields are now renamed with a period (.) and an appended number (**Figure 14.18**).

Figure 14.18 Acrobat automatically renames the signature fields.

To test the fields, click the Hand tool [hand icon] and move the pointer over the field. Since all the fields are copies of the original, all the tooltips are the same at this point (**Figure 14.19**). Erin takes care of that next.

Figure 14.19 Serena–please sign... where exactly? Adjusting the fields' tooltips will make it clear.

Adjusting the Fields' Tooltips

To change a signature's tooltip, just double-click the field to open the Digital Signature Properties dialog. Click the Tooltip field and type the new text. Erin leaves much of the instruction the same, just changing the names for the second and third fields' tooltips to Brian and John.

That's better. But Erin still isn't happy with the appearance, and she decides to underline the fields. That way, the signers can see what they are clicking.

Modifying the Fields' Appearance

It's difficult to determine what is supposed to be signed, in spite of the big Sign Here arrow. Erin can modify the appearance of each field, separately or together as a group, to make the location of the signature fields' areas easier to see.

To modify the appearance of a number of fields at the same time, follow these steps:

1. Shift-click to select all three fields.

2. Right-click/Control-click to open the shortcut menu, and choose Properties to open the Digital Signature Properties dialog.

   You'll see when the dialog opens that there are no values on the General tab because you have selected multiple fields. Only certain properties, such as the appearance, can be modified for a group of fields.

3. Select the Appearance tab (**Figure 14.20**).

4. Click the Border Color color swatch to open the color palette, and choose a color. Erin selects the deep blue used in her office for correspondence and other documents.

5. Click the Line Thickness pull-down arrow and choose an option. Erin chooses the Medium line.

6. Click the Line Style pull-down arrow and choose an option. Erin chooses the Underlined style.

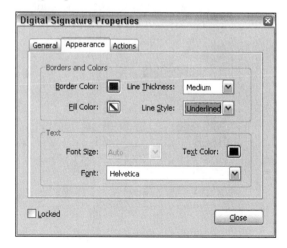

Figure 14.20 *Set the appearance for all fields at once in the Digital Signature Properties dialog.*

7.   Click Close to dismiss the dialog.

8.   Click the Hand tool on the Basic toolbar to deselect the signature fields and show their appearance on the page.

That's better! It's easy to see where the signature fields are.

Now that the fields have been added, Erin turns off the grid by choosing View > Grid. Finally the document is ready for signatures, and she saves it one more time using the same name—that is, CUSTODIAL 05-1937E24.pdf.

At this point, the project is complete except for the signatures. Although the team practiced exchanging certificates in their recent training session, Erin hasn't imported the set of certificates into her system. She'll do that next.

Importing a Certificate

Before Erin can proceed with signing and certifying the tender document, she's got to import the certificates for the signature process.

Download the set of certificate files used in the project. The four files are named **CertExchangeSerenaGarza.fdf**, **CertExchangeJohnTuttle.fdf**, **CertExchangeErinCrowley.fdf**, and **CertExchangeBrianWoo.fdf**.

Here's a summary of what you need to do to include the certificates in Acrobat once you have downloaded them from the Web site:

1.   In Acrobat 7, choose Advanced > Trusted Identities to open the Manage Trusted Identities dialog.

2.   Click Add contacts to open the Choose Contacts to Import dialog.

3.   Click Browse to open a Locate Certificate File dialog.

4.   Locate the certificates you downloaded from the Web site, and select one from the list.

5.   Click Open. The Locate Certificate File dialog closes, and the file is listed in the Contacts area on the Choose Contacts to Import dialog.

6.   Click Browse again, select the next file, and click Open to load it into the Choose Contacts to Import dialog.

7.   Continue until you have loaded all four certificates (**Figure 14.21**).

8.   Click Import to dismiss the Choose Contacts to Import dialog.

Figure 14.21 *Locate and select the certificates you want to import.*

9. The Import Complete dialog displays, showing you a list of the import functions; click OK to dismiss the dialog, returning you to the Manage Trusted Identities dialog.

10. Review the list; you see the new contacts have been added (**Figure 14.22**).

11. Click Close.

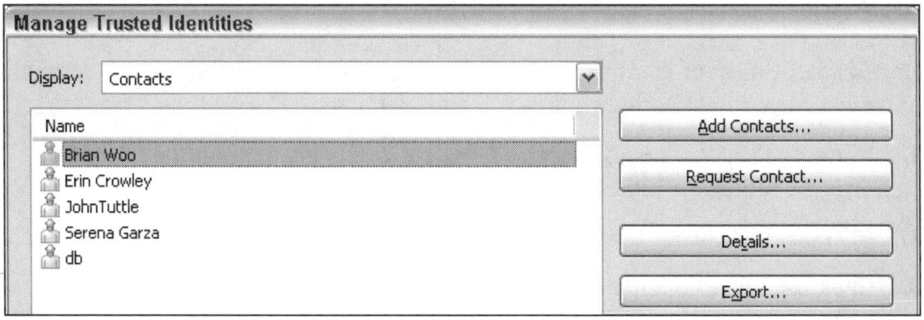

Figure 14.22 *The project certificates are included in the Manage Trusted Identities dialog.*

Erin is going to add her signature to the document first, in the form of a certifying signature, as soon as she takes care of one more bit of housekeeping—flattening the layers in the file.

HOW A DIGITAL ID WORKS

Digital IDs use a key encryption process. For you to share secure documents with others, and for others to share secure documents with you, you need to use Digital IDs.

A Digital ID is composed of two parts: a public key and a private key, which are both created automatically by Acrobat when you create the Digital ID. You have a signature that contains two keys. The private key is yours alone, and Acrobat uses it for signing and certifying your documents, and you share the public key with others. In the same way, another person's Digital ID contains a pair of keys; the private key is maintained by their system, and the public key can be shared with you.

If a coworker has your public key listed in a document, that coworker can share the information with you; if you have that coworker's public key listed in a document, you can share with him. You can share a document and keys with a group because Acrobat lets you use a number of keys for the same document. You don't have to figure which part of the signature is private and which is public—Acrobat takes care of the details for you.

Read more about working with signatures and certificates in Chapter 11's bonus material on the book's Web site.

Modifying the Document's Layers

What? Layers? Where did they come from? The fact is that adding fields and stamps may add a hidden layer to the document as in this project. If you have experimented with replacing pages in a document (as in Chapter 2's project), you have worked with Acrobat layers. Performing an operation such as replacing a page removes the underlying page content and replaces it with a specified page. Any objects you add in Acrobat, such as fields or footers, are retained and are "floating" on their own layer. You don't see the content added to a file in the Layers pane, the way you would with a layered document you create in a program like Microsoft Visio, but it's there!

When you certify a document, Acrobat evaluates its content and structure and displays a warning for any features that may compromise the integrity of your work. Layers will trigger such a warning. And when a recipient opens the file, they'll see the warning too. Erin is afraid the warning will throw the others off, so she decides to flatten the file first.

NOTE The structure of the sample document is the exception rather than the rule as most files won't show a hidden layer that can be flattened. The project's file shows you the connection between document structure and security issues. To see the difference, use a copy of the tender file and run through the steps in the next section to certify the document without following the flattening steps.

Follow these steps to flatten the document:

1. Choose View > Navigation Tabs > Layers to open the Layers pane.

2. Click the Options button on the Layers pane and choose Flatten Layers.

3. Close the Layers pane.

4. Save the file. Acrobat displays a warning that the changes can't be undone. Click OK to dismiss the dialog; the flattened file is saved. Erin saves the file as Signed_CUSTODIAL 05-1937E24.pdf.

All the document features are still available—you'll see the signature fields and stamps as before. Now the file is ready for certifying.

Certifying the Document

Erin hasn't added a big signature field and a Sign Here stamp to the file for her signature. She doesn't need to remind herself to sign the document. In fact, her signature is not even going to be visible on the document. She has, however, decided to sign it for two reasons:

- The first signer of a document is given the choice of signing or certifying the document. Erin's grasp of Acrobat is more extensive than that of her colleagues, and she's afraid the choice between signing and certifying might confuse them.

- She wants to have a signed copy of the document that shows how it existed at the time she completed it—just in case someone tries to sneak in any more changes!

Follow these steps to certify or sign a document invisibly:

1. Click the Sign task button to open its menu, and choose Sign this Document. The Document Is Not Certified dialog opens.

2. As there are no prior signatures on the document, Acrobat displays a message saying the document can be certified (to attest to the contents as they existed when the first signature is added) or signed. Click Certify Document to dismiss the dialog; the Save As Certified Document dialog opens.

3. The dialog offers the choice to get a Digital ID from a third-party source; click OK to dismiss the dialog and open the Save as Certified Document - Choose Allowable Actions dialog.

   A third-party Digital ID is used to control signatures in very large reviews and other secure processes (such as online distribution of content) where each user is granted rights to a document. The third-party company controls the keys for the Digital IDs, rather than the user and recipient having a private and public key, respectively.

4. Click the Allowed Actions pull-down arrow, and choose an option from the list. Erin chooses "Only allow commenting and form fill-in actions on this document" (**Figure 14.23**). She needs to enable the form-filling to allow the others to sign the document, and she wants to give them a choice to add more comments if necessary.

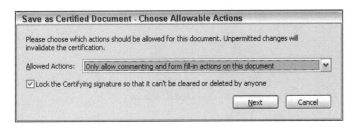

Figure 14.23 Choose the actions you will allow in the certified document.

5. The option "Lock the Certifying signature so that it can't be cleared or deleted by anyone" is selected by default; leave the option selected. Erin thinks the less tampering that can be done with the document, the better.

6. Click Next to show the Save as Certified Document - Warnings dialog. The recipients will see this warning when they open the document, as well as the default Warnings Comment, "I have included this content to make the document more interactive."

   The single warning explains that the use of comments is allowed in the document, which was Erin's choice. This dialog would also warn about layers appearing if the document had not been flattened, but Erin flattened the file in the previous section.

7. Click Next to show the Save as Certified Document - Select Visibility dialog.

8. Click "Do not show Certification on document." Even though Erin decides to hide her signature, the recipients will still be notified that it is certified, and the Certification icon will still display on the program window.

9. Click Next to show the Apply Digital Signature - Digital ID Selection dialog, and select a Digital ID from the list. Erin selects her own certificate, named Erin Crowley.

10. Click OK to go on to the Save as Certified Document - Sign dialog, and then type the Digital ID's password (**Figure 14.24**). Erin uses her password `crowley`.

Figure 14.24 Enter the password for the selected Digital ID, and choose a reason for signing from the list.

11. Click the Reason for Signing Document pull-down arrow, and choose an option from the list. Erin chooses "I attest to the accuracy and integrity of this document." The text selections are active and you can modify the text.

12. Click Sign and Save to save the file with the certification signature. You can also click Sign and Save As to save the file with a different name. Erin saves the file with its current name, Signed_CUSTODIAL 05-1937E24.pdf

13. The Apply Signature to Document dialog displays, saying you've successfully signed the document; click OK to dismiss the dialog and apply the signature.

Now that Erin has signed the document, the Certification icon displays at the lower left of the program window. The only place her signature is visible is in the Signatures pane (**Figure 14.25**). In the Signatures pane you can see the choices she made as she worked through the certification dialogs, such as the actions allowed and the reason for signing.

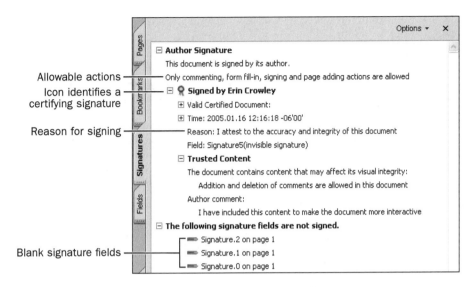

Allowable actions

Icon identifies a
certifying signature

Reason for signing

Blank signature fields

Figure 14.25 *The signature and its features are listed in the Signatures pane.*

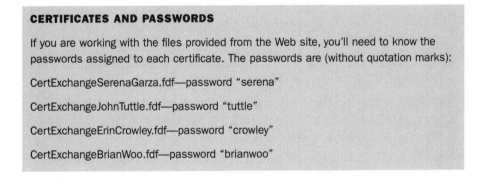

CERTIFICATES AND PASSWORDS

If you are working with the files provided from the Web site, you'll need to know the passwords assigned to each certificate. The passwords are (without quotation marks):

CertExchangeSerenaGarza.fdf—password "serena"

CertExchangeJohnTuttle.fdf—password "tuttle"

CertExchangeErinCrowley.fdf—password "crowley"

CertExchangeBrianWoo.fdf—password "brianwoo"

Routing and Signing the Document

Erin has done a lot of work to complete the document. She prepared and edited several versions of the draft before even starting the PDF review. Now that she's finished a formal review, integrated the changes in the document, and added her certifying signature, she's ready to send it.

Acrobat 7 Professional doesn't provide a wizard for routing an approval process. Instead, Erin will e-mail it to Brian, who will e-mail it to Serena, who will then send it on to John. John will send it back to Erin so she can forward it to the attorney. When the recipients get the file and open it in Acrobat, they'll read through it and then sign it. They can also add comments to the file if they need to, as Erin allowed for them in the certification process.

NOTE The steps don't include adding comments, although all signers did add a comment to the file. You read about working with comments earlier in this chapter and can get more information in Chapters 11 and 13.

Follow these steps to add a signature to an existing signature field:

1. Click the signature field with the Hand tool to open the Apply Digital Signature - Digital ID Selection dialog.

2. Click a Digital ID to select it from the list, and click OK to open the Apply Signature to Document dialog.

3. Type the password for the Digital ID in the Confirm Password field.

NOTE See the sidebar "Certificates and Passwords" to use the Digital IDs and passwords created for this project.

4. Click the Reason for Signing Document pull-down arrow, and choose an option from the list.

5. Click Sign and Save to dismiss the dialog; you'll see the Apply Signature to Document dialog when the process is complete.

6. Click OK to dismiss the dialog and save the file with the new signature. As the new signature is applied, a Signed icon ▨ displays at the lower left of the program window next to the Certification icon.

NOTE If you like, you can also use custom signatures. In the Apply Signature to Document dialog, click Show Options to display further selections, including custom appearances. You can read how to work with custom signature appearances in Chapter 11's bonus material on the Web site.

Once the first approval signature is added, the reviewers will need to forward the document on until all have signed it. Then it will be returned to Erin.

You know those movie scenes where the hero or heroine is gazing reflectively into the camera and the image suddenly goes wavy as some harp music plays? And when the music stops and the screen is clear, it's another day, or even another century? Well, pretend that's happened in this case.

It's the next day, and Erin's got the document back. She's going to take a last look. She'll check out the signature validations, and then she plans to remove the Sign Here stamps along with any other comments the signers may have added.

Working with Signatures

When the document returns to Erin and she opens it in Acrobat, the first thing she'll see is a Document Status dialog explaining that the file has a valid certification and that it also contains signatures. Click Close to dismiss the Document Status dialog.

Download **CUSTODIAL 05-1937E24.pdf** if you'd like to see Erin's version of the file complete with the signature fields; otherwise continue with your copy of the file.

Validating the Signatures

The document's signatures are validated automatically. The three signatures from the document's reviewers are displayed in the Document pane, where they are shown as valid, indicated by the pen-and-checkmark icon at the upper left of the signature field (**Figure 14.26**).

Valid signature icon

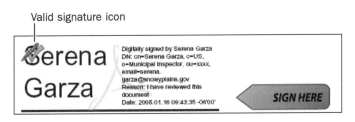

Figure 14.26 The valid signatures are displayed in the fields.

NOTE Information about signatures and their contents are available in many ways in Acrobat. As you learn to work with signatures, you'll see that you can find the same dialogs—such as Certificate Details—by several different paths. It seems overwhelming at first, but if you take the time to read what you are working with, you'll soon find your own best method of finding Digital ID and signature data.

She can find more information about the signatures in the Signatures pane. Choose View > Navigation Tabs > Signatures to open the pane if it's not already displayed in the program. Drag it to dock with the other tabs at the left of the program window.

Examining a Signed Document

Erin is pleased with the process. Being the type of person who really "digs" the software she works with, Erin decides to take a closer look at the signatures' innards.

From the Signatures pane, follow these steps to check out a signature's structure:

1. Click the signature you want to investigate on the Signatures pane to select it (**Figure 14.27**). Erin examines Brian's signature information. To find more information about a signature in the Signatures pane, click the (+) icon to the left of a heading to display its contents.

2. Do one of the following:

   - Click the Options button on the Signatures pane to open its menu, and choose Properties to open the Signature Properties dialog.

   - Right-click/Control-click a signature field on the page or the listing in the Signatures pane, and choose Properties from the shortcut menu to open the Signature Properties dialog.

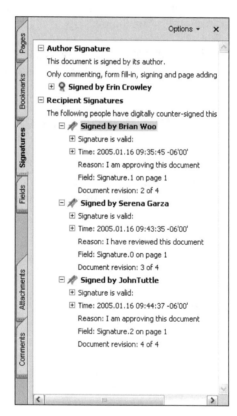

Figure 14.27 Select a signature in the Signatures pane.

The Signature Properties dialog displays the Summary tab by default. The summary shows the name of the person who signed the document as well as the reason for signing and the date. There's also a summary list of validation information, such as changes made and allowed.

3. Select the Document tab. On this tab, you'll find information about the version of the document that has been signed (**Figure 14.28**).

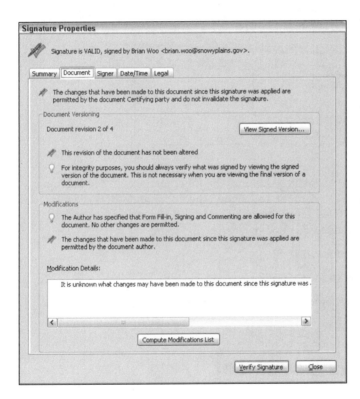

Figure 14.28 The Document tab shows information about the version of the file the signature is applied to.

Each time someone signs a document, another version of the file is saved and appended to the original file. These copies can be seen separately by clicking the View Signed Version on this dialog, or from other commands in the Signatures pane. (Read more about comparing iterations of the file in the bonus material for this chapter on the book's Web site.)

4. Read the information at the bottom of the dialog in the Modification Details section. The default information is shown in Figure 14.28 and says that the changes are unknown.

5. Click Compute Modifications List. Acrobat processes the version of the document you've selected and displays the results in the Modification Details area of the dialog (**Figure 14.29**).

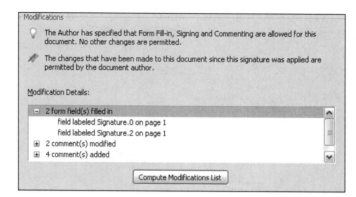

Figure 14.29 Acrobat displays a list of the changes made to the document since the selected signature was applied.

6. Open and collapse the listings to read the modifications. In the example, after Brian added a comment and signed the document, there were two more form fields filled in—the second and third signatures—as well as comments modified and added by Serena and John.

7. Click Close to dismiss the dialog.

Who knew there was so much hidden inside a signature?

The last thing Erin wants to do is strip out the comments and check the file one last time.

Finishing the Document

Erin planned to remove her Sign Here stamps, and she'll also get rid of the comments the signers added. She doesn't think the attorney really needs to read about the organization's personality issues (**Figure 14.30**).

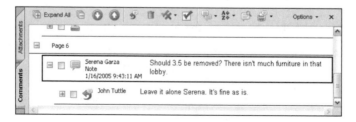

Figure 14.30 Erin decides to remove the comments from the file before sending it to the attorney for review.

THE OTHER TABS ON THE SIGNATURE PROPERTIES DIALOG

There is more information about a signature certificate in the Signature Properties dialog as well:

■ Select Signer to show the name of the person whose signature you're investigating. You'll see a name and e-mail address. The dialog lists Validity Details, such as whether the document has a time limit or revocation date. You'll also find contact information for the person who signed the document if the signer included it in the certificate.

■ Click Show Certificate on the Signer tab to display the specific characteristics of the Digital ID certificate, such as the certificate's serial number, the algorithm used to define the certificate, and the trust status.

■ Select Date/Time to view information about the time stamp used for the signature. If you are using a third-party signature handler, you'll see information about the time management server used to generate a date and time for the signature; otherwise, you'll see that the date and time are taken from the signer's computer.

■ Select Legal to show a summary of information on the legal value of a signature and how certain content included in the document, such as using fields, may compromise the integrity of the document.

■ On the Legal tab, you can click View Document Integrity Properties to show the Certified Document Warnings dialog. This dialog shows items that could compromise the integrity of the file's certification. If you recall, Erin allowed comments, which are listed as a warning item.

Download **Final_CUSTODIAL 05-1937E24.pdf** to see the file in its final form after Erin removes the comments from the file.

Follow these steps to remove the comments:

1. Select the Comments tab to display the Comments pane across the bottom of the program window.

2. Click Collapse All to close the comment listings.

3. Click the first listing on the Comments pane. In Erin's file, there are comments on pages 1 and 6; she selects page 1.

4. Click Delete on the Comments pane to remove the comment from Page 1.

5. The page 6 listing is selected automatically; click Delete again to remove the comments from that page.

6. Save the document. Erin's is saved as Final_CUSTODIAL 05-1937E24.pdf.

She's finished. All that's left to do is send the e-mail to her attorney and attach the signed file.

What Else Can She Do?

Erin's system of commenting works well in her situation since there are only a few people involved in the process. If she were working in a large workgroup, it might be useful for the group to customize their comments' colors and icons. Of course, comments of all colors and appearances can be managed in the Comments pane, but showing them in different colors on the document itself can be a useful tool for the visually inclined. For instance, reviewers from the property management department could use magenta callouts and a circle to identify their comments; reviewers from accounting could use green callouts and a checkmark to identify their comments; and so on.

Erin uses Acrobat's Checkmark feature to manage her work with the comments. These checkmarks are shown on her copy of the document only—the recipients won't see them. If the preparation of the document had required another round of reviewing by the team, she could allow the others to see her actions by setting the comments Review Status to Completed. Read more about working with comments in Chapter 13.

If her situation required it, she could use a set of duplicated fields to copy the signature fields to each page. In some reviews, the approvers have to initial each page of the document; adding a single signature field and then duplicating it across a document's pages is a quick way for a recipient to place an approval signature on each page. You can read more about duplicating fields in Bonus Chapter 4 on the book's Web site.

Erin has set up a small document approval route to make it easy for her recipients to figure out where the file should go next. That might not be the case in some circumstances! In a large approval process, she might want to add some button fields along with the signature fields to route the file. For instance, she could add a button in the same area as the signature field and the Sign Here stamp for a user to click to send the file by e-mail to the next recipient. You can learn how to create buttons in several chapters, including Chapters 4 and 10. You can also see how to use an e-mail action in Bonus Chapter 1 on the book's Web site.

Index